ST PAUL
Sunday Missal
2004

ST PAUL
Sunday Missal
2004

Texts approved for use in
Ireland, England & Wales and Scotland

ST PAULS

Imprimatur:
✠ Michael Smith
Bishop of Meath
10 July 2003

Introductions and Reflections by Gearard Ó Floinn

ST PAULS
Ballykeeran, Athlone, Co. Westmeath
Moyglare Road, Maynooth, Co. Kildare
187 Battersea Bridge Road, London SW11 3AS

ISBN 085439 670 5
© ST PAULS, 2003

Printed in Ireland by the Society of St Paul, Athlone

ST PAULS is an activity of the priests and brothers of the Society of St Paul who proclaim the Gospel through the media of social communication.

CONTENTS

Epiphany: Scotland – 4 January; † *Ascension:* Ireland – 23 May;
** *Corpus Christi:* Ireland & Scotland – 13 June

THE ORDER OF MASS

INTRODUCTORY RITES

ENTRANCE ANTIPHON — *see Mass of the day*

GREETING

In the name of the Father, and of the Son, and of the Holy Spirit.
Amen.

The grace of our Lord Jesus Christ and the love of God and the
fellowship of the Holy Spirit be with you all.
And also with you.

or

The grace and peace of God our Father and the Lord Jesus Christ
be with you.
Blessed be God, the Father of our Lord Jesus Christ.

or

And also with you.

or

The Lord be with you.
And also with you.

The celebrant may briefly introduce the Mass of the day.

RITE OF BLESSING AND SPRINKLING HOLY WATER

*This rite may be used instead of the penitential rite at the beginning of
Mass. The Kyrie is also omitted.*

*The celebrant greets the people. A vessel containing the water to be blessed
is placed before him.*

Dear friends,
this water will be used
to remind us of our baptism.
Let us ask God to bless it
and to keep us faithful
to the Spirit he has given us.

After a brief silence, he joins his hands and continues:

1. God our Father,
   your gift of water
   brings life and freshness to the earth;

it washes away our sins
and brings us eternal life.

We ask you now
to bless ✠ this water,
and to give us your protection on this day
which you have made your own.
Renew the living spring of your life within us
and protect us in spirit and body,
that we may be free from sin
and come into your presence
to receive your gift of salvation.

We ask this through Christ our Lord.

or

2.   Lord God almighty,
      creator of all life,
      of body and soul,
      we ask you to bless ✠ this water:
      as we use it in faith
      forgive our sins
      and save us from all illness
      and the power of evil.

      Lord,
      in your mercy
      give us living water,
      always springing up as a fountain of salvation:
      free us, body and soul, from every danger,
      and admit us to your presence
      in purity of heart.

      Grant this through Christ our Lord.

or (during the Easter season)

3.   Lord God almighty,
      hear the prayers of your people:
      we celebrate our creation and redemption.
      Hear our prayers and bless ✠ this water
      which gives fruitfulness to the fields,
      and refreshment and cleansing to man.
      You chose water to show your goodness
      when you led your people to freedom
      through the Red Sea
      and satisfied their thirst in the desert

with water from the rock.
Water was the symbol used by the prophets
to foretell your new covenant with man.
You made the water of baptism holy
by Christ's baptism in the Jordan:
by it you give us a new birth
and renew us in holiness.
May this water remind us of our baptism
and let us share the joy
of all who have been baptised at Easter.

We ask this through Christ our Lord.

Where it is customary, salt may be mixed with the holy water. The priest blesses the salt, saying:

Almighty God,
we ask you to bless ✠ this salt
as once you blessed the salt scattered over the water
by the prophet Elisha.
Wherever this salt and water are sprinkled,
drive away the power of evil,
and protect us always
by the presence of your Holy Spirit.

We ask this through Christ our Lord.

The priest sprinkles himself, his ministers, and the people. Meanwhile, an antiphon or an appropriate song is sung.

When he returns to his place, the priest says:

May almighty God cleanse us of our sins,
and through the eucharist we celebrate
make us worthy to sit at his table
in his heavenly kingdom.
Amen.

When it is prescribed, the GLORIA *is then sung or said, and the Mass continues.*

PENITENTIAL RITE

The celebrant invites the people to repent of their sins. He may use the following or similar words:

My brothers and sisters,
to prepare ourselves to celebrate the sacred mysteries,
let us call to mind our sins.

or

As we prepare to celebrate the mystery of Christ's love,
let us acknowledge our failures
and ask the Lord for pardon and strength.

or

Coming together as God's family,
with confidence let us ask the Father's forgiveness,
for he is full of gentleness and compassion.

A pause for silent reflection follows. After a brief silence all say:

A

I confess to almighty God,
and to you, my brothers and sisters,
that I have sinned through my own fault

(All strike their breast)

in my thoughts and in my words,
in what I have done,
and in what I have failed to do;
and I ask blessed Mary, ever virgin,
all the angels and saints,
and you, my brothers and sisters,
to pray for me to the Lord our God.

May almighty God have mercy on us,
forgive us our sins,
and bring us to everlasting life.
Amen.

Lord, have mercy.
Lord, have mercy.
Christ, have mercy.
Christ, have mercy.
Lord, have mercy.
Lord, have mercy.

or B

Lord, we have sinned against you:
Lord, have mercy.
Lord, have mercy.
Lord, show us your mercy and love.
And grant us your salvation.
May almighty God have mercy on us,
forgive us our sins,

and bring us to everlasting life.
Amen.

or C (1)

You were sent to heal the contrite:
Lord, have mercy.
Lord, have mercy.

You came to call sinners:
Christ, have mercy.
Christ, have mercy.

You plead for us at the right hand of the Father:
Lord, have mercy.
Lord, have mercy.

May almighty God have mercy on us,
forgive us our sins,
and bring us to everlasting life.
Amen.

or (2)

Lord Jesus, you came to gather the nations
    into the peace of God's kingdom:
Lord, have mercy.
Lord, have mercy.

You come in word and sacrament to strengthen us in holiness:
Christ, have mercy.
Christ, have mercy.

You will come in glory with salvation for your people:
Lord, have mercy.
Lord, have mercy.

May almighty God have mercy on us,
forgive us our sins,
and bring us to everlasting life.
Amen.

or (3)

Lord Jesus, you are mighty God and Prince of peace:
Lord, have mercy.
Lord, have mercy.

Lord Jesus, you are Son of God and Son of Mary:
Christ, have mercy.
Christ, have mercy.

Lord Jesus, you are Word made flesh and splendour of the Father:

Lord, have mercy.
Lord, have mercy.

May almighty God have mercy on us,
forgive us our sins,
and bring us to everlasting life.
Amen.

or (4)

Lord Jesus, you came to reconcile us
        to one another and to the Father:
Lord, have mercy.
Lord, have mercy.

Lord Jesus, you heal the wounds of sin and division:
Christ, have mercy.
Christ, have mercy.

Lord Jesus, you intercede for us with your Father:
Lord, have mercy.
Lord, have mercy.

May almighty God have mercy on us,
forgive us our sins,
and bring us to everlasting life.
Amen.

or (5)

You raise the dead to life in the Spirit:
Lord, have mercy.
Lord, have mercy.

You bring pardon and peace to the sinner:
Christ, have mercy.
Christ, have mercy.

You bring light to those in darkness:
Lord, have mercy.
Lord, have mercy.

May almighty God have mercy on us,
forgive us our sins,
and bring us to everlasting life.
Amen.

or (6)

Lord Jesus, you raise us to new life:
Lord, have mercy.
Lord, have mercy.

Lord Jesus, you forgive us our sins:
Christ, have mercy.
Christ, have mercy.

Lord Jesus, you feed us with your body and blood:
Lord, have mercy.
Lord, have mercy.

May almighty God have mercy on us,
forgive us our sins,
and bring us to everlasting life.
Amen.

or (7)

Lord Jesus, you have shown us the way to the Father:
Lord, have mercy.
Lord, have mercy.

Lord Jesus, you have given us the consolation of the truth:
Christ, have mercy.
Christ, have mercy.

Lord Jesus, you are the Good Shepherd,
      leading us into everlasting life:
Lord, have mercy.
Lord, have mercy.

May almighty God have mercy on us,
forgive us our sins,
and bring us to everlasting life.
Amen.

or (8)

Lord Jesus, you healed the sick:
Lord, have mercy.
Lord, have mercy.

Lord Jesus, you forgave sinners:
Christ, have mercy.
Christ, have mercy.

Lord Jesus, you give us yourself to heal us and bring us strength:
Lord, have mercy.
Lord, have mercy.

May almighty God have mercy on us,
forgive us our sins,
and bring us to everlasting life.
Amen.

GLORIA

Glory to God in the highest,
   and peace to his people on earth.

Lord God, heavenly King,
almighty God and Father,
   we worship you, we give you thanks,
   we praise you for your glory.

Lord Jesus Christ, only Son of the Father,
Lord God, Lamb of God,
you take away the sin of the world:
   have mercy on us;
you are seated at the right hand of the Father:
   receive our prayer.

For you alone are the Holy One,
you alone are the Lord,
you alone are the Most High,
   Jesus Christ,
   with the Holy Spirit,
   in the glory of God the Father. Amen.

OPENING PRAYER

(Turn to the Mass of the day)

LITURGY OF THE WORD

READINGS, RESPONSORIAL PSALM, GOSPEL ACCLAMATION

(Turn to the Mass of the day)

PROFESSION OF FAITH   *(Nicene Creed)*

We believe in one God,
>the Father, the Almighty,
>maker of heaven and earth,
>of all that is, seen and unseen.

We believe in one Lord, Jesus Christ,
>the only Son of God,
>eternally begotten of the Father,
>God from God, Light from Light,
>true God from true God,
>begotten, not made,
>of one Being with the Father.
>Through him all things were made.
>For us men and for our salvation
>>he came down from heaven:

>>*(All bow during these three lines)*

>by the power of the Holy Spirit
>>he became incarnate from the Virgin Mary,
>>and was made man.

For our sake he was crucified under Pontius Pilate;
>he suffered death and was buried.
>On the third day he rose again
>>in accordance with the Scriptures;
>he ascended into heaven
>>and is seated at the right hand of the Father.
>He will come again in glory to judge the living and the
>>dead,
>and his kingdom will have no end.

We believe in the Holy Spirit, the Lord, the giver of life,
>who proceeds from the Father and the Son.
>With the Father and the Son he is worshipped and
>>glorified.
>He has spoken through the Prophets.
>We believe in one holy catholic and apostolic Church.
>We acknowledge one baptism for the forgiveness of sins.
>We look for the resurrection of the dead,
>>and the life of the world to come. Amen.

PROFESSION OF FAITH   *(Apostles' Creed)*

I believe in God, the Father almighty,
    creator of heaven and earth.

I believe in Jesus Christ, his only Son, our Lord.
    He was conceived by the power of the Holy Spirit
        and born of the Virgin Mary.
    He suffered under Pontius Pilate,
        was crucified, died, and was buried.
    He descended to the dead.
    On the third day he rose again.
    He ascended into heaven,
        and is seated at the right hand of the Father.
    He will come again to judge the living and the dead.

I believe in the Holy Spirit,
    the holy catholic Church,
    the communion of saints,
    the forgiveness of sins,
    the resurrection of the body,
    and the life everlasting. Amen.

PRAYER OF THE FAITHFUL

LITURGY OF THE EUCHARIST

PREPARATION OF THE GIFTS

Blessed are you, Lord, God of all creation.
Through your goodness we have this bread to offer,
which earth has given and human hands have made.
It will become for us the bread of life.
Blessed be God for ever.

By the mystery of this water and wine
may we come to share in the divinity of Christ,
who humbled himself to share in our humanity,

Blessed are you, Lord, God of all creation.
Through your goodness we have this wine to offer,
fruit of the vine and work of human hands.
It will become our spiritual drink.
Blessed be God for ever.

Lord God, we ask you to receive us
and be pleased with the sacrifice we offer you
with humble and contrite hearts.

Lord, wash away my iniquity; cleanse me from my sin.

The priest says these or similar words:
Pray, brothers and sisters, that our sacrifice
may be acceptable to God, the almighty Father.

**May the Lord accept the sacrifice at your hands
for the praise and glory of his name,
for our good, and the good of all his Church.**

PRAYER OVER THE GIFTS
(Turn to the Mass of the day)

EUCHARISTIC PRAYER

The Lord be with you
And also with you.
Lift up your hearts.
We lift them up to the Lord.
Let us give thanks to the Lord our God.
It is right to give him thanks and praise.

The celebrant continues alone.

PREFACES

PREFACE OF ADVENT I
(From the First Sunday of Advent until 16 December)

Father, all-powerful and ever-living God,
we do well always and everywhere to give you thanks
through Jesus Christ our Lord.

When he humbled himself to come among us as a man,
he fulfilled the plan you formed long ago
and opened for us the way to salvation.

Now we watch for the day,
hoping that the salvation promised us will be ours
when Christ our Lord will come again in his glory.

And so, with all the choirs of angels in heaven
we proclaim your glory
and join in their unending hymn of praise:

**Holy, holy, holy Lord, God of power and might,
heaven and earth are full of your glory.
Hosanna in the highest.
Blessed is he who comes in the name of the Lord.
Hosanna in the highest.**

PREFACE OF ADVENT II
(17-24 December)

Father, all-powerful and ever-living God,
we do well always and everywhere to give you thanks
through Jesus Christ our Lord.

His future coming was proclaimed by all the prophets.
The virgin mother bore him in her womb with love beyond all
     telling.
John the Baptist was his herald
and made him know when at last he came.

In his love Christ has filled us with joy
as we prepare to celebrate his birth,
so that when he comes he may find us watching in prayer,
our hearts filled with wonder and praise.

And so, with all the choirs of angels in heaven
we proclaim your glory
and join in their unending hymn of praise:

Holy, holy, holy ...

PREFACE OF CHRISTMAS I

Father, all-powerful and ever-living God,
we do well always and everywhere to give you thanks
through Jesus Christ our Lord.

In the wonder of the incarnation
your eternal Word has brought to the eyes of faith
a new and radiant vision of your glory.
In him we see our God made visible
and so are caught up in love of the God we cannot see.

And so, with all the choirs of angels in heaven
we proclaim your glory
and join in their unending hymn of praise:

Holy, holy, holy…

PREFACE OF CHRISTMAS II

Father, all-powerful and ever-living God,
we do well always and everywhere to give you thanks
through Jesus Christ our Lord.

Today you fill our hearts with joy
as we recognise in Christ the revelation of your love.
No eye can see his glory as our God,
yet now he is seen as one like us.

Christ is your Son before all ages,
yet now he is born in time.
He has come to lift up all things to himself,
to restore unity to creation,
and to lead mankind from exile into your heavenly kingdom.

With all the angels of heaven
we sing our joyful hymn of praise:

Holy, holy, holy…

PREFACE OF CHRISTMAS III

Father, all-powerful and ever-living God,
we do well always and everywhere to give you thanks
through Jesus Christ our Lord.

Today in him a new light has dawned upon the world:
God has become one with man,
and man has become one again with God.

Your eternal Word has taken upon himself our human
weakness,
giving our mortal nature immortal value.
So marvellous is this oneness between God and man
that in Christ man restores to man the gift of everlasting life.

In our joy we sing to your glory
with all the choirs of angels:

Holy, holy, holy...

PREFACE OF LENT I

Father, all-powerful and ever-living God,
we do well always and everywhere to give you thanks
through Jesus Christ our Lord.

Each year you give us this joyful season
when we prepare to celebrate the paschal mystery
with mind and heart renewed.
You give us a spirit of loving reverence for you, our Father,
and of willing service to our neighbour.

As we recall the great events that gave us a new life in Christ,
you bring the image of your Son to perfection within us.

Now, with angels and archangels,
and the whole company of heaven,
we sing the unending hymn of your praise.

Holy, holy, holy...

PREFACE OF LENT II

Father, all-powerful and ever-living God,
we do well always and everywhere to give you thanks

This great season of grace is your gift to your family
to renew us in spirit.
You give us strength to purify our hearts,
to control our desires,
and so to serve you in freedom.
You teach us how to live in this passing world,
with our heart set on the world that will never end.

Now, with all the saints and angels,
we praise you for ever:

Holy, holy, holy...

PREFACE OF EASTER II

Father, all-powerful and ever-living God,
we do well always and everywhere to give you thanks
through Jesus Christ our Lord.

We praise you with greater joy than ever in this Easter season,
when Christ became our paschal sacrifice.

He has made us children of the light,
rising to new and everlasting life.
He has opened the gates of heaven
to receive his faithful people.
His death is our ransom from death;
his resurrection is our rising to life.

The joy of the resurrection renews the whole world,
while the choirs of heaven sing for ever to your glory:

Holy, holy, holy...

PREFACE OF EASTER III

Father, all-powerful and ever-living God,
we do well always and everywhere to give you thanks
through Jesus Christ our Lord.

We praise you with greater joy than ever in this Easter season,
when Christ became our paschal sacrifice.

He is still our priest,
our advocate who always pleads our cause.
Christ is the victim who dies no more,
the Lamb, once slain, who lives for ever.

The joy of the resurrection renews the whole world,
while the choirs of heaven sing for ever to your glory:

Holy, holy, holy...

PREFACE OF EASTER IV

Father, all-powerful and ever-living God,
we do well always and everywhere to give you thanks
through Jesus Christ our Lord.

We praise you with greater joy than ever in this Easter season,
when Christ became our paschal sacrifice.

In him a new age has dawned,
the long reign of sin is ended,

a broken world has been renewed,
and man is once again made whole.

The joy of the resurrection renews the whole world,
while the choirs of heaven sing for ever to your glory:

Holy, holy, holy...

PREFACE OF EASTER V

Father, all-powerful and ever-living God,
we do well always and everywhere to give you thanks
through Jesus Christ our Lord.

We praise you with greater joy than ever in this Easter season,
when Christ became our paschal sacrifice.

As he offered his body on the cross,
his perfect sacrifice fulfilled all others.

As he gave himself into your hands for our salvation,
he showed himself to be the priest, the altar, and the lamb of
   sacrifice.

The joy of the resurrection renews the whole world,
while the choirs of heaven sing for ever to your glory:

Holy, holy, holy...

PREFACE OF SUNDAYS IN ORDINARY TIME I

Father, all-powerful and ever-living God,
we do well always and everywhere to give you thanks
through Jesus Christ our Lord.

Through his cross and resurrection
he freed us from sin and death
and called us to the glory that has made us
a chosen race, a royal priesthood,
a holy nation, a people set apart.

Everywhere we proclaim your mighty works
for you have called us out of darkness
into your own wonderful light.

And so, with all the choirs of angels in heaven
we proclaim your glory
and join in their unending hymn of praise:

Holy, holy, holy...

PREFACE OF SUNDAYS IN ORDINARY TIME II

Father, all-powerful and ever-living God,
we do well always and everywhere to give you thanks
through Jesus Christ our Lord.

Out of love for sinful man,
he humbled himself to be born of the Virgin.

By suffering on the cross
he freed us from unending death,
and by rising from the dead
he gave us eternal life.

And so, with all the choirs of angels in heaven
we proclaim your glory
and join in their unending hymn of praise:

Holy, holy, holy...

PREFACE OF SUNDAYS IN ORDINARY TIME III

Father, all-powerful and ever-living God,
we do well always and everywhere to give you thanks.

We see your infinite power
in your loving plan of salvation.
You came to our rescue by your power as God,
but you wanted us to be saved by one like us.
Man refused your friendship,
but man himself was to restore it
through Jesus Christ our Lord.

Through him the angels of heaven offer their prayer of
        adoration
as they rejoice in your presence for ever.
May our voices be one with theirs
in their triumphant hymn of praise:

Holy, holy, holy...

PREFACE OF SUNDAYS IN ORDINARY TIME IV

Father, all-powerful and ever-living God,
we do well always and everywhere to give you thanks
through Jesus Christ our Lord.

By his birth we are reborn.
In his suffering we are freed from sin.

By his rising from the dead we rise to everlasting life.
In his return to you in glory
we enter into your heavenly kingdom.

And so, we join the angels and the saints
as they sing their unending hymn of praise:

Holy, holy, holy...

PREFACE OF SUNDAYS IN ORDINARY TIME V

Father, all-powerful and ever-living God,
we do well always and everywhere to give you thanks.

All things are of your making,
all times and seasons obey your laws,
but you chose to create man in your own image,
setting him over the whole world in all its wonder.
You made man the steward of creation,
to praise you day by day for the marvels of your wisdom and
    power,
through Jesus Christ our Lord.

We praise you, Lord, with all the angels
in their song of joy:

Holy, holy, holy...

PREFACE OF SUNDAYS IN ORDINARY TIME VI

Father, all-powerful and ever-living God,
we do well always and everywhere to give you thanks.

In you we live and move and have our being.
Each day you show us a Father's love;
your Holy Spirit, dwelling within us,
gives us on earth the hope of unending joy.

Your gift of the Spirit,
who raised Jesus from the dead,
is the foretaste and promise
of the paschal feast of heaven.

With thankful praise,
in company with the angels,
we glorify the wonders of your power:

Holy, holy, holy...

PREFACE OF SUNDAYS IN ORDINARY TIME VII

Father, all-powerful and ever-living God,
we do well always and everywhere to give you thanks.

So great was your love
that you gave us your Son as our Redeemer.
You sent him as one like ourselves,
though free from sin,
that you might see and love in us
what you see and love in Christ.
Your gifts of grace, lost by disobedience,
are now restored by the obedience of your Son.

We praise you, Lord, with all the angels and saints
in their song of joy:

Holy, holy, holy...

PREFACE OF SUNDAYS IN ORDINARY TIME VIII

Father, all-powerful and ever-living God,
we do well always and everywhere to give you thanks.

When your children sinned
and wandered far from your friendship,
you reunited them with yourself
through the blood of your Son
and the power of the Holy Spirit.

You gather them into your Church,
to be one as you, Father, are one
with your Son and the Holy Spirit.
You call them to be your people,
to praise your wisdom in all your works.
You make them the body of Christ
and the dwelling-place of the Holy Spirit.

In our joy we sing to your glory
with all the choirs of angels:

Holy, holy, holy...

EUCHARISTIC PRAYERS

EUCHARISTIC PRAYER I

We come to you, Father,
with praise and thanksgiving,
through Jesus Christ your Son.
Through him we ask you to accept and bless ✠
these gifts we offer you in sacrifice.

We offer them for your holy catholic Church,
watch over it, Lord, and guide it;
grant it peace and unity throughout the world.
We offer them for N., our Pope,
for N., our bishop,
and for all who hold and teach the catholic faith
that comes to us from the apostles.

Remember, Lord, your people,
especially those for whom we now pray, N. and N.
Remember all of us gathered here before you.
You know how firmly we believe in you
and dedicate ourselves to you.
We offer you this sacrifice of praise
for ourselves and those who are dear to us.
We pray to you, our living and true God,
for our well-being and redemption.

In union with the whole Church
we honour Mary,
*the ever-virgin mother of Jesus Christ our Lord and God.
We honour Joseph, her husband,
the apostles and martyrs

Special form of In union with the whole Church

Christmas and during the octave

In union with the whole Church
we celebrate that day [night]
when Mary without loss of her virginity
gave the world its Saviour.
We honour her, *

Epiphany

In union with the whole Church
we celebrate that day
when your only Son,

sharing your eternal glory,
showed himself in a human body.
We honour Mary, *

Holy Thursday

In union with the whole Church
we celebrate that day
when Jesus Christ, our Lord,
was betrayed for us.
We honour Mary, *

From the Easter Vigil to the Second Sunday of Easter inclusive

In union with the whole Church
we celebrate that day [night]
when Jesus Christ, our Lord,
rose from the dead in his human body.
We honour Mary, *

Ascension

In union with the whole Church
we celebrate that day
when your only Son, our Lord,
took his place with you
and raised our frail human nature to glory.
We honour Mary, *

Pentecost

In union with the whole Church
we celebrate the day of Pentecost
when the Holy Spirit appeared to the apostles
in the form of countless tongues.
We honour Mary, *

Peter and Paul, Andrew,
[James, John, Thomas,
James, Philip,
Bartholomew, Matthew, Simon and Jude;
we honour Linus, Cletus, Clement, Sixtus,
Cornelius, Cyprian, Lawrence, Chrysogonus,
John and Paul, Cosmas and Damian]
and all the saints.
May their merits and prayers
gain us your constant help and protection.
[Through Christ our Lord. Amen.]

Father, accept this offering *
from your whole family.
Grant us your peace in this life,
save us from final damnation,
and count us among those you have chosen.
[Through Christ our Lord. Amen.]

From the Easter Vigil to the Second Sunday of Easter

Father, accept this offering
from your whole family
and from those born into the new life
of water and the Holy Spirit,
with all their sins forgiven.
Grant us your peace in this life,
save us from final damnation,
and count us among those you have chosen.
[Through Christ our Lord. Amen.]

Bless and approve our offering;
make it acceptable to you,
an offering in spirit and in truth.
Let it become for us
the body and blood of Jesus Christ,
your only Son, our Lord.

The day before he suffered
he took bread in his sacred hands
and looking up to heaven,
to you, his almighty Father,
he gave you thanks and praise.
He broke the bread,
gave it to his disciples, and said:

TAKE THIS, ALL OF YOU, AND EAT IT:
THIS IS MY BODY WHICH WILL BE GIVEN UP FOR YOU.

When supper was ended,
he took the cup.
Again he gave you thanks and praise,
gave the cup to his disciples, and said:

TAKE THIS, ALL OF YOU, AND DRINK FROM IT:
THIS IS THE CUP OF MY BLOOD,
THE BLOOD OF THE NEW AND EVERLASTING COVENANT.
IT WILL BE SHED FOR YOU AND FOR ALL

SO THAT SINS MAY BE FORGIVEN.
DO THIS IN MEMORY OF ME.

Let us proclaim the mystery of faith:

1. **Christ has died,**
   Christ is risen,
   Christ will come again.

2. **Dying you destroyed our death,**
   rising you restored our life.
   Lord Jesus, come in glory.

3. **When we eat this bread and drink this cup,**
   we proclaim your death, Lord Jesus,
   until you come in glory.

4. **Lord, by your cross and resurrection**
   you have set us free.
   You are the Saviour of the world.

5. **My Lord and my God.** *(for Ireland only)*

Father, we celebrate the memory of Christ, your Son.
We, your people and your ministers,
recall his passion,
his resurrection from the dead,
and his ascension into glory;
and from the many gifts you have given us
we offer to you, God of glory and majesty,
this holy and perfect sacrifice:
the bread of life
and the cup of eternal salvation.

Look with favour on these offerings
and accept them as once you accepted
the gifts of your servant Abel,
the sacrifice of Abraham, our father in faith,
and the bread and wine offered by your priest Melchisedech.

Almighty God,
we pray that your angel may take this sacrifice
to your altar in heaven.
Then, as we receive from this altar
the sacred body and blood of your Son,
let us be filled with every grace and blessing.
[Through Christ our Lord. Amen.]

Remember, Lord, those who have died
and have gone before us marked with the sign of faith,
especially those for whom we now pray, N. and N.
May these, and all who sleep in Christ,
find in your presence
light, happiness, and peace.
[Through Christ our Lord. Amen.]

For ourselves, too, we ask
some share in the fellowship of your apostles and martyrs,
with John the Baptist, Stephen, Matthias, Barnabas,
[Ignatius, Alexander, Marcellinus, Peter,
Felicity, Perpetua, Agatha, Lucy,
Agnes, Cecilia, Anastasia]
and all the saints.
Though we are sinners,
we trust in your mercy and love.
Do not consider what we truly deserve,
but grant us your forgiveness.

Through Christ our Lord
you give us all these gifts.
You fill them with life and goodness,
you bless them and make them holy.

Through him,
with him,
in him,
in the unity of the Holy Spirit,
all glory and honour is yours,
almighty Father,
for ever and ever.
Amen.

(Turn to page 54)

EUCHARISTIC PRAYER II

PREFACE *(may be substituted by another)*

Father, it is our duty and our salvation,
always and everywhere
to give you thanks
through your beloved Son, Jesus Christ.

He is the Word through whom you made the universe,
the Saviour you sent to redeem us.
By the power of the Holy Spirit
he took flesh and was born of the Virgin Mary.

For our sake he opened his arms on the cross;
he put an end to death
and revealed the resurrection.
In this he fulfilled your will
and won for you a holy people.

And so we join the angels and the saints
in proclaiming your glory
as we sing (say):

**Holy, holy, holy Lord, God of power and might,
heaven and earth are full of your glory.**
    Hosanna in the highest.
Blessed is he who comes in the name of the Lord.
    Hosanna in the highest.

Lord, you are holy indeed,
the fountain of all holiness.
Let your Spirit come upon these gifts to make them holy,
so that they may become for us
the body ✠ and blood of our Lord, Jesus Christ.

Before he was given up to death,
a death he freely accepted,
he took bread and gave you thanks.
He broke the bread,
gave it to his disciples, and said:

TAKE THIS, ALL OF YOU, AND EAT IT:
THIS IS MY BODY WHICH WILL BE GIVEN UP FOR YOU.

When supper was ended, he took the cup.
Again he gave you thanks and praise,
gave the cup to his disciples, and said:

TAKE THIS, ALL OF YOU, AND DRINK FROM IT:
THIS IS THE CUP OF MY BLOOD,
THE BLOOD OF THE NEW AND EVERLASTING COVENANT.
IT WILL BE SHED FOR YOU AND FOR ALL
SO THAT SINS MAY BE FORGIVEN.
DO THIS IN MEMORY OF ME.

Let us proclaim the mystery of faith:

1. **Christ has died,**
   Christ is risen,
   Christ will come again.

2. **Dying you destroyed our death,**
   rising you restored our life.
   Lord Jesus, come in glory.

3. **When we eat this bread and drink this cup,**
   we proclaim your death, Lord Jesus,
   until you come in glory.

4. **Lord, by your cross and resurrection**
   you have set us free.
   You are the Saviour of the world.

5. **My Lord and my God.** *(for Ireland only)*

In memory of his death and resurrection,
we offer you, Father, this life-giving bread,
this saving cup.
We thank you for counting us worthy
to stand in your presence and serve you.
May all of us who share in the body and blood of Christ
be brought together in unity by the Holy Spirit.

Lord, remember your Church throughout the world;
make us grow in love,
together with N., our Pope,
N., our bishop, and all the clergy.

In Masses for the dead the following may be added:

Remember N., whom you have called from this life.
In baptism he (she) died with Christ:
may he (she) also share his resurrection.

Remember our brothers and sisters
who have gone to their rest
in the hope of rising again;

bring them and all the departed
into the light of your presence.

Have mercy on us all;
make us worthy to share eternal life
with Mary, the virgin Mother of God,
with the apostles, and with all the saints
who have done your will throughout the ages.
May we praise you in union with them,
and give you glory
through your Son, Jesus Christ.

Through him,
with him,
in him,
in the unity of the Holy Spirit,
all glory and honour is yours,
almighty Father,
for ever and ever.
Amen.

(Turn to page 54)

EUCHARISTIC PRAYER III

Father, you are holy indeed,
and all creation rightly gives you praise.
All life, all holiness comes from you
through your Son, Jesus Christ our Lord,
by the working of the Holy Spirit.
From age to age you gather a people to yourself,
so that from east to west
a perfect offering may be made
to the glory of your name.

And so, Father, we bring you these gifts.
We ask you to make them holy by the power of your Spirit,
that they may become the body ✠ and blood
of your Son, our Lord Jesus Christ,
at whose command we celebrate this eucharist.

On the night he was betrayed,
he took bread and gave you thanks and praise.
He broke the bread, gave it to his disciples, and said:

TAKE THIS, ALL OF YOU, AND EAT IT:
THIS IS MY BODY WHICH WILL BE GIVEN UP FOR YOU.

When supper was ended, he took the cup.
Again he gave you thanks and praise,
gave the cup to his disciples, and said:

TAKE THIS, ALL OF YOU, AND DRINK FROM IT:
THIS IS THE CUP OF MY BLOOD,
THE BLOOD OF THE NEW AND EVERLASTING COVENANT.
IT WILL BE SHED FOR YOU AND FOR ALL
SO THAT SINS MAY BE FORGIVEN.
DO THIS IN MEMORY OF ME.

Let us proclaim the mystery of faith:

1. **Christ has died,**
    Christ is risen,
    Christ will come again.

2. **Dying you destroyed our death,**
    rising you restored our life.
    Lord Jesus, come in glory.

3. **When we eat this bread and drink this cup,**
    we proclaim your death, Lord Jesus,
    until you come in glory.

4. **Lord, by your cross and resurrection**
    you have set us free.
    You are the Saviour of the world.

5. **My Lord and my God.** (for Ireland only)

Father, calling to mind the death your Son endured for our
        salvation,
his glorious resurrection and ascension into heaven,
and ready to greet him when he comes again,
we offer you in thanksgiving this holy and living sacrifice.

Look with favour on your Church's offering,
and see the Victim whose death has reconciled us to yourself.
Grant that we, who are nourished by his body and blood,
may be filled with his Holy Spirit,
and become one body, one spirit in Christ.

May he make us an everlasting gift to you
and enable us to share in the inheritance of your saints,
with Mary, the virgin Mother of God;
with the apostles, the martyrs,

(Saint N.) and all your saints,
on whose constant intercession we rely for help.

Lord, may this sacrifice,
which has made our peace with you,
advance the peace and salvation of all the world.
Strengthen in faith and love your pilgrim Church on earth;
your servant, Pope N., our bishop N.,
and all the bishops,
with the clergy and the entire people your Son has gained
        for you.
Father, hear the prayers of the family you have gathered here
        before you.
In mercy and love unite all your children wherever they may be.*
Welcome into your kingdom our departed brothers and sisters,
and all who have left this world in your friendship.
We hope to enjoy for ever the vision of your glory,
through Christ our Lord, from whom all good things come.

In Masses for the dead, the following may be said:

Remember N.
In baptism he (she) died with Christ:
may he (she) share his resurrection,
when Christ will raise our mortal bodies
and make them like his own in glory.
Welcome into your kingdom our departed brothers and sisters,
and all who have left this world in your friendship.
There we hope to share in your glory
when every tear will be wiped away.
On that day we shall see you, our God, as you are.
We shall become like you
and praise you for ever through Christ our Lord,
from whom all good things come.

Through him,
with him,
in him,
in the unity of the Holy Spirit,
all glory and honour is yours,
almighty Father,
for ever and ever.
Amen.

(Turn to page 54)

EUCHARISTIC PRAYER IV

PREFACE

Father in heaven,
it is right that we should give you thanks and glory:
you are the one God, living and true.
Through all eternity you live in unapproachable light.
Source of life and goodness, you have created all things,
to fill your creatures with every blessing
and lead all men to the joyful vision of your light.
Countless hosts of angels stand before you to do your will;
they look upon your splendour
and praise you, night and day.
United with them,
and in the name of every creature under heaven,
we too praise your glory as we sing (say):

**Holy, holy, holy Lord, God of power and might,
heaven and earth are full of your glory.**
　　　Hosanna in the highest.
Blessed is he who comes in the name of the Lord.
　　　Hosanna in the highest.

Father, we acknowledge your greatness:
all your actions show your wisdom and love.
You formed man in your own likeness
and set him over the whole world
to serve you, his creator,
and to rule over all creatures.
Even when he disobeyed you and lost your friendship
you did not abandon him to the power of death,
but helped all men to seek and find you.
Again and again you offered a covenant to man,
and through the prophets taught him to hope for salvation.
Father, you so loved the world
that in the fullness of time you sent your only Son to be
　　　our Saviour.

He was conceived through the power of the Holy Spirit,
and born of the Virgin Mary,
a man like us in all things but sin.
To the poor he proclaimed the good news of salvation,
to prisoners, freedom,
and to those in sorrow, joy.
In fulfilment of your will

he gave himself up to death;
but by rising from the dead,
he destroyed death and restored life.
And that we might live no longer for ourselves but for him,
he sent the Holy Spirit from you, Father,
as his first gift to those who believe,
to complete his work on earth
and bring us the fullness of grace.

Father, may this Holy Spirit sanctify these offerings.
Let them become the body ✠ and blood of Jesus Christ our Lord
as we celebrate the great mystery
which he left us as an everlasting covenant.

He always loved those who were his own in the world.
When the time came for him to be glorified by you,
    his heavenly Father,
he showed the depth of his love.

While they were at supper,
he took bread, said the blessing, broke the bread,
and gave it to his disciples, saying:
TAKE THIS, ALL OF YOU, AND EAT IT:
THIS IS MY BODY WHICH WILL BE GIVEN UP FOR YOU.

In the same way, he took the cup, filled with wine.
He gave you thanks, and giving the cup to his disciples, said:
TAKE THIS, ALL OF YOU, AND DRINK FROM IT:
THIS IS THE CUP OF MY BLOOD,
THE BLOOD OF THE NEW AND EVERLASTING COVENANT.
IT WILL BE SHED FOR YOU AND FOR ALL
SO THAT SINS MAY BE FORGIVEN.
DO THIS IN MEMORY OF ME.

Let us proclaim the mystery of faith:

1. **Christ has died,**
   Christ is risen,
   Christ will come again.

2. **Dying you destroyed our death,**
   rising you restored our life.
   Lord Jesus, come in glory.

3. **When we eat this bread and drink this cup,**
   we proclaim your death, Lord Jesus,
   until you come in glory.

4. **Lord, by your cross and resurrection
    you have set us free.
    You are the Saviour of the world.**

5. **My Lord and my God.** *(for Ireland only)*

Father, we now celebrate this memorial of our redemption.
We recall Christ's death, his descent among the dead,
his resurrection, and his ascension to your right hand;
and, looking forward to his coming in glory,
we offer you his body and blood,
the acceptable sacrifice
which brings salvation to the whole world.

Lord, look upon this sacrifice which you have given to your
    Church;
and by your Holy Spirit, gather all who share this one bread and
    one cup
into the one body of Christ, a living sacrifice of praise.

Lord, remember those for whom we offer this sacrifice,
especially N., our Pope,
N., our bishop, and bishops and clergy everywhere.
Remember those who take part in this offering,
those here present and all your people,
and all who seek you with a sincere heart.

Remember those who have died in the peace of Christ
and all the dead whose faith is known to you alone.
Father, in your mercy grant also to us, your children,
to enter into our heavenly inheritance
in the company of the Virgin Mary, the Mother of God,
and your apostles and saints.
Then, in your kingdom, freed from the corruption of sin and death,
we shall sing your glory with every creature through Christ our
    Lord,
through whom you give us everything that is good.

Through him,
with him,
in him,
in the unity of the Holy Spirit,
all glory and honour is yours,
almighty Father,
for ever and ever. **Amen.**

(Turn to page 54)

EUCHARISTIC PRAYER
FOR MASSES OF RECONCILIATION I

PREFACE

Father, all-powerful and ever-living God,
we do well always and everywhere to give you thanks and praise.
You never cease to call us
to a new and more abundant life.
God of love and mercy,
you are always ready to forgive;
we are sinners
and you invite us
to trust in your mercy.

Time and time again
we broke your covenant,
but you did not abandon us.
Instead, through your Son, Jesus our Lord,
you bound yourself even more closely to the human family
by a bond that can never be broken.

Now is the time
for your people to turn back to you
and to be renewed in Christ your Son,
a time of grace and reconciliation.

You invite us
to serve the family of mankind
by opening our hearts
to the fullness of your Holy Spirit.

In wonder and gratitude,
we join our voices with the choirs of heaven
to proclaim the power of your love
and to sing of our salvation in Christ:
Holy, holy, holy...

Father, from the beginning of time
you have always done what is good for man
so that we may be holy as you are holy.

Look with kindness on your people
gathered here before you:
send forth the power of your Spirit
so that these gifts may become for us
the body and blood of your beloved Son, Jesus the Christ,
in whom we have become your sons and daughters.

When we were lost
and could not find the way to you,
you loved us more than ever:
Jesus, your Son, innocent and without sin,
gave himself into our hands
and was nailed to a cross.
Yet before he stretched out his arms between heaven and earth
in the everlasting sign of your covenant,
he desired to celebrate the Paschal feast
in the company of his disciples.

While they were at supper,
he took bread and gave you thanks and praise.
He broke the bread, gave it to his disciples, and said:
TAKE THIS, ALL OF YOU, AND EAT IT:
THIS IS MY BODY WHICH WILL BE GIVEN UP FOR YOU.

At the end of the meal,
knowing that he was to reconcile all things in himself
by the blood of his cross,
he took the cup, filled with wine.
Again he gave you thanks, handed the cup to his friends,
        and said:
TAKE THIS, ALL OF YOU, AND DRINK FROM IT:
THIS IS THE CUP OF MY BLOOD,
THE BLOOD OF THE NEW AND EVERLASTING COVENANT.
IT WILL BE SHED FOR YOU AND FOR ALL
SO THAT SINS MAY BE FORGIVEN.
DO THIS IN MEMORY OF ME.

Let us proclaim the mystery of faith:

1. **Christ has died,**
    Christ is risen,
    Christ will come again.

2. **Dying you destroyed our death,**
    rising you restored our life.
    Lord Jesus, come in glory.

3. **When we eat this bread and drink this cup,**
    we proclaim your death, Lord Jesus,
    until you come in glory.

4. **Lord, by your cross and resurrection**
    you have set us free.
    You are the Saviour of the world.

5. **My Lord and my God.** (for Ireland only)

We do this in memory of Jesus Christ,
our Passover and our lasting peace.
We celebrate his death and resurrection
and look for the coming of that day
when he will return to give us the fullness of joy.
Therefore we offer you, God ever faithful and true,
the sacrifice which restores man to your friendship.

Father,
look with love
on those you have called
to share in the one sacrifice of Christ.
By the power of your Holy Spirit
make them one body,
healed of all division.

Keep us all
in communion of mind and heart
with N., our Pope, and N., our bishop.
Help us to work together
for the coming of your kingdom,
until at last we stand in your presence
to share the life of the saints,
in the company of the Virgin Mary and the apostles,
and of our departed brothers and sisters
whom we commend to your mercy.

Then, freed from every shadow of death,
we shall take our place in the new creation
and give you thanks
with Christ, our risen Lord.

Through him,
with him,
in him,
in the unity of the Holy Spirit,
all glory and honour is yours,
almighty Father,
for ever and ever.
Amen.

(Turn to page 54)

EUCHARISTIC PRAYER
FOR MASSES OF RECONCILIATION II

PREFACE

Father, all-powerful and ever-living God,
we praise and thank you through Jesus Christ our Lord
for your presence and action in the world.

In the midst of conflict and division,
we know it is you
who turn our minds to thoughts of peace.
Your Spirit changes our hearts:
enemies begin to speak to one another,
those who were estranged join hands in friendship,
and nations seek the way of peace together.

Your Spirit is at work
when understanding puts an end to strife,
when hatred is quenched by mercy,
and vengeance gives way to forgiveness.

For this we should never cease
to thank and praise you.
We join with all the choirs of heaven
as they sing for ever to your glory:
Holy, holy, holy...

God of power and might,
we praise you through your Son, Jesus Christ,
who comes in your name.
He is the Word that brings salvation.
He is the hand you stretch out to sinners.
He is the way that leads to your peace.

God our Father,
we had wandered far from you,
but through your Son you have brought us back.
You gave him up to death
so that we might turn again to you
and find our way to one another.

Therefore we celebrate the reconciliation
Christ has gained for us.
We ask you to sanctify these gifts
by the power of your Spirit,
as we now fulfil your Son's ✠ command.

While he was at supper
on the night before he died for us,
he took bread in his hands,
and gave you thanks and praise.
He broke the bread,
gave it to his disciples, and said:

TAKE THIS, ALL OF YOU, AND EAT IT:
THIS IS MY BODY WHICH WILL BE GIVEN UP FOR YOU.

At the end of the meal he took the cup.
Again he praised you for your goodness,
gave the cup to his disciples, and said:

TAKE THIS, ALL OF YOU, AND DRINK FROM IT:
THIS IS THE CUP OF MY BLOOD,
THE BLOOD OF THE NEW AND EVERLASTING COVENANT.
IT WILL BE SHED FOR YOU AND FOR ALL
SO THAT SINS MAY BE FORGIVEN.
DO THIS IN MEMORY OF ME.

Let us proclaim the mystery of faith:

1. **Christ has died,**
   Christ is risen,
   Christ will come again.

2. **Dying you destroyed our death,**
   rising you restored our life.
   Lord Jesus, come in glory.

3. **When we eat this bread and drink this cup,**
   we proclaim your death, Lord Jesus,
   until you come in glory.

4. **Lord, by your cross and resurrection**
   you have set us free.
   You are the Saviour of the world.

5. **My Lord and my God.** *(for Ireland only)*

Lord our God,
your Son has entrusted to us
this pledge of his love.
We celebrate the memory of his death and resurrection
and bring you the gift you have given us,
the sacrifice of reconciliation.
Therefore, we ask you, Father,
to accept us, together with your Son.

Fill us with his Spirit
through our sharing in this meal.
May he take away all that divides us.

May this Spirit keep us always in communion
with N., our Pope, N., our bishop,
with all the bishops and all your people.
Father, make your Church throughout the world
a sign of unity and an instrument of your peace.

You have gathered us here
around the table of your Son,
in fellowship with the Virgin Mary, Mother of God,
        and all the saints.
In that new world where the fullness of your peace will be
        revealed,
gather people of every race, language, and way of life
to share in the one eternal banquet
with Jesus Christ the Lord.

Through him,
with him,
in him,
in the unity of the Holy Spirit,
all glory and honour is yours,
almighty Father,
for ever and ever.
Amen.

(Turn to page 54)

EUCHARISTIC PRAYER
FOR MASSES WITH CHILDREN I

PREFACE
God our Father,
you have brought us here together
so that we can give you thanks and praise
for all the wonderful things you have done.
We thank you for all that is beautiful in the world
and for the happiness you have given us.
We praise you for daylight
and for your word which lights up our minds.

We praise you for the earth,
and all the people who live on it,
and for our life which comes from you.

We know that you are good.
You love us and do great things for us.
So we all sing (say) together:

**Holy, holy, holy Lord, God of power and might,
heaven and earth are full of your glory.
        Hosanna in the highest.**

Father,
you are always thinking about your people;
you never forget us.
You sent us your Son Jesus,
who gave his life for us
and who came to save us.
He cured sick people;
he cared for those who were poor
and wept with those who were sad.
He forgave sinners
and taught us to forgive each other.
He loved everyone
and showed us how to be kind.
He took children in his arms and blessed them.
So we are glad to sing (say):

**Blessed is he who comes in the name of the Lord.
        Hosanna in the highest.**

God our Father,
all over the world your people praise you.
So now we pray with the whole Church:
with N., our Pope and N., our bishop.
In heaven the blessed Virgin Mary,
the apostles and all the saints
always sing your praise.
Now we join with them and with the angels
to adore you as we sing:

**Holy, holy, holy Lord, God of power and might,
heaven and earth are full of your glory.
        Hosanna in the highest.
Blessed is he who comes in the name of the Lord.
        Hosanna in the highest.**

God our Father,
you are most holy
and we want to show you that we are grateful.
We bring you bread and wine
and ask you to send your Holy Spirit to make these gifts
the body ✠ and blood of Jesus your Son.
Then we can offer to you
what you have given to us.

On the night before he died,
Jesus was having supper with his apostles.
He took bread from the table.
He gave you thanks and praise.
Then he broke the bread,
gave it to his friends, and said:
TAKE THIS, ALL OF YOU, AND EAT IT:
THIS IS MY BODY WHICH WILL BE GIVEN UP FOR YOU.

When supper was ended,
Jesus took the cup that was filled with wine.
He thanked you, gave it to his friends, and said:
TAKE THIS, ALL OF YOU, AND DRINK FROM IT:
THIS IS THE CUP OF MY BLOOD,
THE BLOOD OF THE NEW AND EVERLASTING COVENANT.
IT WILL BE SHED FOR YOU AND FOR ALL
SO THAT SINS MAY BE FORGIVEN.
DO THIS IN MEMORY OF ME.

We do now what Jesus told us to do.
We remember his death and his resurrection
and we offer you, Father, the bread that gives us life,
and the cup that saves us.
Jesus brings us to you;
welcome us as you welcome him.

Let us proclaim the mystery of faith:

1. **Christ has died,**
   Christ is risen,
   Christ will come again.

2. **Dying you destroyed our death,**
   rising you restored our life.
   Lord Jesus, come in glory.

3. **When we eat this bread and drink this cup,**
   we proclaim your death, Lord Jesus,
   until you come in glory.

4. **Lord, by your cross and resurrection**
   you have set us free.
   You are the Saviour of the world.

5. **My Lord and my God.** *(for Ireland only)*

Father,
because you love us,
you invite us to come to your table.
Fill us with the joy of the Holy Spirit
as we receive the body and blood of your Son.

Lord,
you never forget any of your children.
We ask you to take care of those we love,
especially of N. and N.,
and we pray for those who have died.
Remember everyone who is suffering from pain or sorrow.

Remember Christians everywhere
and all other people in the world.
We are filled with wonder and praise
when we see what you do for us
through Jesus your Son,
and so we sing:

Through him,
with him,
in him,
in the unity of the Holy Spirit,
all glory and honour is yours,
almighty Father,
for ever and ever.
Amen.

(Turn to page 54)

EUCHARISTIC PRAYER
FOR MASSES WITH CHILDREN II

PREFACE

God our loving Father,
we are glad to give you thanks and praise
because you love us.
With Jesus we sing your praise:

Glory to God in the highest.

or

Hosanna in the highest.

Because you love us,
you gave us this great and beautiful world.
With Jesus we sing your praise:

Glory to God in the highest.

or

Hosanna in the highest.

Because you love us,
you sent Jesus your Son
to bring us to you
and to gather us around him
as the children of one family.
With Jesus we sing your praise:

Glory to God in the highest.

or

Hosanna in the highest.

For such great love
we thank you with the angels and saints
as they praise you and sing:

Holy, holy, holy Lord, God of power and might,
heaven and earth are full of your glory.
     Hosanna in the highest.
Blessed is he who comes in the name of the Lord.
     Hosanna in the highest.

Blessed be Jesus, whom you sent
to be the friend of children and of the poor.
He came to show us
how we can love you, Father,
by loving one another.

He came to take away sin,
which keeps us from being friends,
and hate, which makes us all unhappy.

He promised to send the Holy Spirit,
to be with us always
so that we can live as your children.

Blessed is he who comes in the name of the Lord.
    Hosanna in the highest.

God our Father,
we now ask you
to send your Holy Spirit
to change these gifts of bread and wine
into the body ✠ and blood
of Jesus Christ, our Lord.

The night before he died,
Jesus your Son showed us how much you love us.
When he was at supper with his disciples,
he took bread,
and gave you thanks and praise.
Then he broke the bread,
gave it to his friends, and said:
TAKE THIS, ALL OF YOU, AND EAT IT:
THIS IS MY BODY WHICH WILL BE GIVEN UP FOR YOU.

Jesus has given his life for us.

When supper was ended,
Jesus took the cup that was filled with wine.
He thanked you, gave it to his friends, and said:
TAKE THIS, ALL OF YOU, AND DRINK FROM IT:
THIS IS THE CUP OF MY BLOOD,
THE BLOOD OF THE NEW AND EVERLASTING COVENANT.
IT WILL BE SHED FOR YOU AND FOR ALL
SO THAT SINS MAY BE FORGIVEN.

Jesus has given his life for us.

Then he said to them:
DO THIS IN MEMORY OF ME.

And so, loving Father,
we remember that Jesus died and rose again
to save the world.
He put himself into our hands
to be the sacrifice we offer you.

We praise you, we bless you, we thank you.

Lord our God,
listen to our prayer.
Send the Holy Spirit
to all of us who share in this meal.
May this Spirit bring us closer together
in the family of the Church,
with N., our Pope,
N., our bishop,
all other bishops,
and all who serve your people.

We praise you, we bless you, we thank you.

Remember, Father, our families and friends (N.)
and all those we do not love as we should.
Remember those who have died (N.)
Bring them home to you
to be with you for ever.

We praise you, we bless you, we thank you.

Gather us all together into your kingdom.
There we shall be happy for ever
with the Virgin Mary, Mother of God and our mother.
There all the friends
of Jesus the Lord will sing a song of joy.

We praise you, we bless you, we thank you.

Through him,
with him,
in him,
in the unity of the Holy Spirit,
all glory and honour is yours,
almighty Father,
for ever and ever.
Amen.

(Turn to page 54)

EUCHARISTIC PRAYER
FOR MASSES WITH CHILDREN III

PREFACE

* We thank you,
God our Father.
You made us to live for you and for each other.
We can see and speak to one another,
and become friends,
and share our joys and sorrows.

* During Easter season

We thank you,
God our Father.
You are the living God;
you have called us to share in your life,
and to be happy with you for ever.
You raised up Jesus, your Son,
the first among us to rise from the dead,
and gave him new life.
You have promised to give us new life also,
a life that will never end,
a life with no more anxiety and suffering.

And so, Father, we gladly thank you
with everyone who believes in you;
with the saints and the angels,
we rejoice and praise you, saying:

Holy, holy, holy ...

Yes, Lord, you are holy;
you are kind to us and to all.
For this we thank you.
We thank you above all for your Son, Jesus Christ.

† You sent him into this world
because people had turned away from you
and no longer loved each other.
He opened our eyes and our hearts
to understand that we are brothers and sisters
and that you are Father of us all.

† During Easter season

He brought us the Good News
of life to be lived with you for ever in heaven.

He showed us the way to that life,
the way of love.
He himself has gone that way before us.

He now brings us together to one table
and asks us to do what he did.

Father,
we ask you to bless these gifts of bread and wine
and make them holy.
Change them for us into the body ✠ and blood of Jesus Christ,
    your Son.
On the night before he died for us,
he had supper for the last time with his disciples.
He took bread and gave you thanks.
He broke the bread
and gave it to his friends, saying:
TAKE THIS, ALL OF YOU, AND EAT IT:
THIS IS MY BODY WHICH WILL BE GIVEN UP FOR YOU.

In the same way he took a cup of wine.
He gave you thanks
and handed the cup to his disciples, saying:
TAKE THIS, ALL OF YOU, AND DRINK FROM IT:
THIS IS THE CUP OF MY BLOOD,
THE BLOOD OF THE NEW AND EVERLASTING COVENANT.
IT WILL BE SHED FOR YOU AND FOR ALL
SO THAT SINS MAY BE FORGIVEN.

Then he said to them:
DO THIS IN MEMORY OF ME.

God our Father,
we remember with joy
all that Jesus did to save us.
In this holy sacrifice,
which he gave as a gift to his Church,
we remember his death and resurrection.

Father in heaven,
accept us together with your beloved Son.
He willingly died for us,
but you raised him to life again.
We thank you and say:

Glory to God in the highest.

Jesus now lives with you in glory,
but he is also here on earth, among us.
We thank you and say:

Glory to God in the highest.

One day he will come in glory
and in his kingdom
there will be no more suffering,
no more tears, no more sadness.
We thank you and say:

Glory to God in the highest.

Father in heaven,
you have called us
to receive the body and blood of Christ at this table
and to be filled with the joy of the Holy Spirit.
Through this sacred meal
give us strength to please you more and more.

Lord, our God,
remember N., our Pope,
N., our bishop, and all other bishops.

* Help all who follow Jesus
to work for peace
and to bring happiness to others.

During Easter season:
Fill all Christians with the gladness of Easter.
Help us to bring this joy
to all who are sorrowful.

Bring us all at last
together with Mary, the Mother of God,
and all the saints,
to live with you
and to be one with Christ in heaven.

Through him,
with him,
in him,
in the unity of the Holy Spirit,
all glory and honour is yours,
almighty Father,
for ever and ever. **Amen.**

COMMUNION RITE

Let us pray with confidence to the Father
in the words our Saviour gave us:

or

Jesus taught us to call God our Father,
and so we have the courage to say:

or

Let us ask our Father to forgive our sins
and to bring us to forgive those who sin against us:

or

Let us pray for the coming of the kingdom
as Jesus taught us:

At the priest's invitation all sing or say the Lord's Prayer.

Our Father, who art in heaven,
hallowed be thy name.
Thy kingdom come.
Thy will be done on earth as it is in heaven.
Give us this day our daily bread,
and forgive us our trespasses,
as we forgive those who trespass against us,
and lead us not into temptation,
but deliver us from evil.

Deliver us, Lord, from every evil,
and grant us peace in our day.
In your mercy keep us free from sin
and protect us from all anxiety
as we wait in joyful hope
for the coming of our Saviour, Jesus Christ.

For the kingdom, the power, and the glory
are yours, now and for ever.

Lord Jesus Christ, you said to your apostles:
I leave you peace, my peace I give you.
Look not on our sins, but on the faith of your Church,
and grant us the peace and unity of your kingdom
where you live for ever and ever. **Amen.**

The peace of the Lord be with you always.
And also with you.

Let us offer each other the sign of peace.

All make a sign of peace according to local custom.

May this mingling of the body and blood of our Lord Jesus Christ
bring eternal life to us who receive it.

Lamb of God, you take away the sins of the world:
have mercy on us.
Lamb of God, you take away the sins of the world:
have mercy on us.
Lamb of God, you take away the sins of the world:
grant us peace.

The priest says quietly:

Lord Jesus Christ, Son of the living God,
by the will of the Father and the work of the Holy Spirit
your death brought life to the world.
By your holy body and blood
free me from all my sins and from every evil.
Keep me faithful to your teaching,
and never let me be parted from you.

or

Lord Jesus Christ,
with faith in your love and mercy
I eat your body and drink your blood.
Let it not bring me condemnation,
but health in mind and body.

Showing the Host to the people, the priest says:

This is the Lamb of God
who takes away the sins of the world.
Happy are those who are called to his supper.

Lord, I am not worthy to receive you,
but only say the word and I shall be healed.

COMMUNION ANTIPHON

(Turn to the Mass of the day)

The communicant is offered the host:

The body of Christ.
Amen.

When the communicant is offered the chalice:

The blood of Christ.
Amen.

PRAYER AFTER COMMUNION

(Turn to the Mass of the day)

CONCLUDING RITE

The Lord be with you.
And also with you.

May almighty God bless you,
the Father, and the Son, ✠ and the Holy Spirit.
Amen.

Go in the peace of Christ.

or

The Mass is ended, go in peace.

or

Go in peace to love and serve the Lord.
Thanks be to God.

SOLEMN BLESSINGS

ADVENT

You believe that the Son of God once came to us;
you look for him to come again.
May his coming bring you the light of his holiness
and free you with his blessing.
Amen.

May God make you steadfast in faith,
joyful in hope, and untiring in love
all the days of your life.
Amen.

You rejoice that our Redeemer came to live with us as man.
When he comes again in glory,
may he reward you with endless life.
Amen.

May almighty God bless you,
the Father, and the Son, ✠ and the Holy Spirit.
Amen.

EASTER SEASON

Through the resurrection of his Son
God has redeemed you and made you his children.
May he bless you with joy.
Amen.

The Redeemer has given you lasting freedom.
May you inherit his everlasting life.
Amen.

By faith you rose with him in baptism.
May your lives be holy,
so that you will be united with him for ever.
Amen.

May almighty God bless you,
the Father, and the Son, ✠ and the Holy Spirit.
Amen.

ORDINARY TIME I: Blessing of Aaron (Numbers 6:24-26)

May the Lord bless you and keep you.
Amen.

May his face shine upon you,
and be gracious to you.
Amen.

May he look upon you with kindness,
and give you his peace.
Amen.

May almighty God bless you,
the Father, and the Son, ✠ and the Holy Spirit.
Amen.

ORDINARY TIME II (Philippians 4:7)

May the peace of God
which is beyond all understanding
keep your hearts and minds
in the knowledge and love of God
and of his Son, our Lord Jesus Christ.
Amen.

May almighty God bless you,
the Father, and the Son, ✠ and the Holy Spirit.
Amen.

ORDINARY TIME III

May almighty God bless you in his mercy,
and make you always aware of his saving wisdom.
Amen.

May he strengthen your faith with proofs of his love,
so that you will persevere in good works. **Amen.**

May he direct your steps to himself,
and show you how to walk in charity and peace.
Amen.

May almighty God bless you,
the Father, and the Son, ✠ and the Holy Spirit.
Amen.

ORDINARY TIME IV

May the God of all consolation
bless you in every way
and grant you peace all the days of your life.
Amen.

May he free you from all anxiety
and strengthen your hearts in his love.
Amen.

May he enrich you with his gifts of faith, hope, and love,
so that what you do in this life
will bring you to the happiness of everlasting life.
Amen.

May almighty God bless you,
the Father, and the Son, ✠ and the Holy Spirit.
Amen.

ORDINARY TIME V

May almighty God keep you from all harm
and bless you with every good gift.
Amen.

May he set his Word in your heart
and fill you with lasting joy.
Amen.

May you walk in his ways,
always knowing what is right and good,
until you enter your heavenly inheritance.
Amen.

May almighty God bless you,
the Father, and the Son, ✠ and the Holy Spirit.
Amen.

LATIN TEXTS

(PEOPLE'S PARTS)

INTRODUCTORY RITES

In nómine Patris, et Fílii, et Spíritus Sancti.
Amen.

or

Dóminus vobíscum.
Et cum spíritu tuo.

CONFITEOR

Confíteor Deo omnipoténti et vobis, fratres,
quia peccávi nimis
cogitatióne, verbo, ópere et omissióne:
(All strike their breast)
mea culpa, mea culpa, mea máxima culpa.
Ideo precor beátam Maríam semper Vírginem,
omnes Angelos et Sanctos,
et vos, fratres, oráre pro me
ad Dóminum Deum nostrum.

KYRIE

Kyrie, eléison. **Kyrie, eléison.**
Christe, eléison. **Christe, eléison.**
Kyrie, eléison. **Kyrie, eléison.**

GLORIA

Glória in excélsis Deo
et in terra pax homínibus bonæ voluntátis.
Laudámus te, benedícimus te,
adorámus te, glorificámus te,
grátias ágimus tibi propter magnam glóriam tuam,
Dómine Deus, Rex cæléstis,
Deus Pater omnípotens.
Dómine Fili unigénite, Iesu Christe,
Dómine Deus, Agnus Dei, Fílius Patris,
qui tollis peccáta mundi, miserére nobis;
qui tollis peccáta mundi,
    súscipe deprecatiónem nostram.
Qui sedes ad déxteram Patris, miserére nobis.
Quóniam tu solus Sanctus, tu solus Dóminus,
    tu solus Altíssimus,

Iesu Christe, cum Sancto Spíritu:
    in glória Dei Patris. Amen.

After the first and second readings
Deo grátias.

Before the Gospel
Dóminus vobíscum.
Et cum spíritu tuo.

Léctio sancti Evangélii secúndum N.
Glória tibi, Dómine.

At the end of the Gospel
Verbum Dómini.
Laus tibi, Christe.

CREDO
Credo in unum Deum,
Patrem omnipoténtem, factórem cæli et terræ,
visibílium ómnium et invisibílium.
Et in unum Dóminum Iesum Christum,
Fílium Dei unigénitum,
et ex Patre natum ante ómnia sæcula.
Deum de Deo, lumen de lúmine,
    Deum verum de Deo vero,
génitum, non factum, consubstantiálem Patri:
per quem ómnia facta sunt.
Qui propter nos hómines
    et propter nostram salútem
descéndit de cælis.

(All bow during the next two lines)

Et incarnátus est de Spíritu Sancto
ex María Vírgine, et homo factus est.
Crucifíxus étiam pro nobis sub Póntio Piláto;
passus et sepúltus est,
et resurréxit tértia die, secúndum Scriptúras,
et ascéndit in cælum, sedet ad déxteram Patris.
Et íterum ventúrus est cum glória,
    iudicáre vivos et mórtuos,
cuius regni non erit finis.
Et in Spíritum Sanctum, Dóminum et vivificántem:
qui ex Patre Filióque procédit.
Qui cum Patre et Fílio simul adorátur
    et conglorificátur:

qui locútus est per prophétas.
Et unam, sanctam, cathólicam et apostólicam Ecclésiam.
Confíteor unum baptísma in remissiónem peccatórum.
Et exspécto resurrectiónem mortuórum,
et vítam ventúri sǽculi. Amen.

Response to offertory prayers
Benedíctus Deus in sǽcula.

Response to the Orate Fratres
**Suscípiat Dóminus sacrifícium de mánibus tuis
ad laudem et glóriam nóminis sui,
ad utilitátem quoque nostram
totiúsque Ecclésiæ suæ sanctæ.**

Dialogue before the Preface
Dóminus vobíscum.
Et cum spíritu tuo.

Sursum corda.
Habémus ad Dóminum.

Grátias agámus Dómino Deo nostro.
Dignum et iustum est.

SANCTUS

**Sanctus, Sanctus, Sanctus Dóminus Deus Sábaoth.
Pleni sunt cæli et terra glória tua.
Hosánna in excélsis.
Benedíctus qui venit in nómine Dómini.
Hosánna in excélsis.**

After the Consecration
Mystérium fidei.

1. **Mortem tuam annuntiámus, Dómine,
   et tuam resurrectiónem confitémur, donec vénias.**

2. **Quotiescúmque manducámus panem hunc
   et cálicem bíbimus,
   mortem tuam annuntiámus, Dómine, donec vénias.**

3. **Salvátor mundi, salva nos,
   qui per crucem et resurrectiónem tuam liberásti nos.**

PATER NOSTER

Præcéptis salutáribus móniti,
et divína institutióne formáti,
audémus dicere:

Pater noster, qui es in cælis:
sanctificétur nomen tuum;
advéniat regnum tuum;
fiat volúntas tua, sicut in cælo, et in terra.
Panem nostrum cotidiánum da nobis hódie;
et dimítte nobis débita nostra,
sicut et nos dimíttimus debitóribus nostris;
et ne nos indúcas in tentatiónem;
sed líbera nos a malo.

Acclamation after the Our Father
Quia tuum est regnum,
et potéstas, et glória
in sǽcula.

At the Pax
Pax Dómini sit semper vobíscum.
Et cum spíritu tuo.

AGNUS DEI
Agnus Dei, qui tollis peccáta mundi:
    miserére nobis.
Agnus Dei, qui tollis peccáta mundi:
    miserére nobis.
Agnus Dei, qui tollis peccáta mundi:
    dona nobis pacem.

Lord, I am not worthy
Domine, non sum dignus ut intres sub tectum meum:
sed tantum dic verbo, et sanabitur ánima mea.

CONCLUSION
Dóminus vobíscum.
Et cum spíritu tuo.

Benedícat vos omnípotens Deus
Pater, et Fílius, ✠ et Spíritus Sanctus
Amen.

Ite, missa est.
Deo grátias.

1 JANUARY
SOLEMNITY OF MARY, MOTHER OF GOD

The first day of the New Year is also the last day of the week-long celebration which began on Christmas Day. The Christmas season itself will continue until the Saturday after the Epiphany. The liturgy today stresses the good purpose of God revealed at the incarnation: to save humanity. On the threshold of a new year, image of mother and the child is put before us as a reminder of how close to us God is and will be throughout the course this year.

ENTRANCE ANTIPHON   *(cf. Is 9:2.6; Lk 1:33)*

A light will shine on us this day, the Lord is born for us: he shall be called Wonderful God, Prince of Peace, Father of the world to come; and his kingship will never end.

or

Hail, holy Mother! The child to whom you gave birth is the King of heaven and earth for ever.

GREETING, PENITENTIAL RITE, GLORIA — *pages 7-14*

OPENING PRAYER

Let us pray
    [that Mary, the mother of the Lord,
    will help us by her prayers]

God our Father,
may we always profit by the prayers
of the Virgin Mother Mary,
for you bring us life and salvation
through Jesus Christ her Son
who lives and reigns with you and the Holy Spirit,
one God, for ever and ever.

or

Let us pray
    [in the name of Jesus,
    born of a virgin and Son of God]

Father,
source of light in every age,
the virgin conceived and bore your Son
who is called Wonderful God, Prince of peace.

May her prayer, the gift of a mother's love,
be your people's joy through all ages.

May her response, born of a humble heart,
draw your Spirit to rest on your people.

FIRST READING   (Nb 6:22-27)

A reading from the book of Numbers.

They are to call down my name on the sons of Israel, and I will bless them.

The Lord spoke to Moses and said, 'Say this to Aaron and his
sons: "This is how you are to bless the sons of Israel. You shall
say to them:

> May the Lord bless you and keep you.
> May the Lord let his face shine on you and be gracious to you.
> May the Lord uncover his face to you and bring you peace."

This is how they are to call down my name on the sons of
Israel, and I will bless them.'

This is the word of the Lord.

RESPONSORIAL PSALM   (Ps 66:2-3.5.6.8)

℟   **O God, be gracious and bless us.**

1.   God, be gracious and bless us
     and let your face shed its light upon us.
     So will your ways be known upon earth
     and all nations learn your saving help. ℟

2.   Let the nations be glad and exult
     for you rule the world with justice.
     With fairness you rule the peoples,
     you guide the nations on earth. ℟

3.   Let the peoples praise you, O God;
     let all the peoples praise you.
     May God still give us his blessing
     till the ends of the earth revere him. ℟

SECOND READING   (Gal 4:4-7)

A reading from the letter of St Paul to the Galatians.

God sent his Son, born of a woman.

When the appointed time came, God sent his Son, born of a
woman, born a subject of the Law, to redeem the subjects of the
Law and to enable us to be adopted as sons. The proof that you
are sons is that God has sent the Spirit of his Son into our hearts:
the Spirit that cries, 'Abba, Father', and it is this that makes you a
son, you are not a slave any more; and if God has made you son,
then he has made you heir.

This is the word of the Lord.

GOSPEL ACCLAMATION *(Heb 1:1-2)*

Alleluia, alleluia!
At various times in the past
and in various different ways,
God spoke to our ancestors through the prophets;
but in our own time, the last days,
he has spoken to us through his Son.
Alleluia!

GOSPEL *(Lk 2:16-21)*

A reading from the holy Gospel according to Luke.

They found Mary and Joseph and the baby... When the eighth day came, they gave him the name Jesus.

The shepherds hurried away to Bethlehem and found Mary and Joseph, and the baby lying in the manger. When they saw the child they repeated what they had been told about him, and everyone who heard it was astonished at what the shepherds had to say. As for Mary, she treasured all these things and pondered them in her heart. And the shepherds went back glorifying and praising God for all they had heard and seen; it was exactly as they had been told.

When the eighth day came and the child was to be circumcised, they gave him the name Jesus, the name the angel had given him before his conception.

This is the Gospel of the Lord.

PROFESSION OF FAITH — *pages 15-16*

PRAYER OVER THE GIFTS

God our Father,
we celebrate at this season
the beginning of our salvation.
On this feast of Mary, the Mother of God,
we ask that our salvation
will be brought to its fulfilment.

PREFACE OF THE BLESSED VIRGIN MARY

Father, all-powerful and ever-living God,
we do well always and everywhere to give you thanks
as we celebrate the motherhood of the Blessed Virgin Mary.

Through the power of the Holy Spirit,
she became the virgin mother of your only Son,
our Lord Jesus Christ,
who is for ever the light of the world.

Through him the choirs of angels
and all the powers of heaven
praise and worship your glory.
May our voices blend with theirs
as we join in their unending hymn:
Holy, holy, holy...

COMMUNION ANTIPHON   *(Heb 13:8)*

Jesus Christ is the same yesterday, today, and for ever.

PRAYER AFTER COMMUNION

Father,
as we proclaim the Virgin Mary
to be the mother of Christ and the mother of the Church,
may our communion with her Son
bring us to salvation.

SOLEMN BLESSING

Every good gift comes from the Father of light.
May he grant you his grace and every blessing,
and keep you safe throughout the coming year.
Amen.

May he grant you unwavering faith,
constant hope, and love that endures to the end.
Amen.

May he order your days and work in his peace,
hear your every prayer,
and lead you to everlasting life and joy.
Amen.

May almighty God bless you,
the Father, and the Son, ✠ and the Holy Spirit.
Amen.

REFLECTION

Today we are invited by the Church to look on Mary as the
Mother of God. The role of Mary in the Church is always
connected with the person and work of her Son. This
extraordinary title of Mary's which we are presented with in
today's liturgy points to one of the basic truth about her Son,
that he is the Son of God.

4 JANUARY

SECOND SUNDAY AFTER CHRISTMAS

(In Scotland the Epiphany *is celebrated
on this Sunday — see page 71)*

Today's celebration, coming as it does between Christmas Day
and the Epiphany contains themes which are connected to
these feasts. Though Christmas Day and the Epiphany form
part of the Church's season of Christmas tide, there is a
difference of emphasis. Christmas Day celebrates the coming
of the Son of God as a human being and the Epiphany
highlights the revealing of this truth to all the nations of the
earth. Both themes are echoed in today's prayers.

ENTRANCE ANTIPHON   *(Ws 18:14-15)*

**When peaceful silence lay over all, and night had run half of
her swift course, your all-powerful word, O Lord, leaped
down from heaven, from the royal throne.**

GREETING, PENITENTIAL RITE, GLORIA — *pages 7-14*

OPENING PRAYER

Let us pray
    [that all humankind may be enlightened by the gospel]

God of power and life,
glory of all who believe in you,
fill the world with your splendour
and show the nations the light of your truth.

or

Let us pray
    [aware of the dignity to which we are called
    by the love of Christ]

Father of our Lord Jesus Christ,
our glory is to stand before the world
as your own sons and daughters.

May the simple beauty of Jesus' birth
summon us always to love what is most deeply human,
and to see your Word made flesh
reflected in those whose lives we touch.

FIRST READING   *(Si 24:1-2.8-12)*

A reading from the book of Ecclesiasticus.

The wisdom of God has pitched her tent among the chosen people.

Wisdom speaks her own praises,
in the midst of her people she glories in herself.
She opens her mouth in the assembly of the Most High,
she glories in herself in the presence of the Mighty One.

'Then the creator of all things instructed me,
and he who created me fixed a place for my tent.
He said, "Pitch your tent in Jacob,
make Israel your inheritance."
From eternity, in the beginning, he created me,
and for eternity I shall remain.
I ministered before him in the holy tabernacle,
and thus was I established on Zion.
In the beloved city he has given me rest,
and in Jerusalem I wield my authority.
I have taken root in a privileged people
in the Lord's property, in his inheritance.'
This is the word of the Lord.

RESPONSORIAL PSALM   *(Ps 147:12-15.19-20)*

℟   **The Word was made flesh, and lived among us.**
or **Alleluia!**

1. O praise the Lord, Jerusalem!
    Zion, praise your God!
    He has strengthened the bars of your gates,
    he has blessed the children within you. ℟

2. He established peace on your borders,
    he feeds you with finest wheat.
    He sends out his word to the earth
    and swiftly runs his command. ℟

3. He makes his word known to Jacob,
    to Israel his laws and decrees.
    He has not dealt thus with other nations;
    he has not taught them his decrees. ℟

SECOND READING   *(Eph 1:3-6.15-18)*
A reading from the letter of St Paul to the Ephesians.
He determined that we should become his adopted sons through Jesus.

Blessed be God the Father of our Lord Jesus Christ, who has
blessed us with all the spiritual blessings of heaven in Christ.
Before the world was made, he chose us, chose us in Christ, to
be holy and spotless, and to live through love in his presence,
determining that we should become his adopted sons, through

Jesus Christ, for his own kind purposes, to make us praise the glory of his grace, his free gift to us in the Beloved.

That will explain why I, having once heard about your faith in the Lord Jesus, and the love that you show towards all the saints, have never failed to remember you in my prayers and to thank God for you. May the God of our Lord Jesus Christ, the Father of glory, give you a spirit of wisdom and perception of what is revealed, to bring you to full knowledge of him. May he enlighten the eyes of your mind so that you can see what hope his call holds for you, what rich glories he has promised the saints will inherit.

This is the word of the Lord.

GOSPEL ACCLAMATION   *(cf. 1 Tm 3:16)*

Alleluia, alleluia!
Glory be to you, O Christ, proclaimed to the pagans;
Glory be to you, O Christ, believed in by the world.
Alleluia!

GOSPEL   *(Jn 1:1-18)*

(For Shorter Form, *read between* ◗ ◖*)*

A reading from the holy Gospel according to John.

The Word was made flesh, and lived among us.

◗In the beginning was the Word:
the Word was with God
and the Word was God.
He was with God in the beginning.
Through him all things came to be,
not one thing had its being but through him.
All that came to be had life in him
and that life was the light of men,
a light that shines in the dark,
a light that darkness could not overpower.◖

A man came, sent by God.
His name was John.
He came as a witness,
as a witness to speak for the light,
so that everyone might believe through him.
He was not the light,
only a witness to speak for the light.

◗The Word was the true light
that enlightens all men;
and he was coming into the world.

He was in the world
that had its being through him,
and the world did not know him.
He came to his own domain
and his own people did not accept him.
But to all who did accept him
he gave power to become children of God,
to all who believe in the name of him
who was born not out of human stock
or urge of the flesh
or will of man
but of God himself.
The Word was made flesh,
he lived among us,
and we saw his glory,
the glory that is his as the only Son of the Father,
full of grace and truth.◀

John appears as his witness. He proclaims:
'This is the one of whom I said:
He who comes after me
ranks before me
because he existed before me'.

Indeed, from his fullness we have, all of us, received—
yes, grace in return for grace,
since, though the Law was given through Moses,
grace and truth have come through Jesus Christ.
No one has ever seen God;
it is the only Son, who is nearest to the Father's heart,
who has made him known.

   ▶This is the Gospel of the Lord.◀

PROFESSION OF FAITH — *pages 15-16*

PRAYER OVER THE GIFTS
Lord, make holy these gifts
through the coming of your Son,
who shows us the way of truth
and promises the life of your kingdom.

PREFACE OF CHRISTMAS I-III — *page 19*

COMMUNION ANTIPHON   *(Jn 1:12)*
He gave to all who accepted him the power to become
children of God.

PRAYER AFTER COMMUNION
Lord,
hear our prayers.
By this eucharist free us from sin
and keep us faithful to your word.

SOLEMN BLESSING — *page 400*

REFLECTION

> God's Son has become a human being with the conception
> and birth of Jesus. But this truth is not just an abstract one. It
> has a meaning for the human race. It was to show God's love
> for every human being that God's Son was born and the
> proclamation of this truth to the nations of the earth, in the
> persons of the Magi, at an early stage after his birth, is to
> underline this aspect of the incarnation.

═══ 6 JANUARY ═══

THE EPIPHANY OF THE LORD

'Epiphany' comes from the word 'to disclose' or 'to show'. What
is involved in today's liturgy through the story of the wise men
is that the Son of God has been shown to people of other races
and through them to all the people of the earth. God's plan is
no longer confined to any one people but to all of humanity.

ENTRANCE ANTIPHON   *(cf. Ml 3:1; I Ch 19:12)*
**The Lord and ruler is coming; kingship is his, and
government and power.**

GREETING, PENITENTIAL RITE, GLORIA — *pages 7-14*

OPENING PRAYER
Let us pray
    [that we will be guided by the light of faith]
Father,
you revealed your Son to the nations
by the guidance of a star.
Lead us to your glory in heaven
by the light of faith.
or

Let us pray
> [grateful for the glory revealed today
> through God made man]

Father of light, unchanging God,
today you reveal to men of faith
the resplendent fact of the Word made flesh.

Your light is strong,
your love is near;
draw us beyond the limits which this world imposes,
to the life where your Spirit makes all life complete.

FIRST READING   (Is 60:1-6)

A reading from the prophet Isaiah.

Above you the glory of the Lord appears.

Arise, shine out Jerusalem, for your light has come,
the glory of the Lord is rising on you,
though night still covers the earth
and darkness the peoples.

Above you the Lord now rises
and above you his glory appears.
The nations come to your light
and kings to your dawning brightness.

Lift up your eyes and look round:
all are assembling and coming towards you,
your sons from far away
and daughters being tenderly carried.

At this sight you will grow radiant,
your heart throbbing and full;
since the riches of the sea will flow to you;
the wealth of the nations come to you;

camels in throngs will cover you,
and dromedaries of Midian and Ephah;
everyone in Sheba will come,
bringing gold and incense
and singing the praise of the Lord.

> This is the word of the Lord.

RESPONSORIAL PSALM   (Ps 71:1-2.7-8.10-13)

℞ **All nations shall fall prostrate before you, O Lord.**

1.   O God, give your judgement to the king,
     to a king's son your justice,

that he may judge your people in justice
and your poor in right judgement. ℟

2. In his days justice shall flourish
    and peace till the moon fails.
    He shall rule from sea to sea,
    from the Great River to earth's bounds. ℟

3. The kings of Tarshish and the sea coasts
    shall pay him tribute.
    The kings of Sheba and Seba
    shall bring him gifts.
    Before him all kings shall fall prostrate,
    all nations shall serve him. ℟

4. For he shall save the poor when they cry
    and the needy who are helpless.
    He will have pity on the weak
    and save the lives of the poor. ℟

SECOND READING   (Eph 3:2-3.5-6)

A reading from the letter of St Paul to the Ephesians.

It has now been revealed that pagans share the same inheritance.

You have probably heard how I have been entrusted by God
with the grace he meant for you, and that it was by a revelation
that I was given the knowledge of the mystery. This mystery that
has now been revealed through the Spirit to his holy apostles
and prophets was unknown to any men in past generations; it
means that pagans now share the same inheritance, that they are
parts of the same body, and that the same promise has been
made to them, in Christ Jesus, through the gospel.

This is the word of the Lord.

GOSPEL ACCLAMATION   (Mt 2:2)

Alleluia, alleluia!
We saw his star as it rose
and have come to do the Lord homage.
Alleluia!

GOSPEL   (Mt 2:1-12)

A reading from the holy Gospel according to Matthew.

We saw his star and have come to do the king homage.

After Jesus had been born at Bethlehem in Judaea during the
reign of King Herod, some wise men came to Jerusalem from the
east. 'Where is the infant king of the Jews?' they asked. 'We saw

his star as it rose and have come to do him homage.' When King
Herod heard this he was perturbed, and so was the whole of
Jerusalem. He called together all the chief priests and the scribes
of the people, and enquired of them where the Christ was to be
born. 'At Bethlehem in Judaea', they told him 'for this is what
the prophet wrote:

> And you, Bethlehem, in the land of Judah,
> you are by no means least among the leaders of Judah,
> for out of you will come a leader
> who will shepherd my people Israel.'

Then Herod summoned the wise men to see him privately. He
asked them the exact date on which the star had appeared, and
sent them on to Bethlehem. 'Go and find out all about the
child', he said 'and when you have found him, let me know, so
that I too may go and do him homage.' Having listened to what
the king had to say, they set out. And there in front of them was
the star they had seen rising; it went forward and halted over the
place where the child was. The sight of the star filled them with
delight, and going into the house they saw the child with his
mother Mary, and falling to their knees they did him homage.
Then, opening their treasures, they offered him gifts of gold and
frankincense and myrrh. But they were warned in a dream not
to go back to Herod, and returned to their own country by a
different way.

This is the Gospel of the Lord.

PROFESSION OF FAITH — *pages 15-16*

PRAYER OVER THE GIFTS
Lord,
accept the offerings of your Church,
not gold, frankincense and myrrh,
but the sacrifice and food they symbolise:
Jesus Christ, who is Lord for ever and ever.

PREFACE OF THE EPIPHANY
Father, all-powerful and ever-living God,
we do well always and everywhere to give you thanks.

Today you revealed in Christ your eternal plan of salvation
and showed him as the light of all peoples.
Now that his glory has shone among us
you have renewed humanity in his immortal image.
Now, with angels and archangels,

and the whole company of heaven,
we sing the unending hymn of your praise:
Holy, holy, holy…

COMMUNION ANTIPHON   *(cf. Mt 2:2)*
We have seen his star in the east, and have come with gifts to adore the Lord.

PRAYER AFTER COMMUNION
Father,
guide us with your light.
Help us to recognise Christ in this eucharist
and welcome him with love,
for he is Lord for ever and ever.

SOLEMN BLESSING
God has called you out of darkness,
into his wonderful light.
May you experience his kindness and blessings,
and be strong in faith, in hope, and in love.
Amen.

Because you are followers of Christ,
who appeared on this day as a light shining in darkness,
may he make you a light to all your sisters and brothers.
Amen.

The wise men followed the star,
and found Christ who is light from light.
May you too find the Lord
when your pilgrimage is ended.
Amen.

May almighty God bless you,
the Father, and the Son, ✠ and the Holy Spirit.
Amen.

REFLECTION
The wise men, or the Magi, have two qualities which are
impressive. First their openness. They did not rule out the fact
that they might have to look beyond the familiar, in their
search for life. Secondly, they were prepared to get up and go.
It was not merely a journey of the mind but one which called
for a response of the whole person. They in turn must have
been impressed by what they had already experienced of God.

11 JANUARY
THE BAPTISM OF THE LORD

Today's feast marks the dividing line between the hidden and
the public life of Jesus. No sooner does Christmastide end
than we move directly into the last three years of Jesus' life.
The liturgy, like the scriptures, pass quickly over the thirty or
so years in between.

ENTRANCE ANTIPHON   *(Mt 3:16-17)*

**When the Lord had been baptised, the heavens opened, and
the Spirit came down like a dove to rest on him. Then the
voice of the Father thundered: This is my beloved Son, with
him I am well pleased.**

GREETING, PENITENTIAL RITE, GLORIA — *pages 7-14*

OPENING PRAYER
Let us pray
    [that we will be faithful to our baptism]
Almighty, eternal God,
when the Spirit descended upon Jesus
at his baptism in the Jordan,
you revealed him as your own beloved Son.
Keep us, your children born of water and the Spirit,
faithful to our calling.
or
Father,
your only Son revealed himself to us by becoming man.
May we who share his humanity
come to share his divinity,
for he lives and reigns with you and the Holy Spirit,
one God for ever and ever.
or
Let us pray
    [as we listen to the voice of God's Spirit]
Father in heaven,
you revealed Christ as your Son
by the voice that spoke over the waters of the Jordan.
May all who share in the sonship of Christ
follow in his path of service to man,
and reflect the glory of his kingdom

even to the ends of the earth,
for he is Lord for ever and ever.

FIRST READING *(Is 40:1-5.9-11)*

A reading from the prophet Isaiah.

The glory of the Lord shall be revealed and all mankind shall see it.

'Console my people, console them'
says your God.
'Speak to the heart of Jerusalem
and call to her
that her time of service is ended,
that her sin is atoned for,
that she has received from the hand of the Lord
double punishment for her crimes.'

A voice cries, 'Prepare in the wilderness
a way for the Lord.
Make a straight highway for our God
across the desert.
Let every valley be filled in,
every mountain and hill be laid low,
let every cliff become a plain,
and the ridges a valley;
then the glory of the Lord shall be revealed
and all mankind shall see it;
for the mouth of the Lord has spoken.'

Go up on a high mountain,
joyful messenger to Zion.
Shout with a loud voice,
joyful messenger to Jerusalem.
Shout without fear,
say to the towns of Judah,
'Here is your God.'

Here is the Lord coming with power,
his arm subduing all things to him.
The prize of his victory is with him,
his trophies all go before him.
He is like a shepherd feeding his flock,
gathering lambs in his arms,
holding them against his breast
and leading to their rest the mother ewes.

This is the word of the Lord.

RESPONSORIAL PSALM   *(Ps 103:1-4.24-25.27-30)*

℟   **Bless the Lord, my soul!**
    Lord God, how great you are.

1. Lord God, how great you are,
    clothed in majesty and glory,
    wrapped in light as in a robe!
    You stretch out the heavens like a tent. ℟

2. Above the rains you build your dwelling.
    You make the clouds your chariot,
    you walk on the wings of the wind,
    you make the winds your messengers
    and flashing fire your servants. ℟

3. How many are your works, O Lord!
    In wisdom you have made them all.
    The earth is full of your riches.
    There is the sea, vast and wide,
    with its moving swarms past counting,
    living things great and small. ℟

4. All of these look to you
    to give them their food in due season.
    You give it, they gather it up:
    you open your hand, they have their fill. ℟

5. You take back your spirit, they die,
    returning to the dust from which they came.
    You send forth your spirit, they are created;
    and you renew the face of the earth. ℟

SECOND READING   *(Tt 2:11-14.3:4-7)*

A reading from the letter of St Paul to Titus.

He saved us by the cleansing water of rebirth and by renewing us with
the Holy Spirit.

God's grace has been revealed, and it has made salvation
possible for the whole human race and taught us that what we
have to do is to give up everything that does not lead to God,
and all our worldly ambitions; we must be self-restrained and
live good and religious lives here in this present world, while we
are waiting in hope for the blessing which will come with the
Appearing of the glory of our great God and saviour Christ Jesus.
He sacrificed himself for us in order to set us free from all
wickedness and to purify a people so that it could be his very
own and would have no ambition except to do good.

When the kindness and love of God our saviour for mankind were revealed, it was not because he was concerned with any righteous actions we might have done ourselves; it was for no reason except his own compassion that he saved us, by means of the cleansing water of rebirth and by renewing us with the Holy Spirit which he has so generously poured over us through Jesus Christ our saviour. He did this so that we should be justified by his grace, to become heirs looking forward to inheriting eternal life.

This is the word of the Lord.

GOSPEL ACCLAMATION *(cf. Lk 3:16)*
Alleluia, alleluia!
Someone is coming, said John, someone greater than I.
He will baptize you with the Holy Spirit and with fire.
Alleluia!

GOSPEL *(Lk 3:15-16.21-22)*
A reading from the holy Gospel according to Luke.
While Jesus after his own baptism was at prayer, heaven opened.
A feeling of expectancy had grown among the people, who were beginning to think that John might be the Christ, so John declared before them all, 'I baptise you with water, but someone is coming, someone who is more powerful than I am and I am not fit to undo the strap of his sandals; he will baptise you with the Holy Spirit and fire.'

Now when all the people had been baptised and while Jesus after his own baptism was at prayer, heaven opened and the Holy Spirit descended on him in bodily shape, like a dove. And a voice came from heaven, 'You are my Son, the Beloved; my favour rests on you.'

This is the Gospel of the Lord.

PROFESSION OF FAITH — *pages 15-16*

PRAYER OVER THE GIFTS
Lord,
we celebrate the revelation of Christ your Son
who takes away the sins of the world.
Accept our gifts
and let them become one with his sacrifice,
for he is Lord for ever and ever.

PREFACE OF BAPTISM OF THE LORD
Father, all-powerful and ever-living God,
we do well always and everywhere to give you thanks.

You celebrated your new gift of baptism
by signs and wonders at the Jordan.
Your voice was heard from heaven
to awaken faith in the presence among us
of the Word made man.

Your Spirit was seen as a dove,
revealing Jesus as your servant,
and anointing him with joy as the Christ,
sent to bring to the poor
the good news of salvation.

In our unending joy we echo on earth
the song of the angels in heaven
as they praise your glory for ever:
Holy, holy, holy...

COMMUNION ANTIPHON   (Jn 1: 32.34)
**This is he of whom John said: I have seen and have given
witness that this is the Son of God.**

PRAYER AFTER COMMUNION
Lord,
you feed us with bread from heaven.
May we hear your Son with faith
and become your children in name and in fact.

SOLEMN BLESSING — *pages 57-58*

REFLECTION
> The dynamic and marvellous aspect of baptism is largely toned
> down by our celebration of baptism by pouring a little water
> over the person's head. Only in baptism by immersion as in
> today's scripture is the symbolism really effective. Baptism is
> closely associated with new life. The water which completely
> covers the person symbolises the womb and coming up out of
> the water, the bursting forth into a new form of life, full of
> possibility and choice.

18 JANUARY
2nd SUNDAY IN ORDINARY TIME

In its Jewish context 'Peace' or 'Shalom' captures the idea of life, the promotion of all that is truly human. Where human beings are flourishing the kingdom of God is there. Wedding, bridegroom and wine combine to draw attention to one aspect of peace: good relations between people. This is particularly apt as we begin this week the Week of Prayer and work for Christian Unity.

ENTRANCE ANTIPHON   *(Ps 65:4)*

May all the earth give you worship and praise, and break into song to your name, O God, Most High.

GREETING, PENITENTIAL RITE, GLORIA — *pages 7-14*

OPENING PRAYER

Let us pray
    [to our Father for the gift of peace]
Father of heaven and earth,
hear our prayers,
and show us the way to peace in the world.

or

Let us pray
    [for the gift of peace]
Almighty and ever-present Father,
your watchful care reaches from end to end
and orders all things in such power
that even the tensions and the tragedies of sin
cannot frustrate your loving plans.

Help us to embrace your will,
give us the strength to follow your call,
so that your truth may live in our hearts
and reflect peace to those who believe in your love.

FIRST READING   *(Is 62:1-5)*

A reading from the prophet Isaiah.

The bridegroom rejoices in his bride.

About Zion I will not be silent,
about Jerusalem I will not grow weary,
until her integrity shines out like the dawn
and her salvation flames like a torch.

The nations then will see your integrity,
all the kings your glory,
and you will be called by a new name,
one which the mouth of the Lord will confer.
You are to be a crown of splendour in the hand of the Lord,
a princely diadem in the hand of your God;
no longer are you to be named 'Forsaken',
nor your land 'Abandoned',
but you shall be called 'My Delight'
and your land 'The Wedded''
for the Lord takes delight in you
and your land will have its wedding.
Like a young man marrying a virgin,
so will the one who built you wed you,
and as the bridegroom rejoices in his bride,
so will your God rejoice in you.

> This is the word of the Lord.

RESPONSORIAL PSALM   (Ps 95:1-3.7-10)

℟ **Proclaim the wonders of the Lord
   among all the peoples.**

1. O sing a new song to the Lord,
    sing to the Lord all the earth.
    O sing to the Lord, bless his name. ℟

2. Proclaim his help day by day,
    tell among the nations his glory
    and his wonders among all the peoples. ℟

3. Give the Lord, you families of peoples,
    give the Lord glory and power,
    give the Lord the glory of his name. ℟

4. Worship the Lord in his temple.
    O earth, tremble before him.
    Proclaim to the nations: 'God is king.'
    He will judge the peoples in fairness. ℟

SECOND READING   (1 Cor 12:4-11)

A reading from the first letter of St Paul to the Corinthians.

One and the same Spirit, who distributes gifts to different people just as
he chooses.

There is a variety of gifts but always the same Spirit; there are all
sorts of service to be done, but always to the same Lord; working
in all sorts of different ways in different people, it is the same

God who is working in all of them. The particular way in which the Spirit is given to each person is for a good purpose. One may have the gift of preaching with wisdom given him by the Spirit; another may have the gift of preaching instruction given him by the same Spirit; another again the gift of faith given by the same Spirit; another again the gift of healing, through this one Spirit; one, the power of miracles; another, prophecy; another the gift of recognising spirits; another the gift of tongues and another the ability to interpret them. All these are the work of one and the same Spirit, who distributes different gifts to different people just as he chooses.

This is the word of the Lord

GOSPEL ACCLAMATION   *(cf. Jn 6:63.68)*
Alleluia, alleluia!
Your words are spirit, Lord,
and they are life:
you have the message of eternal life.
Alleluia!

or   *(cf. 2 Thess 2:14)*

Alleluia, alleluia!
Through the Good News God called us
to share the glory of our Lord Jesus Christ.
Alleluia!

GOSPEL   *(Jn 2:1-11)*
A reading from the holy Gospel according to John.
This was the first of the signs given by Jesus: it was given at Cana in Galilee.
There was a wedding at Cana in Galilee. The mother of Jesus was there, and Jesus and his disciples had also been invited. When they ran out of wine, since the wine provided for the wedding was all finished, the mother of Jesus said to him, 'They have no wine.' Jesus said, 'Woman, why turn to me? My hour has not come yet.' His mother said to the servants, 'Do whatever he tells you.' There were six stone water jars standing there, meant for the ablutions that are customary among the Jews; each could hold twenty or thirty gallons. Jesus said to the servants, 'Fill the jars with water,' and they filled them to the brim. 'Draw some out now' he told them 'and take it to the steward.' They did this; the steward tasted the water, and it had turned into wine. Having no idea where it came from — only the servants who had drawn the water knew — the steward called the bridegroom

and said, 'People generally serve the best wine first, and keep the cheaper sort till the guests have had plenty to drink; but you have kept the best wine till now.'

This was the first of the signs given by Jesus: it was given at Cana in Galilee. He let his glory be seen, and his disciples believed in him.

This is the Gospel of the Lord.

PROFESSION OF FAITH — *pages 15-16*

PRAYER OVER THE GIFTS

Father,
may we celebrate the eucharist
with reverence and love,
for when we proclaim the death of the Lord
you continue the work of his redemption,
who is Lord for ever and ever.

PREFACE OF SUNDAYS IN ORDINARY TIME — *pages 22-25*

COMMUNION ANTIPHON   *(Ps 22:5)*

The Lord has prepared a feast for me: given wine in plenty for me to drink.

PRAYER AFTER COMMUNION

Lord,
you have nourished us with bread from heaven.
Fill us with your Spirit,
and make us one in peace and love.

SOLEMN BLESSING — *pages 57-58*

REFLECTION

Heaven and earth, God and humanity, are wedded in the person of Jesus. He is frequently presented as a bridegroom who is close to the community of the Church which is his bride. In any human relationship either party can be unfaithful, but in the case of God and his people only one can be. God is always faithful.

25 JANUARY

3rd SUNDAY IN ORDINARY TIME

Today until the end of the Liturgical Year we hear the Gospel of Luke being read. He presents Jesus as one who has a particular concern for the poor, the sick, the weak, the suffering, those in any kind of need and those on the margins of society.

ENTRANCE ANTIPHON   *(Ps 95:1.6)*

Sing a new song to the Lord! Sing to the Lord, all the earth. Truth and beauty surround him, he lives in holiness and glory.

GREETING, PENITENTIAL RITE, GLORIA — *pages 7-14*

OPENING PRAYER

Let us pray
    [for unity and peace]
All-powerful and ever-living God,
direct your love that is within us,
that our efforts in the name of your Son
may bring humankind to unity and peace.

or

Let us pray
    [pleading that our vision
    may overcome our weakness]
Almighty Father,
the love you offer
always exceeds the furthest expression of our human longing,
for you are greater than the human heart.

Direct each thought, each effort of our life,
so that the limits of our faults and weaknesses
may not obscure the vision of your glory
or keep us from the peace you have promised.

FIRST READING   *(Ne 8:2-6.8-10)*

A reading from the book of Nehemiah.

Ezra read from the law of God and the people understood what was read.

Ezra the priest brought the Law before the assembly, consisting of men, women, and children old enough to understand. This was the first day of the seventh month. On the square before the Water Gate, in the presence of the men and women, and children old enough to understand, he read from the book from early morning till noon; all the people listened attentively to the Book of the Law.

Ezra the scribe stood on a wooden dais erected for the purpose. In full view of all the people — since he stood higher than all the people — Ezra opened the book; and when he opened it all the people stood up. Then Ezra blessed the Lord, the great God, and all the people raised their hands and answered, 'Amen! Amen!'; then they bowed down and, face to the ground, prostrated themselves before the Lord. And Ezra read from the Law of God, translating and giving the sense, so that the people understood what was read.

Then Nehemiah — His Excellency — and Ezra, priest and scribe (and the Levites who were instructing the people) said to all the people, 'This day is sacred to the Lord your God. Do not be mournful, do not weep.' For the people were all in tears as they listened to the words of the Law.

He then said, 'Go, eat the fat, drink the sweet wine, and send a portion to the man who has nothing prepared ready. For this day is sacred to our Lord. Do not be sad: the joy of the Lord is your stronghold.'

This is the word of the Lord.

RESPONSORIAL PSALM   (Ps 18:8-10.15)

℟   **Your words are spirit, Lord, and they are life.**

1.   The law of the Lord is perfect,
     it revives the soul.
     The rule of the Lord is to be trusted,
     it gives wisdom to the simple. ℟

2.   The precepts of the Lord are right,
     they gladden the heart.
     The command of the Lord is clear,
     it gives light to the eyes. ℟

3.   The fear of the Lord is holy,
     abiding for ever.
     The decrees of the Lord are truth
     and all of them just. ℟

4.   May the spoken words of my mouth,
     the thoughts of my heart,
     win favour in your sight, O Lord,
     my rescuer, my rock! ℟

SECOND READING   *(1 Cor 12:12-30)*

(For Shorter Form, read between ◗ ◖)

A reading from the first letter of St Paul to the Corinthians.

You together are Christ's body; but each of you is a different part of it.

◗Just as a human body, though it is made up of many parts, is a single unit because all these parts, though many, make one body, so it is with Christ. In the one Spirit we were all baptised, Jews as well as Greeks, slaves as well as citizens, and one Spirit was given to us all to drink.

Nor is the body to be identified with any one of its many parts.◖ If the foot were to say, 'I am not a hand and so I do not belong to the body', would that mean that it stopped being part of the body? If the ear were to say, 'I am not an eye, and so I do not belong to the body,' would that mean that it is not a part of the body? If your whole body was just one eye, how would you hear anything? If it was just one ear, how would you smell anything?

Instead of that, God put all the separate parts into the body on purpose. If all the parts were the same, how could it be a body? As it is, the parts are many but the body is one. The eye cannot say to the hand, 'I do not need you,' nor can the head say to the feet, 'I do not need you.'

What is more, it is precisely the parts of the body that seem to be the weakest which are the indispensable ones; and it is the least honourable parts of the body that we clothe with the greatest care. So our more improper parts get decorated in a way that our more proper parts do not need. God has arranged the body so that more dignity is given to the parts which are without it, and so that there may not be disagreements inside the body, but that each part may be equally concerned for all the others. If one part is hurt, all parts are hurt with it. If one part is given special honour, all parts enjoy it.

◗Now you together are Christ's body; but each of you is a different part of it.◖ In the Church, God has given the first place to apostles, the second to prophets, the third to teachers; after them, miracles, and after them the gift of healing; helpers, good leaders, those with many languages. Are all of them apostles, or all of them prophets, or all of them teachers? Do they all have the gift of miracles, or all have the gift of healing? Do all speak strange languages, and all interpret them?

◗This is the word of the Lord.◖

GOSPEL ACCLAMATION   *(Lk 4:18)*

Alleluia, alleluia!
The Lord has sent me to bring the Good News to the poor,
to proclaim liberty to captives.
Alleluia!

GOSPEL   *(Lk 1:1-4; 4:14-21)*

A reading from the holy Gospel according to Luke.

This text is being fulfilled today.

Seeing that many others have undertaken to draw up accounts of
the events that have taken place among us, exactly as these were
handed down to us by those who from the outset were eye-witnesses
and ministers of the word, I in my turn, after carefully going
over the whole story from the beginning, have decided to write
an ordered account for you, Theophilus, so that your Excellency
may learn how well founded the teaching is that you have received.

Jesus, with the power of the Spirit in him, returned to Galilee;
and his reputation spread throughout the countryside. He taught
in their synagogues and everyone praised him.

He came to Nazara, where he had been brought up, and
went into the synagogue on the sabbath day as he usually did.
He stood up to read, and they handed him the scroll of the prophet
Isaiah. Unrolling the scroll he found the place where it is written:

The spirit of the Lord has been given to me,
for he has anointed me.
He has sent me to bring the good news to the poor,
to proclaim liberty to captives
and to the blind new sight,
to set the downtrodden free,
to proclaim the Lord's year of favour.

He then rolled up the scroll, gave it back to the assistant and sat
down. And all eyes in the synagogue were fixed on him. Then he
began to speak to them, 'This text is being fulfilled today even as
you listen.'

This is the Gospel of the Lord.

PROFESSION OF FAITH — *pages 15-16*

PRAYER OVER THE GIFTS

Lord, receive our gifts.
Let our offerings make us holy
and bring us salvation.

PREFACE OF SUNDAYS IN ORDINARY TIME — *pages 22-25*

COMMUNION ANTIPHON   (Ps 33:6)
**Look up at the Lord with gladness and smile; your face will
never be ashamed.**

or   (Jn 8:12)
**I am the light of the world, says the Lord; the man who
follows me will have the light of life.**

PRAYER AFTER COMMUNION
God, all-powerful Father,
may the new life you give us increase our love
and keep us in the joy of your kingdom.

SOLEMN BLESSING — *pages 57-58*

REFLECTION
> Throughout this year as we hear the Gospel of Luke being read
> we cannot but be impressed by his portrait of Jesus, whose
> inclusive concern knows no boundaries. In his second volume,
> The Acts of the Apostles, he portrays Paul as building on that
> outlook and inviting all nations into the plan of God. God
> has no favourites but loves all equally.

═══════════════ 1 FEBRUARY ═══════════════

4th SUNDAY IN ORDINARY TIME

> One of the reasons why the liturgical calendar was rearranged
> by decree of the Second Vatican Council was to restore to
> Sunday one of its principal roles, the celebration of the
> mysteries of the Lord throughout the year. Who is Christ?
> What was he doing on earth? What is his role today? These are
> some of the questions which the Liturgy of the Word and of
> the Eucharist can help to answer.

ENTRANCE ANTIPHON   (Ps 105:47)
**Save us, Lord our God, and gather us together from the
nations, that we may proclaim your holy name and glory in
your praise.**

OPENING PRAYER
Let us pray

> [for a greater love of God
> and of our fellow men]

Lord our God,
help us to love you with all our hearts
and to love all as you love them.

or

Let us pray

[joining in the praise of the living God
for we are his people]
Father in heaven,
from the days of Abraham and Moses
until this gathering of your Church in prayer,
you have formed a people in the image of your Son.

Bless this people with the gift of your kingdom.
May we serve you with our every desire
and show love for one another
even as you have loved us.

FIRST READING   (Jer 1:4-5.17-19)
A reading from the prophet Jeremiah.
I have appointed you as prophet to the nations.
In the days of Josiah, the word of the Lord was addressed to me,
saying,

'Before I formed you in the womb I knew you;
before you came to birth I consecrated you;
I have appointed you as prophet to the nations.
So now brace yourself for action.
Stand up and tell them
all I command you.
Do not be dismayed at their presence,
or in their presence I will make you dismayed.
I, for my part, today will make you
into a fortified city,
a pillar of iron,
and a wall of bronze
to confront all this land:
the kings of Judah, its princes,
its priests and the country people.
They will fight against you
but shall not overcome you,
for I am with you to deliver you —
it is the Lord who speaks.
This is the word of the Lord.

RESPONSORIAL PSALM *(Ps 70:1-6.15.17)*

℞ **My lips will tell of your help.**

1. In you, O Lord, I take refuge;
   let me never be put to shame.
   In your justice rescue me, free me:
   pay heed to me and save me. ℞

2. Be a rock where I can take refuge,
   a mighty stronghold to save me;
   for you are my rock, my stronghold.
   Free me from the hand of the wicked. ℞

3. It is you, O Lord, who are my hope,
   my trust, O Lord, since my youth.
   On you I have leaned from my birth,
   from my mother's womb you have been my help. ℞

4. My lips will tell of your justice
   and day by day of your help.
   O God, you have taught me from my youth
   and I proclaim your wonders still. ℞

SECOND READING *(1 Cor 12:31—13:13)*

(For Shorter Form, read between ♦ ♦)

A reading from the first letter of St Paul to the Corinthians.

There are three things that last: faith, hope and love; and the greatest of these is love.

Be ambitious for the higher gifts. And I am going to show you a way that is better than any of them.

If I have all the eloquence of men or of angels, but speak without love, I am simply a gong booming or a cymbal clashing. If I have the gift of prophecy, understanding all the mysteries there are, and knowing everything, and if I have faith in all its fullness, to move mountains, but without love, then I am nothing at all. If I give away all that I possess, piece by piece, and if I even let them take my body to burn it, but am without love, it will do me no good whatever.

♦Love is always patient and kind: it is never jealous; love is never boastful or conceited; it is never rude or selfish; it does not take offence, and is not resentful. Love takes no pleasure in other people's sins but delights in the truth; it is always ready to excuse, to trust, to hope, and to endure whatever comes.

Love does not come to an end. But if there are gifts of prophecy, the time will come when they must fail; or the gift of languages, it will not continue for ever; and knowledge — for this, too, the time will come when it must fail. For our knowledge is imperfect and our prophesying is imperfect; but once perfection comes, all imperfect things will disappear. When I was a child, I used to talk like a child and think like a child, and argue like a child, but now I am a man, all childish ways are put behind me. Now we are seeing a dim reflection in a mirror; but then we shall be seeing face to face. The knowledge that I have now is imperfect; but then I shall know as fully as I am known.

In short, there are three things that last: faith, hope and love; and the greatest of these is love.

This is the word of the Lord.◀

GOSPEL ACCLAMATION   *(Jn 14:2)*
Alleluia, alleluia!
I am the Way, the Truth and the Life, says the Lord;
no one can come to the Father except through me.
Alleluia!

or   *(Lk 4:18)*
Alleluia, alleluia!
The Lord has sent me to bring the good news to the poor,
to proclaim liberty to captives.
Alleluia!

GOSPEL   *(Lk 4:21-30)*
A reading from the holy Gospel according to Luke.
Like Elijah and Elisha, Jesus is not sent to the Jews only.

Jesus began to speak in the synagogue, 'This text is being fulfilled today even as you listen.' And he won the approval of all, and they were astonished by the gracious words that came from his lips.

They said, 'This is Joseph's son, surely?' But he replied, 'No doubt you will quote me the saying, "Physician, heal yourself" and tell me, "We have heard all that happened in Capernaum, do the same here in your own countryside." ' And he went on, 'I tell you solemnly, no prophet is ever accepted in his own country.

'There were many widows in Israel, I can assure you, in Elijah's day, when heaven remained shut for three years and six months and a great famine raged throughout the land, but Elijah was not sent to any one of these: he was sent to a widow at Zarephath, a Sidonian town. And in the prophet Elisha's time there were many lepers in Israel, but none of these was cured, except the Syrian, Naaman.'

When they heard this everyone in the synagogue was enraged. They sprang to their feet and hustled him out of the town; and they took him up to the brow of the hill their town was built on, intending to throw him down the cliff, but he slipped through the crowd and walked away.

This is the Gospel of the Lord.

PROFESSION OF FAITH — *pages 15-16*

PRAYER OVER THE GIFTS
Lord,
be pleased with the gifts we bring to your altar,
and make them the sacrament of our salvation.

PREFACE OF SUNDAYS IN ORDINARY TIME — *pages 22-25*

COMMUNION ANTIPHON   *(Ps 30:17-18)*
Let your face shine on your servant, and save me by your love.
Lord, keep me from shame, for I have called to you.
or   *(Mt 5:3-4)*
Happy are the poor in spirit; the kingdom of heaven is theirs!
Happy are the lowly; they shall inherit the land.

PRAYER AFTER COMMUNION
Lord,
you invigorate us with this help to our salvation.
By this eucharist give the true faith continued growth
throughout the world.

SOLEMN BLESSING — *pages 57-58*

REFLECTION

In his life Jesus reached out to people beyond the narrow boundaries imposed by the culture of his day. This challenged the presumptions of his native place. There are many versions of the caste system and all are equally opposed to what Jesus perceived to be God's plan for the human race.

8 FEBRUARY
5th SUNDAY IN ORDINARY TIME

The Mass is composed of two principal parts: word and sacrament.
In the first part, we are invited to listen to God's word, not a
passive response but an activity which can transform us. Our
scriptures come from a Jewish background. When the Jewish
people were celebrating an event of the past it was as if that event
were present to them at the moment of celebration. As we celebrate
the Lord's supper today that event is made real for us now.

ENTRANCE ANTIPHON   *(Ps 94:6-7)*
**Come, let us worship the Lord. Let us bow down in the presence
of our maker, for he is the Lord our God.**

GREETING, PENITENTIAL RITE, GLORIA — *pages 7-14*

OPENING PRAYER
Let us pray
    [that God will watch over us and protect us]
Father,
watch over your family
and keep us safe in your care,
for all our hope is in you.

or

Let us pray
    [with reverence in the presence of the living God]

In faith and love we ask you, Father,
to watch over your family gathered here.
In your mercy and loving kindness
no thought of ours is left unguarded,
no tear unheeded, no joy unnoticed.

Through the prayer of Jesus
may the blessings promised to the poor in spirit
lead us to the treasures of your heavenly kingdom.

FIRST READING   *(Is 6:1-8)*
A reading from the prophet Isaiah.
Here I am, send me.
In the year of King Uzziah's death I saw the Lord seated on a
high throne; his train filled the sanctuary; above him stood seraphs,
each one with six wings. And they cried out one to another in
this way,

'Holy, holy, holy is the Lord of hosts.
His glory fills the whole earth.'

The foundations of the threshold shook with the voice of the one who cried out, and the Temple was filled with smoke. I said:

'What a wretched state I am in! I am lost,
for I am a man of unclean lips
and I live among a people of unclean lips,
and my eyes have looked at the King, the Lord of hosts.'

Then one of the seraphs flew to me, holding in his hand a live coal which he had taken from the altar with a pair of tongs. With this he touched my mouth and said:

'See now, this has touched your lips,
your sin is taken away,
your iniquity is purged.'

Then I heard the voice of the Lord saying:
'Whom shall I send? Who will be our messenger?'

I answered, 'Here I am, send me.'
This is the word of the Lord.

RESPONSORIAL PSALM   *(Ps 137:1-5.7-8)*

℟ **Before the angels I will bless you, O Lord.**

1. I thank you, Lord, with all my heart,
    you have heard the words of my mouth.
    Before the angels I will bless you.
    I will adore before your holy temple. ℟

2. I thank you for your faithfulness and love
    which excel all we ever knew of you.
    On the day I called, you answered;
    you increased the strength of my soul. ℟

3. All earth's kings shall thank you
    when they hear the words of your mouth.
    They shall sing of the Lord's ways:
    'How great is the glory of the Lord!' ℟

4. You stretch out your hand and save me,
    your hand will do all things for me.
    Your love, O Lord, is eternal,
    discard not the work of your hand. ℟

SECOND READING   *(1 Cor 15:1-11)*
(For Shorter Form, *read between ◗ ◖)*
A reading from the first letter of St Paul to the Corinthians.
I preach what they preach, and this is what you all believed.
Brothers, I want to remind you of the gospel I preached to you,
the gospel that you received and in which you are firmly
established; because the gospel will save you only if you keep
believing exactly what I preached to you — believing anything
else will not lead to anything.

Well then, ◗in the first place, I taught you what I had been
taught myself, namely that Christ died for our sins, in accordance
with the scriptures; that he was buried; and that he was raised to
life on the third day, in accordance with the scriptures; that he
appeared first to Cephas and secondly to the Twelve. Next he
appeared to more than five hundred of the brothers at the same
time, most of whom are still alive, though some have died; then
he appeared to James, and then to all the apostles; and last of all
he appeared to me too; it was as though I was born when no
one expected it.◖

I am the least of the apostles; in fact, since I persecuted the
Church of God, I hardly deserve the name apostle; but by God's
grace that is what I am, and the grace that he gave me has not been
fruitless. On the contrary, I, or rather the grace of God that is with
me, have worked harder than any of the others; ◗but what matters
is that I preach what they preach, and this is what you all believed.

This is the word of the Lord.◖

GOSPEL ACCLAMATION   *(Jn 15:15)*
Alleluia, alleluia!
I call you friends, says the Lord,
because I have made known to you
everything I have learnt from my Father. Alleluia!
or   *(Mt 4:19)*
Alleluia, alleluia!
Follow me, says the Lord,
and I will make you fishers of men. Alleluia!

GOSPEL   *(Lk 5:1-11)*
A reading from the holy Gospel according to Luke.
They left everything and followed him.
Jesus was standing one day by the Lake of Gennesaret, with the
crowd pressing round him listening to the word of God, when he
caught sight of two boats close to the bank. The fishermen had

gone out of them and were washing their nets. He got into one of the boats — it was Simon's — and asked him to put out a little from the shore. Then he sat down and taught the crowds from the boat.

When he had finished speaking he said to Simon, 'Put out into deep water and pay out your nets for a catch.' 'Master,' Simon replied, 'we worked hard all night long and caught nothing, but if you say so, I will pay out the nets.' And when they had done this they netted such a huge number of fish that their nets began to tear, so they signalled to their companions in the other boats to come and help them; when these came, they filled the two boats to sinking point.

When Simon Peter saw this he fell at the knees of Jesus saying, 'Leave me, Lord; I am a sinful man.' For he and all his companions were completely overcome by the catch they had made; so also were James and John, sons of Zebedee, who were Simon's partners. But Jesus said to Simon, 'Do not be afraid; from now on it is men you will catch.' Then, bringing their boats back to land, they left everything and followed him.

This is the Gospel of the Lord.

PROFESSION OF FAITH — *pages 15-16*

PRAYER OVER THE GIFTS
Lord our God,
may the bread and wine
you give us for our nourishment on earth
become the sacrament of our eternal life.

PREFACE OF SUNDAYS IN ORDINARY TIME — *pages 22-25*

COMMUNION ANTIPHON   *(Ps 106:8-9)*
Give praise to the Lord for his kindness, for his wonderful deeds towards men. He has filled the hungry with good things, he has satisfied the thirsty.
or   *(Mt 5:5-6)*
Happy are the sorrowing; they shall be consoled. Happy those who hunger and thirst for what is right; they shall be satisfied.

PRAYER AFTER COMMUNION
God our Father,
you give us a share in the one bread and the one cup
and make us one in Christ.
Help us to bring your salvation and joy
to all the world.

SOLEMN BLESSING — *pages 57-58*

REFLECTION

Faith has traditionally been called a theological virtue because its presence in a human being prepares and enables that person to share in God's life. Biblical faith is not simply agreeing with a particular belief but is a commitment to God freely given in response to God's prior gift to the believer.

15 FEBRUARY

6th SUNDAY IN ORDINARY TIME

The second part of the Mass, the Liturgy of the Eucharist, was originally a special meal of bread and wine following the last supper. It took place at the end of a larger meal. As time went by, the first meal was replaced by the Liturgy of the Word. And so the present two-fold shape of the Mass goes back to at least the early Second Century.

ENTRANCE ANTIPHON   (Ps 30:3-4)

Lord, be my rock of safety, the stronghold that saves me. For the honour of your name, lead me and guide me.

GREETING, PENITENTIAL RITE, GLORIA — *pages 7-14*

OPENING PRAYER

Let us pray
    [that everything we do
    will be guided by God's law of love]
God our Father,
you have promised to remain for ever
with those who do what is just and right.
Help us to live in your presence.

or

Let us pray
    [for the wisdom that is greater than human words]
Father in heaven,
the loving plan of your wisdom took flesh in Jesus Christ,
and changed humankind's history
by his command of perfect love.

May our fulfilment of his command reflect your wisdom
and bring your salvation to the ends of the earth.

FIRST READING *(Jer 17:5-8)*

A reading from the prophet Jeremiah.

A curse on the man who puts his trust in man, a blessing on the man who puts his trust in the Lord.

The Lord says this:

'A curse on the man who puts his trust in man,
who relies on things of flesh,
whose heart turns from the Lord.
He is like dry scrub in the wastelands:
if good comes, he has no eyes for it,
he settles in the parched places of the wilderness,
a salt land, uninhabited.

'A blessing on the man who puts his trust in the Lord,
with the Lord for his hope.
He is like a tree by the waterside
that thrusts its roots to the stream:
when the heat comes it feels no alarm,
its foliage stays green;
it has no worries in a year of drought,
and never ceases to bear fruit.'

This is the word of the Lord.

RESPONSORIAL PSALM *(Ps 1:1-4.6)*

℞ **Happy the man who has placed
his trust in the Lord.**

1. Happy indeed is the man
   who follows not the counsel of the wicked;
   nor lingers in the way of sinners
   nor sits in the company of scorners,
   but whose delight is the law of the Lord
   and who ponders his law day and night. ℞

2. He is like a tree that is planted
   beside the flowing waters,
   that yields its fruit in due season
   and whose leaves shall never fade;
   and all that he does shall prosper. ℞

3. Not so are the wicked, not so!
   For they like winnowed chaff
   shall be driven away by the wind.
   For the Lord guards the way of the just
   but the way of the wicked leads to doom. ℞

SECOND READING   *(1 Cor 15:12.16-20)*

A reading from the first letter of St Paul to the Corinthians.

If Christ has not been raised, your believing is useless.

If Christ raised from the dead is what has been preached, how can some of you be saying that there is no resurrection of the dead? For if the dead are not raised, Christ has not been raised, and if Christ has not been raised, you are still in your sins. And what is more serious, all who have died in Christ have perished. If our hope in Christ has been for this life only, we are the most unfortunate of all people.

But Christ has in fact been raised from the dead, the first-fruits of all who have fallen asleep.

This is the word of the Lord.

GOSPEL ACCLAMATION   *(cf. Mt 11:25)*

Alleluia, alleluia!
Blessed are you, Father,
Lord of heaven and earth,
for revealing the mysteries of the kingdom
to mere children.
Alleluia!

or   *(Lk 6:23)*

Alleluia, alleluia!
Rejoice and be glad:
your reward will be great in heaven.
Alleluia!

GOSPEL   *(Lk 6:17.20-26)*

A reading from the holy Gospel according to Luke.

How happy are you who are poor. Alas for you who are rich.

Jesus came down with the Twelve and stopped at a piece of level ground where there was a large gathering of his disciples with a great crowd of people from all parts of Judaea and from Jerusalem and from the coastal region of Tyre and Sidon who had come to hear him and to be cured of their diseases.

Then fixing his eyes on his disciples he said:

'How happy are you who are poor; yours is the kingdom of God. Happy you who are hungry now: you shall be satisfied. Happy you who weep now: you shall laugh.

'Happy are you when people hate you, drive you out, abuse you, denounce your name as criminal, on account of the Son of Man. Rejoice when that day comes and dance for joy, for then your reward will be great in heaven. This was the way their ancestors treated the prophets.

'But alas for you who are rich: you are having your consolation now.

Alas for you who have your fill now: you shall go hungry.

Alas for you who laugh now: you shall mourn and weep.

'Alas for you when the world speaks well of you! This was the way their ancestors treated the false prophets.'

This is the Gospel of the Lord.

PROFESSION OF FAITH — *pages 15-16*

PRAYER OVER THE GIFTS
Lord,
we make this offering in obedience to your word.
May it cleanse and renew us,
and lead us to our eternal reward.

PREFACE OF SUNDAYS IN ORDINARY TIME — *pages 22-25*

COMMUNION ANTIPHON   *(Ps 77:29-30)*
They ate and were filled; the Lord gave them what they wanted: they were not deprived of their desire.
or   *(Jn 3:16)*
God loved the world so much, he gave his only Son, that all who believe in him might not perish, but might have eternal life.

PRAYER AFTER COMMUNION
Lord,
you give us food from heaven.
May we always hunger for the bread of life.

SOLEMN BLESSING — *pages 57-58*

REFLECTION

Hope is also termed a theological virtue. It is God and the Kingdom of God which is the object of Christian hope. Every human being longs for happiness. This longing is met in this life when the values of the Kingdom of God are being put into practice and in the next life when we shall see God face to face.

22 FEBRUARY
7th SUNDAY IN ORDINARY TIME

At the beginning of each Mass we are invited to remember our
sin before the priest asks God to forgive us. Sin has been
described as a positive concept because it involves our being
aware of our estrangement from God and a desire to do
something about it.

ENTRANCE ANTIPHON   *(Ps 12:6)*

**Lord, your mercy is my hope, my heart rejoices in your saving
power. I will sing to the Lord, for his goodness to me.**

GREETING, PENITENTIAL RITE, GLORIA — *pages 7-14*

OPENING PRAYER

Let us pray
      [that God will make us more like Christ, his Son]
Father,
keep before us the wisdom and love
you have revealed in your Son.
Help us to be like him
in word and deed,
for he lives and reigns with you and the Holy Spirit,
one God, for ever and ever.

or

Let us pray
      [to the God of power and might, for his mercy is our hope]
Almighty God,
Father of our Lord Jesus Christ,
faith in your word is the way to wisdom,
and to ponder your divine plan is to grow in the truth.

Open our eyes to your deeds,
our ears to the sound of your call,
so that our every act may increase our sharing
in the life you have offered us.

FIRST READING   *(1 Sam 26:2.7-9.12-13.22-23)*

A reading from the first book of Samuel.

The Lord put you in my power, but I would not raise my hand.

Saul set off and went down to the wilderness of Ziph,
accompanied by three thousand men chosen from Israel to
search for David in the wilderness of Ziph.

So in the dark David and Abishai made their way towards the force, where they found Saul asleep inside the camp, his spear stuck in the ground beside his head, with Abner and the troops lying round him.

Then Abishai said to David, 'Today God has put your enemy in your power; so now let me pin him to the ground with his own spear. Just one stroke! I will not need to strike him twice.' David answered Abishai, 'Do not kill him, for who can lift his hand against the Lord's anointed and be without guilt?' David took the spear and the pitcher of water from beside Saul's head, and they made off. No one saw, no one knew, no one woke up; they were all asleep, for a deep sleep from the Lord had fallen on them.

David crossed to the other side and halted on the top of the mountain a long way off; there was a wide space between them. David then called out, 'Here is the king's spear. Let one of the soldiers come across and take it. The Lord repays everyone for his uprightness and loyalty. Today the Lord put you in my power, but I would not raise my hand against the Lord's anointed.'

This is the word of the Lord.

RESPONSORIAL PSALM   *(Ps 102:1-4.8.10.12-13)*

℟ **The Lord is compassion and love.**

1. My soul, give thanks to the Lord,
    all my being, bless his holy name.
    My soul, give thanks to the Lord
    and never forget all his blessings. ℟

2. It is he who forgives all your guilt,
    who heals every one of your ills,
    who redeems your life from the grave,
    who crowns you with love and compassion. ℟

3. The Lord is compassion and love,
    slow to anger and rich in mercy.
    He does not treat us according to our sins
    nor repay us according to our faults. ℟

4. As far as the east is from the west
    so far does he remove our sins.
    As a father has compassion on his sons,
    the Lord has pity on those who fear him. ℟

SECOND READING   *(1 Cor 15:45-49)*

A reading from the first letter of St Paul to the Corinthians.

We who have been modelled on the earthly man will be modelled on the heavenly man.

The first man, Adam, as scripture says, became a living soul; but the last Adam has become a life-giving spirit. That is, first the one with the soul, not the spirit, and after that, the one with the spirit. The first man, being from the earth, is earthly by nature; the second man is from heaven. As this earthly man was, so are we on earth; and as the heavenly man is, so are we in heaven. And we, who have been modelled on the earthly man, will be modelled on the heavenly man.

This is the word of the Lord.

GOSPEL ACCLAMATION   *(cf. Acts 16:14)*

Alleluia, alleluia!
Open our heart, O Lord,
to accept the words of your Son.
Alleluia!

or   *(Jn 13:34)*

Alleluia, alleluia!
I give you a new commandment:
love one another,
just as I have loved you,
says the Lord.
Alleluia!

GOSPEL   *(Lk 6:27-38)*

A reading from the holy Gospel according to Luke.

Be compassionate as your Father is compassionate.

Jesus said to his disciples: 'I say this to you who are listening: Love your enemies, do good to those who hate you, bless those who curse you, pray for those who treat you badly. To the man who slaps you on one cheek, present the other cheek too; to the man who takes your cloak from you, do not refuse your tunic. Give to everyone who asks you, and do not ask for your property back from the man who robs you. Treat others as you would like them to treat you. If you love those who love you, what thanks can you expect? Even sinners love those who love them. And if you do good to those who do good to you, what thanks can you expect? For even sinners do that much. And if you lend to those from whom you hope to receive, what thanks can you expect? Even sinners lend to sinners to get back the same amount.

Instead, love your enemies and do good, and lend without any hope of return. You will have a great reward, and you will be sons of the Most High, for he himself is kind to the ungrateful and the wicked.

'Be compassionate as your Father is compassionate. Do not judge, and you will not be judged yourselves; do not condemn, and you will not be condemned yourselves; grant pardon, and you will be pardoned. Give, and there will be gifts for you: a full measure, pressed down, shaken together, and running over, will be poured into your lap; because the amount you measure out is the amount you will be given back.'

This is the Gospel of the Lord.

PROFESSION OF FAITH — *pages 15-16*

PRAYER OVER THE GIFTS
Lord,
as we make this offering,
may our worship in Spirit and truth
bring us salvation.

PREFACE OF SUNDAYS IN ORDINARY TIME — *pages 22-25*

COMMUNION ANTIPHON   *(Ps 9:2-3)*
I will tell all your marvellous works. I will rejoice and be glad in you, and sing to your name, Most High.

or   *(Jn 11:27)*
Lord, I believe that you are the Christ, the Son of God, who was to come into this world.

PRAYER AFTER COMMUNION
Almighty God,
help us to live the example of love
we celebrate in this eucharist,
that we may come to its fulfilment in your presence.

SOLEMN BLESSING — *pages 57-58*

REFLECTION
The difference between faith, hope and love is that the first two are for this present life only. They will pass away. But love which Paul called 'the greatest of these' is the primary mark of the Christian and will endure. It will not pass away. Even though it is not named as such, the kingdom of God is present wherever people love one another.

25 FEBRUARY
ASH WEDNESDAY

Today we begin the season of Lent which will last for forty
days and which will be followed by Holy Week. Over the next
three months we shall celebrate these two seasons which will
be followed by the great feast of Easter which will last for fifty
days. Today and Good Friday are days of Fast and Abstinence.

ENTRANCE ANTIPHON   *(cf. Ws 11:24-25.27)*

**Lord, you are merciful to all, and hate nothing you have
created. You overlook the sins of men to bring them to
repentance. You are the Lord our God.**

(The penitential rite is replaced by the giving of ashes — see below. The
Gloria *is omitted.)*

OPENING PRAYER

Let us pray
    [for the grace to keep Lent faithfully]

Lord,
protect us in our struggle against evil.
As we begin the discipline of Lent,
make this season holy by our self-denial.

or

Let us pray
    [in quiet remembrance of our need for redemption]

Father in heaven,
the light of your truth bestows sight
to the darkness of sinful eyes.
May this season of repentance
bring us the blessing of your forgiveness
and the gift of your light.

FIRST READING   *(Joel 2:12-18)*

A reading from the prophet Joel.

Let your hearts be broken, not your garments torn.

'Now, now — it is the Lord who speaks —
come back to me with all your heart,
fasting, weeping, mourning.'
Let your hearts be broken not your garments torn,
turn to the Lord your God again,
for he is all tenderness and compassion,

slow to anger, rich in graciousness,
and ready to relent.
Who knows if he will not turn again, will not relent,
will not leave a blessing as he passes,
oblation and libation
for the Lord your God?
Sound the trumpet in Zion!
Order a fast,
proclaim a solemn assembly,
call the people together,
summon the community,
assemble the elders,
gather the children,
even the infants at the breast.
Let the bridegroom leave his bedroom
and the bride her alcove.
Between vestibule and altar let the priests,
the ministers of the Lord, lament.
Let them say,
'Spare your people, Lord!
Do not make your heritage a thing of shame,
a byword for the nations.
Why should it be said among the nations,
"Where is their God?" '
Then the Lord, jealous on behalf of his land,
took pity on his people.

This is the word of the Lord.

RESPONSORIAL PSALM   (Ps 50:3-6.12-14.17)

℟   **Have mercy on us, O Lord, for we have sinned.**

1.   Have mercy on me, God, in your kindness.
      In your compassion blot out my offence.
      O wash me more and more from my guilt
      and cleanse me from my sin. ℟

2.   My offences truly I know them;
      my sin is always before me.
      Against you, you alone, have I sinned:
      what is evil in your sight I have done. ℟

3.   A pure heart create for me, O God,
      put a steadfast spirit within me.
      Do not cast me away from your presence,
      nor deprive me of your holy spirit. ℟   *(continued)*

4. Give me again the joy of your help;
    with a spirit of fervour sustain me.
    O Lord, open my lips
    and my mouth shall declare your praise. ℞

℞ **Have mercy on us, O Lord, for we have sinned.**

SECOND READING   *(2 Cor 5:20–6:2)*

A reading from the second letter of St Paul to the Corinthians.

Be reconciled to God... now is the favourable time.

We are ambassadors for Christ; it is as though God were appealing through us, and the appeal that we make in Christ's name is: be reconciled to God. For our sake God made the sinless one into sin, so that in him we might become the goodness of God. As his fellow workers, we beg you once again not to neglect the grace of God that you have received. For he says: At the favourable time, I have listened to you; on the day of salvation I came to your help. Well, now is the favourable time; this is the day of salvation.

    This is the word of the Lord.

GOSPEL ACCLAMATION   *(Ps 50:12.14)*

Praise to you, O Christ, king of eternal glory!
A pure heart create for me, O God,
and give me again the joy of your help.
Praise to you, O Christ, king of eternal glory!

or   *(cf. Ps 94:8)*

Praise to you, O Christ, king of eternal glory!
Harden not your hearts today,
but listen to the voice of the Lord.
Praise to you, O Christ, King of eternal glory!

GOSPEL   *(Mt 6:1-6.16-18)*

A reading from the holy Gospel according to Matthew.

Your Father, who sees all that is done in secret, will reward you.

Jesus said to his disciples:

    'Be careful not to parade your good deeds before men to attract their notice; by doing this you will lose all reward from your Father in heaven. So when you give alms, do not have it trumpeted before you; this is what the hypocrites do in the synagogues and in the streets to win men's admiration. I tell you solemnly, they have had their reward. But when you give alms, your left hand must not know what your right is doing; your almsgiving must be secret, and your Father who sees all that is done in secret will reward you.

'And when you pray, do not imitate the hypocrites: they love to say their prayers standing up in the synagogues and at the street corners for people to see them. I tell you solemnly, they have had their reward. But when you pray go to your private room and, when you have shut your door, pray to your Father who is in that secret place, and your Father who sees all that is done in secret will reward you.

'When you fast do not put on a gloomy look as the hypocrites do: they pull long faces to let men know they are fasting. I tell you solemnly, they have had their reward. But when you fast, put oil on your head and wash your face, so that no one will know you are fasting except your Father who sees all that is done in secret; and your Father who sees all that is done in secret will reward you.'

This is the Gospel of the Lord.

CEREMONY OF ASHES

In the Bible to cover one's head with ashes, to wear sackcloth and to fast are penitential signs; they express the sinner's repentance imploring the divine mercy.

So, our reception of ashes at the beginning of Lent means we recognise ourselves as sinners. We ask God's pardon for his Church and show our sincere desire to change our ways. Faith in the Lord's word makes us pass with him from death to life.

BLESSING AND GIVING OF ASHES

After the homily the priest joins his hands and says:

Dear friends in Christ,
let us ask our Father
to bless these ashes
which we will use
as the mark of our repentance.

Silent prayer

Lord,
bless the sinner who asks for your forgiveness
and bless ✠ all those who receive these ashes.
May they keep this lenten season
in preparation for the joy of Easter.

or

Lord,
bless these ashes ✠
by which we show that we are dust.

Pardon our sins
and keep us faithful to the discipline of Lent,
for you do not want sinners to die
but to live with the risen Christ,
who reigns with you for ever and ever.

He sprinkles the ashes with holy water in silence. The priest then places ashes on those who come forward, saying to each:

Turn away from sin and be faithful to the gospel.

or

Remember, you are dust
and to dust you will return.

Meanwhile some of the following antiphons or other appropriate songs are sung.

ANTIPHON 1   *(cf. Joel 2:13)*

Come back to the Lord with all your heart;
leave the past in ashes,
and turn to God with tears and fasting,
for he is slow to anger and ready to forgive.

ANTIPHON 2   *(cf. Joel 2:17; Est 13:17)*

Let the priests and ministers of the Lord
lament before his altar, and say:
Spare us, Lord; spare your people!
Do not let us die for we are crying out to you.

ANTIPHON 3   *(Ps 50:3)*

Lord, take away our wickedness.

These may be repeated after each verse of Psalm 50, 'Have mercy on me, God' (page 107).

RESPONSORY   *(cf. Ba 3:5; Ps 78:9)*

Direct our hearts to better things, O Lord;
heal our sin and ignorance.
Lord, do not face us suddenly with death,
but give us time to repent.

℟   Turn to us with mercy, Lord; we have sinned against you.
℣   Help us, God our Saviour, rescue us for the honour of
      your name.
℟   Turn to us with mercy, Lord; we have sinned against you.

The rite concludes with the Prayer of the Faithful. The Profession of Faith is not said.

PRAYER OVER THE GIFTS
Lord,
help us to resist temptation
by our lenten works of charity and penance.
By this sacrifice
may we be prepared to celebrate
the death and resurrection of Christ our Saviour
and be cleansed from sin and renewed in spirit.

PREFACE OF LENT IV
Father, all-powerful and ever-living God,
we do well always and everywhere to give you thanks.

Through our observance of Lent
you correct our faults and raise our minds to you,
you help us grow in holiness,
and offer us the reward of everlasting life
through Jesus Christ our Lord.

Through him the angels and all the choirs of heaven
worship in awe before your presence.
May our voices be one with theirs
as they sing with joy the hymn of your glory:
Holy, holy, holy...

COMMUNION ANTIPHON   *(Ps 1:2-3)*
**The man who meditates day and night on the law of the Lord
will yield fruit in due season.**

PRAYER AFTER COMMUNION
Lord,
through this communion
may our lenten penance give you glory
and bring us your protection.

REFLECTION
Prayer, fasting and alms-giving are traditional Lenten activities.
When they are freely undertaken they are ways in which a person
actively turns towards God and signals one's willingness to
journey with the Lord on the road to Jerusalem and from there
to participate in his mission to the ends of the earth.

29 FEBRUARY
FIRST SUNDAY OF LENT

Lent is the springtime of the Church's year. The word itself
probably comes from the Old English *lencten*, which refers to
the lengthening of the daytime hours. Spring is a good image
for what this season means: new life, hope, joy in the gifts of
God that surround us.

ENTRANCE ANTIPHON   *(Ps 90:15-16)*

**When he calls to me, I will answer; I will rescue him and give
him honour. Long life and contentment will be his.**

GREETING, PENITENTIAL RITE — *pages 7-13*

The Gloria is omitted.

OPENING PRAYER

Let us pray

[that this Lent will help us reproduce in our lives
the self-sacrificing love of Christ]

Father, through our observance of Lent,
help us to understand the meaning
of your Son's death and resurrection,
and teach us to reflect it in our lives.

or

Let us pray

[at the beginning of Lent
for the spirit of repentance]

Lord our God, you formed man from the clay of the earth
and breathed into him the spirit of life,
but he turned from your face and sinned.

In this time of repentance
we call out for your mercy.
Bring us back to you
and to the life your Son won for us
by his death on the cross.
for he lives and reigns for ever and ever.

FIRST READING   *(Deut 26:4-10)*

A reading from the book of Deuteronomy.
The creed of the chosen people.

Moses said to the people: 'The priest shall take the pannier from your hand and lay it before the altar of the Lord your God. Then, in the sight of the Lord your God, you must make this pronouncement:

"My father was a wandering Aramaean. He went down into Egypt to find refuge there, few in numbers; but there he became a nation, great, mighty, and strong. The Egyptians ill-treated us, they gave us no peace and inflicted harsh slavery on us. But we called on the Lord, the God of our fathers. The Lord heard our voice and saw our misery, our toil and our oppression; and the Lord brought us out of Egypt with mighty hand and outstretched arm, with great terror, and with signs and wonders. He brought us here and gave us this land, a land where milk and honey flow. Here then I bring the first-fruits of the produce of the soil that you, Lord, have given me." You must then lay them before the Lord your God, and bow down in the sight of the Lord your God.'

This is the word of the Lord.

RESPONSORIAL PSALM   *(Ps 90:1-2. 10-15)*

℟   **Be with me, O Lord, in my distress.**

1.   He who dwells in the shelter of the Most High
     and abides in the shade of the Almighty
     says to the Lord: 'My refuge,
     my stronghold, my God in whom I trust!' ℟

2.   Upon you no evil shall fall,
     no plague approach where you dwell.
     For you has he commanded his angels,
     to keep you in all your ways. ℟

3.   They shall bear you upon their hands
     lest you strike your foot against a stone.
     On the lion and the viper you will tread
     and trample the young lion and the dragon. ℟

4.   His love he set on me, so I will rescue him;
     protect him for he knows my name.
     When he calls I shall answer: 'I am with you.'
     I will save him in distress and give him glory. ℟

SECOND READING   *(Rom 10:8-13)*

A reading from the letter of St Paul to the Romans.

The creed of the Christian.

Scripture says: The word, that is the faith we proclaim, is very near to you, it is on your lips and in your heart. If your lips confess that Jesus is Lord and if you believe in your heart that God raised him from the dead, then you will be saved. By believing from the heart you are made righteous; by confessing with your lips you are saved. When scripture says: those who believe in him will have no cause for shame, it makes no distinction between Jew and Greek: all belong to the same Lord who is rich enough, however many ask for his help, for everyone who calls on the name of the Lord will be saved.

This is the word of the Lord.

GOSPEL ACCLAMATION   (Mt 4:4)
Praise to you, O Christ, king of eternal glory!
Man does not live on bread alone.
but on every word that comes from the mouth of God.
Praise to you, O Christ, king of eternal glory!

GOSPEL   (Lk 4:1-13)
A reading from the holy Gospel according to Luke.
Jesus was led by the Spirit through the wilderness and was tempted there.
Filled with the Holy Spirit, Jesus left the Jordan and was led by the Spirit through the wilderness, being tempted there by the devil for forty days. During that time he ate nothing and at the end he was hungry. Then the devil said to him, 'If you are the Son of God, tell this stone to turn into a loaf.' But Jesus replied, 'Scripture says: Man does not live on bread alone.'

Then leading him to a height, the devil showed him in a moment of time all the kingdoms of the world and said to him, 'I will give you all this power and the glory of these kingdoms, for it has been committed to me and I give it to anyone I choose. Worship me, then, and it shall all be yours.' But Jesus answered him. 'Scripture says:

You must worship the Lord your God,
and serve him alone.'

Then he led him to Jerusalem and made him stand on the parapet of the Temple. 'If you are the Son of God', he said to him 'throw yourself down from here, for scripture says:
He will put his angels in charge of you to guard you,
and again:
They will hold you up on their hands
in case you hurt your foot against a stone.'
But Jesus answered him, 'It has been said:

You must not put the Lord your God to the test.'
Having exhausted all these ways of tempting him, the devil left
him, to return at the appointed time.

This is the Gospel of the Lord.

PROFESSION OF FAITH — *pages 15-16*

PRAYER OVER THE GIFTS

Lord, make us worthy to bring you these gifts.
May this sacrifice
help to change our lives.

PREFACE OF FIRST SUNDAY OF LENT

Father, all-powerful and ever-living God,
we do well always and everywhere to give you thanks
through Jesus Christ our Lord.

His fast of forty days
makes this a holy season of self-denial.
By rejecting the devil's temptations
he has taught us
to rid ourselves of the hidden corruption of evil,
and so to share his paschal meal in purity of heart,
until we come to its fulfilment
in the promised land of heaven.

Now we join the angels and the saints
as they sing their unending hymn of praise:
Holy, holy, holy...

COMMUNION ANTIPHON   *(Mt 4:4)*

**Man does not live on bread alone, but on every word that
comes from the mouth of God.**

PRAYER AFTER COMMUNION

Father, you increase our faith and hope,
you deepen our love in this communion.
Help us to live by your words
and to seek Christ, our bread of life,
who is Lord for ever and ever.

REFLECTION

> 'To repent' means basically to change one's mind or attitude. For
> those who have not done so this could mean to take on board
> the God-dimension to life, while for those who already have, it
> might mean to do so at a deeper level. To accept God into
> one's plan for life will certainly mean a change of some sort.

1 MARCH
ST DAVID
(Patron of Wales)

The celebration of the feast of Saint David reminds us that the history of the Church is made up of countless people who handed on the faith in their own time to the people of their own place and beyond it. In this chain every link is important. When someone does what they can to promote the Good News, many others benefit.

ENTRANCE ANTIPHON   *(Is 59:21, 56:7)*

My teaching, which I have put in your mouth, will never fail, says the Lord; the gifts which you offered on my altar will be accepted.

or   *(Ps 15:5-6)*

You, Lord, are my portion and cup, you restore my inheritance to me; the way of life you marked out for me has made my heritage glorious.

GREETINGS, PENITENTIAL RITE, GLORIA — *pages 7-14*

OPENING PRAYER

God our Father,
you gave the bishop David to the Welsh Church
to uphold the faith
and to be an example of Christian perfection.
In this changing world
may he help us to hold fast to the values
which bring eternal life.

FIRST READING   *(Ph 3:8-14)*

A reading from the letter of St Paul to the Philippians.

I am racing for the finish, for the prize to which God calls us upwards to receive in Christ Jesus.

I believe nothing can happen that will outweigh the supreme advantage of knowing Christ Jesus my Lord. For him I have accepted the loss of everything, and I look on everything as so much rubbish if only I can have Christ and be given a place in him. I am no longer trying for perfection by my own efforts, the perfection that comes from the Law, but I want only the perfection that comes through faith in Christ, and is from God and based on faith. All I want is to know Christ and the power of his resurrection and to share his sufferings by reproducing the pattern of his death. That is the way I can hope to take my place in the resurrection of the dead. Not that I have become perfect yet: I have not yet won, but I am still running, trying to capture the prize for which Christ Jesus captured me. I can assure you my brothers, I am far from thinking that I have already won. All I can say is that I forget the past and I strain ahead for what is still to come; I am racing for the finish, for the prize to which God calls us upwards to receive in Christ Jesus.

This is the word of the Lord.

RESPONSORIAL PSALM   *(Ps 1:1-4.6)*

℟   **Happy the man who has placed
    his trust in the Lord.**

1. Happy indeed is the man
    who follows not the counsel of the wicked,
    nor lingers in the way of sinners
    nor sits in the company of scorners,
    but whose delight is the law of the Lord
    and who ponders his law day and night. ℟

2. He is like a tree that is planted
    beside the flowing waters,
    that yields its fruit in due season
    and whose leaves shall never fade;
    and all that he does shall prosper. ℟

3. Not so are the wicked, not so!
    For they like winnowed chaff
    shall be driven away by the wind;
    for the Lord guards the way of the just
    but the way of the wicked leads to doom. ℟

GOSPEL ACCLAMATION   *(Jn 8:31-32)*
**Glory to you, O Christ, you are the Word of God.
If you make my word your home
you will indeed be my disciples,
and you will learn the truth, says the Lord.
Glory to you, O Christ, you are the Word of God.**

GOSPEL   *(Mt 5:13-16)*
A reading from the holy Gospel according to Matthew.
You are the light of the world.
Jesus said to his disciples: 'You are the salt of the earth. But if salt becomes tasteless, what can make it salty again? It is good for nothing, and can only be thrown out to be trampled underfoot by men.

'You are the light of the world. A city built on a hill-top cannot be hidden. No one lights a lamp to put it under a tub; they put it on the lamp-stand where it shines for everyone in the house. In the same way your light must shine in the sight of men, so that, seeing your good works, they may give the praise to your Father in heaven.'

This is the Gospel of the Lord.

PROFESSION OF FAITH — *pages 15-16*

PRAYER OVER THE GIFTS

Lord, accept the gifts we bring
on the feast of Saint David.
We offer them to win your forgiveness
and to give honour to your name.

PREFACE OF HOLY MEN AND WOMEN I

Father, all-powerful and ever-living God,
we do well always and everywhere to give you thanks.

You are glorified in your saints,
for their glory is the crowning of your gifts.
In their lives on earth
you give us an example.
In your communion with them,
you give us their friendship.
In their prayer for the Church
you give us strength and protection.
This great company of witnesses spurs us on to victory,
to share their prize of everlasting glory,
through Jesus Christ our Lord.

With angels and archangels
and the whole company of saints
we sing our unending hymn of praise:
Holy, holy, holy...

COMMUNION ANTIPHON   (Mk 10:45)
The Son of Man came to give his life as a ransom for all.
or   (cf. Mt 19:27.29)
I assure you who left all and followed me: you will receive a hundredfold in return and inherit eternal life.

PRAYER AFTER COMMUNION

All-powerful God,
you have strengthened us with this sacrament.

May we learn from Saint David's example
to seek you above all things,
and to live always as new men in Christ,
who lives and reigns for ever and ever.

REFLECTION

>Today there are many people who have not had the light of
>faith shine on them. The missionary aspect of the Church is
>one which will continue until the end of time. It is the nature
>of the Kingdom of God that it press outwards all the time so
>that no one is excluded from its promises. Saint David played
>his part in furthering God's kingdom. The men and women of
>today who are heirs of his preaching are called on to hand on
>the faith in their turn.

—————— 7 MARCH ——————

SECOND SUNDAY OF LENT

>Three of the activities which have become associated with Lent
>are: prayer, fasting and alms-giving. Prayer is simply moving towards
>God who is already close to us. In Luke's gospel, Jesus encourages
>us to do this all the time and not to lose heart. The gospels
>present Jesus to us as someone who gave prayer an important
>place in his life. No matter how far removed from God we may
>think we are that gap is bridged when we begin to pray.

ENTRANCE ANTIPHON   *(Ps 24:6.3.22)*
**Remember your mercies, Lord, your tenderness from ages
past. Do not let our enemies triumph over us; O God, deliver
Israel from all her distress.**
or   *(Ps 26:8-9)*
**My heart has prompted me to seek your face; I seek it, Lord;
do not hide from me.**

GREETING, PENITENTIAL RITE — *pages 7-13*

The Gloria is omitted.

OPENING PRAYER

Let us pray
      [for the grace to respond to
      the Word of God]
God our Father,
help us to hear your Son.

Enlighten us with your word,
that we may find the way to your glory.

or

Let us pray
     [in this season of Lent
     for the gift of integrity]

Father of light,
in you is found no shadow of change
but only the fulness of life and limitless truth.

Open our hearts to the voice of your Word
and free us from the original darkness that shadows our vision.
Restore our sight that we may look upon your Son
who calls us to repentance and a change of heart,
for he lives and reigns with you for ever and ever.

FIRST READING   *(Gen 15:5-12.17-18)*
A reading from the book of Genesis.
God enters into a Covenant with Abraham, the man of faith.

Taking Abram outside the Lord said, 'Look up to heaven and count
the stars if you can. Such will be your descendants' he told him. Abram
put his faith in the Lord, who counted this as making him justified.

     'I am the Lord' he said to him 'who brought you out of Ur of
the Chaldaeans to make you heir to this land.' 'My Lord, the Lord'
Abram replied 'how am I to know that I shall inherit it?' He said
to him, 'Get me a three-year-old heifer, a three-year-old goat, a
three-year-old ram, a turtledove and a young pigeon.' He brought
him all these, cut them in half and put half on one side and half
facing it on the other; but the birds he did not cut in half. Birds
of prey came down on the carcasses but Abram drove them off.

     Now as the sun was setting Abram fell into a deep sleep,
and terror seized him. When the sun had set and darkness had
fallen, there appeared a smoking furnace and a firebrand that
went between the halves. That day the Lord made a Covenant
with Abram in these terms:

     'To your descendants I give this land,
     from the wadi of Egypt to the Great River.'

     This is the word of the Lord.

RESPONSORIAL PSALM   *(Ps 26:1.7-9.13-14)*

℟   **The Lord is my light and my help.**
1.   The Lord is my light and my help;
     whom shall I fear?

The Lord is the stronghold of my life;
before whom shall I shrink? ℟

2. O Lord, hear my voice when I call;
have mercy and answer.
Of you my heart has spoken:
'Seek his face.' ℟

3. It is your face, O Lord, that I seek;
hide not your face.
Dismiss not your servant in anger;
you have been my help. ℟

4. I am sure I shall see the Lord's goodness
in the land of the living.
Hope in him, hold firm and take heart.
Hope in the Lord! ℟

SECOND READING *(Ph 3:17-4:1)*

A reading from the letter of St Paul to the Philippians.

Christ will transfigure our bodies into copies of his glorious body.

My brothers, be united in following my rule of life. Take as your models everybody who is already doing this and study them as you used to study us. I have told you often, and I repeat it today with tears, there are many who are behaving as the enemies of the cross of Christ. They are destined to be lost. They make foods into their god and they are proudest of something they ought to think shameful; the things they think important are earthly things. For us, our homeland is in heaven, and from heaven comes the saviour we are waiting for, the Lord Jesus Christ, and he will transfigure these wretched bodies of ours into copies of his glorious body. He will do that by the same power with which he can subdue the whole universe.

So then, my brothers and dear friends, do not give way but remain faithful in the Lord. I miss you very much, dear friends; you are my joy and my crown.

This is the word of the Lord.

GOSPEL ACCLAMATION *(Mt 17:5)*

Glory and praise to you, O Christ!
From the bright cloud the Father's voice was heard:
'This is my Son, the Beloved. Listen to him!'
Glory and praise to you, O Christ!

GOSPEL   (Lk 9:28-36)

A reading from the holy Gospel according to Luke.

As Jesus prayed, the aspect of his face was changed.

Jesus took with him Peter and John and James and went up the mountain to pray. As he prayed, the aspect of his face was changed and his clothing became brilliant as lightning. Suddenly there were two men there talking to him; they were Moses and Elijah appearing in glory, and they were speaking of his passing which he was to accomplish in Jerusalem. Peter and his companions were heavy with sleep, but they kept awake and saw his glory and the two men standing with him. As these were leaving him, Peter said to Jesus, 'Master, it is wonderful for us to be here; so let us make three tents, one for you, one for Moses and one for Elijah.'— He did not know what he was saying. As he spoke, a cloud came and covered them with shadow; and when they went into the cloud the disciples were afraid. And a voice came from the cloud saying, 'This is my Son, the Chosen One. Listen to him'. And after the voice had spoken, Jesus was found alone. The disciples kept silence and, at that time, told no one what they had seen.

    This is the Gospel of the Lord.

PROFESSION OF FAITH — *pages 15-16*

PRAYER OVER THE GIFTS

Lord, make us holy.
May this eucharist take away our sins
that we may be prepared
to celebrate the resurrection.

PREFACE OF SECOND SUNDAY OF LENT

Father, all-powerful and ever-living God,
we do well always and everywhere to give you thanks
through Jesus Christ our Lord.

On your holy mountain he revealed himself in glory
in the presence of his disciples.
He had already prepared them for his approaching death.
He wanted to teach them through the Law and the Prophets
that the promised Christ had first to suffer
and so come to the glory of his resurrection.

In our unending joy we echo on earth
the song of the angels in heaven
as they praise your glory for ever:

Holy, holy, holy...

COMMUNION ANTIPHON   (Mt 17:5)

This is my Son, my beloved, in whom is all my delight: listen to him.

PRAYER AFTER COMMUNION

Lord,
we give thanks for these holy mysteries
which bring to us here on earth
a share in the life to come,
through Christ our Lord.

REFLECTION

There are many kinds of prayer: public and private, spoken
and silent, calm and passionate, confident and demoralised.
The psalms provide us with examples of all of these. There was
no human situation which wouldn't allow the psalmist to call
out to the Lord. Today there is no life situation which can prevent
us from raising our minds and hearts to God.

─────────── 14 MARCH ───────────

THIRD SUNDAY OF LENT

In an age when so many are hungry while there is so much
surplus food around, fasting can be looked at cynically. It has a
special connection with Lent. It has something to recommend
it still. Maybe the money spared could be given to someone in
need. To be aware of hunger can be to experience something
which is shared by many today.

ENTRANCE ANTIPHON   (Ps 24:15-16)

**My eyes are ever fixed on the Lord, for he releases my feet
from the snare. O look at me and be merciful, for I am wretched
and alone.**

or   (Ez 36:23-26)

**I will prove my holiness through you. I will gather you from
the ends of the earth. I will pour clean water on you and wash
away all your sins. I will give you a new spirit within you, says
the Lord.**

GREETING, PENITENTIAL RITE — *pages 7-13*

The Gloria is omitted.

OPENING PRAYER

Let us pray
> [for confidence in the love of God
> and the strength to overcome all our weakness]

Father, you have taught us to overcome our sins
by prayer, fasting and works of mercy.
When we are discouraged by our weakness,
give us confidence in your love.

or

Let us pray
> [to the Father and ask him
> to form a new heart within us]

God of all compassion, Father of all goodness,
to heal the wounds our sins and selfishness bring upon us
you bid us turn to fasting, prayer, and sharing with our brothers.

We acknowledge our sinfulness, our guilt is ever before us:
when our weakness causes discouragement,
let your compassion fill us with hope
and lead us through a Lent of repentance to the beauty of Easter joy.

FIRST READING   *(Ex 3:1-8.13-15)*

A reading from the book of Exodus.

I Am has sent me to you.

Moses was looking after the flock of Jethro, his father-in-law,
priest of Midian. He led his flock to the far side of the wilderness
and came to Horeb, the mountain of God. There the angel of the
Lord appeared to him in the shape of a flame of fire, coming
from the middle of a bush. Moses looked; there was the bush
blazing but it was not being burnt up. 'I must go and look at this
strange sight,' Moses said 'and see why the bush is not burnt.'
Now the Lord saw him go forward to look, and God called to
him from the middle of the bush. 'Moses, Moses!' he said. 'Here
I am' he answered. 'Come no nearer' he said. 'Take off your shoes,
for the place on which you stand is holy ground. I am the God of
your father,' he said 'the God of Abraham, the God of Isaac and the
God of Jacob.' At this Moses covered his face, afraid to look at God.

And the Lord said, 'I have seen the miserable state of my
people in Egypt. I have heard their appeal to be free of their
slave-drivers. Yes, I am well aware of their sufferings. I mean to
deliver them out of the hands of the Egyptians and bring them
up out of that land to a land rich and broad, a land where milk
and honey flow.'

Then Moses said to God, 'I am to go, then, to the sons of Israel and say to them, "The God of your fathers has sent me to you." But if they ask me what his name is, what am I to tell them?' And God said to Moses, 'I Am who I Am. This' he added 'is what you must say to the sons of Israel: "The Lord, the God of your fathers, the God of Abraham, the God of Isaac, and the God of Jacob, has sent me to you." This is my name for all time; by this name I shall be invoked for all generations to come.'

This is the word of the Lord.

RESPONSORIAL PSALM   *(Ps 102:1-4.6-8.11)*

℟   **The Lord is compassion and love.**

1.   My soul, give thanks to the Lord,
     all my being, bless his holy name.
     My soul, give thanks to the Lord
     and never forget all his blessings. ℟

2.   It is he who forgives all your guilt,
     who heals every one of your ills,
     who redeems your life from the grave,
     who crowns you with love and compassion. ℟

3.   The Lord does deeds of justice,
     gives judgement for all who are oppressed.
     He made known his ways to Moses
     and his deeds to Israel's sons. ℟

4.   The Lord is compassion and love,
     slow to anger and rich in mercy.
     For as the heavens are high above the earth
     so strong is his love for those who fear him. ℟

SECOND READING   *(1 Cor 10:1-6.10-12)*

A reading from the first letter of St Paul to the Corinthians.

The life of the people under Moses in the desert was written down to be a lesson for us.

I want to remind you, brothers, how our fathers were all guided by a cloud above them and how they all passed through the sea. They were all baptised into Moses in this cloud and in this sea; all ate the same spiritual food and all drank the same spiritual drink, since they all drank from the spiritual rock that followed them as they went, and that rock was Christ. In spite of this, most of them failed to please God and their corpses littered the desert.

These things all happened as warnings for us, not to have the wicked lusts for forbidden things that they had. You must never complain: some of them did, and they were killed by the Destroyer.

All this happened to them as a warning and it was written down to be a lesson for us who are living at the end of the age. The man who thinks he is safe must be careful that he does not fall.

This is the word of the Lord.

GOSPEL ACCLAMATION   (Mt 4:17)
Glory to you, O Christ, you are the Word of God!
Repent, says the Lord,
for the kingdom of heaven is close at hand.
Glory to you, O Christ, you are the Word of God!

GOSPEL   (Lk 13:1-9)
A reading from the holy Gospel according to Luke.
Unless you repent you will all perish as they did.

Some people arrived and told Jesus about the Galileans whose blood Pilate had mingled with that of their sacrifices. At this he said to them, 'Do you suppose these Galileans who suffered like that were greater sinners than any other Galileans? They were not, I tell you. No; but unless you repent you will all perish as they did. Or those eighteen on whom the tower at Siloam fell and killed them? Do you suppose that they were more guilty than all the other people living in Jerusalem? They were not, I tell you. No; but unless you repent you will all perish as they did.'

He told this parable: 'A man had a fig tree planted in his vineyard and he came looking for fruit on it but found none. He said to the man who looked after the vineyard, "Look here, for three years now I have been coming to look for fruit on this fig tree and finding none. Cut it down: why should it be taking up the ground?" "Sir," the man replied "leave it one more year and give me time to dig round it and manure it: it may bear fruit next year; if not, then you can cut it down." '

This is the Gospel of the Lord.

PROFESSION OF FAITH — *pages 15-16*

PRAYER OVER THE GIFTS
Lord,
by the grace of this sacrifice
may we who ask forgiveness
be ready to forgive one another.

PREFACE OF LENT I or II — *page 20*

COMMUNION ANTIPHON *(Ps 83:4-5)*

The sparrow even finds a home, the swallow finds a nest wherein to place her young, near to your altars, Lord of hosts, my King, my God! How happy they who dwell in your house! For ever they are praising you.

PRAYER AFTER COMMUNION

Lord,
in sharing this sacrament
may we receive your forgiveness
and be brought together in unity and peace.

REFLECTION

> To deny oneself food is no virtue in itself. The reason is all important. When people fast for reasons of faith it can be to increase their awareness of the people of God who are hungry. Or it can help to turn their mind to God when they become aware of their own hunger.

═══════════ 17 MARCH ═══════════

ST PATRICK
(Patron of Ireland)

> Patrick is a link through which the people of Ireland and the people of God were brought together. Throughout their history, the people of Israel considered that they and they alone were God's people. With the teaching of the prophets this narrow outlook gradually opened out so that by the time of Jesus, the stage was set for the expansion of God's word to the ends of the earth.

ENTRANCE ANTIPHON *(Gen 12:1-2)*

Go from your country and your kindred and your father's house to the land that I will show you; and I will make you the father of a great people.

GREETING, PENITENTIAL RITE, GLORIA — *pages 7-14*

OPENING PRAYER

Let us pray
[that like Saint Patrick the missionary,
we will be fearless witnesses
to the gospel of Jesus Christ]

God our Father,
you sent Saint Patrick
to preach your glory to the people of Ireland.
By the help of his prayers,
may all Christians proclaim your love to all.

or

Let us pray
    [that, like Saint Patrick,
    we may be loyal to our faith in Christ]

Father in heaven,
you sent the great bishop Patrick
to the people of Ireland to share his faith
and to spend his life in loving service.
May our lives bear witness
to the faith we profess,
and our love bring others
to the peace and joy of your gospel.

FIRST READING   *(Jer 1:4-9)*

A reading from the prophet Jeremiah.

Go now to those to whom I send you.

The word of the Lord was addressed to me, saying,

    'Before I formed you in the womb I knew you;
    before you came to birth I consecrated you;
    I have appointed you as prophet to the nations.

    I said, 'Ah, Lord God; look, I do not know how to speak: I am
a child!'

But the Lord replied,

    'Do not say, "I am a child."
    Go now to those to whom I send you
    and say whatever I command you.
    Do not be afraid of them,
    for I am with you to protect you —
    it is the Lord who speaks!'

    Then the Lord put out his hand and touched my mouth and
said to me:

    'There! I am putting my words into your mouth.'

    This is the word of the Lord.

RESPONSORIAL PSALM *(Ps 116)*

℞ **Go out to all the world,
and tell the Good News.**

1. O praise the Lord, all you nations,
acclaim him all you peoples. ℞

2. Strong is his love for us;
he is faithful for ever. ℞

SECOND READING *(Acts 13:46-49)*

A reading from the Acts of the Apostles.

We must turn to the pagans.

Paul and Barnabas spoke out boldly to the Jews, 'We had to proclaim the word of God to you first, but since you have rejected it, since you do not think yourselves worthy of eternal life, we must turn to the pagans. For this is what the Lord commanded us to do when he said:

'I have made you a light for the nations,
so that my salvation may reach the ends of the earth.'

It made the pagans very happy to hear this and they thanked the Lord for his message; all who were destined for eternal life became believers. Thus the word of the Lord spread through the whole countryside.

This is the word of the Lord.

GOSPEL ACCLAMATION *(Lk 4:18-19)*

**Praise and honour to you, Lord Jesus!
The Lord sent me to bring Good News to the poor,
and freedom to prisoners.
Praise and honour to you, Lord Jesus!**

GOSPEL *(Lk 10:1-12.17-20)*

A reading from the holy Gospel according to Luke.

Your peace will rest on that man.

The Lord appointed seventy-two others and sent them out ahead of him, in pairs, to all the towns and places he himself was to visit. He said to them, 'The harvest is rich but the labourers are few, so ask the Lord of the harvest to send labourers to his harvest. Start off now, but remember, I am sending you out like lambs among wolves. Carry no purse, no haversack, no sandals. Salute no one on the road. Whatever house you go into, let your first words be, "Peace to this house!" And if a man of peace lives there, your peace will go and rest on him; if not, it will come back to you. Stay in the same house, taking what food and drink they have to offer, for the labourer deserves his wages; do not move from house to house. Whenever you go into a town where they make you welcome, eat what is set before you. Cure those in it who are sick, and say, "The kingdom of God is very near to you." But whenever you enter a town and they do not make you welcome, go out into its streets and say, "We wipe off the very dust of your town that clings to our feet, and leave it with you. Yet be sure of this: the kingdom of God is very near." I tell you, on that day it will not go as hard with Sodom as with that town.'

The seventy-two came back rejoicing. 'Lord,' they said, 'even the devils submit to us when we use your name.' He said to them, 'I watched Satan fall like lightning from heaven. Yes, I have given you power to tread underfoot serpents and scorpions and the whole strength of the enemy; nothing shall ever hurt you. Yet do not rejoice that the spirits submit to you; rejoice rather that your names are written in heaven.'

This is the Gospel of the Lord.

PROFESSION OF FAITH — *pages 15-16*

PRAYER OVER THE GIFTS

Lord our God,
by the power of this sacrament
deepen our love
and strengthen our faith:
as we celebrate the feast of Saint Patrick
bind us more and more to each other
in unity and peace.

PREFACE OF HOLY MEN AND WOMEN I

Father, all-powerful and ever-living God,
we do well always and everywhere to give you thanks.

You are glorified in your saints,
for their glory is the crowning of your gifts.
In their lives on earth
you give us an example.
In your communion with them,
you give us their friendship.
In their prayer for the Church
you give us strength and protection.
This great company of witnesses spurs us on to victory,

to share their prize of everlasting glory,
through Jesus Christ our Lord.

With angels and archangels
and the whole company of saints
we sing our unending hymn of praise:
Holy, holy, holy…

COMMUNION ANTIPHON   *(cf. Lk 10:1.9)*
**The Lord sent disciples to proclaim to the people: the
Kingdom of God is very near to you.**
or   *(Lk 4:18-19)*
**The Lord sent me to bring the good news to the poor, to
proclaim liberty to captives.**

PRAYER AFTER COMMUNION
Lord,
by the power of this sacrament
strengthen our faith:
may all we do or say
proclaim your truth
in imitation of Saint Patrick,
who did not spare himself
but gave his whole life
to the preaching of your Word.

REFLECTION

> In Patrick's writings, especially in his Breastplate, Christ comes
> across as central to everything. He was very much aware of his
> mission in life. Like Paul, he believed that God had appointed
> him as an apostle to bring the gospel where it had not yet been
> heard. It was Patrick's choice to accept this mission. His
> response could have been otherwise.

21 MARCH
FOURTH SUNDAY OF LENT

Sometimes the joy of the Lenten season may become obscured
by the passion and death of Jesus but today's liturgy, from its
very first word, reminds us once again that we are in a season
of joy. Our celebration of Lent is from a post-Easter point of
view. Even in these days of the impending shadow of the cross,
Christ has risen. The Father has vindicated him.

ENTRANCE ANTIPHON   *(Is 66:10-11)*
**Rejoice Jerusalem! Be glad for her, you who love her; rejoice
with her, you who mourned for her, and you will find
contentment at her consoling breasts.**

GREETING, PENITENTIAL RITE — *pages 7-13*

The Gloria is omitted.

OPENING PRAYER
Let us pray
     [for a greater faith and love]
Father of peace,
we are joyful in your Word,
your Son Jesus Christ,
who reconciles us to you.
Let us hasten toward Easter
with the eagerness of faith and love.

or

Let us pray
     [that by growing in love this lenten season
     we may bring the peace of Christ to our world]
God our Father,
your Word, Jesus Christ, spoke peace to a sinful world
and brought humankind the gift of reconciliation
by the suffering and death he endured.

Teach us, the people who bear his name,
to follow the example he gave us:
may our faith, hope, and charity
turn hatred to love, conflict to peace, death to eternal life.

FIRST READING   *(Jos 5:9-12)*

A reading from the book of Joshua.

The People of God keep the Passover on their entry into the promised land.

The Lord said to Joshua, 'Today I have taken the shame of Egypt away from you.'

The Israelites pitched their camp at Gilgal and kept the Passover there on the fourteenth day of the month, at evening in the plain of Jericho. On the morrow of the Passover they tasted the produce of that country, unleavened bread and roasted ears of corn, that same day. From that time, from their first eating of the produce of that country, the manna stopped falling. And having manna no longer, the Israelites fed from that year onwards on what the land of Canaan yielded.

This is the word of the Lord.

RESPONSORIAL PSALM   *(Ps 33:2-7)*

℟ **Taste and see that the Lord is good.**

1. I will bless the Lord at all times,
    his praise always on my lips;
    in the Lord my soul shall make its boast.
    The humble shall hear and be glad. ℟

2. Glorify the Lord with me.
    Together let us praise his name.
    I sought the Lord and he answered me;
    from all my terrors he set me free. ℟

3. Look towards him and be radiant;
    let your faces not be abashed.
    This poor man called; the Lord heard him
    and rescued him from all his distress. ℟

SECOND READING   *(2 Cor 5:17-21)*

A reading from the second letter of St Paul to the Corinthians.

God reconciled us to himself through Christ.

For anyone who is in Christ, there is a new creation; the old creation has gone, and now the new one is here. It is all God's work. It was God who reconciled us to himself through Christ and gave us the work of handing on his reconciliation. In other words, God in Christ was reconciling the world to himself, not holding men's faults against them, and he has entrusted to us the news that they are reconciled. So we are ambassadors for Christ; it is as though God were appearing through us, and the appeal that we make in Christ's name is: be reconciled to God. For our sake God made the sinless one into sin, so that in him we might become the goodness of God.

This is the word of the Lord.

GOSPEL ACCLAMATION   (Lk 15:18)
Praise and honour to you, Lord Jesus!
I will leave this place and go to my father and say:
'Father, I have sinned against heaven and against you.'
Praise and honour to you, Lord Jesus!

GOSPEL   (Lk 15:1-3.11-32)
A reading from the holy Gospel according to Luke.
Your brother here was dead and has come to life.

The tax collectors and the sinners were all seeking the company of Jesus to hear what he had to say, and the Pharisees and the scribes complained. 'This man' they said 'welcomes sinners and eats with them.' So he spoke this parable to them:

'A man had two sons. The younger said to his father, "Father, let me have the share of the estate that would come to me." So the father divided the property between them. A few days later, the younger son got together everything he had and left for a distant country where he squandered his money on a life of debauchery.

'When he had spent it all, that country experienced a severe famine, and now he began to feel the pinch, so he hired himself out to one of the local inhabitants who put him on his farm to feed the pigs. And he would willingly have filled his belly with the husks the pigs were eating but no one offered him anything. Then he came to his senses and said, "How many of my father's paid servants have more food than they want, and here am I dying of hunger! I will leave this place and go to my father and say: Father, I have sinned against heaven and against you; I no longer deserve to be called your son; treat me as one of your paid servants." So he left the place and went back to his father.

'While he was still a long way off, his father saw him and was moved with pity. He ran to the boy, clasped him in his arms and kissed him tenderly. Then his son said, "Father, I have sinned against heaven and against you. I no longer deserve to be called your Son." But the father said to his servants, "Quick! Bring out the best robe and put it on him; put a ring on his finger and sandals on his feet. Bring the calf we have been fattening, and kill it; we are going to have a feast, a celebration, because this son of mine was dead and has come back to life; he was lost and is found." And they began to celebrate.

'Now the elder son was out in the fields, and on his way back, as he drew near the house, he could hear music and dancing. Calling one of the servants he asked what it was all about. "Your brother has come" replied the servant "and your father has killed the calf we had fattened because he has got him back safe and sound." He was angry then and refused to go in, and his father came out to plead with him; but he answered his father, "Look, all these years I have slaved for you and never once disobeyed your orders, yet you never offered me so much as a kid for me to celebrate with my friends. But for this son of yours, when he comes back after swallowing up your property — he and his women — you kill the calf we had been fattening."

'The father said, "My son, you are with me always and all I have is yours. But it is only right we should celebrate and rejoice, because your brother here was dead and has come to life; he was lost and is found." '

This is the Gospel of the Lord.

PROFESSION OF FAITH — *pages 15-16*

PRAYER OVER THE GIFTS
Lord,
we offer you these gifts
which bring us peace and joy.
Increase our reverence by this eucharist,
and bring salvation to the world.

PREFACE OF LENT I or II — *page 20*

COMMUNION ANTIPHON   (Lk 15:32)
**My son, you should rejoice, because your brother was dead
and has come back to life; he was lost and is found.**

PRAYER AFTER COMMUNION
Father,
you enlighten all who come into the world.
Fill our hearts with the light of your gospel,
that our thoughts may please you,
and our love be sincere.

REFLECTION
    The language of the letters of Paul has caused some people to
    detect in them the contortions of spirit which the author must
    have gone through in order to leave behind him the life of a

pious and zealous Jew and to accept Jesus as the Christ. His life is the story of the elder brother of the prodigal son who was converted by his father's words and actions to leave his comfortable existence and to spend the rest of his days in search of his lost brothers and sisters.

28 MARCH

FIFTH SUNDAY OF LENT

The giving of alms is the third activity associated particularly with Lent. From the earliest times when Christians came together to celebrate the eucharist they were aware of those in their community who had little or nothing. They wished to do something about this. Sometimes it took the form of bringing a gift which was distributed to those in need. Or as time went on, they contributed money to a fund for those in want. By doing this they were expressing the truth that we are all part of the same family.

ENTRANCE ANTIPHON   (Ps 42:1-2)

Give me justice, O God, and defend my cause against the wicked; rescue me from deceitful and unjust men. You, O God, are my refuge.

GREETING, PENITENTIAL RITE — pages 7-13

The Gloria *is omitted.*

OPENING PRAYER

Let us pray
    [for the courage to follow Christ]
Father,
help us to be like Christ your Son,
who loved the world and died for our salvation.
Inspire us by his love,
guide us by his example,
who lives and reigns with you and the Holy Spirit,
one God, for ever and ever.

or

Let us pray
    [for the courage to embrace the world
    in the name of Christ]

Father in heaven,
the love of your Son led him to accept the suffering of the cross
that his brothers might glory in new life.
Change our selfishness into self-giving.
Help us to embrace the world you have given us,
that we may transform the darkness of its pain
into the life and joy of Easter.

FIRST READING   *(Is 43:16-21)*

A reading from the prophet Isaiah.

See, I am doing a new deed, and I will give my chosen people drink.

Thus says the Lord,
who made a way through the sea,
a path in the great waters;
who put chariots and horse in the field
and a powerful army,
which lay there never to rise again,
snuffed out, put out like a wick:

No need to recall the past,
no need to think about what was done before.
See, I am doing a new deed,
even now it comes to light; can you not see it?
Yes, I am making a road in the wilderness,
paths in the wilds.
The wild beasts will honour me,
jackals and ostriches,
because I am putting water in the wilderness
(rivers in the wild)
to give my chosen people drink.
The people I have formed for myself
will sing my praises.

This is the word of the Lord.

RESPONSORIAL PSALM   *(Ps 125)*

℞ **What marvels the Lord worked for us!**
   Indeed we were glad.

1. When the Lord delivered Zion from bondage,
   it seemed like a dream.
   Then was our mouth filled with laughter,
   on our lips there were songs. ℞

2. The heathens themselves said: 'What marvels
   the Lord worked for them!'   *(continued)*

What marvels the Lord worked for us!
Indeed we were glad. ℟

℟ **What marvels the Lord worked for us!
Indeed we were glad.**

3. Deliver us, O Lord, from our bondage
    as streams in dry land.
    Those who are sowing in tears
    will sing when they reap. ℟

4. They go out, they go out, full of tears,
    carrying seed for the sowing:
    they come back, they come back, full of song,
    carrying their sheaves. ℟

SECOND READING   *(Phil 3:8-14)*

A reading from the letter of St Paul to the Philippians.

Reproducing the pattern of his death, I have accepted the loss of everything for Christ.

I believe nothing can happen that will outweigh the supreme advantage of knowing Christ Jesus my Lord. For him I have accepted the loss of everything, and I look on everything as so much rubbish if only I can have Christ and be given a place in him. I am no longer trying for perfection by my own efforts, the perfection that comes from the Law, but I want only the perfection that comes through faith in Christ, and is from God and based on faith. All I want is to know Christ and the power of his resurrection and to share his sufferings by reproducing the pattern of his death. That is the way I can hope to take my place in the resurrection of the dead. Not that I have become perfect yet: I have not yet won, but I am still running, trying to capture the prize for which Christ Jesus captured me. I can assure you my brothers, I am far from thinking that I have already won. All I can say is that I forget the past and I strain ahead for what is still to come; I am racing for the finish, for the prize to which God calls us upwards to receive in Christ Jesus.

This is the word of the Lord.

GOSPEL ACCLAMATION   *(cf. Amos 5:14)*

**Praise to you, O Christ, king of eternal glory!
Seek good and not evil so that you may live,
and that the Lord God of hosts may really be with you.
Praise to you, O Christ, king of eternal glory!**

GOSPEL (*Jn 8:1-11*)

A reading from the holy Gospel according to John.

If there is one of you who has not sinned, let him be the first to throw a stone at her.

Jesus went to the Mount of Olives. At daybreak he appeared in the Temple again; and as all the people came to him, he sat down and began to teach them.

The scribes and Pharisees brought a woman along who had been caught committing adultery; and making her stand there in full view of everybody, they said to Jesus, 'Master, this woman was caught in the very act of committing adultery, and Moses has ordered us in the Law to condemn women like this to death by stoning. What have you to say?' They asked him this as a test, looking for something to use against him. But Jesus bent down and started writing on the ground with his finger. As they persisted with their question, he looked up and said, 'If there is one of you who has not sinned, let him be the first to throw a stone at her.' Then he bent down and wrote on the ground again. When they heard this they went away one by one, beginning with the eldest, until Jesus was left alone with the woman, who remained standing there. He looked up and said, 'Woman, where are they? Has no one condemned you?' 'No one, sir,' she replied. 'Neither do I condemn you,' said Jesus 'go away, and don't sin any more.'

This is the Gospel of the Lord.

PROFESSION OF FAITH — *pages 15-16*

PRAYER OVER THE GIFTS

Almighty God,
may the sacrifice we offer
take away the sins of those
whom you enlighten with the Christian faith.

PREFACE OF LENT I or II — *page 20*

COMMUNION ANTIPHON (*Jn 8:10-11*)

Has no one condemned you? The woman answered: No one, Lord. Neither do I condemn you: go and do not sin again.

PRAYER AFTER COMMUNION

Almighty Father,
by this sacrifice
may we always remain one with your Son, Jesus Christ,
whose body and blood we share,
for he is Lord for ever and ever.

REFLECTION

Christianity is not simply a matter of a relationship between
the individual and God. It is equally concerned with the
relationship between people. It has social consequences. This
aspect goes back to the days of Moses and the covenant on
Mount Sinai. It was because they were sharers in the same
covenant with the Lord rather than for any ties of family or
race that the children of Israel had an obligation to look after
one another as well as an obligation to God.

--------------------------------- 4 APRIL ---------------------------------

PASSION (PALM) SUNDAY

Holy Week, in the Irish language, 'The Great Week' begins today.
At one end Passion Sunday and at the other the Easter Triduum
of Holy Thursday, Good Friday and Easter Saturday and the
Easter vigil. Today we hear the passion story according to Luke.
On Good Friday we shall hear John's account of the same event.
Luke presents Jesus' passion as a confrontation with Satan, which
acts as an echo of the temptation scene at the beginning of his gospel.

COMMEMORATION OF THE LORD'S ENTRANCE
INTO JERUSALEM

FIRST FORM: THE PROCESSION

*The congregation assembles in a secondary church or chapel or in some
other suitable place distinct from the church to which the procession will
move. Palm branches are carried.*

*While the priest and ministers go to the place where the people have
assembled, the following antiphon or any other appropriate song is sung.*

ANTIPHON   *(Mt 2:9)*

Hosanna to the Son of David,
the King of Israel.
Blessed is he who comes
in the name of the Lord.
Hosanna in the highest.

The priest then greets the people in these or similar words:

Dear friends in Christ, for five weeks of Lent we have been
preparing, by works of charity and self-sacrifice, for the
celebration of our Lord's paschal mystery. Today we come
together to begin this solemn celebration in union with the

whole Church throughout the world. Christ entered in triumph into his own city, to complete his work as our Messiah: to suffer, to die, and to rise again. Let us remember with devotion this entry which began his saving work and follow him with a lively faith. United with him in his suffering on the cross, may we share his resurrection and new life.

Then the priest says one of the following prayers:

Let us pray.

Almighty God,
we pray you
bless ✠ these branches
and make them holy.
Today we joyfully acclaim Jesus our Messiah and King.
May we reach one day the happiness of the new and everlasting
    Jerusalem
by faithfully following him
who lives and reigns for ever and ever.

or

Let us pray.

Lord, increase the faith of your people
and listen to our prayers.
Today we honour Christ our triumphant King
by carrying these branches.
May we honour you every day
by living always in him,
for he is Lord for ever and ever.

The priest sprinkles the branches with holy water in silence. The account of the Lord's entrance into Jerusalem is proclaimed.

GOSPEL   (Lk 19:28-40)

A reading from the holy Gospel according to Luke.

Blessings on him who comes in the name of the Lord.

Jesus went on ahead, going up to Jerusalem. Now when he was near Bethphage and Bethany, close by the Mount of Olives as it is called, he sent two of the disciples, telling them, 'Go off to the village opposite, and as you enter it you will find a tethered colt that no one has yet ridden. Untie it and bring it here. If anyone asks you, "Why are you untying it?" you are to say this, "The Master needs it".' The messengers went off and found everything just as he had told them. As they were untying the colt, its owner said, 'Why are you untying that colt?' and they answered, 'The Master needs it.'

So they took the colt to Jesus, and throwing their garments over its back they helped Jesus on to it. As he moved off, people spread their cloaks in the road, and now, as he was approaching the downward slope of the Mount of Olives, the whole group of disciples joyfully began to praise God at the top of their voices for all the miracles they had seen. They cried out:

'Blessings on the King who comes,
in the name of the Lord!
Peace in heaven
and glory in the highest heavens!'

Some Pharisees in the crowd said to him, 'Master, check your disciples,' but he answered, 'I tell you, if these keep silence the stones will cry out.'

This is the Gospel of the Lord.

PROCESSION

Before the procession begins, the celebrant or suitable minister may address the people in these or similar words:

Let us go forth in peace,
praising Jesus our Messiah,
as did the crowds who welcomed him to Jerusalem.

The procession to the church where Mass will be celebrated then begins. During the procession the following or some other appropriate songs are sung.

ANTIPHON

The children of Jerusalem
welcomed Christ the King.
They carried olive branches
and loudly praised the Lord:
Hosanna in the highest.

(The Antiphon *may be repeated between verses of psalm 23)*

PSALM 23

1. The Lord's is the earth and its fullness,
    the world and all its peoples.
    It is he who set it on the seas;
    on the waters he made it firm. *(Ant.)*

2. Who shall climb the mountain of the Lord?
    Who shall stand in his holy place?
    The man with clean hands and pure heart,
    who desires not worthless things,
    (who has not sworn so as to deceive his neighbour). *(Ant.)*

3. He shall receive blessings from the Lord
   and reward from the God who saves him.
   Such are the men who seek him,
   seek the face of the God of Jacob. *(Ant.)*

4. O gates, lift high your heads:
   grow higher, ancient doors.
   Let him enter, the king of glory! *(Ant.)*

5. Who is the king of glory?
   The Lord, the mighty, the valiant,
   the Lord, the valiant in war. *(Ant.)*

6. O gates, lift high your heads;
   grow higher, ancient doors.
   Let him enter, the king of glory! *(Ant.)*

7. Who is he, the king of glory?
   He, the Lord of armies,
   he is the king of glory. *(Ant.)*

A hymn in honour of Christ is sung during the procession.

*As the procession enters the church, the following responsory or another
song which refers to the Lord's entrance is sung.*

℟ **The children of Jerusalem
   welcomed Christ the King.
   They proclaimed the resurrection of life,
   and, waving olive branches,
   they loudly praised the Lord:
   Hosanna in the highest.**

℣ **When the people heard that Jesus
   was entering Jerusalem;
   they went to meet him
   and, waving olive branches,
   they loudly praised the Lord:
   Hosanna in the highest.**

The priest goes to the chair and says the Opening Prayer *of the Mass,
which concludes the procession. Mass then continues in the usual way.*

SECOND FORM: THE SOLEMN ENTRANCE

*If the procession cannot be held outside the church, the commemoration of
the Lord's entrance may be celebrated within the church. The faithful,
carrying palm branches, assemble either in front of the church door or
inside the church.*

THIRD FORM: THE SIMPLE ENTRANCE

If the solemn entrance is not held, the Lord's entrance is commemorated with the following simple entrance. While the celebrant goes to the altar, the entrance antiphon with its psalm (see below) or another song with the same theme, is sung. Mass continues in the usual way.

ENTRANCE ANTIPHON

Six days before the solemn passover the Lord came to Jerusalem, and children waving palm branches ran out to welcome him. They loudly praised the Lord: Hosanna in the highest. Blessed are you who have come to us so rich in love and mercy.

PSALM   (23:9-10)

Open wide the doors and gates.
Lift high the ancient portals.
The King of glory enters.

Who is the King of glory?
He is God the mighty Lord.

Hosanna in the highest.
Blessed are you who have come to us
so rich in love and mercy.

THE MASS

OPENING PRAYER

Let us pray
   [for a closer union with Christ
   during this holy season]

Almighty, ever-living God,
you have given the human race Jesus Christ our Saviour
as a model of humility.
He fulfilled your will
by becoming man and giving his life on the cross.
Help us to bear witness to you
by following his example of suffering
and make us worthy to share in his resurrection.

or

Let us pray
   [as we accompany our King to Jerusalem]

Almighty Father of our Lord Jesus Christ,
you sent your Son
to be born of woman and to die on a cross,

so that through the obedience of one man,
estrangement might be dissolved for all.

Guide our minds by his truth
and strengthen our lives by the example of his death,
that we may live in union with you
in the kingdom of your promise.
Grant this through Christ our Lord.

FIRST READING   *(Is 50:4-7)*

A reading from the prophet Isaiah.

I did not cover my face against insult — I know I shall not be shamed.

The Lord has given me
a disciple's tongue.
So that I may know how to reply to the wearied,
he provides me with speech.
Each morning he wakes me to hear,
to listen like a disciple.
The Lord has opened my ear.

For my part, I made no resistance,
neither did I turn away.
I offered my back to those who struck me,
my cheeks to those who tore at my beard;
I did not cover my face
against insult and spittle.

The Lord comes to my help,
so that I am untouched by the insults.
So, too, I set my face like flint;
I know I shall not be shamed.

    This is the word of the Lord.

RESPONSORIAL PSALM   *(Ps 21:8-9.17-20.23-24)*

℟ **My God, my God, why have you forsaken me?**

1. All who see me deride me.
    They curl their lips, they toss their heads.
    'He trusted in the Lord, let him save him:
    let him release him if this is his friend.' ℟

2. Many dogs have surrounded me,
    a band of the wicked beset me.
    They tear holes in my hands and my feet,
    I can count every one of my bones. ℟   *(continued)*

3.   They divide my clothing among them.
     They cast lots for my robe.
     O Lord, do not leave me alone,
     my strength, make haste to help me! ℞

℞   **My God, my God, why have you forsaken me?**

4.   I will tell of your name to my brethren
     and praise you where they are assembled.
     'You who fear the Lord give him praise;
     all sons of Jacob, give him glory.
     Revere him, Israel's sons.' ℞

SECOND READING   (Phil 2:6-11)

A reading from the letter of St Paul to the Philippians.

He humbled himself, but God raised him high.

His state was divine,
yet Christ Jesus did not cling
to his equality with God
but emptied himself
to assume the condition of a slave,
and became as men are;
and being as all men are,
he was humbler yet,
even to accepting death,
death on a cross.
But God raised him high
and gave him the name
which is above all other names
so that all beings
in the heavens, on earth and in the underworld,
should bend the knee at the name of Jesus
and that every tongue should acclaim
Jesus Christ as Lord,
to the glory of God the Father.

     This is the word of the Lord.

GOSPEL ACCLAMATION   (Phil 2:8-9)

Praise to you, O Christ, King of eternal glory!
Christ was humbler yet,
even to accepting death,
death on a cross,
But God raised him high
and gave him the name which is above all names.
Praise to you, O Christ, king of eternal glory.

GOSPEL   *(Lk 22:14-23:56)*

(For Shorter Form, read between ◗ ◖*)*

(N. Narrator; J. Jesus; O. other individual voices; C. the 'crowd' — **bold types***)*

The passion of our Lord Jesus Christ according to Luke.

N. When the hour came Jesus took his place at table, and the apostles with him. And he said to them,

J. I have longed to eat this passover with you before I suffer; because, I tell you, I shall not eat it again until it is fulfilled in the kingdom of God.

N. Then, taking a cup, he gave thanks and said,

J. Take this and share it among you, because from now on, I tell you, I shall not drink wine until the kingdom of God comes.

N. Then he took some bread, and when he had given thanks, broke it and gave it to them, saying,

J. This is my body which will be given for you; do this as a memorial of me.

N. He did the same with the cup after supper, and said,

J. This cup is the new covenant in my blood which will be poured out for you.

     And yet, here with me on the table is the hand of the man who betrays me. The Son of Man does indeed go to his fate even as it has been decreed, but alas for that man by whom he is betrayed!

N. And they began to ask one another which of them it could be who was to do this thing.

     A dispute arose also between them about which should be reckoned the greatest, but he said to them,

J. Among pagans it is the kings who lord it over them, and those who have authority over them are given the title Benefactor. This must not happen with you. No; the greatest among you must behave as if he were the youngest, the leader as if he were the one who serves. For who is the greater: the one at table or the one who serves? The one at table, surely? Yet here I am among you as one who serves!

     You are the men who have stood by me faithfully in my trials; and now I confer a kingdom on you, just as my Father conferred one on me: you will eat and drink at my table in my kingdom, and you will sit on thrones to judge the twelve tribes of Israel.

    Simon, Simon! Satan, you must know, has got his wish to sift you all like wheat; but I have prayed for you, Simon, that your faith may not fail, and once you have recovered, you in your turn must strengthen your brothers.

N. He answered,

O. Lord, I would be ready to go to prison with you, and to death.

N. Jesus replied,

J. I tell you, Peter, by the time the cock crows today you will have denied three times that you know me.

N. He said to them,

J. When I sent you out without purse or haversack or sandals, were you short of anything?

N. They answered,

C. **No.**

N. He said to them,

J. But now if you have a purse, take it: if you have a haversack, do the same; if you have no sword, sell your cloak and buy one, because I tell you these words of scripture have to be fulfilled in me: He let himself be taken for a criminal. Yes, what scripture says about me is even now reaching its fulfilment.

N. They said,

C. **Lord, there are two swords here now.**

N. He said to them,

J. That is enough!

N. He then left the upper room to make his way as usual to the Mount of Olives, with the disciples following. When they reached the place he said to them,

J. Pray not to be put to the test.

N. Then he withdrew from them, about a stone's throw away, and knelt down and prayed, saying,

J. Father, if you are willing, take this cup away from me. Nevertheless, let your will be done, not mine.

N. Then an angel appeared to him coming from heaven to give him strength. In his anguish he prayed even more earnestly, and his sweat fell to the ground like great drops of blood.

    When he rose from prayer he went to the disciples and found them sleeping for sheer grief. He said to them,

J.   Why are you asleep? Get up and pray not to be put to the
       test.

N.   He was still speaking when a number of men appeared, and
       at the head of them the man called Judas, one of the Twelve,
       who went up to Jesus to kiss him. Jesus said,

J.   Judas, are you betraying the Son of Man with a kiss?

N.   His followers, seeing what was happening, said,

C.   **Lord, shall we use our swords?**

N.   And one of them struck out at the high priest's servant, and
       cut off his right ear. But at this Jesus spoke,

J.   Leave off! That will do!

N.   And touching the man's ear he healed him.
              Then Jesus spoke to the chief priests and captains of the
       Temple guard and elders who had come for him. He said,

J.   Am I a brigand that you had to set out with swords and
       clubs? When I was among you in the Temple day after day
       you never moved to lay hands on me. But this is your hour;
       this is the reign of darkness.

N.   They seized him then and led him away, and they took him
       to the high priest's house. Peter followed at a distance. They
       had lit a fire in the middle of the courtyard and Peter sat
       down among them, and as he was sitting there by the blaze
       a servant-girl saw him, peered at him and said,

O.   This person was with him too.

N.   But he denied it, saying,

O.   Woman, I do not know him.

N.   Shortly afterwards, someone else saw him and said,

O.   You are another of them.

N.   But Peter replied,

O.   I am not, my friend.

N.   About an hour later, another man insisted, saying,

O.   This fellow was certainly with him. Why, he is a Galilean.

N.   Peter said,

O.   My friend, I do not know what you are talking about.

N.   At that instant, while he was still speaking, the cock crew,
       and the Lord turned and looked straight at Peter, and Peter
       remembered what the Lord had said to him, 'Before the
       cock crows today, you will have disowned me three times'.
       And he went outside and wept bitterly.

Meanwhile the men who guarded Jesus were mocking and beating him. They blindfolded him and questioned him, saying,

C. **Play the prophet. Who hit you then?**

N. And they continued heaping insults on him.

When day broke there was a meeting of the elders of the people, attended by the chief priests and scribes. He was brought before their council, and they said to him,

C. **If you are the Christ, tell us.**

N. He replied,

J. If I tell you, you will not believe me, and if I question you, you will not answer. But from now on, the Son of Man will be seated at the right hand of the Power of God.

N. Then they all said,

C. **So you are the Son of God then?**

N. He answered,

J. It is you who say I am.

N. They said,

C. **What need of witnesses have we now? We have heard it for ourselves from his own lips.**

N. ♦The whole assembly then rose, and they brought him before Pilate.

They began their accusation by saying,

C. **We found this man inciting our people to revolt, opposing payment of tribute to Caesar, and claiming to be Christ, a king.**

N. Pilate put to him this question,

O. Are you the king of the Jews?

N. He replied,

J. It is you who say it.

N. Pilate then said to the chief priests and the crowd,

O. I find no case against this man.

N. But they persisted,

C. **He is inflaming the people with his teaching all over Judaea; it has come all the way from Galilee, where he started, down to here.**

N. When Pilate heard this, he asked if the man were a Galilean; and finding that he came under Herod's jurisdiction he passed him over to Herod who was also in Jerusalem at that time.

Herod was delighted to see Jesus; he had heard about him and had been wanting for a long time to set eyes on him; moreover, he was hoping to see some miracle worked by him. So he questioned him at some length; but without getting any reply. Meanwhile the chief priests and the scribes were there, violently pressing their accusations. Then Herod, together with his guards, treated him with contempt and made fun of him; he put a rich cloak on him and sent him back to Pilate. And though Herod and Pilate had been enemies before, they were reconciled that same day.

Pilate then summoned the chief priests and the leading men and the people. He said,

O. You brought this man before me as a political agitator. Now I have gone into the matter myself in your presence and found no case against him. Nor has Herod either, since he has sent him back to us. As you can see, the man has done nothing that deserves death, so I shall have him flogged and then let him go.

N. But as one man they howled,

C. **Away with him! Give us Barabbas!**

N. This man had been thrown into prison for causing a riot in the city and for murder.

Pilate was anxious to set Jesus free and addressed them again, but they shouted back.

C. **Crucify him! Crucify him!**

N. And for the third time he spoke to them,

O. Why? What harm has this man done? I have found no case against him that deserves death, so I shall have him punished and let him go.

N. But they kept on shouting at the top of their voices, demanding that he should be crucified, and their shouts were growing louder.

Pilate then gave his verdict: their demand was to be granted. He released the man they asked for, who had been imprisoned for rioting and murder, and handed Jesus over to them to deal with as they pleased.

As they were leading him away they seized on a man, Simon from Cyrene, who was coming in from the country, and made him shoulder the cross and carry it behind Jesus. Large numbers of people followed him, and of women too who mourned and lamented for him. But Jesus turned to them and said,

J. Daughters of Jerusalem, do not weep for me; weep rather for
    yourselves and for your children. For the days will surely
    come when people will say, 'Happy are those who are barren,
    the wombs that have never borne, the breasts that have never
    suckled!' Then they will begin to say to the mountains, 'Fall
    on us!'; to the hills, 'Cover us!' For if men use the green
    wood like this, what will happen when it is dry?

N. Now with him they were also leading out two other criminals
    to be executed.

       When they reached the place called The Skull, they
    crucified him there and the criminals also, one on the right,
    the other on the left. Jesus said,

J. Father, forgive them; they do not know what they are doing.

N. Then they cast lots to share out his clothing. The people
    stayed there watching him. As for the leaders, they jeered at
    him, saying,

C. **He saved others; let him save himself if he is the Christ of
    God, the Chosen One.**

N. The soldiers mocked him too, and when they approached to
    offer him vinegar they said,

C. **If you are the king of the Jews, save yourself.**

N. Above him there was an inscription: 'This is the King of the Jews.'

       One of the criminals hanging there abused him, saying,

O. Are you not the Christ? Save yourself and us as well.

N. But the other spoke up and rebuked him,

O. Have you no fear of God at all? You got the same sentence
    as he did, but in our case we deserved it: we are paying for
    what we did. But this man has done nothing wrong. Jesus,
    remember me when you come into your kingdom.

N. He replied,

J. Indeed, I promise you, today you will be with me in paradise.

N. It was now about the sixth hour and, with the sun eclipsed,
    a darkness came over the whole land until the ninth hour.
    The veil of the Temple was torn right down the middle; and
    when Jesus had cried out in a loud voice, he said,

J. Father, into your hands I commit my spirit.

N. With these words he breathed his last.

                    All kneel and pause a moment.

When the centurion saw what had taken place, he gave praise to God and said,

O. This was a great and good man.

N. And when all the people who had gathered for the spectacle saw what had happened, they went home beating their breasts.

All his friends stood at a distance; so also did the women who had accompanied him from Galilee, and they saw all this happen. ◖

Then a member of the council arrived, an upright and virtuous man named Joseph. He had not consented to what the others had planned and carried out. He came from Arimathaea, a Jewish town, and he lived in the hope of seeing the kingdom of God. This man went to Pilate and asked for the body of Jesus. He then took it down, wrapped it in a shroud and put him in a tomb which was hewn in stone in which no one had yet been laid. It was Preparation Day and the sabbath was imminent.

Meanwhile the women who had come from Galilee with Jesus were following behind. They took note of the tomb and of the position of the body.

Then they returned and prepared spices and ointments. And on the sabbath day they rested, as the law required.

PROFESSION OF FAITH — *pages 15-16*

PRAYER OVER THE GIFTS

Lord, may the suffering and death of Jesus, your only Son,
make us pleasing to you.
Alone we can do nothing,
but may this perfect sacrifice
win us mercy and love.

PREFACE OF PASSION (PALM) SUNDAY

Father, all-powerful and ever-living God,
we do well always and everywhere to give you thanks
through Jesus Christ our Lord.

Though he was sinless, he suffered willingly for sinners.
Though innocent, he accepted death to save the guilty.
By his dying, he has destroyed our sins.
By his rising, he has raised us up to holiness of life.

We praise you, Lord, with all the angels and saints
in their song of joy:
Holy, holy, holy...

COMMUNION ANTIPHON   *(Mt 26:42)*

Father, if this cup may not pass, but I must drink it, then your will be done.

PRAYER AFTER COMMUNION

Lord,
you have satisfied our hunger with this eucharistic food.
The death of your Son gives us hope and strengthens our faith.
May his resurrection give us perseverance
and lead us to salvation.

SOLEMN BLESSING

Bow your heads and pray for God's blessing.

The Father of mercies has given us an example of unselfish love
in the sufferings of his only Son.
Through your service of God and neighbour
may you receive his countless blessings.
Amen.

You believe that by his dying
Christ destroyed death for ever.
May he give you everlasting life.
Amen.

He humbled himself for our sakes.
May you follow his example
and share in his resurrection.
Amen.

May almighty God bless you,
the Father, and the Son, ✠ and the Holy Spirit.
Amen.

REFLECTION

Luke's story of the passion is concerned with values which
Jesus lived during his life. In his second volume, the Acts of the
Apostles, he continues this approach showing that the true
disciple is one who lives the values which Jesus did. Stephen is
a perfect example of this. He dies, as Jesus does and as we hear
today, forgiving others.

8 APRIL
HOLY THURSDAY
EVENING MASS OF THE LORD'S SUPPER

This evening we begin the three day celebration which is the
high point of the Church's liturgical year. Evening Mass of the
Lord's Supper recalls the institution of the Eucharist, and of the
Priesthood. In some places today is called 'Maundy Thursday' in
recognition of Jesus' words: 'A new commandment I give you;
love one another as I have loved you.'

ENTRANCE ANTIPHON   (Ga 6:14)

We should glory in the cross of our Lord Jesus Christ, for he
is our salvation, our life and our resurrection; through him
we are saved and made free.

GREETING, PENITENTIAL RITE, GLORIA — *pages 7-14*

OPENING PRAYER

Let us pray.
God our Father,
we are gathered here to share in the supper
which your only Son left to his Church to reveal his love.
He gave it to us when he was about to die
and commanded us to celebrate it as the new and eternal sacrifice.
We pray that in this eucharist
we may find the fullness of love and life.

FIRST READING   (Ex 12:1-8.11-14)

A reading from the book of Exodus.

Instructions concerning the Passover meal.

The Lord said to Moses and Aaron in the land of Egypt, 'This
month is to be the first of all the others for you, the first month
of your year. Speak to the whole community of Israel and say,
"On the tenth day of this month each man must take an animal
from the flock, one for each family: one animal for each
household. If the household is too small to eat the animal, a
man must join with his neighbour, the nearest to his house, as
the number of persons requires. You must take into account
what each can eat in deciding the number for the animal. It
must be an animal without blemish, a male one year old; you
may take it from either sheep or goats. You must keep it till the

fourteenth day of the month when the whole assembly of the
community of Israel shall slaughter it between the two evenings.
Some of the blood must then be taken and put on the two
doorposts and the lintel of the houses where it is eaten. That
night, the flesh is to be eaten, roasted over the fire; it must be
eaten with unleavened bread and bitter herbs. You shall eat it
like this: with a girdle round your waist, sandals on your feet, a
staff in your hand. You shall eat it hastily: it is a passover in
honour of the Lord. That night, I will go through the land of
Egypt and strike down all the first-born in the land of Egypt,
man and beast alike, and I shall deal out punishment to all the
gods of Egypt, I am the Lord. The blood shall serve to mark the
houses that you live in. When I see the blood I will pass over
you and you shall escape the destroying plague when I strike the
land of Egypt. This day is to be a day of remembrance for you,
and you must celebrate it as a feast in the Lord's honour. For all
generations you are to declare it a day of festival, for ever." '

This is the word of the Lord.

RESPONSORIAL PSALM   (Ps 115:12-13.15-18)

℟ **The blessing-cup that we bless**
   is a communion with the blood of Christ.

1. How can I repay the Lord
    for his goodness to me?
    The cup of salvation I will raise;
    I will call on the Lord's name. ℟

2. O precious in the eyes of the Lord
    is the death of his faithful.
    Your servant, Lord, your servant am I;
    you have loosened my bonds. ℟

3. A thanksgiving sacrifice I make:
    I will call on the Lord's name.
    My vows to the Lord I will fulfil
    before all his people. ℟

SECOND READING   (1 Cor 11:23-26)

A reading from the first letter of St. Paul to the Corinthians.

Every time you eat this bread and drink this cup, you are proclaiming
the death of the Lord.

This is what I received from the Lord, and in turn passed on to
you: that on the same night that he was betrayed, the Lord Jesus
took some bread, and thanked God for it and broke it, and he

said, 'This is my body, which is for you; do this as a memorial of me.' In the same way he took the cup after supper, and said, 'This cup is the new covenant in my blood. Whenever you drink it, do this as a memorial of me.' Until the Lord comes, therefore, every time you eat this bread and drink this cup, you are proclaiming his death.

This is the word of the Lord.

GOSPEL ACCLAMATION   *(Jn 13:34)*

Praise and honour to you, Lord Jesus!
I give you a new commandment:
love one another just as I have loved you, says the Lord.
Praise and honour to you, Lord Jesus!

GOSPEL   *(Jn 13:1-15)*

A reading from the holy Gospel according to John.

Now he showed how perfect his love was.

It was before the festival of the Passover, and Jesus knew that the hour had come for him to pass from this world to the Father. He had always loved those who were his in the world, but now he showed how perfect his love was.

They were at supper, and the devil had already put it into the mind of Judas Iscariot son of Simon, to betray him. Jesus knew that the Father had put everything into his hands, and that he had come from God and was returning to God, and he got up from table, removed his outer garment and, taking a towel, wrapped it round his waist; he then poured water into a basin and began to wash the disciples' feet and to wipe them with the towel he was wearing.

He came to Simon Peter, who said to him, 'Lord, are you going to wash my feet?' Jesus answered, 'At the moment you do not know what I am doing, but later you will understand.' 'Never!' said Peter. 'You shall never wash my feet.' Jesus replied, 'If I do not wash you, you can have nothing in common with me.' 'Then, Lord,' said Simon Peter 'not only my feet, but my hands and my head as well!' Jesus said, 'No one who has taken a bath needs washing, he is clean all over. You too are clean, though not all of you are.' He knew who was going to betray him, that was why he said, 'though not all of you are.'

When he had washed their feet and put on his clothes again he went back to the table. 'Do you understand,' he said, 'what I have done to you? You call me Master and Lord, and rightly; so I am. If I, then, the Lord and Master, have washed your feet, you should wash each other's feet. I have given you an example so that you may copy what I have done to you.'

This is the Gospel of the Lord.

WASHING OF FEET

If the ceremony of the Washing of Feet is conducted, it follows the homily. During the washing of feet the following antiphons or other appropriate hymns are sung.

ANTIPHON 1   *(cf. Jn 13:4.5.15)*

The Lord Jesus,
when he had eaten with his disciples,
poured water into a basin
and began to wash their feet, saying:
This example I leave you.

ANTIPHON 2   *(Jn 13:6.7.8)*

Lord, do you wash my feet?
Jesus said to him:
If I do not wash your feet,
you can have no part with me.

℣ So he came to Simon Peter,
who said to him:
Lord, do you wash my feet?

℣ Now you do not know what I am doing,
but later you will understand.
Lord, do you wash my feet?

ANTIPHON 3   *(cf. Jn 13:14)*

If I, your Lord and Teacher, have washed your feet,
then surely you must wash one another's feet.

ANTIPHON 4   *(Jn 13:35)*

If there is this love among you,
all will know that you are my disciples.

℣ Jesus said to his disciples:
If there is this love among you,
all will know that you are my disciples.

ANTIPHON 5   *(Jn 13:34)*

I give you a new commandment:
love one another as I have loved you, says the Lord.

ANTIPHON 6   *(1Cor 13:13)*

**Faith, hope, and love,
let these endure among you;
and the greatest of these is love.**

The Profession of Faith *is not said. Priest introduces the* Prayer of the Faithful.

PRAYER OVER THE GIFTS

Lord,
make us worthy to celebrate these mysteries.
Each time we offer this memorial sacrifice,
the work of our redemption is accomplished.

PREFACE OF THE HOLY EUCHARIST I

Father, all-powerful and ever-living God,
we do well always and everywhere to give you thanks
through Jesus Christ our Lord.

He is the true and eternal priest
who established this unending sacrifice.
He offered himself as a victim for our deliverance
and taught us to make this offering in his memory.
As we eat his body which he gave for us,
we grow in strength.
As we drink his blood which he poured out for us,
we are washed clean.

Now, with angels and archangels,
and the whole company of heaven,
we sing the unending hymn of your praise:

Holy, holy, holy...

COMMUNION ANTIPHON   *(1Cor 11:24-25)*

**This body will be given for you. This is the cup of the new
covenant in my blood; whenever you receive them, do so in
remembrance of me.**

PRAYER AFTER COMMUNION

Almighty God,
we receive new life
from the supper your Son gave us in this world.
May we find full contentment
in the meal we hope to share
in your eternal kingdom.

TRANSFER OF THE HOLY EUCHARIST

After the Prayer after Communion, *takes place the solemn transfer of the Blessed Sacrament. During the procession the hymn* Pange, lingua *or some other eucharistic song is sung.*

Pange, lingua gloriosi
Corporis mysterium,
Sanguinisque pretiosi,
Quem in mundi pretium
Fructus ventris generosi
Rex effudit gentium

In supremae nocte coenae,
Recumbens cum fratribus,
Observata lege plene
Cibis in legalibus,
Cibum turbae duodenae
Se dat suis manibus.

Nobis datus, nobis natus
Ex intacta virgine,
Et in mundo conversatus
Sparso verbi semine,
Sui moras incolatus
Miro clausit ordine.

Verbum caro, panem verum,
Verbo carnem efficit:
Fitque sanguis Christi merum:
Et si sensus deficit,
Ad firmandum cor sincerum
Sola fides sufficit.

When the procession reaches the place of reposition, the priest sets the ciborium down. Then he puts incense in the thurible and, kneeling, incenses the Blessed Sacrament, while Tantum ergo sacramentum *is sung. The tabernacle of reposition is then closed.*

Tantum ergo sacramentum
Veneremur cernui:
Et antiquum documentum
Novo cedat ritui;
Praestet fides supplementum
Sensuum defectui.

Genitori, Genitoque
Laus et jubilatio,
Salus, honor, virtus quoque
Sit et benedictio:
Procedenti ab utroque
Compar sit laudatio. Amen.

After a period of silent adoration, the priest and ministers genuflect and return to the sacristy. Then the altar is stripped and, if possible, the crosses are removed from the church. It is desirable to cover any crosses which remain in the church.

The faithful are encouraged to continue adoration before the Blessed Sacrament for a suitable period of time during the night, according to local circumstances, but there should be no solemn adoration after midnight.

REFLECTION

The washing of the feet is the striking image which remains from this evening's liturgy. It is an act of lowly service which mirrors the attitude which God has towards his people. Anything done for the sake of a neighbour takes on a deeper significance in that it makes the Kingdom of God present in that place.

9 APRIL
GOOD FRIDAY
CELEBRATION OF THE LORD'S PASSION

Like his gospel in general, John's account of the passion of Jesus is very different from those of the other three gospel writers, principally in this respect: they highlight the agony of Jesus while he emphasises his glory. This is a side which can only be seen with the eyes of faith. Jesus' passion is his glorious return to the Father. Three times the armed group which comes to arrest him is presented as 'falling' down before him, a word which in a biblical context refers to the worship of God.

All pray silently for a while. Then the priest says:

PRAYER
Lord,
by shedding his blood for us,
your Son, Jesus Christ,
established the paschal mystery.
In your goodness, make us holy
and watch over us always.

or

Lord,
by the suffering of Christ your Son
you have saved us all from the death
we inherited from sinful Adam.
By the law of nature
we have borne the likeness of his manhood.
May the sanctifying power of grace
help us to put on the likeness of our Lord in heaven,
who lives and reigns for ever and ever.

I. LITURGY OF THE WORD

FIRST READING   *(Is 52:13—53:12)*
A reading from the prophet Isaiah.
He was pierced through for our faults.
See, my servant will prosper,
he shall be lifted up, exalted, rise to great heights.

As the crowds were appalled on seeing him
— so disfigured did he look

that he seemed no longer human —
so will the crowds be astonished at him,
and kings stand speechless before him;
for they shall see something never told
and witness something never heard before:
'Who could believe what we have heard,
and to whom has the power of the Lord been revealed?'

Like a sapling he grew up in front of us,
like a root in arid ground.
Without beauty, without majesty (we saw him),
no looks to attract our eyes;
a thing despised and rejected by men,
a man of sorrows and familiar with suffering,
a man to make people screen their faces;
he was despised and we took no account of him.

And yet ours were the sufferings he bore,
ours the sorrows he carried.
But we, we thought of him as someone punished,
struck by God, and brought low.
Yet he was pierced through for our faults,
crushed for our sins.
On him lies a punishment that brings us peace,
and through his wounds we are healed.

We had all gone astray like sheep,
each taking his own way,
and the Lord burdened him
with the sins of all of us.
Harshly dealt with, he bore it humbly,
he never opened his mouth,
like a lamb that is led to the slaughter-house,
like a sheep that is dumb before its shearers
never opening its mouth.

By force and by law he was taken;
would anyone plead his cause?
Yes, he was torn away from the land of the living;
for our faults struck down in death.
They gave him a grave with the wicked,
a tomb with the rich,
though he had done no wrong
and there had been no perjury in his mouth.
The Lord has been pleased to crush him with suffering.
If he offers his life in atonement,

he shall see his heirs, he shall have a long life
and through him what the Lord wishes will be done.

His soul's anguish over
he shall see the light and be content.
By his sufferings shall my servant justify many,
taking their faults on himself.

Hence I will grant whole hordes for his tribute,
he shall divide the spoil with the mighty,
for surrendering himself to death
and letting himself be taken for a sinner,
while he was bearing the faults of many
and praying all the time for sinners.

This is the word of the Lord.

RESPONSORIAL PSALM *(Ps 30:2-6.12-13.15-17.25)*

℞ **Father, into your hands I commend my spirit.**

1. In you, O Lord, I take refuge.
   Let me never be put to shame.
   In your justice, set me free.
   Into your hands I commend my spirit.
   It is you who will redeem me, Lord. ℞

2. In the face of all my foes
   I am a reproach,
   an object of scorn to my neighbours
   and of fear to my friends. ℞

3. Those who see me in the street
   run far away from me.
   I am like a dead man, forgotten in men's hearts,
   like a thing thrown away. ℞

4. But as for me, I trust in you, Lord,
   I say: 'You are my God.'
   My life is in your hands, deliver me
   from the hands of those who hate me. ℞

5. Let your face shine on your servant.
   Save me in your love.
   Be strong, let your heart take courage,
   all who hope in the Lord. ℞

SECOND READING   *(Heb 4:14-16; 5:7-9)*

A reading from the letter to the Hebrews.

He learnt to obey through suffering and became for all who obey him the source of eternal salvation.

Since in Jesus, the Son of God, we have the supreme high priest who has gone through to the highest heaven, we must never let go of the faith that we have professed. For it is not as if we had a high priest who was incapable of feeling our weaknesses with us; but we have one who has been tempted in every way that we are, though he is without sin. Let us be confident, then, in approaching the throne of grace, that we shall have mercy from him and find grace when we are in need of help.

During his life on earth, he offered up prayer and entreaty, aloud and in silent tears, to the one who had the power to save him out of death, and he submitted so humbly that his prayer was heard. Although he was Son, he learnt to obey through suffering; but having been made perfect, he became for all who obey him the source of eternal salvation.

This is the word of the Lord.

GOSPEL ACCLAMATION   *(Ph 2:8-9)*

Glory and praise to you, O Christ!
Christ was humbler yet,
even to accepting death, death on a cross.
But God raised him high
and gave him the name that is above all names.
Glory and praise to you, O Christ!

GOSPEL   *(Jn 18:1-19:42)*

(N. Narrator; J. Jesus; O. other individual voices; C. the 'crowd' — bold types.)

The passion of our Lord Jesus Christ according to John.

N. Jesus left with his disciples and crossed the Kedron valley. There was a garden there, and he went into it with his disciples. Judas the traitor knew the place well, since Jesus had often met his disciples there, and he brought the cohort to this place together with a detachment of guards sent by the chief priests and the Pharisees, all with lanterns and torches and weapons. Knowing everything that was going to happen to him, Jesus then came forward and said,

J. Who are you looking for?

N. They answered,

C. **Jesus the Nazarene.**

N. He said,

J. I am he.

N. Now Judas the traitor was standing among them. When Jesus said, 'I am he', they moved back and fell to the ground. He asked them a second time,

J. Who are you looking for?

N. They said,

C. **Jesus the Nazarene.**

N. Jesus replied,

J. I have told you that I am he. If I am the one you are looking for, let these others go.

N. This was to fulfil the words he had spoken, 'Not one of those you gave me have I lost.'

   Simon Peter, who carried a sword, drew it and wounded the high priest's servant, cutting off his right ear. The servant's name was Malchus. Jesus said to Peter,

J. Put your sword back in its scabbard; am I not to drink the cup that the Father has given me?

N. The cohort and its captain and the Jewish guards seized Jesus and bound him. They took him first to Annas, because Annas was the father-in-law of Caiaphas, who was high priest that year. It was Caiaphas who had suggested to the Jews, 'It is better for one man to die for the people.'

   Simon Peter, with another disciple, followed Jesus. This disciple, who was known to the high priest, went with Jesus into the high priest's palace, but Peter stayed outside the door. So the other disciple, the one known to the high priest, went out, spoke to the woman who was keeping the door and brought Peter in. The maid on duty at the door said to Peter,

O. Aren't you another of that man's disciples?

N. He answered,

O. I am not.

N. Now it was cold, and the servants and guards had lit a charcoal fire and were standing there warming themselves; so Peter stood there too, warming himself with the others.

   The high priest questioned Jesus about his disciples and his teaching. Jesus answered,

J. I have spoken openly for all the world to hear; I have always taught in the synagogue and in the Temple where all the

Jews meet together: I have said nothing in secret. But why ask me? Ask my hearers what I taught: they know what I said.

N. At these words, one of the guards standing by gave Jesus a slap in the face, saying.

O. Is that the way to answer the high priest?

N. Jesus replied,

J. If there is something wrong in what I said, point it out; but if there is no offence in it, why do you strike me?

N. Then Annas sent him, still bound, to Caiaphas the high priest.

As Simon Peter stood there warming himself, someone said to him,

O. Aren't you another of his disciples?

N. He denied it saying,

O. I am not.

N. One of the high priest's servants, a relation of the man whose ear Peter had cut off, said,

O. Didn't I see you in the garden with him?

N. Again Peter denied it; and at once a cock crew.

They then led Jesus from the house of Caiaphas to the Prætorium. It was now morning. They did not go into the Prætorium themselves or they would be defiled and unable to eat the passover. So Pilate came outside to them and said,

O. What charge do you bring against this man?

N. They replied,

C. **If he were not a criminal, we should not be handing him over to you.**

N. Pilate said,

O. Take him yourselves, and try him by your own Law.

N. The Jews answered,

C. **We are not allowed to put a man to death.**

N. This was to fulfil the words Jesus had spoken indicating the way he was going to die.

So Pilate went back into the Prætorium and called Jesus to him, and asked,

O. Are you the king of the Jews?

N. Jesus replied,

J. Do you ask this of your own accord, or have others spoken to you about me?

N. Pilate answered,

O. Am I a Jew? It is your own people and the chief priests who have handed you over to me: what have you done?'

N. Jesus replied,

J. Mine is not a kingdom of this world; if my kingdom were of this world, my men would have fought to prevent my being surrendered to the Jews. But my kingdom is not of this kind.

N. Pilate said,

O. So you are a king then?

N. Jesus answered,

J. It is you who say it. Yes, I am a king. I was born for this, I came into the world for this: to bear witness to the truth; and all who are on the side of truth listen to my voice.

N. Pilate said,

O. Truth? What is that?

N. And with that he went out again to the Jews and said,

O. I find no case against him. But according to a custom of yours I should release one prisoner at the Passover; would you like me, then, to release the king of the Jews?

N. At this they shouted:

C. **Not this man, but Barabbas.**

N. Barabbas was a brigand.

Pilate then had Jesus taken away and scourged; and after this, the soldiers twisted some thorns into a crown and put it on his head, and dressed him in a purple robe. They kept coming up to him and saying,

C. **Hail, king of the Jews!**

N. and they slapped him in the face.

Pilate came outside again and said to them,

O. Look, I am going to bring him out to you to let you see that I find no case.

N. Jesus then came out wearing the crown of thorns and the purple robe. Pilate said,

O. Here is the man.

N. When they saw him the chief priests and the guards shouted,

C. **Crucify him! Crucify him!**

N. Pilate said,

O. Take him yourselves and crucify him: I can find no case against him.

N. The Jews replied,

C. **We have a Law, and according to that Law he ought to die, because he has claimed to be the Son of God.**

N. When Pilate heard them say this his fears increased. Re-entering the Prætorium, he said to Jesus,

O. Where do you come from?

N. But Jesus made no answer. Pilate then said to him,

O. Are you refusing to speak to me? Surely you know I have power to release you and I have power to crucify you?

N. Jesus replied,

J. You would have no power over me if it had not been given you from above; that is why the one who handed me over to you has the greater guilt.

N. From that moment Pilate was anxious to set him free, but the Jews shouted,

C. **If you set him free you are no friend of Caesar's; anyone who makes himself king is defying Caesar.**

N. Hearing these words, Pilate had Jesus brought out, and seated himself on the chair of judgement at a place called the Pavement, in Hebrew Gabbatha. It was Passover Preparation Day, about the sixth hour. Pilate said to the Jews,

O. Here is your king.

N. They said,

C. **Take him away, take him away! Crucify him!**

N. Pilate said,

O. Do you want me to crucify your king?

N. The chief priests answered,

C. **We have no king except Caesar.**

N. So in the end Pilate handed him over to them to be crucified.

They then took charge of Jesus, and carrying his own cross he went out of the city to the place of the skull or, as it was called in Hebrew, Golgotha, where they crucified him with two others, one on either side with Jesus in the middle. Pilate wrote out a notice and had it fixed to the cross; it ran 'Jesus the Nazarene, King of the Jews.' This notice was read by many of the Jews, because the place where Jesus was crucified was not far from the city, and the writing was in Hebrew, Latin and Greek. So the Jewish chief priests said to Pilate,

C. **You should not write "King of the Jews", but "This man said: I am King of the Jews".**

N.   Pilate answered,

O.   What I have written, I have written.

N.   When the soldiers had finished crucifying Jesus they took his clothing and divided it into four shares, one for each soldier. His undergarment was seamless, woven in one piece from neck to hem; so they said to one another,

C.   **Instead of tearing it, let's throw dice to decide who is to have it.**

N.   In this way the words of scripture were fulfilled:

     'They shared out my clothing among them.

     They cast lots for my clothes.'

     This is exactly what the soldiers did.

     Near the cross of Jesus stood his mother and his mother's sister, Mary the wife of Clopas, and Mary of Magdala. Seeing his mother and the disciple he loved standing near her, Jesus said to his mother,

J.   Woman, this is your son.

N.   Then to the disciple he said,

J.   This is your mother.

N.   And from that moment the disciple made a place for her in his home.

     After this, Jesus knew that everything had now been completed, and to fulfil the scripture perfectly he said:

J.   I am thirsty.

N.   A jar full of vinegar stood there, so putting a sponge soaked in vinegar on a hyssop stick they held it up to his mouth. After Jesus had taken the vinegar he said,

J.   It is accomplished.

N.   And bowing his head he gave up his spirit.

                    (All kneel and pause a moment)

It was Preparation Day, and to prevent the bodies remaining on the cross during the sabbath — since that sabbath was a day of special solemnity — the Jews asked Pilate to have the legs broken and the bodies taken away. Consequently the soldiers came and broke the legs of the first man who had been crucified with him and then of the other. When they came to Jesus, they found he was already dead, and so instead of breaking his legs one of the soldiers pierced his side with a lance; and immediately there came out blood and water. This is the evidence of one who saw it — trustworthy evidence,

and he knows he speaks the truth — and he gives it so that
you may believe as well. Because all this happened to fulfil
the words of scripture:
    'Not one bone of his will be broken,'
and again, in another place scripture says:
    'They will look on the one whom they have pierced.'
    After this, Joseph of Arimathaea, who was a disciple of
Jesus — though a secret one because he was afraid of the
Jews — asked Pilate to let him remove the body of Jesus.
Pilate gave permission, so they came and took it away.
Nicodemus came as well — the same one who had first
come to Jesus at night-time — and he brought a mixture of
myrrh and aloes, weighing about a hundred pounds. They
took the body of Jesus and wrapped it with the spices in
linen cloths, following the Jewish burial custom. At the
place where he had been crucified there was a garden, and
in this garden a new tomb in which no one had yet been
buried. Since it was the Jewish Day of Preparation and the
tomb was near at hand, they laid Jesus there.

GENERAL INTERCESSIONS

1. FOR THE CHURCH

Let us pray, dear friends,
for the holy Church of God throughout the world,
that God the almighty Father
guide it and gather it together
so that we may worship him
in peace and tranquillity.
Silent prayer. Then the priest says:
Almighty and eternal God,
you have shown your glory to all nations in Christ, your Son.
Guide the work of your Church.
Help it to persevere in faith,
proclaim your name,
and bring your salvation to people everywhere.
We ask this through Christ our Lord. **Amen.**

2. FOR THE POPE

Let us pray
for our Holy Father, Pope N.,
that God who chose him to be bishop
may give him health and strength

to guide and govern God's holy people.

Silent prayer. Then the priest says:

Almighty and eternal God,
you guide all things by your word,
you govern all Christian people.
In your love protect the Pope you have chosen for us.
Under his leadership deepen our faith
and make us better Christians.
We ask this through Christ our Lord. **Amen.**

3. FOR THE CLERGY AND LAITY OF THE CHURCH

Let us pray
for N., our bishop,
for all bishops, priests, and deacons;
for all who have a special ministry
in the Church and for all God's people.

Silent prayer. Then the priest says:

Almighty and eternal God,
your Spirit guides the Church
and makes it holy.
Listen to our prayers
and help each of us
in his own vocation
to do your work more faithfully.
We ask this through Christ our Lord.
Amen.

4. FOR THOSE PREPARING FOR BAPTISM

Let us pray
for those (among us) preparing for baptism,
that God in his mercy
make them responsive to his love,
forgive their sins through the waters of new birth,
and give them life in Jesus Christ our Lord.

Silent prayer. Then the priest says:

Almighty and eternal God,
you continually bless your Church with new members.
Increase the faith and understanding
of those (among us) preparing for baptism.
Give them a new birth in these living waters
and make them members of your chosen family.
We ask this through Christ our Lord.
Amen.

5. FOR THE UNITY OF CHRISTIANS

Let us pray
for all our brothers and sisters
who share our faith in Jesus Christ,
that God may gather and keep together in one Church
all those who seek the truth with sincerity.

Silent prayer. Then the priest says:

Almighty and eternal God,
you keep together those you have united.
Look kindly on all who follow Jesus your Son.
We are all consecrated to you by our common baptism.
Make us one in the fullness of faith,
and keep us one in the fellowship of love.
We ask this through Christ our Lord.
Amen.

6. FOR THE JEWISH PEOPLE

Let us pray
for the Jewish people,
the first to hear the word of God,
that they may continue to grow in the love of his name
and in faithfulness to his covenant.

Silent prayer. Then the priest says:

Almighty and eternal God,
long ago you gave your promise to Abraham and his posterity.
Listen to your Church as we pray
that the people you first made your own
may arrive at the fullness of redemption.
We ask this through Christ our Lord.
Amen.

7. FOR THOSE WHO DO NOT BELIEVE IN CHRIST

Let us pray
for those who do not believe in Christ,
that the light of the Holy Spirit
may show them the way to salvation.

Silent prayer. Then the priest says:

Almighty and eternal God,
enable those who do not acknowledge Christ
to find the truth
as they walk before you in sincerity of heart.
Help us to grow in love for one another,
to grasp more fully the mystery of your godhead,

and to become more perfect witnesses of your love
in the sight of men.
We ask this through Christ our Lord.
Amen.

8. FOR THOSE WHO DO NOT BELIEVE IN GOD

Let us pray
for those who do not believe in God,
that they may find him
by sincerely following all that is right.

Silent Prayer. Then the priest says:

Almighty and eternal God,
you created mankind
so that all might long to find you
and have peace when you are found.
Grant that, in spite of the hurtful things
that stand in their way,
they may all recognize in the lives of Christians
the tokens of your love and mercy,
and gladly acknowledge you
as the one true God and Father of us all.
We ask this through Christ our Lord.
Amen.

9. FOR ALL IN PUBLIC OFFICE

Let us pray
for those who serve us in public office,
that God may guide their minds and hearts,
so that all men may live in true peace and freedom.

Silent prayer. Then the priest says:

Almighty and eternal God,
you know the longings of men's hearts
and you protect their rights.
In your goodness
watch over those in authority,
so that people everywhere may enjoy
religious freedom, security, and peace.
We ask this through Christ our Lord.
Amen.

10. FOR THOSE IN SPECIAL NEED

Let us pray, dear friends,
that God the almighty Father
may heal the sick,

comfort the dying,
give safety to travellers,
free those unjustly deprived of liberty,
and rid the world of falsehood,
hunger, and disease.
Silent prayer. Then the priest says:
Almighty, ever-living God,
you give strength to the weary
and new courage to those who have lost heart.
Hear the prayers of all who call on you in any trouble
that they may have the joy of receiving your help in their need.
We ask this through Christ our Lord.
Amen.

II. VENERATION OF THE CROSS

The showing of the Cross takes place in three stages. Three times the priest says:

This is the wood of the cross,
on which hung the Saviour of the world.

All reply:

Come, let us worship.

During the veneration of the Cross, the antiphon, We worship you, Lord, *the* Reproaches *or other suitable hymns are sung. Numbers 1 and 2 indicate first and second choirs.*

ANTIPHON

1 and 2:	**We worship you, Lord,**
	we venerate your cross,
	we praise your resurrection.
	Through the cross you brought joy to the world.

(Ps 66:2)

1.	May God be gracious and bless us;
	and let his face shed its light upon us.

(Choirs 1 and 2 repeat Antiphon)

REPROACHES I

1 and 2:	My people, what have I done to you?
	How have I offended you? Answer me!
1:	I led you out of Egypt, from slavery to freedom,
	but you led your Saviour to the cross.

| 2: | My people, what have I done to you? |
| | How have I offended you? Answer me! |

| 1: | Holy is God! |

| 2: | Holy and strong! |

| 1: | Holy immortal One, |
| | have mercy on us! |

1 and 2:	For forty years I led you safely through the desert.
	I fed you with manna from heaven,
	and brought you to a land of plenty;
	but you led your Saviour to the cross.

| 1: | Holy is God! |

| 2: | Holy and strong! |

| 1: | Holy immortal One, |
| | have mercy on us! |

1 and 2:	What more could I have done for you?
	I planted you as my fairest vine,
	but you yielded only bitterness:
	when I was thirsty you gave me vinegar to drink,
	and you pierced your Saviour with a lance.

| 1: | Holy is God! |

| 2: | Holy and strong! |

| 1: | Holy immortal One, |
| | have mercy on us! |

REPROACHES II

| 1: | For your sake I scourged your captors and their first born sons, |
| | but you brought your scourges down on me. |

| 2: | My people, what have I done to you? |
| | How have I offended you? Answer me! |

1:	I led you from slavery to freedom
	and drowned your captors in the sea,
	but you handed me over to your high priests.

| 2: | My people, what have I done to you? |
| | How have I offended you? Answer me! |

| 1: | I opened the sea before you, |
| | but you opened my side with a spear. |

| 2: | My people, what have I done to you? |
| | How have I offended you? Answer me! |

1:   I led you on your way in a pillar of cloud,
       but you led me to Pilate's court.

2:   My people, what have I done to you?
       How have I offended you? Answer me!

1:   I bore you up with manna in the desert,
       but you struck me down and scourged me.

2:   My people, what have I done to you?
       How have I offended you? Answer me!

1:   I gave you saving water from the rock,
       but you gave me gall and vinegar to drink.

2:   My people, what have I done to you?
       How have I offended you? Answer me!

1:   For you I struck down the kings of Canaan,
       but you struck my head with a reed.

2:   My people, what have I done to you?
       How have I offended you? Answer me!

1:   I gave you a royal sceptre,
       but you gave me a crown of thorns.

2:   My people, what have I done to you?
       How have I offended you? Answer me!

1:   I raised you to the height of majesty,
       but you have raised me high on a cross.

2:   My people, what have I done to you?
       How have I offended you? Answer me!

III. HOLY COMMUNION

The Blessed Sacrament is brought from the place of reposition to the altar.
Then the priest says:

Let us pray with confidence to the Father in the words our
Saviour gave us:
Our Father, who art in heaven,
hallowed be thy name.
Thy kingdom come.
Thy will be done on earth as it is in heaven.
Give us this day our daily bread,
and forgive us our trespasses,
as we forgive those who trespass against us,
and lead us not into temptation,
but deliver us from evil.

Deliver us, Lord, from every evil,
and grant us peace in our day.
In your mercy keep us free from sin
and protect us from all anxiety
as we wait in joyful hope
for the coming of our Saviour, Jesus Christ.
For the kingdom, the power, and the glory are yours,
now and for ever.

Lord Jesus Christ, with faith in your love and mercy I eat your
body and drink your blood. Let it not bring me condemnation,
but health in mind and body.

This is the Lamb of God
who takes away the sins of the world.
Happy are those who are called to his supper.
Lord, I am not worthy to receive you,
but only say the word and I shall be healed.

After the Communion a period of silence may be observed. Then the priest
says:

Let us pray.
Almighty and eternal God,
you have restored us to life
by the triumphant death and resurrection of Christ.
Continue this healing work within us.
May we who participate in this mystery
never cease to serve you.
We ask this through Christ our Lord.
Amen.

For the dismissal the priest extends his hands towards the people and says
the following Prayer over the People.

PRAYER OVER THE PEOPLE

Lord,
send down your abundant blessing,
upon your people who have devoutly recalled the death of your
    Son
in the sure hope of the resurrection.
Grant them pardon; bring them comfort.
May their faith grow stronger
and their eternal salvation be assured.
We ask this through Christ our Lord.
Amen.

REFLECTION

In John's account of the passion the glory of Jesus is underlined by the fact that no one has taken his life from him. He has handed it over willingly. Jesus died because of what he stood for during his life. His death reinforced what he taught and did during his life. It was his most effective means of preaching. According to John the core of this preaching is that in Jesus God is revealed to humanity.

All depart in silence.

---

10 APRIL

THE EASTER VIGIL

Tonight's celebration is the very apex of the liturgical life of the Church. It is the night in which Christians, remembering their Jewish heritage, celebrate their liberation from death to life, from oppression to liberty. The liberation from Egypt at the beginning of the Hebrew bible shows that freedom is part of God's plan for every human being. The resurrection of the Lord calls to mind that what God has done for Jesus he will do also for us.

I. THE SERVICE OF LIGHT

All the lights in the church are put out. Fire is prepared in a suitable place outside the church. When the people have assembled the priest goes there with the ministers, one of whom carries the Easter candle. The priest greets the congregation in these or similar words:

Dear friends in Christ,
on this most holy night,
when our Lord Jesus Christ passed from death to life,
the Church invites her children throughout the world
to come together in vigil and prayer.
This is the passover of the Lord:
if we honour the memory of his death and resurrection
by hearing his word and celebrating his mysteries,
then we may be confident
that we shall share his victory over death
and live with him for ever in God.

Then the fire is blessed.

Let us pray.
Father,
we share in the light of your glory
through your Son, the light of the world.
Make this new fire ✠ holy, and inflame us with new hope.
Purify our minds by this Easter celebration
and bring us one day to the feast of eternal light.
We ask this through Christ our Lord.
Amen.

PREPARATION AND LIGHTING OF THE CANDLE

After the blessing of the new fire the Easter candle is brought to the celebrant, who cuts a cross in the wax. Then he traces the Greek letters alpha and omega and numerals of the current year. Meanwhile he says:

1. Christ yesterday and today
2. the beginning and the end
3. Alpha
4. and Omega
5. all time belongs to him
6. and all the ages
7. to him be glory and power
8. through every age for ever. Amen.

Then he may insert five grains of incense into the candle in the form of a cross, saying:

1. By his holy
2. and glorious wounds
3. may Christ our Lord
4. guard us
5. and keep us. Amen.

The priest lights the candle from the new fire, saying:

May the light of Christ, rising in glory,
dispel the darkness of our hearts and minds.

PROCESSION

The deacon (or the priest) takes the Easter candle, lifts high and sings:

Christ our light.

All answer:

Thanks be to God.

At the church door the deacon lifts the candle high and sings a second time:

Christ our light.

All answer:

Thanks be to God.

All light their candles from the Easter candle and continue the procession. When the deacon arrives before the altar, he faces the people and sings a third time:

Christ our light.

All answer:

Thanks be to God.

The lights in the church are put on.

The Easter candle is placed in the middle of the sanctuary. The book and the candle may be incensed. The deacon or the priest now sings the Easter Proclamation. *All stand with their candles lit.*

EASTER PROCLAMATION (EXSULTET)

(Parts given within [ ] *may be omitted)*

Rejoice, heavenly powers! Sing, choirs of angels!
    Exult, all creation around God's throne!
    Jesus Christ, our King, is risen!
    Sound the trumpet of salvation!

Rejoice, O earth, in shining splendour,
    radiant in the brightness of your King!
    Christ has conquered! Glory fills you!
    Darkness vanishes for ever!

Rejoice, O Mother Church! Exult in glory!
    The risen Saviour shines upon you!
    Let this place resound with joy,
    echoing the mighty song of all God's people!

[My dearest friends, standing with me in this holy light,
    join me in asking God for mercy,
    that he may give his unworthy minister
    grace to sing his Easter praises.]

The Lord be with you.
And also with you.

Lift up your hearts.
We lift them up to the Lord.

Let us give thanks to the Lord our Lord.
It is right to give him thanks and praise.

It is truly right
    that with full hearts and minds and voices
    we should praise the unseen God, the all-powerful Father,
    and his only Son, our Lord Jesus Christ.

For Christ has ransomed us with his blood,
    and paid for us the price of Adam's sin

to our eternal Father!

This is our passover feast,
    when Christ, the true Lamb, is slain,
    whose blood consecrates the homes of all believers.

This is the night when first you saved our fathers:
    you freed the people of Israel from their slavery
    and led them dry-shod through the sea.

[This is the night when the pillar of fire
    destroyed the darkness of sin!]

This is the night when Christians everywhere,
    washed clean of sin
    and freed from all defilement,
    are restored to grace and grow together in holiness.

This is the night when Jesus Christ
    broke the chains of death
    and rose triumphant from the grave.

[What good would life have been to us,
    had Christ not come as our Redeemer?]

Father, how wonderful your care for us!
    How boundless your merciful love!
    To ransom a slave
    you gave away your Son.

O happy fault, O necessary sin of Adam,
    which gained for us so great a Redeemer!
    [Most blessed of all nights, chosen by God
    to see Christ rising from the dead!

Of this night scripture says:
    'The night will be as clear as day:
    it will become my light, my joy.']

The power of this holy night
    dispels all evil, washes guilt away,
    restores lost innocence, brings mourners joy.
    [It casts out hatred, brings us peace, and humbles earthly
        pride.]

Night truly blessed when heaven is wedded to earth
    and man is reconciled with God!

Therefore, heavenly Father, in the joy of this night,
    receive our evening sacrifice of praise,
    your Church's solemn offering.

Accept this Easter candle,

[a flame divided but undimmed,
a pillar of fire that glows to the honour of God.
Let it mingle with the lights of heaven
    and continue bravely burning]
    to (may it always) dispel the darkness of this night!
    May the Morning Star which never sets find this flame still
        burning:
    Christ, that Morning Star, who came back from the dead,
    and shed his peaceful light on all mankind,
    your Son who lives and reigns for ever and ever.
    Amen.

II. LITURGY OF THE WORD

After the Easter Proclamation *candles are extinguished. The priest gives
an introduction in these or similar words. All sit.*

Dear friends in Christ,
we have begun our solemn vigil.
Let us now listen attentively to the word of God,
recalling how he saved his people throughout history
and, in the fullness of time,
sent his own Son to be our Redeemer.
Through this Easter celebration,
may God bring to perfection
the saving work he has begun in us.

*Nine readings are given. For pastoral reasons the number may be reduced
but one of the readings must always be reading 3 from Exodus.*

*A reader goes to the lectern and proclaims the first reading. Then the
cantor leads the psalm and the people respond. All rise and the priest sings
or says,* Let us pray. *All pray silently for a while and then the priest sings
or says the prayer. Instead of the responsorial psalm a period of silence
may be observed.*

FIRST READING   *(Gen 1:1-2:2)*

(For Shorter Form, *read between* ◗ ◖*)*

A reading from the book of Genesis.

God saw all he had made, and indeed it was very good.

◗In the beginning God created the heavens and the earth.◖ Now
the earth was a formless void, there was darkness over the deep,
and God's spirit hovered over the water.

God said, 'Let there be light', and there was light. God saw
that light was good, and God divided light from darkness. God
called light 'day', and darkness he called 'night'. Evening came
and morning came: the first day.

God said, 'Let there be a vault in the waters to divide the waters in two.' And so it was. God made the vault, and it divided the waters above the vault from the waters under the vault. God called the vault 'heaven'. Evening came and morning came: the second day.

God said, 'Let the waters under heaven come together into a single mass, and let dry land appear.' And so it was. God called the dry land 'earth' and the mass of waters 'seas', and God saw that it was good.

God said, 'Let the earth produce vegetation: seed-bearing plants, and fruit trees bearing fruit with their seed inside, on the earth.' And so it was. The earth produced vegetation: plants bearing seed in their several kinds, and trees bearing fruit with their seed inside in their several kinds. God saw that it was good. Evening came and morning came: the third day.

God said, 'Let there be lights in the vault of heaven to divide day from night, and let them indicate festivals, days and years. Let them be lights in the vault of heaven to shine on the earth.' And so it was. God made the two great lights: the greater light to govern the day, the smaller light to govern the night, and the stars. God set them in the vault of heaven to shine on the earth, to govern the day and the night and to divide light from darkness. God saw that it was good. Evening came and morning came: the fourth day.

God said, 'Let the waters teem with living creatures, and let birds fly above the earth within the vault of heaven.' And so it was. God created great sea-serpents and every kind of living creature with which the waters teem, and every kind of winged creature. God saw that it was good. God blessed them, saying 'Be fruitful, multiply, and fill the waters of the seas; and let the birds multiply upon the earth.' Evening came and morning came: the fifth day.

God said, 'Let the earth produce every kind of living creature: cattle, reptiles, and every kind of wild beast.' And so it was. God made every kind of wild beast, every kind of cattle, and every kind of land reptile. God saw that it was good.

▶God said, 'Let us make man in our own image, in the likeness of ourselves, and let them be masters of the fish of the sea, the birds of heaven, the cattle, all the wild beasts and all the reptiles that crawl upon the earth.'

God created man in the image of himself,
in the image of God he created him,
male and female he created them.

God blessed them, saying to them, 'Be fruitful, multiply, fill the earth and conquer it. Be masters of the fish of the sea, the

birds of heaven and all living animals on the earth.' God said,
'See, I give you all the seed-bearing plants that are upon the
whole earth, and all the trees with seed-bearing fruit; this shall
be your food. To all wild beasts, all birds of heaven and all living
reptiles on the earth I give all the foliage of plants for food.' And
so it was. God saw all he had made, and indeed it was very
good.◗ Evening came and morning came: the sixth day.

Thus heaven and earth were completed with all their array.
On the seventh day God completed the work he had been doing.
He rested on the seventh day after all the work he had been doing.

◗This is the word of the Lord.◗

RESPONSORIAL PSALM   *(Ps 103:1-2.5-6.10.12-14.24.35)*

℟ **Send forth your spirit, O Lord,**
    and renew the face of the earth.

1. Bless the Lord, my soul!
    Lord God, how great you are,
    clothed in majesty and glory,
    wrapped in light as in a robe! ℟

2. You founded the earth on its base,
    to stand firm from age to age.
    You wrapped it with the ocean like a cloak:
    the waters stood higher than the mountains. ℟

3. You make springs gush forth in the valleys:
    they flow in between the hills.
    On their banks dwell the birds of heaven;
    from the branches they sing their song. ℟

4. From your dwelling you water the hills;
    earth drinks its fill of your gift.
    You make the grass grow for the cattle
    and the plants to serve man's needs. ℟

5. How many are your works, O Lord!
    In wisdom you have made them all.
    The earth is full of your riches.
    Bless the Lord, my soul! ℟

ALTERNATIVE PSALM   *(Ps 32:4-7.12-13.20.22)*

℟ **The Lord fills the earth with his love.**

1. The word of the Lord is faithful
    and all his works to be trusted.

The Lord loves justice and right
and fills the earth with his love. ℟

2. By his word the heavens were made,
   by the breath of his mouth all the stars.
   He collects the waves of the ocean;
   he stores up the depths of the sea. ℟

3. They are happy, whose God is the Lord,
   the people he has chosen as his own.
   From the heavens the Lord looks forth,
   he sees all the children of men. ℟

4. Our soul is waiting for the Lord.
   The Lord is our help and our shield.
   May your love be upon us, O Lord,
   as we place all our hope in you. ℟

All stand for the prayer.
Let us pray.
Almighty and eternal God,
you created all things in wonderful beauty and order.
Help us now to perceive
how still more wonderful is the new creation
by which in the fullness of time you redeemed your people
through the sacrifice of our passover, Jesus Christ,
who lives and reigns for ever and ever. **Amen.**
or
Let us pray.
Lord God,
the creation of man was a wonderful work,
his redemption still more wonderful.
May we persevere in right reason
against all that entices to sin
and so attain to everlasting joy.
We ask this through Christ our Lord. **Amen.**

SECOND READING   *(Gen 22:1-18)*

(*For Shorter Form, read between* ◗ ◖)
A reading from the book of Genesis.
The sacrifice of Abraham, our father in faith.

◗God put Abraham to the test. 'Abraham, Abraham,' he called.
'Here I am' he replied. 'Take your son,' God said, 'your only
child Isaac, whom you love, and go to the land of Moriah. There

you shall offer him as a burnt-offering, on a mountain I will point out to you.'◀

Rising early next morning Abraham saddled his ass and took with him two of his servants and his son Isaac. He chopped wood for the burnt-offering and started on his journey to the place God had pointed out to him. On the third day Abraham looked up and saw the place in the distance. Then Abraham said to his servants, 'Stay here with the donkey. The boy and I will go over there; we will worship and come back to you.'

Abraham took the wood for the burnt-offering, loaded it on Isaac, and carried in his own hands the fire and the knife. Then the two of them set out together. Isaac spoke to his father Abraham, 'Father', he said. 'Yes, my son', he replied. 'Look,' he said 'here are the fire and the wood, but where is the lamb for the burnt-offering?' Abraham answered, 'My son, God himself will provide the lamb for the burnt-offering.' Then the two of them went on together.

▶When they arrived at the place God had pointed out to him, Abraham built an altar there, and arranged the wood. Then he bound his son Isaac and put him on the altar on top of the wood. Abraham stretched out his hand and seized the knife to kill his son.

But the angel of the Lord called to him from heaven, 'Abraham, Abraham' he said. 'I am here' he replied. 'Do not raise your hand against the boy' the angel said. 'Do not harm him, for now I know you fear God. You have not refused me your son, your only son.' Then looking up, Abraham saw a ram caught by its horns in a bush. Abraham took the ram and offered it as a burnt-offering in place of his son.◀

Abraham called this place 'The Lord provides', and hence the saying today: On the mountain the Lord provides.

▶The angel of the Lord called Abraham a second time from heaven. 'I swear by my own self — it is the Lord who speaks — because you have done this, because you have not refused me your son, your only son, I will shower blessings on you, I will make your descendants as many as the stars of heaven and the grains of sand on the seashore. Your descendants shall gain possession of the gates of their enemies. All the nations of the earth shall bless themselves by your descendants, as a reward for your obedience.'

This is the word of the Lord.◀

RESPONSORIAL PSALM   *(Ps 15:5.8-11)*

℟ **Preserve me, God, I take refuge in you.**

1. O Lord, it is you who are my portion and cup;
   it is you yourself who are my prize.
   I keep the Lord ever in my sight:
   since he is at my right hand, I shall stand firm. ℟

2. And so my heart rejoices, my soul is glad;
   even my body shall rest in safety.
   For you will not leave my soul among the dead,
   nor let your beloved know decay. ℟

3. You will show me the path of life,
   the fullness of joy in your presence,
   at your right hand happiness for ever. ℟

All stand for the prayer.

Let us pray.
God and Father of all who believe in you,
you promised Abraham that he would become the father of all
      nations,
and through the death and resurrection of Christ you fulfil that
      promise:
everywhere throughout the world you increase your chosen people.
May we respond to your call
by joyfully accepting your invitation to the new life of grace.
We ask this through Christ our Lord.

Amen.

(The following reading is obligatory)

THIRD READING   *(Ex 14:15-15:1)*

A reading from the book of Exodus.

The sons of Israel went on dry ground right into the sea.

The Lord said to Moses, 'Why do you cry to me so? Tell sons of
Israel to march on. For yourself, raise your staff and stretch out
your hand over the sea and part it for the sons of Israel to walk
through the sea on dry ground. I for my part will make the heart
of the Egyptians so stubborn that they will follow them. So shall
I win myself glory at the expense of Pharaoh, of all his army, his
chariots, his horsemen. And when I have won glory for myself,
at the expense of Pharaoh and his chariots and his army, the
Egyptians will learn that I am the Lord.'
      Then the angel of the Lord, who marched at the front of the
army of Israel, changed station and moved to their rear. The

pillar of cloud changed station from the front to the rear of them, and remained there. It came between the camp of the Egyptians and the camp of Israel. The cloud was dark, and the night passed without the armies drawing any closer the whole night long. Moses stretched out his hand over the sea. The Lord drove back the sea with a strong easterly wind all night, and he made dry land of the sea. The waters parted and the sons of Israel went on dry ground right into the sea, walls of water to right and to left of them. The Egyptians gave chase: after them they went, right into the sea, all Pharaoh's horses, his chariots, and his horsemen. In the morning watch, the Lord looked down on the army of the Egyptians from the pillar of fire and of cloud, and threw the army into confusion. He so clogged their chariot wheels that they could scarcely make headway. 'Let us flee from the Israelites,' the Egyptians cried 'the Lord is fighting for them against the Egyptians!' 'Stretch out your hand over the sea,' the Lord said to Moses 'that the waters may flow back on the Egyptians and their chariots and their horsemen.' Moses stretched out his hand over the sea and, as day broke, the sea returned to its bed. The fleeing Egyptians marched right into it, and the Lord overthrew the Egyptians in the very middle of the sea. The returning waters overwhelmed the chariots and the horsemen of Pharaoh's whole army, which had followed the Israelites into the sea; not a single one of them was left. But the sons of Israel had marched through the sea on dry ground, walls of water to right and to left of them. That day, the Lord rescued Israel from the Egyptians, and Israel saw the Egyptians lying dead on the shore. Israel witnessed the great act that the Lord had performed against the Egyptians, and the people venerated the Lord; they put their faith in the Lord and in Moses, his servant.

It was then that Moses and the sons of Israel sang this song in honour of the Lord:

(The Responsorial Psalm follows immediately)

RESPONSORIAL PSALM   *(Ex 15:1-6.17-18)*

℟   **I will sing to the Lord, glorious his triumph!**

1.   I will sing to the Lord, glorious his triumph!
     Horse and rider he has thrown into the sea!
     The Lord is my strength, my song, my salvation.
     This is my God and I extol him,
     my father's God and I give him praise.   ℟

2. The Lord is a warrior! The Lord is his name.
   The chariots of Pharaoh he hurled into the sea,
   the flower of his army is drowned in the sea.
   The deeps hide them; they sank like a stone. ℟

3. Your right hand, Lord, glorious in its power,
   your right hand, Lord, has shattered the enemy.
   In the greatness of your glory you crushed the foe. ℟

4. You will lead your people and plant them on your mountain,
   the place, O Lord, where you have made your home,
   the sanctuary, Lord, which your hands have made.
   The Lord will reign for ever and ever. ℟

All stand for the prayer.

Let us pray.
Father, even today we see the wonders
of the miracles you worked long ago.
You once saved a single nation from slavery,
and now you offer that salvation to all through baptism.
May the peoples of the world become true sons of Abraham
and prove worthy of the heritage of Israel.
We ask this through Christ our Lord. **Amen.**

or

Let us pray.
Lord God,
in the new covenant
you shed light on the miracles you worked in ancient times:
the Red Sea is a symbol of our baptism,
and the nation you freed from slavery
is a sign of your Christian people.
May every nation
share the faith and privilege of Israel
and come to new birth in the Holy spirit.
We ask this through Christ our Lord. **Amen.**

FOURTH READING   *(Is 54:5-14)*

A reading from the prophet Isaiah.

With everlasting love the Lord your redeemer has taken pity on you.

Thus says the Lord:

> Now your creator will be your husband,
> his name, the Lord of hosts;
> your redeemer will be the Holy One of Israel,
> he is called the God of the whole earth.

Yes, like a forsaken wife, distressed in spirit,
the Lord calls you back.
Does a man cast off the wife of his youth?
says your God.
I did forsake you for a brief moment,
but with great love will I take you back.
In excess of anger, for a moment
I hid my face from you.
But with everlasting love I have taken pity on you,
says the Lord, your redeemer.

I am now as I was in the days of Noah
when I swore that Noah's waters
should never flood the world again.
So now I swear concerning my anger with you
and the threats I made against you;
for the mountains may depart,
the hills be shaken,
but my love for you will never leave you
and my covenant of peace with you will never be shaken,
says the Lord who takes pity on you.

Unhappy creature, storm-tossed, disconsolate,
see, I will set your stones on carbuncles
and your foundations on sapphires.
I will make rubies your battlements,
your gates crystal,
and your entire wall precious stones.
Your sons will all be taught by the Lord.
The prosperity of your sons will be great.
You will be founded on integrity;
remote from oppression, you will have nothing to fear;
remote from terror, it will not approach you.

This is the word of the Lord.

RESPONSORIAL PSALM   *(Ps 29:2.4-6.11-13)*

℟ **I will praise you, Lord, you have rescued me.**

1. I will praise you, Lord, you have rescued me
    and have not let my enemies rejoice over me.
    O Lord, you have raised my soul from the dead,
    restored me to life from those who sink into the grave. ℟

2. Sing psalms to the Lord, you who love him,
    give thanks to his holy name.

His anger lasts but a moment; his favour through life.
At night there are tears, but joy comes with dawn. ℞

3. The Lord listened and had pity.
   The Lord came to my help.
   For me you have changed my mourning into dancing,
   O Lord my God, I will thank you for ever. ℞

All stand for the prayer.

Let us pray.
Almighty and eternal God,
glorify your name by increasing your chosen people
as you promised long ago.
In reward for their trust,
may we see in the Church the fulfilment of your promise.
We ask this through Christ our Lord. **Amen.**

FIFTH READING   *(Is 55:1-11)*

A reading from the prophet Isaiah.

Come to me and your soul will live, and I will make an everlasting
covenant with you.

Thus says the Lord:

> Oh, come to the water all you who are thirsty;
> though you have no money, come!
> Buy corn without money, and eat,
> and, at no cost, wine and milk.
> Why spend money on what is not bread,
> your wages on what fails to satisfy?
> Listen, listen to me, and you will have good things to eat
> and rich food to enjoy.
> Pay attention, come to me;
> listen, and your soul will live.
> With you I will make an everlasting covenant
> out of the favours promised to David.
> See, I have made of you a witness to the peoples,
> a leader and a master of the nations.
> See, you will summon a nation you never knew,
> those unknown will come hurrying to you,
> for the sake of the Lord your God,
> of the Holy One of Israel who will glorify you.
> Seek the Lord while he is still to be found,
> call to him while he is still near.
> Let the wicked man abandon his way,

the evil man his thoughts.
Let him turn back to the Lord who will take pity on him,
to our God who is rich in forgiving;
for my thoughts are not your thoughts,
my ways not your ways — it is the Lord who speaks.
Yes, the heavens are as high above earth
as my ways are above your ways,
my thoughts above your thoughts.

Yes, as the rain and the snow come down from the heavens and do not return without watering the earth, making it yield and giving growth to provide seed for the sower and bread for the eating, so the word that goes from my mouth does not return to me empty, without carrying out my will and succeeding in what it was sent to do.

This is the word of the Lord.

RESPONSORIAL PSALM   (Is 12:2-6)

℟   **With joy you will draw water
    from the wells of salvation.**

1.   Truly God is my salvation,
     I trust, I shall not fear.
     For the Lord is my strength, my song,
     he became my saviour.
     With joy you will draw water
     from the wells of salvation. ℟

2.   Give thanks to the Lord, give praise to his name!
     Make his mighty deeds known to the peoples,
     declare the greatness of his name. ℟

3.   Sing a psalm to the Lord
     for he has done glorious deeds,
     make them known to all the earth!
     People of Zion, sing and shout for joy
     for great in your midst is the Holy One of Israel. ℟

All stand for the prayer.
Let us pray.
Almighty, ever-living God,
only hope of the world,
by the preaching of the prophets
you proclaimed the mysteries we are celebrating tonight.
Help us to be your faithful people,
for it is by your inspiration alone

that we can grow in goodness.
We ask this through Christ our Lord. **Amen**.

SIXTH READING   *(Ba 3:9-15.32-4:4)*
A reading from the prophet Baruch.
In the radiance of the Lord make your way to light.

Listen, Israel, to commands that bring life;
hear, and learn what knowledge means.
Why, Israel, why are you in the country of your enemies,
growing older and older in an alien land,
sharing defilement with the dead,
reckoned with those who go to Sheol?
Because you have forsaken the fountain of wisdom.
Had you walked in the way of God,
you would have lived in peace for ever.
Learn where knowledge is, where strength,
where understanding, and so learn
where length of days is, where life,
where the light of the eyes and where peace.
But who has found out where she lives,
who has entered her treasure house?
But the One who knows all knows her,
he has grasped her with his own intellect,
he has set the earth firm for ever
and filled it with four-footed beasts,
he sends the light — and it goes,
he recalls it — and trembling it obeys;
the stars shine joyfully at their set times:
when he calls them, they answer, 'Here we are';
they gladly shine for their creator.
It is he who is our God,
no other can compare with him.
He has grasped the whole way of knowledge,
and confided it to his servant Jacob,
to Israel his well-beloved;
so causing her to appear on earth
and move among men.

This is the book of the commandments of God,
the Law that stands for ever;
those who keep her live,
those who desert her die.
Turn back, Jacob, seize her,

in her radiance make your way to light:
do not yield your glory to another,
your privilege to a people not your own.
Israel, blessed are we:
what pleases God has been revealed to us.

This is the word of the Lord.

RESPONSORIAL PSALM   *(Ps 18:8-11)*

℟ **You have the message of eternal life, O Lord.**

1. The law of the Lord is perfect,
    it revives the soul.
    The rule of the Lord is to be trusted,
    it gives wisdom to the simple. ℟

2. The precepts of the Lord are right,
    they gladden the heart.
    The command of the Lord is clear,
    it gives light to the eyes. ℟

3. The fear of the Lord is holy,
    abiding for ever.
    The decrees of the Lord are truth
    and all of them just. ℟

4. They are more to be desired than gold,
    than the purest of gold
    and sweeter are they than honey,
    than honey from the comb. ℟

All stand for the prayer.
Let us pray.
Father,
you increase your Church
by continuing to call all people to salvation.
Listen to our prayers
and always watch over those you cleanse in baptism.
We ask this through Christ our Lord.
Amen.

SEVENTH READING   *(Ezk 36:16-28)*
A reading from the prophet Ezekiel.
I shall pour clean water over you, and I shall give you a new heart.
The word of the Lord was addressed to me as follows: 'Son of
man, the members of the House of Israel used to live in their
own land, but they defiled it by their conduct and actions. I then

discharged my fury at them because of the blood they shed in their land and the idols with which they defiled it. I scattered them among the nations and dispersed them in foreign countries. I sentenced them as their conduct and actions deserved. And now they have profaned my holy name among the nations where they have gone, so that people say of them, "These are the people of the Lord; they have been exiled from his land." But I have been concerned about my holy name, which the House of Israel has profaned among the nations where they have gone. And so, say to the House of Israel, "The Lord says this: I am not doing this for your sake, House of Israel, but for the sake of my holy name, which you have profaned among the nations where you have gone. I mean to display the holiness of my great name, which has been profaned among the nations, which you have profaned among them. And the nations will learn that I am the Lord — it is the Lord who speaks — when I display my holiness for your sake before their eyes. Then I am going to take you from among the nations and gather you together from all the foreign countries, and bring you home to your own land. I shall pour clean water over you and you will be cleansed; I shall cleanse you of all your defilement and all your idols. I shall give you a new heart, and put a new spirit in you; I shall remove the heart of stone from your bodies and give you a heart of flesh instead. I shall put my spirit in you, and make you keep my laws and sincerely respect my observances. You will live in the land which I gave your ancestors. You shall be my people and I will be your God." '

This is the word of the Lord.

RESPONSORIAL PSALM   *(Ps 41:3.5; 42:3.4)*

℟   **Like the deer that yearns for running streams,
so my soul is yearning for you, my God.**

1. My soul is thirsting for God,
    the God of my life;
    when can I enter and see
    the face of God? ℟

2. These things will I remember
    as I pour out my soul:
    how I would lead the rejoicing crowd
    into the house of God,
    amid cries of gladness and thanksgiving,
    the throng wild with joy. ℟.

(continued)

3.   O send forth your light and your truth;
     let these be my guide.
     Let them bring me to your holy mountain
     to the place where you dwell. ℞

℞   **Like the deer that yearns for running streams,
    so my soul is yearning for you, my God**

4.   And I will come to the altar of God,
     the God of my joy.
     My redeemer, I will thank you on the harp,
     O God, my God. ℞

*If a Baptism takes place, the Responsorial Psalm which follows the Fifth
Reading above (page 192) is used or Ps 50 as follows.*

RESPONSORIAL PSALM   *(Ps 50:12-15.18-19)*

℞   **A pure heart create for me, O God.**

1.   A pure heart create for me, O God,
     put a steadfast spirit within me.
     Do not cast me away from your presence,
     nor deprive me of your holy spirit. ℞

2.   Give me again the joy of your help;
     with a spirit of fervour sustain me,
     that I may teach transgressors your ways
     and sinners may return to you. ℞

3.   For in sacrifice you take no delight,
     burnt offering from me you would refuse,
     my sacrifice, a contrite spirit.
     A humbled, contrite heart you will not spurn. ℞

All stand for the prayer.
Let us pray.
God of unchanging power and light,
look with mercy and favour on your entire Church.
Bring lasting salvation to humankind,
so that the world may see
the fallen lifted up,
the old made new,
and all things brought to perfection,
through him who is their origin,
our Lord Jesus Christ,
who lives and reigns for ever and ever. **Amen.**
or

Let us pray.
Father,
you teach us in both the Old and the New Testament
to celebrate this passover mystery.
Help us to understand your great love for us.
May the goodness you now show us
confirm our hope in your future mercy.
We ask this through Christ our Lord. **Amen.**

or (if there are candidates to be baptised)
Let us pray.
Almighty and eternal God,
be present in this sacrament of your love.
Send your Spirit of adoption
on those to be born again in baptism.
And may the work of our humble ministry
be brought to perfection by your mighty power.
We ask this through Christ our Lord. **Amen.**

*After the last reading from the Old Testament with its responsory and prayer,
the altar candles are lighted, and the priest intones the* Gloria *(see page 14)
which is taken up by all. The church bells are rung, according to local custom.*

OPENING PRAYER
Let us pray.
Lord God, you have brightened this night
with the radiance of the risen Christ.
Quicken the spirit of sonship in your Church;
renew us in mind and body
to give you whole-hearted service.

EPISTLE   *(Rm 6:3-11)*
A reading from the letter of St Paul to the Romans.
Christ, having been raised from the dead, will never die again.
When we were baptized in Christ Jesus we were baptized in his
death; in other words, when we were baptized we went into the
tomb with him and joined him in death, so that as Christ was
raised from the dead by the Father's glory, we too might live a
new life.

If in union with Christ we have imitated his death, we shall
also imitate him in his resurrection. We must realise that our
former selves have been crucified with him to destroy this sinful
body and to free us from the slavery of sin. When a man dies, of
course, he has finished with sin.

But we believe that having died with Christ we shall return

to life with him: Christ, as we know, having been raised from the dead will never die again. Death has no power over him any more. When he died, he died, once for all, to sin, so his life now is life with God; and in that way, you too must consider yourselves to be dead to sin but alive for God in Christ Jesus.

This is the word of the Lord.

After the Epistle all rise. The priest solemnly intones the Alleluia *which is repeated by all.*

RESPONSORIAL PSALM   *(Ps 117:1-2.16-17.22-23)*

℟   **Alleluia, alleluia, alleluia!**

1.   Give thanks to the Lord for he is good,
     for his love has no end.
     Let the sons of Israel say:
     'His love has no end'. ℟

2.   The Lord's right hand has triumphed;
     his right hand raised me up.
     I shall not die, I shall live
     and recount his deeds. ℟

3.   The stone which the builders rejected
     has become the corner stone.
     This is the work of the Lord,
     a marvel in our eyes. ℟

GOSPEL   *(Lk 24:1-12)*

A reading from the holy Gospel according to Luke.

Why look among the dead for someone who is alive.

On the first day of the week, at the first sign of dawn, the women went to the tomb with the spices they had prepared. They found that the stone had been rolled away from the tomb, but on entering discovered that the body of the Lord Jesus was not there. As they stood there not knowing what to think, two men in brilliant clothes suddenly appeared at their side. Terrified, the women lowered their eyes. But the two men said to them, 'Why look among the dead for someone who is alive? He is not here; he has risen. Remember what he told you when he was still in Galilee: that the Son of Man had to be handed over into the power of sinful men and be crucified, and rise again on the third day?' And they remembered his words.

When the women returned from the tomb they told all this to the Eleven and to all the others. The women were Mary of

Magdala, Joanna, and Mary the mother of James. The other women with them also told the apostles, but this story of theirs seemed pure nonsense and they did not believe them.

Peter, however, went running to the tomb. He bent down and saw the binding cloths, but nothing else; he then went back home, amazed at what had happened.

This is the Gospel of the Lord.

III. LITURGY OF BAPTISM

The priest goes with the ministers to the baptismal font, if this can be seen by the congregation. Otherwise a vessel of water is placed in the sanctuary.

If there are candidates to be baptised, they are called forward and presented by their godparents. If they are children, the parents and godparents bring them forward in front of the congregation.

Then the priest speaks to the people in these or similar words.

(If there are candidates to be baptised:)
Dear friends in Christ,
as our brothers and sisters approach the waters of rebirth,
let us help them by our prayers
and ask God, our almighty Father,
to support them with his mercy and love.

(If the font is to be blessed, but there is no one to be baptized:)
Dear friends in Christ,
let us ask God, the almighty Father,
to bless this font, that those reborn in it
may be made one with his adopted children in Christ.

All present stand and answer. If there is no one to be baptized and the font is not to be blessed the litany is omitted, and the blessing of water takes place at once.

Lord, have mercy	**Lord, have mercy**
Christ, have mercy	**Christ, have mercy**
Lord, have mercy	**Lord, have mercy**
Holy Mary, Mother of God	**pray for us**
Saint Michael	**pray for us**
Holy angels of God	"
Saint John the Baptist	"
Saint Joseph	"
Saint Peter and Saint Paul	"
Saint Andrew	"
Saint John	"

Saint Mary Magdalene	**pray for us**
Saint Stephen	"
Saint Ignatius.	"
Saint Lawrence	"
Saint Perpetua and Saint Felicity	"
Saint Agnes	"
Saint Gregory	"
Saint Augustine	"
Saint Athanasius	"
Saint Basil	"
Saint Martin	"
Saint Benedict	"
Saint Francis and Saint Dominic	"
Saint Francis Xavier	"
Saint John Vianney	"
Saint Catherine	"
Saint Teresa	"
All holy men and women	"
Lord, be merciful	**Lord, save your people**
From all evil	"
From every sin	"
From everlasting death	"
By your coming as man	"
By your death and rising to new life	"
By your gift of the Holy Spirit	"
Be merciful to us sinners	**Lord, hear our prayer**

(If there are candidates to be baptized.)
Give new life to these chosen ones by the grace of baptism
Lord, hear our prayer

(If there is no one to be baptized.)
By your grace bless this font where your children will be reborn
Lord, hear our prayer

Jesus, Son of the living God	**Lord, hear our prayer**
Christ, hear us	**Christ, hear us**
Lord Jesus, hear our prayer	**Lord Jesus, hear our prayer**

BLESSING OF BAPTISMAL WATER

The priest then blesses the baptismal water, saying:

Father, you give us grace through sacramental signs,
    which tell us of the wonders of your unseen power.

In baptism we use your gift of water,

which you have made a rich symbol
of the grace you give us in this sacrament.

At the very dawn of creation
your Spirit breathed on the waters,
making them the wellspring of all holiness.

The waters of the great flood
you made a sign of the waters of baptism,
that make an end of sin and a new beginning of goodness.

Through the waters of the Red Sea
you led Israel out of slavery,
to be an image of God's holy people,
set free from sin by baptism.

In the waters of the Jordan
your Son was baptized by John
and anointed with the Spirit.

Your Son willed that water and blood
should flow from his side
as he hung upon the cross.

After his resurrection he told his disciples:
'Go out and teach all nations,
baptizing them in the name of the Father
and of the Son and of the Holy Spirit.'

Father, look now with love upon your Church,
and unseal for her the fountain of baptism.

By the power of the Spirit
give to the water of this font
the grace of your Son.

You created man in your own likeness:
cleanse him from sin in a new birth of innocence
by water and the Spirit.

The priest may lower the Easter candle into the water either once or three times, as he continues:

We ask you, Father, with your Son
to send the Holy Spirit upon the waters of this font.

He holds the candle in the water:

May all who are buried with Christ
in the death of baptism
rise also with him to newness of life.

We ask this through Christ our Lord.
Amen.

The candle is taken out of the water as the people sing this (or any other appropriate) acclamation:

Springs of water, bless the Lord.
Give him glory and praise for ever.

Those who are to be baptised renounce the devil individually. Then they are questioned about their faith and are baptised. Adults are confirmed immediately after baptism if a bishop or a priest with the faculty to confirm is present.

If no one is to be baptized and the font is not to be blessed, the priest blesses the water with the following prayer:

My brothers and sisters,
let us ask the Lord our God
to bless this water he has created,
which we shall use to recall our baptism.
May he renew us
and keep us faithful to the Spirit
we have all received.

All pray silently for a short while. The priest then continues:

Lord our God,
this night your people keep prayerful vigil.
Be with us as we recall the wonder of our creation
and the greater wonder of our redemption.
Bless this water: it makes the seed to grow,
it refreshes us and makes us clean.
You have made of it a servant of your loving kindness:
through water you set your people free,
and quenched their thirst in the desert.
With water the prophets announced a new covenant
that you would make with man.
By water, made holy by Christ in Jordan,
you made our sinful nature new
in the bath that gives rebirth.
Let this water remind us of our baptism;
let us share the joys of our brothers
who are baptized this Easter.
We ask this through Christ our Lord.
Amen.

RENEWAL OF BAPTISMAL PROMISES

When the rite of baptism (and confirmation) has been completed or, if there is no baptism, immediately after the blessing of the water, all present stand with lighted candles and renew their baptismal profession of faith.

Dear friends,
through the paschal mystery
we have been buried with Christ in baptism,
so that we may rise with him to a new life.
Now that we have completed our lenten observance,
let us renew the promise we made in baptism
when we rejected Satan and his works,
and promised to serve God faithfully
in his holy Catholic Church.

And so:

Do you reject Satan?
I do.
And all his works?
I do.
And all his empty promises?
I do.

or

Do you reject sin, so as to live in the freedom of God's children?
I do.
Do you reject the glamour of evil, and refuse to be mastered by
    sin?
I do.
Do you reject Satan, father of sin and prince of darkness?
I do.

Then the priest continues:

Do you believe in God, the Father almighty,
creator of heaven and earth?
I do.
Do you believe in Jesus Christ, his only Son, our Lord, who was
born of the Virgin Mary, was crucified, died, and was buried,
rose from the dead, and is now seated at the right hand of the
Father?
I do.
Do you believe in the Holy Spirit, the holy Catholic Church, the
communion of saints, the forgiveness of sins, the resurrection of
the body, and life everlasting? **I do.**
God, the all-powerful Father of our Lord Jesus Christ,
has given us a new birth by water and the Holy Spirit,
and forgiven all our sins.
May he also keep us faithful to our Lord Jesus Christ for ever
and ever. **Amen.**

The priest sprinkles the people with the blessed water, while all sing the
following or any other suitable hymn.

I saw water flowing
from the side of the temple, alleluia.
It brought God's life and his salvation,
and the people sang in joyful praise:
alleluia, alleluia.

After the people have been sprinkled, the priest returns to the chair. The
Profession of Faith *is omitted, and the priest directs the* Prayer of the Faithful.

IV. LITURGY OF THE EUCHARIST

PRAYER OVER THE GIFTS
Lord,
accept the prayers and offerings of your people.
With your help
may this Easter mystery of our redemption
bring to perfection the saving work you have begun in us.

PREFACE OF EASTER I
Father, all-powerful and ever-living God,
we do well always and everywhere to give you thanks
through Jesus Christ our Lord.

We praise you with greater joy than ever
on this Easter night (day),
when Christ became our paschal sacrifice.

He is the true Lamb who took away the sins of the world.
By dying he destroyed our death;
by rising he restored our life.

And so, with all the choirs of angels in heaven
we proclaim your glory
and join in their unending hymn of praise:

Holy, holy, holy…

COMMUNION ANTIPHON   *(1 Cor 5:7-8)*
Christ has become our paschal sacrifice; let us feast with the
unleavened bread of sincerity and truth, alleluia.

PRAYER AFTER COMMUNION
Lord, you have nourished us with your Easter sacraments.
Fill us with your Spirit,
and make us one in peace and love.

SOLEMN BLESSING

May almighty God bless you on this solemn feast of Easter,
and may he protect you against all sin. **Amen**.

Through the resurrection of his Son
God has granted us healing.
May he fulfil his promises,
and bless you with eternal life. **Amen**.

You have mourned for Christ's sufferings;
now you celebrate the joy of his resurrection.
May you come with joy to the feast which lasts for ever. **Amen**.

May almighty God bless you,
the Father, and the Son, ✠ and the Holy Spirit. **Amen**.

REFLECTION

A person writing on the liturgy said recently that when the people
are on their way out of the church, if they are not leaving with
a sense of how wonderful God is, then the celebration has
failed. If that is true of Mass on a Sunday throughout the year
it applies even more so on this night, the greatest in the
Church's year. The mystery of the resurrection of the Lord is
our main reason for proclaiming: 'Isn't God great'.

═══════════ 11 APRIL ═══════════

EASTER SUNDAY

'ALLELUIA' or, more exactly 'HALLELUYAH' is the catchcry of
an Easter people. It means 'praise the Lord'. The resurrection of
Jesus, which we celebrate every Sunday of the year is the chief
reason why God is to be praised. God did not turn his back on
his Son even though on Calvary it appeared that he was dying
alone. A faithful God and a faithful servant cannot be separated
from each other.

ENTRANCE ANTIPHON   *(Ps 138:18.5-6)*
**I have risen: I am with you once more; you placed your hand
on me to keep me safe. How great is the depth of your wisdom,
alleluia!**

or   *(Lk 24:34;Rv 1:6)*
**The Lord has indeed risen, alleluia. Glory and kingship be his
for ever and ever.**

GREETING, PENITENTIAL RITE, GLORIA — *pages 7-14*

OPENING PRAYER

Let us pray
  [that the risen Christ will raise us up
  and renew our lives]

God our Father, by raising Christ your Son
you conquered the power of death
and opened for us the way to eternal life.
Let our celebration today
raise us up and renew our lives
by the Spirit that is within us.

or

Let us pray
  [on this Easter morning for the life
  that never again shall see darkness]

God our Father, creator of all,
today is the day of Easter joy.
This is the morning on which the Lord appeared to men
who had begun to lose hope
and opened their eyes to what the scriptures foretold:
that first he must die, and then he would rise
and ascend into his Father's glorious presence.

May the risen Lord
breathe on our minds and open our eyes
that we may know him in the breaking of bread
and follow him in his risen life.

FIRST READING   (Acts 10:34.37-43)

A reading from the Acts of the Apostles.
We have eaten and drunk with him after his resurrection.

Peter addressed Cornelius and his household: 'You must have
heard about the recent happenings in Judaea: about Jesus of Nazareth
and how he began in Galilee, after John had been preaching baptism.
God had anointed him with the Holy Spirit and with power,
and because God was with him, Jesus went about doing good
and curing all who had fallen into the power of the devil. Now I,
and those with me, can witness to everything he did throughout
the country-side of Judaea and in Jerusalem itself: and also to
the fact that they killed him by hanging him on a tree, yet three
days afterwards God raised him to life and allowed him to be
seen, not by the whole people but only by certain witnesses God
had chosen beforehand. Now we are those witnesses — we have
eaten and drunk with him after his resurrection from the dead —

and he has ordered us to proclaim this to his people and to tell them that God has appointed him to judge everyone, alive or dead. It is to him that all the prophets bear this witness: that all who believe in Jesus will have their sins forgiven through his name.'

This is the word of the Lord.

RESPONSORIAL PSALM   *(Ps 117:1-2.16-17.22-23)*

℟ **This day was made by the Lord;**
   we rejoice and are glad.

or **Alleluia, alleluia, alleluia!**

1. Give thanks to the Lord for he is good,
    for his love has no end.
    Let the sons of Israel say:
    'His love has no end.' ℟

2. The Lord's right hand has triumphed;
    his right hand raised me up.
    I shall not die, I shall live
    and recount his deeds. ℟

3. The stone which the builders rejected
    has become the corner stone.
    This is the work of the Lord,
    a marvel in our eyes. ℟

SECOND READING   *(Col 3:1-4)*

A reading from the letter of St. Paul to the Colossians.

You must look for the things that are in heaven, where Christ is.

Since you have been brought back to true life with Christ, you must look for the things that are in heaven, where Christ is, sitting at God's right hand. Let your thoughts be on heavenly things, not on the things that are on the earth, because you have died, and now the life you have is hidden with Christ in God. But when Christ is revealed — and he is your life — you too will be revealed in all your glory with him.

This is the word of the Lord.

Alternative Second Reading   *(1 Cor 5:6-8)*

A reading from the first letter of St Paul to the Corinthians.

Get rid of the old yeast, make yourselves into a completely new batch of bread.

You must know how even a small amount of yeast is enough to leaven all the dough, so get rid of all the old yeast, and make yourselves into a completely new batch of bread, unleavened as you are meant to be. Christ, our passover, has been sacrificed; let us celebrate the feast, by getting rid of all the old yeast of evil and wickedness, having only the unleavened bread of sincerity and truth.

This is the word of the Lord.

SEQUENCE

Christians, to the Paschal Victim offer sacrifice and praise.
The sheep are ransomed by the Lamb;
and Christ, the undefiled,
hath sinners to his Father reconciled.
Death with life contended; combat strangely ended!
Life's own Champion, slain, yet lives to reign.
Tell us, Mary: say what thou didst see upon the way.
The tomb the Living did enclose;
I saw Christ's glory as he rose!
The angels there attesting,
shroud with grave-clothes resting.
Christ, my hope, has risen: he goes before you into Galilee.
That Christ is truly risen from the dead we know.
Victorious king, thy mercy show!

GOSPEL ACCLAMATION   *(1Cor 5:7-8)*

Alleluia, alleluia!
Christ, our passover, has been sacrificed;
let us celebrate the feast then, in the Lord.
Alleluia!

GOSPEL   *(Jn 20:1-9)*
(Instead of the following Gospel, that of the Easter Vigil may be used.)
A reading from the holy Gospel according to John.
He must rise from the dead.

It was very early on the first day of the week and still dark, when Mary of Magdala came to the tomb. She saw that the stone had been moved away from the tomb and came running to Simon Peter and the other disciple, the one Jesus loved. 'They have taken the Lord out of the tomb' she said 'and we don't know where they have put him.'

So Peter set out with the other disciple to go to the tomb. They ran together, but the other disciple, running faster than Peter, reached the tomb first; he bent down and saw the linen cloths lying on the ground, but did not go in. Simon Peter who was following now came up, went right into the tomb, saw the linen cloths on the ground, and also the cloth that had been over his head; this was not with the linen cloths but rolled up in a place by itself. Then the other disciple who had reached the tomb first also went in; he saw and he believed. Till this moment they had failed to understand the teaching of scripture, that he must rise from the dead.

This is the Gospel of the Lord.

The rite of the Renewal of Baptismal Promises (page 203) is desirable after the homily. The Profession of Faith is then omitted.

PRAYER OVER THE GIFTS

Lord,
with Easter joy we offer you the sacrifice
by which your Church is reborn and nourished
through Christ our Lord.

PREFACE OF EASTER I — *page 204*

COMMUNION ANTIPHON   *(1Cor 5:7-8)*

Christ has become our paschal sacrifice; let us feast with the unleavened bread of sincerity and truth, alleluia.

PRAYER AFTER COMMUNION

Father of love,
watch over your Church
and bring us to the glory of the resurrection
promised by this Easter sacrament.

SOLEMN BLESSING — *page 205*

REFLECTION

> Christianity stands or falls on this basis: that Christ has been raised from the dead. This is a great mystery which the community of the Church has pondered over in every age. No one could have expected that God's plan for the human race goes beyond death. In his passage from death to life Jesus, the Christ, is the first of many brothers and sisters. This is what we will celebrate for the next fifty days.

18 APRIL
SECOND SUNDAY OF EASTER
(Divine Mercy Sunday)

The Easter or Paschal candle is a reminder to us of the presence of the risen Lord among his people when they assemble in his name. Its flame is bright and alive. His presence among us is dynamic and empowering. It gives light in the darkness. Jesus as the light of the world is the clearest revelation of God that has ever been or will ever be.

ENTRANCE ANTIPHON   *(1 Pt 2:2)*

Like newborn children you should thirst for milk, on which your spirit can grow to strength, alleluia.

or   *(4 Ezra 2:36-37)*

Rejoice to the full in the glory that is yours, and give thanks to God who called you to his kingdom, alleluia.

GREETING, PENITENTIAL RITE, GLORIA — *pages 7-14*

OPENING PRAYER

Let us pray
    [for a deeper awareness of our Christian baptism]

God of mercy,
you wash away our sins in water,
you give us new birth in the Spirit,
and redeem us in the blood of Christ.
As we celebrate Christ's resurrection
increase our awareness of these blessings,
and renew your gift of life within us.

or

Let us pray
    [as Christians thirsting for the risen life]

Heavenly Father and God of mercy,
we no longer look for Jesus among the dead,
for he is alive and has become the Lord of life.
From the waters of death you raise us with him
and renew your gift of life within us.

Increase in our minds and hearts
the risen life we share with Christ
and help us to grow as your people

toward the fullness of eternal life with you.

FIRST READING   (Acts 5:12-16)

A reading from the Acts of the Apostles.

The numbers of men and women who came to believe in the Lord increased steadily.

The faithful all used to meet by common consent in the Portico of Solomon. No one else ever dared to join them, but the people were loud in their praise and the numbers of men and women who came to believe in the Lord increased steadily. So many signs and wonders were worked among the people at the hands of the apostles that the sick were even taken out into the streets and laid on beds and sleeping-mats in the hope that at least the shadow of Peter might fall across some of them as he went past. People even came crowding in from the towns round about Jerusalem, bringing with them their sick and those tormented by unclean spirits, and all of them were cured.

    This is the word of the Lord.

RESPONSORIAL PSALM   (Ps 117:2-4.22-27)

℟   **Give thanks to the Lord for he is good,**
     for his love has no end.

or **Alleluia, alleluia, alleluia!**

1. Let the sons of Israel say:
    'His love has no end.'
    Let the sons of Aaron say:
    'His love has no end.'
    Let those who fear the Lord say:
    'His love has no end.' ℟

2. The stone which the builders rejected
    has become the corner stone.
    This is the work of the Lord,
    a marvel in our eyes.
    This day was made by the Lord;
    we rejoice and are glad. ℟

3. O Lord, grant us salvation;
    O Lord grant success.
    Blessed in the name of the Lord
    is he who comes.
    We bless you from the house of the Lord;
    the Lord God is our light. ℟

SECOND READING   *(Apoc 1:9-13.17-19)*

A reading from the book of the Apocalypse.

I was dead and now I am to live for ever and ever.

My name is John, and through our union in Jesus I am your
brother and share your sufferings, your kingdom, and all you
endure. I was on the island of Patmos for having preached God's
word and witnessed for Jesus; it was the Lord's day and the Spirit
possessed me, and I heard a voice behind me, shouting like a
trumpet, 'Write down all that you see in a book.' I turned round
to see who had spoken to me, and when I turned I saw seven
golden lamp-stands and, surrounded by them, a figure like a
Son of man, dressed in a long robe tied at the waist with a
golden girdle.

When I saw him, I fell in a dead faint at his feet, but he
touched me with his right hand and said, 'Do not be afraid; it is
I, the First and the Last; I am the Living One. I was dead and
now I am to live for ever and ever, and I hold the keys of death
and of the underworld. Now write down all that you see of
present happenings and things that are still to come.'

This is the word of the Lord.

GOSPEL ACCLAMATION   *(Jn 20:29)*

Alleluia, alleluia!
Jesus said: 'You believe because you can see me.
Happy are those who have not seen and yet believe.'
Alleluia!

GOSPEL   *(Jn 20:19-31)*

A reading from the holy Gospel according to John.

Eight days later, Jesus came.

In the evening of that same day, the first day of the week, the
doors were closed in the room where the disciples were, for fear
of the Jews. Jesus came and stood among them. He said to them,
'Peace be with you,' and showed them his hands and his side.
The disciples were filled with joy when they saw the Lord, and
he said to them again, 'Peace be with you.

'As the Father sent me,
so am I sending you.'

After saying this he breathed on them and said:

'Receive the Holy Spirit.
For those whose sins you forgive,
they are forgiven;

for those whose sins you retain,
they are retained.'

Thomas, called the Twin, who was one of the Twelve, was not with them when Jesus came. When the disciples said, 'We have seen the Lord', he answered, 'Unless I see the holes that the nails made in his hands and can put my finger into the holes they made, and unless I can put my hand into his side, I refuse to believe.' Eight days later the disciples were in the house again and Thomas was with them. The doors were closed, but Jesus came in and stood among them. 'Peace be with you' he said. Then he spoke to Thomas, 'Put your finger here; look, here are my hands. Give me your hand; put it into my side. Doubt no longer but believe.' Thomas replied, 'My Lord and my God!' Jesus said to him:

'You believe because you can see me.
Happy are those who have not seen and yet believe.'

There were many other signs that Jesus worked and the disciples saw, but they are not recorded in this book. These are recorded so that you may believe that Jesus is the Christ, the Son of God, and that believing this you may have life through his name.

This is the Gospel of the Lord.

PROFESSION OF FAITH — *page 15*

PRAYER OVER GIFTS
Lord,
through faith and baptism
we have become a new creation.
Accept the offerings of your people
(and of those born again in baptism)
and bring us to eternal happiness.

PREFACE OF EASTER I — *page 204*

COMMUNION ANTIPHON   *(Jn 20:27)*
Jesus spoke to Thomas: Put your hand here, and see the place of the nails. Doubt no longer, but believe, alleluia.

PRAYER AFTER COMMUNION
Almighty God,
may the Easter sacraments we have received
live for ever in our minds and hearts.

SOLEMN BLESSING — *page 205*

REFLECTION

In the Easter season we celebrate our Redemption. What does this mean? The biblical background sheds much light on it. If a Hebrew person were sold into slavery because of debt his nearest relative would redeem him, that is, would pay what was needed in order to restore him to freedom. Redemption begins in this life when people can worship God in conditions that are worthy of their dignity as human beings and it continues into the next when the glory of Christ's resurrection will be theirs.

─────────────── 23 APRIL ───────────────

ST GEORGE
(Patron of England)

The patron of England and a martyr, very little is known about the life of George. His historical existence, though it has sometimes been disputed, is now generally accepted. It is likely that he suffered before the time of Constantine in the Fourth Century but it wasn't until the Sixth Century that devotion to him became popular. In 1415 his Feast became one of the chief holidays of the year in England. It was around this time that Saint George's arms, a red cross on a white background, became a kind of uniform for soldiers.

ENTRANCE ANTIPHON   *(cf. 4 Ezra 2:35)*
Light for ever will shine on your saints, O Lord, alleluia.

GREETING, PENITENTIAL RITE, GLORIA – *pages 7-14*

OPENING PRAYER

Lord, hear the prayers of those who praise your mighty power.
As Saint George was ready to follow Christ in suffering and death, so may he be ready to help us in our weakness.

FIRST READING   *(Apo 12:10-12)*
A reading from the book of the Apocalypse.
In the face of death they would not cling to life.
I, John, heard a voice shout from heaven, 'Victory and power and empire for ever have been won by our God, and all authority for his Christ, now that the persecutor, who accused our brothers day and night before our God, has been brought down. They have triumphed over him by the blood of the Lamb

and by the witness of their martyrdom, because even in the face of death they would not cling to life. Let the heavens rejoice and all who live there.'

This is the word of the Lord.

RESPONSORIAL PSALM *(Ps 125)*

℟ **Those who are sowing in tears**
   will sing when they reap.

1. When the Lord delivered Zion from bondage,
   it seemed like a dream.
   Then was our mouth filled with laughter,
   on our lips there were songs. ℟

2. The heathens themselves said:
   'What marvels the Lord worked for them!'
   What marvels the Lord worked for us!
   Indeed we were glad. ℟

3. Deliver us, O Lord, from our bondage
   as streams in dry land.
   Those who are sowing in tears
   will sing when they reap. ℟

4. They go out, they go out, full of tears,
   carrying seed for the sowing;
   they come back, they come back, full of song,
   carrying their sheaves. ℟

GOSPEL ACCLAMATION *(Jm 1:12)*

Alleluia, alleluia!
Happy the man who stands firm,
for he has proved himself,
and will win the crown of life.
Alleluia!

GOSPEL *(Jn 15:18-21)*

A reading from the holy Gospel according to John.

If they persecuted me, they will persecute you.

Jesus said to his disciples:

'If the world hates you,
remember that it hated me before you.
If you belonged to the world,
the world would love you as its own;
but because you do not belong to the world,
because my choice withdrew you from the world,

therefore the world hates you.
Remember the words I said to you:
A servant is not greater than his master.
If they persecuted me,
they will persecute you too;
if they kept my word,
they will keep yours as well.
But it will be on my account that they will do this,
because they do not know the one who sent me.'
This is the Gospel of the Lord.

PRAYER OVER THE GIFTS
Lord, bless our offerings and make them holy.
May these gifts fill our hearts
with the love which gave Saint George victory
over all his suffering.

PREFACE OF MARTYRS
Father, all powerful and ever-living God,
we do well always and everywhere to give you thanks.
Your holy martyr N. followed the example of Christ,
and gave his life for the glory of your name.
His death reveals your power
shining through our human weakness.
You choose the weak and make them strong
in bearing witness to you,
through Jesus Christ our Lord.
In our unending joy we echo on earth
the song of the angels in heaven
as they praise your glory for ever:
Holy, holy, holy...

COMMUNION ANTIPHON   (Jn 12:20-21)
I tell you solemnly: unless a grain of wheat falls on the
ground and dies, it remains a single grain; but if it dies, yields
a rich harvest, alleluia.

PRAYER AFTER COMMUNION
Lord,
we receive your gifts from heaven
at this joyful feast.
May we who proclaim at this holy table
the death and resurrection of your Son

come to share his glory with Saint George
and all your holy martyrs.

REFLECTION

Since the Second Vatican Council the Church has renewed its
awareness of its Jewish background. This is something which
tended to be forgotten. The Jewish influence may be clearly
seen in the liturgy as, for example, in the division of the week
into 7 and the designation of the first day of the week as a day
of rest. Sunday, the day of Resurrection, is both a day of rest
and a day of worship.

━━━━━━━━━━━━━━ 25 APRIL ━━━━━━━━━━━━━━

THIRD SUNDAY OF EASTER

The resurrection of the Lord dominates our celebration in
these days of Eastertide. Today's liturgy provides an example of
the transforming power of the resurrection. Peter's threefold
confession of faith reverses his threefold denial of Jesus during
the passion. Jesus' forgiveness of his disciple here is intended
to assure disciples of every age of his forgiveness.

ENTRANCE ANTIPHON *(Ps 65:1-2)*

**Let all the earth cry out to God with joy; praise the glory of
his name; proclaim his glorious praise, alleluia.**

GREETING, PENITENTIAL RITE, GLORIA — *pages 7-14*

OPENING PRAYER

Let us pray
     [that Christ will give us
     a share in the glory of his unending life]

God our Father,
may we look forward with hope to our resurrection,
for you have made us your sons and daughters,
and restored the joy of our youth.

or

Let us pray
     [in confident peace and Easter hope]

Father in heaven, author of all truth,
a people once in darkness has listened to your Word
and followed your Son as he rose from the tomb.

Hear the prayer of this newborn people
and strengthen your Church to answer your call.
May we rise and come forth into the light of day
to stand in your presence until eternity dawns.

FIRST READING   *(Acts 5:27-32.40-41)*

A reading from the Acts of the Apostles.

We are witnesses of all this, we and the Holy Spirit.

The high priest demanded an explanation of the apostles. 'We gave you a formal warning,' he said 'not to preach in this name, and what have you done? You have filled Jerusalem with your teaching, and seem determined to fix the guilt of this man's death on us.' In reply Peter and the apostles said, 'Obedience to God comes before obedience to men; it was the God of our ancestors who raised up Jesus, but it was you who had him executed by hanging on a tree. By his own right hand God has now raised him up to be leader and saviour, to give repentance and forgiveness of sins through him to Israel. We are witnesses to all this, we and the Holy Spirit whom God has given to those who obey him.' They warned the apostles not to speak in the name of Jesus and released them. And so they left the presence of the Sanhedrin glad to have had the honour of suffering humiliation for the sake of the name.

    This is the word of the Lord.

RESPONSORIAL PSALM   *(Ps 29:2.4-6.11-13)*

℟   **I will praise you, Lord, you have rescued me.**

or   **Alleluia!**

1.   I will praise you, Lord, you have rescued me
      and have not let my enemies rejoice over me.
      O Lord, you have raised my soul from the dead,
      restored me to life from those who sink into the grave. ℟

2.   Sing psalms to the Lord, you who love him,
      give thanks to his holy name.
      His anger lasts but a moment; his favour through life.
      At night there are tears, but joy comes with dawn. ℟

3.   The Lord listened and had pity.
      The Lord came to my help.
      For me you have changed my mourning into dancing;
      O Lord my God, I will thank you for ever. ℟

SECOND READING   *(Apo 5:11-14)*
A reading from the book of the Apocalypse.
The Lamb that was sacrificed is worthy to be given riches and power.

In my vision, I, John, heard the sound of an immense number of
angels gathered round the throne and the animals and the
elders; there were ten thousand times ten thousand of them and
thousands upon thousands, shouting, 'The Lamb that was
sacrificed is worthy to be given power, riches, wisdom, strength,
honour, glory and blessing.' Then I heard all the living things in
creation — everything that lives in the air and on the ground,
and under the ground, and in the sea, crying, 'To the One who is
sitting on the throne and to the Lamb, be all praise, honour,
glory and power, for ever and ever.' And the four animals said,
'Amen'; and the elders prostrated themselves to worship.

This is the word of the Lord.

GOSPEL ACCLAMATION   *(cf. Lk 24:32)*
Alleluia, alleluia!
Lord Jesus, explain the scriptures to us.
Make our hearts burn within us as you talk to us. Alleluia!
or
Alleluia, alleluia!
Christ has risen: he who created all things,
and has granted his mercy to men. Alleluia!

GOSPEL   *(Jn 21:1-19)*
(For Shorter Form, *read between* ◗ ◖*)*
A reading from the holy Gospel according to John.
*Jesus stepped forward, took the bread and gave it to them, and the same
with the fish.*

◗Jesus showed himself again to the disciples. It was by the Sea of
Tiberias, and it happened like this: Simon Peter, Thomas called
the Twin, Nathanael from Cana in Galilee, the sons of Zebedee
and two more of his disciples were together. Simon Peter said,
'I'm going fishing.' They replied, 'We'll come with you.' They
went out and got into the boat but caught nothing that night.

It was light by now and there stood Jesus on the shore,
though the disciples did not realise that it was Jesus. Jesus called
out, 'Have you caught anything, friends?' And when they
answered, 'No', he said, 'Throw the net out to starboard and
you'll find something.' So they dropped the net, and there were
so many fish that they could not haul it in. The disciple Jesus
loved said to Peter, 'It is the Lord.' At these words 'It is the Lord',

Simon Peter, who had practically nothing on, wrapped his cloak round him and jumped into the water. The other disciples came on in the boat, towing the net and the fish; they were only about a hundred yards from land.

As soon as they came ashore they saw that there was some bread there, and a charcoal fire with fish cooking on it. Jesus said, 'Bring some of the fish you have just caught.' Simon Peter went aboard and dragged the net to the shore, full of big fish, one hundred and fifty-three of them; and in spite of there being so many the net was not broken. Jesus said to them, 'Come and have breakfast.' None of the disciples was bold enough to ask, 'Who are you?'; they knew quite well it was the Lord. Jesus then stepped forward, took the bread and gave it to them, and the same with the fish. This was the third time that Jesus showed himself to the disciples after rising from the dead.◀

After the meal Jesus said to Simon Peter, 'Simon son of John, do you love me more than these others do?' He answered, 'Yes Lord, you know I love you.' Jesus said to him, 'Feed my lambs.' A second time he said to him, 'Simon son of John, do you love me?' He replied 'Yes Lord you know I love you.' Jesus said to him, 'Look after my sheep.' Then he said to him a third time, 'Simon son of John, do you love me?' Peter was upset that he asked him the third time, 'Do you love me?' and said, 'Lord, you know everything; you know I love you.' Jesus said to him, 'Feed my sheep.

'I tell you most solemnly,
when you were young
you put on your own belt
and walked where you liked;
but when you grow old
you will stretch out your hands,
and somebody else will put a belt round you
and take you where you would rather not go.'

In these words he indicated the kind of death by which Peter would give glory to God. After this he said, 'Follow me.'

◀This is the Gospel of the Lord.◀

PROFESSION OF FAITH — *pages 15-16*

PRAYER OVER THE GIFTS

Lord, receive these gifts from your Church.
May the great joy you give us
come to perfection in heaven.

PREFACE OF EASTER II-V — *pages 21-22*

COMMUNION ANTIPHON   *(Jn 21:12-13)*

Jesus said to his disciples: Come and eat. And he took the bread, and gave it to them, alleluia.

PRAYER AFTER COMMUNION

Lord, look on your people with kindness
and by these Easter mysteries
bring us to the glory of the resurrection.

SOLEMN BLESSING — *page 56*

REFLECTION

> The extraordinary catch of fish in today's scripture is intended by the writer to instil in his hearers confidence for the task ahead. It is not by their own efforts alone but by the power of the Spirit that the work will bear fruit. They shared a meal with Jesus on the shore of the sea. Today we share a similar meal with him and with one another. His presence among us is our principal source of confidence.

— 2 MAY —

FOURTH SUNDAY OF EASTER

Each celebration of the Eucharist begins with the sign of the cross in the name of the Blessed Trinity. In these days of Eastertide we await the coming of the Holy Spirit on Pentecost Sunday. The Holy Spirit is adored and glorified with the Father and the Son. It is from Jesus that the Church has learnt the name of the Holy Spirit and it is in this name as well as that of the Father and the Son that each new child of the Church is baptised.

ENTRANCE ANTIPHON   *(Ps 32:5-6)*

The earth is full of the goodness of the Lord; by the word of the Lord the heavens were made, alleluia.

GREETING, PENITENTIAL RITE, GLORIA — *pages 7-14*

OPENING PRAYER

Let us pray

> [that Christ our shepherd
> will lead us through the difficulties of this life]

Almighty and ever-living God,

give us new strength
from the courage of Christ our shepherd,
and lead us to join the saints in heaven,
where he lives and reigns with you and the Holy Spirit,
one God, for ever and ever.

or

Let us pray

   [to God our helper in time of distress]

God and Father of our Lord Jesus Christ,
though your people walk in the valley of darkness,
no evil should they fear;
for they follow in faith the call of the shepherd
whom you have sent for their hope and strength.

Attune our minds to the sound of his voice,
lead our steps in the path he has shown,
that we may know the strength of his outstretched arm
and enjoy the light of your presence for ever.

FIRST READING   *(Acts 13:14.43-52)*
A reading from the Acts of the Apostles.

We must turn to the pagans.

Paul and Barnabas carried on from Perga till they reached
Antioch in Pisidia. Here they went to synagogue on the sabbath
and took their seats.

   When the meeting broke up, many Jews and devout
converts joined Paul and Barnabas, and in their talks with them
Paul and Barnabas urged them to remain faithful to the grace
God had given them.

   The next sabbath almost the whole town assembled to hear
the word of God. When they saw the crowds, the Jews,
prompted by jealousy, used blasphemies and contradicted
everything Paul said. Then Paul and Barnabas spoke out boldly,
'We had to proclaim the word of God to you first, but since you
have rejected it, since you do not think yourselves worthy of
eternal life, we must turn to the pagans. For this is what the Lord
commanded us to do when he said:

   I have made you a light for the nations,
   so that my salvation may reach the ends of the earth.'

   It made the pagans very happy to hear this and they
thanked the Lord for his message; all who were destined for
eternal life became believers. Thus the word of the Lord spread

through the whole countryside.

But the Jews worked upon some of the devout women of the upper classes and the leading men of the city and persuaded them to turn against Paul and Barnabas and expel them from their territory. So they shook the dust from their feet in defiance and went off to Iconium; but the disciples were filled with joy and the Holy Spirit.

This is the word of the Lord.

RESPONSORIAL PSALM   *(Ps 99:1-3.5.)*

℟   **We are his people, the sheep of his flock.**

or   **Alleluia!**

1.   Cry out with joy to the Lord, all the earth.
      Serve the Lord with gladness.
      Come before him, singing for joy. ℟

2.   Know that he, the Lord, is God.
      He made us, we belong to him,
      we are his people, the sheep of his flock. ℟

3.   Indeed, how good is the Lord,
      eternal his merciful love.
      He is faithful from age to age. ℟

SECOND READING   *(Apo 7:9.14-17)*

A reading from the book of the Apocalypse.

The Lamb will be their shepherd and will lead them to springs of living water.

I, John, saw a huge number, impossible to count, of people from every nation, race, tribe and language; they were standing in front of the throne and in front of the Lamb, dressed in white robes and holding palms in their hands. One of the elders said to me, 'These are the people who have been through the great persecution, and because they have washed their robes white again in the blood of the Lamb, they now stand in front of God's throne and serve him day and night in his sanctuary; and the One who sits on the throne will spread his tent over them. They will never hunger or thirst again; neither the sun nor scorching wind will ever plague them, because the Lamb who is at the throne will be their shepherd and will lead them to springs of living water; and God will wipe away all tears from their eyes.'

This is the word of the Lord.

GOSPEL ACCLAMATION   *(Jn 10:14)*
Alleluia, alleluia!
I am the good shepherd, says the Lord;
I know my own sheep and my own know me. Alleluia!

GOSPEL   *(Jn 10:27-30)*
A reading from the holy Gospel according to John.
I give eternal life to the sheep that belong to me.
Jesus said:

> 'The sheep that belong to me listen to my voice;
> I know them and they follow me.
> I give them eternal life;
> they will never be lost
> and no one will ever steal them from me.
> The Father who gave them to me is greater than anyone,
> and no one can steal from the Father.
> The Father and I are one.'
> This is the Gospel of the Lord.

PROFESSION OF FAITH — *pages 15-16*

PRAYER OVER THE GIFTS
Lord, restore us by these Easter mysteries.
May the continuing work of our Redeemer
bring us eternal joy.

PREFACE OF EASTER II-V — *pages 21-22*

COMMUNION ANTIPHON
The Good Shepherd is risen! He who laid down his life for
his sheep, who died for his flock, he is risen, alleluia.

PRAYER AFTER COMMUNION
Father, eternal shepherd,
watch over the flock redeemed by the blood of Christ
and lead us to the promised land.

SOLEMN BLESSING — *page 56*

REFLECTION
> The word 'spirit' translates a Hebrew word which primarily
> means breath, air, wind. Jesus himself used the image of the
> wind to suggest the power, freedom and newness of the one
> who is the breath of God, the Holy Spirit. It is this Spirit which
> is given to each of us at our baptism and which remains with
> us throughout our life.

9 MAY
FIFTH SUNDAY OF EASTER

At the Last Supper, Jesus announces and promises the Holy
Spirit to the disciples. He calls the Spirit 'the paraclete', literally
'the one who is called to be at your side'. Sometimes the word
is translated as 'consoler'. What greater consolation can anyone
give than the consolation of their presence through thick and thin.

ENTRANCE ANTIPHON   *(Ps 97:1-2)*
**Sing to the Lord a new song, for he has done marvellous deeds;
he has revealed to the nations his saving power, alleluia.**

GREETING, PENITENTIAL RITE, GLORIA — *pages 7-14*

OPENING PRAYER

Let us pray
    [that we may enjoy true freedom]
God our Father,
look upon us with love.
You redeem us and make us your children in Christ.
Give us true freedom
and bring us to the inheritance you promised.
or
Let us pray
    [in the freedom of the children of God]
Father of our Lord Jesus Christ,
you have revealed to the nations your saving power
and filled all ages with the words of a new song.
Hear the echo of this hymn.
Give us voice to sing your praise
throughout this season of joy.

FIRST READING   *(Acts 14:21-27)*
A reading from the Acts of the Apostles.
They gave an account to the church of all that God had done with them.
Paul and Barnabas went back through Lystra and Iconium to
Antioch. They put fresh heart into the disciples, encouraging
them to persevere in the faith. 'We all have to experience many
hardships' they said 'before we enter the kingdom of God.' In
each of these churches they appointed elders, and with prayer
and fasting they commended them to the Lord in whom they
had come to believe.

They passed through Pisidia and reached Pamphylia. Then after proclaiming the word at Perga they went down to Attalia and from there sailed for Antioch, where they had originally been commended to the grace of God for the work they had now completed.

On their arrival they assembled the church and gave an account of all that God had done with them, and how he had opened the door of faith to the pagans.

This is the word of the Lord.

RESPONSORIAL PSALM   (Ps 144:8-13)

℞ **I will bless your name for ever, O God my King.**

or **Alleluia!**

1. The Lord is kind and full of compassion,
    slow to anger, abounding in love.
    How good is the Lord to all,
    compassionate to all his creatures. ℞

2. All your creatures shall thank you, O Lord,
    and your friends shall repeat their blessing.
    They shall speak of the glory of your reign
    and declare your might, O God,
    to make known to men your mighty deeds
    and the glorious splendour of your reign. ℞

3. Yours is an everlasting kingdom;
    your rule lasts from age to age. ℞

SECOND READING   (Apo 21:1-5)

A reading from the book of the Apocalypse.

God will wipe away all tears from their eyes.

I, John, saw a new heaven and a new earth; the first heaven and the first earth had disappeared now, and there was no longer any sea. I saw the holy city, and the new Jerusalem, coming down from God out of heaven, as beautiful as a bride all dressed for her husband. Then I heard a loud voice call from the throne, 'You see this city? Here God lives among men. He will make his home among them; they shall be his people, and he will be their God; his name is God-with-them. He will wipe away all tears from their eyes; there will be no more death, and no more mourning or sadness. The world of the past has gone.'

Then the One sitting on the throne spoke: 'Now I am making the whole of creation new'.

This is the word of the Lord.

GOSPEL ACCLAMATION   *(Jn 13:34)*

Alleluia, alleluia!
Jesus said: 'I give you a new commandment:
love one another, just as I have loved you.'
Alleluia!

GOSPEL   *(Jn 13:31-35)*

A reading from the holy Gospel according to John.

I give you a new commandment: love one another.

When Judas had gone Jesus said:

> 'Now has the Son of Man been glorified,
> and in him God has been glorified.
> If God has been glorified in him,
> God will in turn glorify him in himself,
> and will glorify him very soon.
> My little children,
> I shall not be with you much longer.
> I give you a new commandment:
> love one another;
> just as I have loved you,
> you also must love one another.
> By this love you have for one another,
> everyone will know that you are my disciples.'
> This is the Gospel of the Lord.

PROFESSION OF FAITH — *pages 15-16*

PRAYER OVER THE GIFTS

Lord God,
by this holy exchange of gifts
you share with us your divine life.
Grant that everything we do
may be directed by the knowledge of your truth.

PREFACE OF EASTER II-V — *pages 21-22*

COMMUNION ANTIPHON   *(Jn 15:5)*

I am the vine and you are the branches, says the Lord; he who
lives in me, and I in him, will bear much fruit, alleluia!

PRAYER AFTER COMMUNION

Merciful Father,
may these mysteries give us new purpose
and bring us to a new life in you.

SOLEMN BLESSING — *page 56*

REFLECTION

One of the ancient poems of the Christian tradition offers a rich understanding of the Holy Spirit. In it the Spirit is referred to as father of the poor, giver of gifts, light of hearts, greatest consoler, kind guest of the soul, pleasant coolness, relaxation in labour, moderate temperature in the summer heat, consolation in grief, most happily received light.

---

16 MAY

SIXTH SUNDAY OF EASTER

The Holy Spirit has been called by the Lord 'the Spirit of truth'. Since Jesus was not able to tell his disciples everything they needed to know the Holy Spirit which has been given to them will do so. The principal truth which the Spirit teaches is about Jesus himself, that he is the real revelation of God the Father and that it is he who speaks the words of God.

ENTRANCE ANTIPHON   *(Is 48:20)*

Speak out with a voice of joy; let it be heard to the ends of the earth: The Lord has set his people free, alleluia.

GREETING, PENITENTIAL RITE, GLORIA — *pages 7-14*

OPENING PRAYER

Let us pray
[that we may practise in our lives
the faith we profess]

Ever-living God,
help us to celebrate our joy
in the resurrection of the Lord
and to express in our lives
the love we celebrate.

or

Let us pray
[in silence, reflecting on the joy of Easter]

God our Father, maker of all,
the crown of your creation was the Son of Man,
born of a woman, but without beginning;
he suffered for us but lives for ever.

May our mortal lives be crowned with the ultimate joy of rising
    with him,
who is Lord for ever and ever.

FIRST READING *(Acts 15:1-2.22-29)*

A reading from the Acts of the Apostles.

*It has been decided by the Holy Spirit and by ourselves not to saddle
you with any burden beyond these essentials.*

Some men came down from Judaea and taught the brothers, 'Unless
you have yourselves circumcised in the tradition of Moses you
cannot be saved.' This led to disagreement, and after Paul and
Barnabas had had a long argument with these men it was arranged
that Paul and Barnabas and others of the church should go up to
Jerusalem and discuss the problem with the apostles and elders.

    Then the apostles and elders decided to choose delegates to
send to Antioch with Paul and Barnabas; the whole church
concurred with this. They chose Judas known as Barsabbas and
Silas, both leading men in the brotherhood, and gave them this
letter to take with them:

    'The apostles and elders, your brothers, send greetings to the
brothers of pagan birth in Antioch, Syria and Cilicia. We hear
that some of our members have disturbed you with their
demands and have unsettled your minds. They acted without
any authority from us, and so we have decided unanimously to
elect delegates and to send them to you with Barnabas and Paul,
men we highly respect who have dedicated their lives to the
name of our Lord Jesus Christ. Accordingly we are sending you
Judas and Silas, who will confirm by word of mouth what we
have written in this letter. It has been decided by the Holy Spirit
and by ourselves not to saddle you with any burden beyond
these essentials: you are to abstain from food sacrificed to idols,
from blood, from the meat of strangled animals and from
fornication. Avoid these, and you will do what is right. Farewell.'

    This is the word of the Lord.

RESPONSORIAL PSALM *(Ps 66:2-3.5-6.8)*

℞ **Let the peoples praise you, O God;**
    let all the peoples praise you.

or **Alleluia!**

1. O God, be gracious and bless us
    and let your face shed its light upon us.
    So will your ways be known upon earth
    and all nations learn your saving help. ℞

(continued)

2. Let the nations be glad and exult
    for you rule the world with justice.
    With fairness you rule the peoples,
    you guide the nations on earth. ℟

℟ **Let the peoples praise you, O God;
    let all the peoples praise you.**

or **Alleluia!**

3. Let the peoples praise you, O God;
    let all the peoples praise you.
    May God still give us his blessing
    till the ends of the earth revere him. ℟

SECOND READING   *(Apo 21:10-14.22-23)*

A reading from the book of the Apocalypse.

He showed me the holy city coming down out of heaven.

In the spirit, the angel took me to the top of an enormous high
mountain and showed me Jerusalem, the holy city, coming down
from God out of heaven. It had all the radiant glory of God and
glittered like some precious jewel of crystal-clear diamond. The
walls of it were of a great height, and had twelve gates; at each of
the twelve gates there was an angel, and over the gates were written
the names of the twelve tribes of Israel; on the east there were
three gates, on the north three gates, on the south three gates,
and on the west three gates. The city walls stood on twelve foundation
stones, each one of which bore the name of one of the twelve
apostles of the Lamb.

I saw that there was no temple in the city since the Lord God
Almighty and the Lamb were themselves the temple, and the city
did not need the sun or the moon for light, since it was lit by the
radiant glory of God and the Lamb was a lighted torch for it.

This is the word of the Lord.

GOSPEL ACCLAMATION   *(Jn 14:23)*

Alleluia! alleluia!
**Jesus said: 'If anyone loves me, he will keep my word, and my
Father will love him, and we shall come to him. Alleluia!**

GOSPEL   *(Jn 14:23-29)*

A reading from the holy Gospel according to John.

The Holy Spirit will remind you of all I have said to you.

Jesus said to his disciples:

'If anyone loves me he will keep my word,
    and my Father will love him,

and we shall come to him
and make our home with him.
Those who do not love me do not keep my words.
And my word is not my own;
it is the word of the one who sent me.
I have said these things to you
while still with you;
but the Advocate, the Holy Spirit,
whom the Father will send in my name,
will teach you everything
and remind you of all I have said to you.
Peace I bequeath to you,
my own peace I give you,
a peace the world cannot give, this is my gift to you.
Do not let your hearts be troubled or afraid.
You heard me say:
I am going away, and shall return.
If you loved me you would have been glad to know
that I am going to the Father,
for the Father is greater than I.
I have told you this now before it happens,
so that when it does happen you may believe.'
This is the Gospel of the Lord.

PROFESSION OF FAITH — *pages 15-16*

PRAYER OVER THE GIFTS
Lord, accept our prayers and offerings.
Make us worthy of your sacraments of love
by granting us your forgiveness.

PREFACE OF EASTER II-V — *pages 21-22*

COMMUNION ANTIPHON   *(Jn 14:15-16)*
If you love me, keep my commandments, says the Lord. The Father will send you the Holy Spirit, to be with you for ever, alleluia.

PRAYER AFTER COMMUNION
Almighty and ever-living Lord,
you restored us to life
by raising Christ from death.
Strengthen us by this Easter sacrament.

SOLEMN BLESSING — *page 56*

REFLECTION

The Holy Spirit's presence with the Church is the guarantee
that when the Church is open to the Spirit it will be guided in
all truth. This requires an attitude of openness, a listening ear
and a willingness to discern. The community of the Church
like all its members has its sinful as well as its glorious history.
Not every decision that the Church has made in the past has
reflected the promptings of the Spirit of truth. That is why 'the
Church always in need of reform' is an ancient proverb. But
the promise of the Lord that the Spirit will always remain with
the Church is its source of consolation.

━━━━━━━━━━━━━━━ 20 MAY ━━━━━━━━━━━━━━━

THE ASCENSION OF THE LORD

(Celebrated in Ireland next Sunday – 23 May)

The Ascension marks the transition from the first part of the
Easter season to the second. In the first, the emphasis was on
the appearances of the risen Lord and on the identity of this
same Lord with the Jesus of Nazareth who was with the
disciples during his public life. Today marks the close of this
stage when Jesus is no longer visibly present to his Church. He
is now exalted, at God's right hand, and it is from there that he
exercises his authority over heaven and earth.

ENTRANCE ANTIPHON   *(Acts 1:11)*
**Men of Galilee, why do you stand looking in the sky? The
Lord will return, just as you have seen him ascend, alleluia.**

GREETING, PENITENTIAL RITE, GLORIA — *pages 7-14*

OPENING PRAYER
Let us pray
    [that the risen Christ will lead us to eternal life]
God our Father,
make us joyful in the ascension of your Son Jesus Christ.
May we follow him into the new creation,
for his ascension is our glory and our hope.

or

Let us pray
[on this day of Ascension
as we watch and wait for Jesus' return]
Father in heaven,
our minds were prepared for the coming of your kingdom
when you took Christ beyond our sight
so that we might seek him in his glory.

May we follow where he has led
and find our hope in his glory,
for he is Lord for ever.

FIRST READING   *(Acts 1:1-11)*
A reading from the Acts of the Apostles.
He was lifted up while they looked on.

In my earlier work, Theophilus, I dealt with everything Jesus had done and taught from the beginning until the day he gave his instructions to the apostles he had chosen through the Holy Spirit, and was taken up to heaven. He had shown himself alive to them after his Passion by many demonstrations: for forty days he had continued to appear to them and tell them about the kingdom of God. When he had been at table with them, he had told them not to leave Jerusalem, but to wait there for what the Father had promised. 'It is,' he had said, 'what you have heard me speak about: John baptised with water but you, not many days from now, will be baptised with the Holy Spirit.'

Now having met together, they asked him, 'Lord, has the time come? Are you going to restore the kingdom to Israel?' He replied, 'It is not for you to know times or dates that the Father has decided by his own authority, but you will receive power when the Holy Spirit comes on you, and then you will be my witnesses not only in Jerusalem but throughout Judaea and Samaria, and indeed to the ends of the earth.'

As he said this he was lifted up while they looked on, and a cloud took him from their sight. They were still staring into the sky when suddenly two men in white were standing near them and they said, 'Why are you men from Galilee standing here looking into the sky? Jesus who has been taken up from you into heaven, this same Jesus will come back in the same way as you have seen him go there.'

This is the word of the Lord.

RESPONSORIAL PSALM   *(Ps 46:2-3.6-7.8-9)*

℟   **God goes up with shouts of joy;**
     the Lord goes up with trumpet blast.

or   **Alleluia!**

1.   All peoples, clap your hands,
      cry to God with shouts of joy!
      For the Lord, the Most High, we must fear,
      great king over all the earth. ℟

2.   God goes up with shouts of joy;
      the Lord goes up with trumpet blast.
      Sing praise for God, sing praise,
      sing praise to our king, sing praise. ℟

3.   God is king of all the earth.
      Sing praise with all your skill.
      God is king over the nations;
      God reigns on his holy throne. ℟

SECOND READING   *(Heb 9:24-28.10.19-23)*

A reading from the letter to the Hebrews.

Christ entered into heaven itself.

It is not as though Christ had entered a man-made sanctuary
which was only modelled on the real one; but it was heaven
itself, so that he could appear in the actual presence of God on
our behalf. And he does not have to offer himself again and again,
like the high priest going into the sanctuary year after year with
the blood that is not his own, or else he would have had to suffer
over and over again since the world began. Instead of that, he
has made his appearance once and for all, now at the end of the
last age, to do away with sin by sacrificing himself. Since men
only die once, and after that comes judgement, so Christ, too,
offers himself only once to take the faults of many on himself,
and when he appears a second time, it will not be to deal with
sin but to reward with salvation those who are waiting for him.

In other words, brothers, through the blood of Jesus we
have the right to enter the sanctuary, by a new way which he had
opened for us, a living opening through the curtain, that is to
say, his body. And we have the supreme high priest over all the
house of God. So as we go in, let us be sincere in heart and filled
with faith, our minds sprinkled and free from any trace of bad
conscience and our bodies washed with pure water. Let us keep
firm in the hope we profess, because the one who made the

promise is faithful.

This is the word of the Lord.

(The following Second Reading of Year A, Eph 1:17-23, may be used instead of the above.)

A reading from the letter of St Paul to the Ephesians.

He made him sit at his right hand in heaven.

May the God of our Lord Jesus Christ, the Father of glory, give you a spirit of wisdom and perception of what is revealed, to bring you to full knowledge of him. May he enlighten the eyes of your mind so that you can see what hope his call holds for you, what rich glories he has promised the saints will inherit and how infinitely great is the power that he has exercised for us believers. This you can tell from the strength of his power at work in Christ, when he used it to raise him from the dead and to make him sit at his right hand, in heaven, far above every Sovereignty, Authority, Power, or Domination, or any other name that can be named, not only in this age, but also in the age to come. He has put all things under his feet, and made him as the ruler of everything, the head of the Church; which is his body, the fullness of him who fills the whole creation.

This is the word of the Lord.

GOSPEL ACCLAMATION   *(Mt 28:19.20)*

Alleluia, alleluia!
Go, make disciples of all the nations;
I am with you always; yes, to the end of time.
Alleluia!

GOSPEL   *(Lk 24:46-53)*

A reading from the holy Gospel according to Luke.

As he blessed them he was carried up to heaven.

Jesus said to his disciples: 'You see how it is written that the Christ would suffer and on the third day rise from the dead, and that, in his name, repentance for the forgiveness of sins would be preached to all the nations, beginning from Jerusalem. You are witnesses to this.

'And now I am sending down to you what the Father has promised. Stay in the city then, until you are clothed with the power from on high.' Then he took them out as far as the outskirts of Bethany, and lifting up his hands he blessed them. Now as he blessed them, he withdrew from them and was carried up to heaven. They worshipped him and then went back to Jerusalem full of joy; and they were continually in the Temple praising God.

This is the Gospel of the Lord.

PROFESSION OF FAITH — *pages 15-16*

PRAYER OVER THE GIFTS

Lord, receive our offering
as we celebrate the ascension of Christ your Son.
May his gifts help us rise with him
to the joys of heaven,
where he lives and reigns for ever and ever.

PREFACE OF THE ASCENSION I

Father, all-powerful and ever-living God,
we do well always and everywhere to give you thanks.

[Today] the Lord Jesus, the King of glory,
the conqueror of sin and death,
ascended to heaven while the angels sang his praises.

Christ, the mediator between God and man,
judge of the world and Lord of all,
has passed beyond our sight,
not to abandon us but to be our hope.
Christ is the beginning, the head of the Church;
where he has gone, we hope to follow.

The joy of the resurrection and ascension renews the whole world,
while the choirs of heaven sing for ever to your glory:
Holy, holy, holy...

COMMUNION ANTIPHON   *(Mt 28:20)*

I, the Lord, am with you always, until the end of the world, alleluia.

PRAYER AFTER COMMUNION

Father, in this eucharist
we touch the divine life you give to the world.
Help us to follow Christ with love
to eternal life where he is Lord for ever and ever.

SOLEMN BLESSING

May almighty God bless you on this day
when his only Son ascended into heaven
to prepare a place for you.
Amen.

After his resurrection, Christ was seen by his disciples.
When he appears as judge
may you be pleasing for ever in his sight. **Amen.**

You believe that Jesus has taken his seat in majesty
at the right hand of the Father.
May you have the joy of experiencing
that he is also with you to the end of time,
according to his promise. **Amen.**

May almighty God bless you,
the Father, and the Son, ✠ and the Holy Spirit. **Amen.**

REFLECTION

> The Ascension is not an event to be thought about in isolation.
> It is part of the mystery of the resurrection. It is the means
> whereby Jesus is with each member of the Church in a way
> that would have been impossible had he remained in bodily
> form here on earth. The sadness of his leave taking is replaced
> by the joy of his sure presence until the end of time.

───────────────── 23 MAY ─────────────────

SEVENTH SUNDAY OF EASTER

During these days we see how the early Church transferred the
use of the word 'Lord' from referring to God the Father alone
to include the exalted one, Jesus whom God had made both
Lord and Christ. This is uppermost in Luke's account of the
martyrdom of Stephen. On his lips we have the title 'Lord Jesus'
and when he raised his eyes to heaven he saw the heavens thrown
open and the Son of Man standing at the right hand of God.

ENTRANCE ANTIPHON   *(Ps 26:7-9)*

**Lord, hear my voice when I call to you. My heart has prompted
me to seek your face; I seek it, Lord; do not hide from me, alleluia.**

GREETING, PENITENTIAL RITE, GLORIA — *pages 7-14*

OPENING PRAYER

Let us pray
  [that we may recognise the presence of Christ in our midst]

Father, help us keep in mind that Christ our Saviour
lives with you in glory
and promised to remain with us until the end of time.
or

Let us pray
     [to our Father who has raised us to life in Christ]
Eternal Father,
reaching from end to end of the universe,
and ordering all things with your mighty arm:
for you, time is the unfolding of truth that already is,
the unveiling of beauty that is yet to be.

Your Son has saved us in history
by rising from the dead,
so that transcending time he might free us from death.
May his presence among us
lead to the vision of unlimited truth
and unfold the beauty of your love.

FIRST READING   *(Acts 7:55-60)*
A reading from the Acts of the Apostles.
I can see the Son of Man standing at the right hand of God.

Stephen, filled with the Holy Spirit, gazed into heaven and saw
the glory of God, and Jesus standing at God's right hand. 'I can
see heaven thrown open' he said 'and the Son of Man standing
at the right hand of God.' At this all the members of the council
shouted out and stopped their ears with their hands; then they
all rushed at him, sent him out of the city and stoned him. The
witnesses put down their clothes at the feet of a young man
called Saul. As they were stoning him, Stephen said in
invocation, 'Lord Jesus, receive my spirit.' Then he knelt down
and said aloud, 'Lord, do not hold this sin against them'; and
with these words he fell asleep.

     This is the word of the Lord.

RESPONSORIAL PSALM   *(Ps 96:1-2.6-7.9)*

℟   **The Lord is king, most high above all the earth.**

or   **Alleluia!**

1.   The Lord is king, let earth rejoice,
     the many coastlands be glad.
     His throne is justice and right.   ℟

2.   The skies proclaim his justice;
     all peoples see his glory.
     All you spirits, worship him.   ℟

3.   For you indeed are the Lord
     most high above all the earth
     exalted far above all spirits.   ℟

SECOND READING   *(Apo 22:12-14.16-17.20)*
A reading from the book of Apocalypse.
Come, Lord Jesus!

I, John, heard a voice speaking to me: 'Very soon now, I shall be
with you again, bringing the reward to be given to every man
according to what he deserves. I am the Alpha and the Omega,
the First and the Last, the Beginning and the End. Happy are
those who will have washed their robes clean, so that they will
have the right to feed on the tree of life and can come through
the gates into the city.'

I, Jesus, have sent my angel to make these revelations to you
for the sake of the churches. I am of David's line, the root of
David and the bright star of the morning.

The Spirit and the Bride say, 'Come.' Let everyone who
listens answer, 'Come.' Then let all who are thirsty come; all
who want it may have the water of life, and have it free.

The one who guarantees these revelations repeats his promise:
I shall indeed be with you soon. Amen; come, Lord Jesus.

This is the word of the Lord.

GOSPEL ACCLAMATION   *(cf. Jn 14:18)*
Alleluia, alleluia!
I will not leave you orphans, says the Lord;
I will come back to you, and your hearts will be full of joy.
Alleluia!

GOSPEL   *(Jn 17:20-26)*
A reading from the holy Gospel according to John.
May they be completely one.

Jesus raised his eyes to heaven and said:

'Holy Father,
I pray not only for these,
but for those also
who through their words will believe in me.
May they all be one.
Father, may they be one in us,
as you are in me and I am in you,
so that the world may believe it was you who sent me.
I have given them the glory you gave to me,
that they may be one as we are one.
With me in them and you in me,
may they be so completely one
that the world will realise that it was you who sent me

and that I have loved them as much as you loved me.
Father,
I want those you have given me
to be with me where I am,
so that they may always see the glory
you have given me
because you loved me
before the foundation of the world.
Father, Righteous One,
the world has not known you,
but I have known you,
and these have known
that you have sent me.
I have made your name known to them
and will continue to make it known,
so that the love with which you loved me may be in them,
and so that I may be in them.'
This is the Gospel of the Lord.

PROFESSION OF FAITH — *pages 15-16*

PRAYER OVER THE GIFTS

Lord,
accept the prayers and gifts
we offer in faith and love.
May this eucharist
bring us to your glory.

PREFACE OF THE ASCENSION II

Father, all-powerful and ever-living God,
we do well always and everywhere to give you thanks
through Jesus Christ our Lord.

In his risen body he plainly showed himself to his disciples
and was taken up to heaven in their sight
to claim for us a share in his divine life.

And so, with all the choirs of angels in heaven
we proclaim your glory
and join in their unending hymn of praise:

Holy, holy, holy...

COMMUNION ANTIPHON   *(Jn 17:22)*
**This is the prayer of Jesus: that his believers may become one
as he is one with the Father, alleluia.**

PRAYER AFTER COMMUNION

God our Saviour, hear us,
and through this holy mystery give us hope
that the glory you have given Christ
will be given to the Church, his body,
for he is Lord for ever and ever.

SOLEMN BLESSING — *page 56*

REFLECTION

> Like Jesus, Stephen dies forgiving those responsible for his
> death. Like Jesus also, who died rather than renounce what he
> had spent his life preaching and teaching, Stephen bears
> witness to what he believed by his death. This is the root
> meaning of the word martyr. He was prepared to give his life
> to indicate how firmly he believed in Jesus. For those who
> were looking on it was a powerful statement of how Jesus is.

=========== 30 MAY ===========

PENTECOST SUNDAY
VIGIL MASS

The feast of Pentecost was originally a Jewish harvest feast
celebrating the first fruits of the season. In our celebration this
evening we rejoice at the outpouring of the Spirit on the Church
which is a celebration of the first fruits of the Easter season.

ENTRANCE ANTIPHON   *(cf Rm 5:5; 8:11)*

**The love of God has been poured into our hearts by his Spirit
living in us, alleluia.**

GREETING, PENITENTIAL RITE, GLORIA — *pages 7-14*

OPENING PRAYER

Let us pray
    [that the Holy Spirit
    may bring peace and unity to all humankind]

Almighty and ever-living God,
you fulfilled the Easter promise
by sending us your Holy Spirit.
May that Spirit unite the races and nations on earth
to proclaim your glory.

or

God our Father,
you have given us new birth.
Strengthen us with your Holy Spirit
and fill us with your light.

or

Let us pray
       [that the flame of the Spirit will descend upon us]

Father in heaven,
fifty days have celebrated the fullness
of the mystery of your revealed love.

See your people gathered in prayer,
open to receive the Spirit's flame.
May it come to rest in our hearts
and dispense the divisions of word and tongue.
With one voice and one song
may we praise your name in joy and thanksgiving.

FIRST READING   *(Gen 11:1-9)*
A reading from the book of Genesis.

It was named Babel because there the language of the whole earth was confused.

Throughout the earth men spoke the same language, with the same vocabulary. Now as they moved eastwards they found a plain in the land of Shinar where they settled. They said to one another, "Come, let us make bricks and bake them in the fire." — For stone they used bricks, and for mortar they used bitumen. — 'Come,' they said, 'let us build ourselves a town and a tower with its top reaching heaven. Let us make a name for ourselves, so that we may not be scattered about the whole earth.'

Now the Lord came down to see the town and the tower that the sons of man had built. 'So they are all a single people with a single language!' said the Lord. 'This is but the start of their undertakings! There will be nothing too hard for them to do. Come, let us go down and confuse their language on the spot so that they can no longer understand one another.' The Lord scattered them thence over the whole face of the earth, and they stopped building the town. It was named Babel therefore, because there the Lord confused the language of the whole earth. It was from there that the Lord scattered them over the whole face of the earth.

This is the word of the Lord.

RESPONSORIAL PSALM *(Ps 103:1-2.24.27-30.35)*

℟ **Send forth your Spirit, O Lord,**
   and renew the face of the earth.

or **Alleluia!**

1. Bless the Lord, my soul!
   Lord God, how great you are,
   clothed in majesty and glory,
   wrapped in light as in a robe! ℟

2. How many are your works, O Lord!
   In wisdom you have made them all.
   The earth is full of your riches.
   Bless the Lord, my soul. ℟

3. All of these look to you
   to give them their food in due season.
   You give it, they gather it up:
   you open your hand, they have their fill. ℟

4. You take back your spirit, they die,
   returning to the dust from which they came.
   You send forth your spirit, they are created;
   and you renew the face of the earth. ℟

SECOND READING *(Rom 8:22-27)*

A reading from the letter of St Paul to the Romans.

The Spirit himself expresses our plea in a way that could never be put into words.

From the beginning till now the entire creation, as we know, has been groaning in one great act of giving birth; and not only creation, but all of us who possess the first-fruits of the Spirit, we too groan inwardly as we wait for our bodies to be set free. For we must be content to hope that we shall be saved — our salvation is not in sight, we should not have to be hoping for it if it were — but, as I say, we must hope to be saved since we are not saved yet — it is something we must wait for with patience.

   The Spirit too comes to help us in our weakness. For when we cannot choose words in order to pray properly, the Spirit himself expresses our plea in a way that could never be put into words, and God who knows everything in our hearts knows perfectly well what he means, and that the pleas of the saints expressed by the Spirit are according to the mind of God.

   This is the word of the Lord.

GOSPEL ACCLAMATION

Alleluia, alleluia!
Come, Holy Spirit, fill the hearts of your faithful,
and kindle in them the fire of your love. Alleluia!

GOSPEL   *(Jn 7:37-39)*

A reading from the holy Gospel according to John.

From his breast shall flow fountains of living water.

On the last day and greatest day of the festival, Jesus stood there
and cried out:

'If any man is thirsty, let him come to me!
Let the man come and drink who believes in me!'

As scripture says: From his breast shall flow fountains of living water.

He was speaking of the Spirit which those who believed in
him were to receive; for there was no Spirit as yet because Jesus
had not yet been glorified.

This is the Gospel of the Lord.

PROFESSION OF FAITH — *pages 15-16*

PRAYER OVER THE GIFTS

Lord,
Send your Spirit on these gifts
and through them help the Church you love
to show your salvation to all the world.

PREFACE OF PENTECOST — *page 250*

COMMUNION ANTIPHON   *(Jn 7:37)*

On the last day of the festival, Jesus stood and cried aloud: If
anyone is thirsty, let him come to me and drink, alleluia.

PRAYER AFTER COMMUNION

Lord, through this eucharist,
send the Holy Spirit of Pentecost into our hearts
to keep us always in your love.

SOLEMN BLESSING — *page 250*

REFLECTION

At times in our life we are aware of God's presence with us and
among us. At other times it is the absence of God which seems
to dominate our conscious moments. At one point in time the
Israelites rejoiced in their covenant with God, at another they
had to face the crisis of exile. The Holy One, blessed be he, is
forever with us through his Spirit.

MASS DURING THE DAY

In the Jewish calendar there was a tradition of celebrating the
fiftieth day after Passover, which they called Pentecost. Today
the Christian Church reaches the fiftieth and final day of the
Easter season when we commemorate the gift of the Holy Spirit.
In the scriptures the Spirit is also known as 'the Spirit of the
promise', 'the Spirit of adoption', 'the Spirit of the Lord', 'the
Spirit of Christ', 'the Spirit of God' and 'the Spirit of Glory'.

ENTRANCE ANTIPHON   *(Wis 1:7)*

**The Spirit of the Lord fills the whole world. It holds all things
together and knows every word spoken by man, alleluia.**
or
**The love of God has been poured into our hearts by his Spirit
living in us, alleluia.**

GREETING, PENITENTIAL RITE, GLORIA — *pages 7-14*

OPENING PRAYER

Let us pray
    [that the Spirit will work through our lives
    to bring Christ to the world]
God our Father,
let the Spirit you sent on your Church
to begin the teaching of the gospel
continue to work in the world
through the hearts of all who believe.
or
Let us pray
    [in the Spirit who dwells within us]
Father of light, from whom every good gift comes,
send your Spirit into our lives
with the power of a mighty wind,
and by the flame of your wisdom
open the horizons of our minds.

Loosen our tongues to sing your praise
in words beyond the power of speech,
for without your Spirit
man could never raise his voice in words of peace
or announce the truth that Jesus is Lord,
who lives and reigns with you and the Holy Spirit
one God, for ever and ever.

FIRST READING   *(Acts 2:1-11)*

A reading from the Acts of the Apostles.

They were all filled with the Holy Spirit and began to speak.

When Pentecost day came round, the apostles had all met in one room, when suddenly they heard what sounded like a powerful wind from heaven, the noise of which filled the entire house in which they were sitting; and something appeared to them that seemed like tongues of fire; these separated and came to rest on the head of each of them. They were all filled with the Holy Spirit, and began to speak foreign languages as the Spirit gave them the gift of speech.

Now there were devout men living in Jerusalem from every nation under heaven, and at this sound they all assembled, each one bewildered to hear these men speaking his own language. They were amazed and astonished. 'Surely' they said 'all these men speaking are Galileans? How does it happen that each of us hears them in his own native language? Parthians, Medes and Elamites; people from Mesopotamia, Judaea and Cappadocia, Pontus and Asia, Phrygia and Pamphylia, Egypt and the parts of Libya round Cyrene; as well as visitors from Rome — Jews and proselytes alike — Cretans and Arabs; we hear them preaching in our own language about the marvels of God.'

This is the word of the Lord.

RESPONSORIAL PSALM   *(Ps 103:1.24.29-31.34)*

℟ **Send forth your Spirit, O Lord,**
   and renew the face of the earth.

or **Alleluia!**

1. Bless the Lord, my soul!
    Lord God, how great you are,
    How many are your works, O Lord!
    The earth is full of your riches. ℟

2. You take back your spirit, they die,
    returning to the dust from which they came.
    You send forth your spirit, they are created;
    and you renew the face of the earth. ℟

3. May the glory of the Lord last for ever!
    May the Lord rejoice in his works!
    May my thoughts be pleasing to him.
    I find my joy in the Lord. ℟

SECOND READING   (Rm 8:8-17)

A reading from the letter of St Paul to the Romans.

Everyone moved by the Spirit is a son of God.

People who are interested only in unspiritual things can never be pleasing to God. Your interests, however, are not in the unspiritual, but in the spiritual, since the Spirit of God has made his home in you. In fact, unless you possessed the Spirit of Christ you would not belong to him. Though your body may be dead it is because of sin, but if Christ is in you then your spirit is life itself because you have been justified; and if the Spirit of him who raised Jesus from the dead is living in you, then he who raised Jesus from the dead will give life to your own mortal bodies through his Spirit living in you.

So then, my brothers, there is no necessity for us to obey our unspiritual selves or to live unspiritual lives. If you do live in that way, you are doomed to die; but if by the Spirit you put an end to the misdeeds of the body you will live.

Everyone moved by the Spirit is a son of God. The spirit you received is not the spirit of slaves bringing fear into your lives again; it is the spirit of sons, and it makes us cry out, 'Abba, Father!' The Spirit himself and our spirit bear united witness that we are children of God. And if we are children we are heirs as well: heirs of God and coheirs with Christ, sharing his sufferings so as to share his glory.

This is the word of the Lord.

(The following Second Reading of Year A, 1 Cor 12:3-7.12-13, may be used instead of the above.)

A reading from the first letter of St Paul to the Corinthians.

In the one Spirit we were all baptised.

No one can say, 'Jesus is Lord' unless he is under the influence of the Holy Spirit.

There is a variety of gifts but always the same Spirit; there are all sorts of service to be done, but always to the same Lord; working in all sorts of different ways in different people, it is the same God who is working in all of them. The particular way in which the Spirit is given to each person is for a good purpose.

Just as a human body, though it is made up of many parts, is a single unit because all these parts, though many, make one body, so it is with Christ. In the one Spirit we were all baptised, Jews as well as Greeks, slaves as well as citizens, and one Spirit was given to us all to drink.

This is the word of the Lord.

SEQUENCE
(The sequence may be said or sung.)
Holy Spirit, Lord of light,
From the clear celestial height
Thy pure beaming radiance give.

Come, thou Father of the poor,
Come with treasures which endure;
Come, thou light of all that live!

Thou, of all consolers best,
Thou, the soul's delightful guest,
Dost refreshing peace bestow.

Thou in toil art comfort sweet;
Pleasant coolness in the heat;
Solace in the midst of woe.

Light immortal, light divine,
Visit thou these hearts of thine,
And our inmost being fill:

If thou take thy grace away,
Nothing pure in man will stay;
All his good is turned to ill.

Heal our wounds, our strength renew;
On our dryness pour thy dew;
Wash the stains of guilt away:

Bend the stubborn heart and will;
Melt the frozen, warm the chill;
Guide the steps that go astray.

Thou, on us who evermore
Thee confess and thee adore,
With thy sevenfold gifts descend:

Give us comfort when we die;
Give us life with thee on high;
Give us joys that never end.

GOSPEL ACCLAMATION
Alleluia, alleluia!
Come, Holy Spirit, fill the hearts of your faithful,
and kindle in them the fire of your love.
Alleluia!

GOSPEL   *(Jn 14:15-16.23-26)*
A reading from the holy Gospel according to John.
The Holy Spirit will teach you everything.

Jesus said to his disciples:

'If you love me you will keep my commandments.
I shall ask the Father
and he will give you another Advocate
to be with you for ever.
'If anyone loves me he will keep my word,
and my Father will love him,
and we shall come to him
and make our home with him.
Those who do not love me do not keep my words.
And my word is not my own;
it is the word of the one who sent me.
I have said these things to you
while still with you;
but the Advocate, the Holy Spirit,
whom the Father will send in my name,
will teach you everything
and remind you of all I have said to you.
This is the Gospel of the Lord.

(The following Gospel of Year A, Jn 20:19-23, may be used instead of the above.)

A reading from the holy Gospel according to John.

As the Father sent me, so am I sending you: receive the Holy Spirit.

In the evening of the first day of the week, the doors were closed in the room where the disciples were, for fear of the Jews. Jesus came and stood among them. He said to them, 'Peace be with you,' and showed them his hands and his side. The disciples were filled with joy when they saw the Lord, and he said to them again, 'Peace be with you'.

'As the Father sent me,
so am I sending you.'

After saying this he breathed on them and said:

'Receive the Holy Spirit.
For those whose sins you forgive,
they are forgiven;
for those whose sins you retain,
they are retained.'
This is the Gospel of the Lord

PROFESSION OF FAITH — *pages 15-16*

PRAYER OVER THE GIFTS

Lord, may the Spirit you promised
lead us into all truth
and reveal to us the full meaning of this sacrifice.

PREFACE OF PENTECOST

Father, all-powerful and ever-living God,
we do well always and everywhere to give you thanks.

Today you sent the Holy Spirit
on those marked out to be your children
by sharing the life of your only Son,
and so you brought the paschal mystery to its completion.

Today we celebrate the great beginning of your Church
when the Holy Spirit made known to all peoples the one true God,
and created from the many languages of man
one voice to profess one faith.

The joy of the resurrection renews the whole world,
while the choirs of heaven sing for ever to your glory:
Holy, holy, holy...

COMMUNION ANTIPHON   *(Ac 2:4.11)*

**They were all filled with the Holy Spirit, and they spoke of the
great things God had done, alleluia.**

PRAYER AFTER COMMUNION

Father, may the food we receive in the eucharist
help our eternal redemption.
Keep within us the vigour of your Spirit
and protect the gifts you have given to your Church.

SOLEMN BLESSING

[This day] the Father of light
has enlightened the minds of the disciples
by the out pouring of the Holy Spirit.
May he bless you
and give you the gifts of the Spirit for ever. **Amen.**

May that fire which hovered over the disciples
as tongues of flame
burn out all evil from our hearts
and make them glow with pure light. **Amen.**

God inspired speech in different tongues
to proclaim one faith.
May he strengthen your faith
and fulfil your hope of seeing him face to face. **Amen.**

May almighty God bless you,
the Father, and the Son, ✠ and the Holy Spirit. **Amen.**

REFLECTION

The Church is the Body of Christ and the Temple of the Holy
Spirit. The mission of Christ and of the Spirit and now also of
the Church is to bring humankind to share in the communion
which Father, Son and Spirit share. It is the Spirit who makes present
the mystery of Christ, particularly at the Eucharist in order to
reconcile humanity and to bring them into relationship with God.

═══════════════ 6 JUNE ═══════════════

THE MOST HOLY TRINITY

One of the most profound and unsearchable mysteries of
Christianity is the mystery of the Trinity. It is a mystery which
was revealed over time, in the pages of the Hebrew Scriptures
which we sometimes call the Old Testament and in the life, death
and resurrection of Jesus of Nazareth. It is Christianity's answer
to the question: who is God? In the New Testament there is
evidence that first two and then three persons were proclaimed
as being part of God. This belief was given fuller elaboration in
the following centuries. God is three yet God is one.

ENTRANCE ANTIPHON

**Blessed be God the Father and his only-begotten Son and the
Holy Spirit: for he has shown that he loves us.**

GREETING, PENITENTIAL RITE, GLORIA — *pages 7-14*

OPENING PRAYER

Let us pray

[to the one God, Father, Son and Spirit,
that our lives may bear witness to our faith]

Father, you sent your Word to bring us truth
and your Spirit to make us holy.
Through them we come to know the mystery of your life.
Help us to worship you, one God in three Persons,
by proclaiming and living our faith in you.

or

Let us pray

[to our God who is Father, Son, and Holy Spirit]

God, we praise you:
Father all-powerful, Christ Lord and Saviour, Spirit of love.
You reveal yourself in the depths of our being,
drawing us to share in your life and your love.
One God, three Persons,
be near to the people formed in your image,
close to the world your love brings to life.

FIRST READING   *(Pr 8:22-31)*

A reading from the book of Proverbs.

Before the earth came into being, Wisdom was born.

The Wisdom of God cries aloud:

> The Lord created me when his purpose first unfolded,
> before the oldest of his works.
> From everlasting I was firmly set,
> from the beginning, before earth came into being.
> The deep was not, when I was born,
> there were no springs to gush with water.
> Before the mountains were settled,
> before the hills, I came to birth;
> before he made the earth, the countryside,
> or the first grains of the world's dust.
> When he fixed the heavens firm, I was there,
> when he drew a ring on the surface of the deep,
> when he thickened the clouds above,
> when he fixed fast the springs of the deep,
> when he assigned the sea its boundaries
> — and the waters will not invade the shore —
> when he laid down the foundations of the earth,
> I was by his side, a master craftsman,
> delighting him day after day,
> ever at play in his presence,
> at play everywhere in his world,
> delighting to be with the sons of men.

This is the word of the Lord.

RESPONSORIAL PSALM   *(Ps 8:4-9)*

℟ **How great is your name, O Lord our God,
   through all the earth!**

1. When I see the heavens, the work of your hands,
    the moon and the stars which you arranged,
    what is man that you should keep him in mind,
    mortal man that you care for him? ℟

2. Yet you have made him little less than a god;
    with glory and honour you crowned him,
    gave him power over the works of your hand,
    put all things under his feet. ℞

3. All of them, sheep and cattle,
    yes, even the savage beasts,
    birds of the air, and fish
    that make their way through the waters. ℞

SECOND READING   *(Rm 5:1-5)*

A reading from the letter of St Paul to the Romans.

To God, through Christ, in the love poured out by the Spirit.

Through our Lord Jesus Christ, by faith we are judged righteous
and at peace with God, since it is by faith and through Jesus that
we have entered this state of grace in which we can boast about
looking forward to God's glory. But that is not all we can boast
about; we can boast about our sufferings. These sufferings bring
patience, as we know, and patience brings perseverance, and
perseverance brings hope, and this hope is not deceptive,
because the love of God has been poured into our hearts by the
Holy Spirit which has been given us.

    This is the word of the Lord.

GOSPEL ACCLAMATION   *(Rev 1:8)*

Alleluia, alleluia!
Glory be to the Father, and to the Son, and to the Holy Spirit,
the God who is, who was, and who is to come. Alleluia!

GOSPEL   *(Jn 16:12-15)*

A reading from the holy Gospel according to John.

Everything the Father has is mine: all the Spirit tells you will be taken
from what is mine.

Jesus said to his disciples:

    'I still have many things to say to you
    but they would be too much for you now.
    But when the Spirit of truth comes
    he will lead you to the complete truth,
    since he will not be speaking as from himself
    but will say only what he has learnt;
    and he will tell you of the things to come.
    He will glorify me
    since all he tells you
    will be taken from what is mine.
    Everything the Father has is mine;

that is why I said:
All he tells you
will be taken from what is mine.'
This is the Gospel of the Lord.

PROFESSION OF FAITH — *pages 15-16*

PRAYER OVER THE GIFTS
Lord our God,
make these gifts holy,
and through them
make us a perfect offering to you.

PREFACE OF THE HOLY TRINITY
Father, all-powerful and ever-living God,
we do well always and everywhere to give you thanks.

We joyfully proclaim our faith
in the mystery of your Godhead.
You have revealed your glory
as the glory also of your Son
and of the Holy Spirit:
three Persons equal in majesty,
undivided in splendour,
yet one Lord, one God,
ever to be adored in your everlasting glory.

And so, with all the choirs of angels in heaven
we proclaim your glory
and join in their unending hymn of praise:
Holy, holy, holy...

COMMUNION ANTIPHON   *(Gal 4:6)*
**You are the sons of God, so God has given you the Spirit of
his Son to form your hearts and make you cry out: Abba, Father.**

PRAYER AFTER COMMUNION
Lord God,
we worship you, a Trinity of Persons, one eternal God.
May our faith and the sacrament we receive
bring us health of mind and body.

REFLECTION
God has been addressed as Father, Son and Spirit from the
time of the apostles even before the implications of this belief
were worked out in formal doctrines. As time went on, the Church
understood its own faith in this mystery by degrees, culminating
in the formulas of the Fourth Century, especially the Nicene

Creed which we profess at Mass on Sundays. The short prayer
'In the name of the Father and of the Son and of the Holy Spirit.
Amen,' is one of the richest of the Church's treasury of prayer.

───────────── **10 JUNE** ─────────────

THE BODY AND BLOOD OF CHRIST
(CORPUS CHRISTI)
(Celebrated in Ireland and Scotland next Sunday – 13 June)

Since the Fourteenth Century the Church of the West has celebrated
this feast in every place where she is established. It commemorates
the institution of the Body and Blood of the Lord in the Eucharist
and so it is closely linked with Holy Thursday. It was felt that
other elements of the celebration of the Easter Triduum tended
to obscure the aspect of the Eucharist. Therefore it was considered
that a special day outside the Easter season in which the focus
would be on this aspect would be useful. And so today's feast.

ENTRANCE ANTIPHON   *(Ps 80:17)*
**The Lord fed his people with the finest wheat and honey;
their hunger was satisfied.**

GREETING, PENITENTIAL RITE, GLORIA — *pages 7-14*

OPENING PRAYER
Let us pray
   [to the Lord who gives himself in the eucharist,
    that this sacrament may bring us salvation and peace]

Lord Jesus Christ,
you gave us the eucharist
as the memorial of your suffering and death.
May our worship of this sacrament of your body and blood
help us to experience the salvation you won for us
and the peace of the kingdom
where you live with the Father and the Holy Spirit,
one God, for ever and ever.
or
Let us pray
   [for the willingness to make present in our world
    the love of Christ shown to us in the eucharist]

Lord Jesus Christ,
we worship you living among us
in the sacrament of your body and blood.

May we offer to our Father in heaven
a solemn pledge of undivided love.
May we offer to our brothers and sisters
a life poured out in loving service of that kingdom
where you live with the Father and the Holy Spirit,
one God, for ever and ever.

FIRST READING   *(Gen 14:18-20)*

A reading from the book of Genesis.

He brought bread and wine.

Melchizedek king of Salem brought bread and wine; he was a
priest of God Most High. He pronounced this blessing:

> 'Blessed be Abraham by God Most High, creator of heaven
>   and earth,
> and blessed be God Most High for handing over your
>   enemies to you.'

And Abraham gave him a tithe of everything.

> This is the word of the Lord.

RESPONSORIAL PSALM   *(Ps 109:1-4)*

℟   **You are a priest for ever,**
     a priest like Melchizedek of old.

1.   The Lord's revelation to my Master:
     'Sit on my right:
     I will put your foes beneath your feet.' ℟

2.   The Lord will send from Zion
     your sceptre of power:
     rule in the midst of all your foes. ℟

3.   A prince from the day of your birth
     on the holy mountains;
     from the womb before the daybreak I begot you. ℟

4.   The Lord has sworn an oath he will not change.
     'You are a priest for ever,
     a priest like Melchizedek of old.' ℟

SECOND READING   *(1 Cor 11:23-26)*

A reading from the first letter of St Paul to the Corinthians.

Every time you eat this bread and drink this cup, you are proclaiming
the Lord's death.

This is what I received from the Lord, and in turn passed on to
you: that on the same night that he was betrayed, the Lord Jesus
took some bread, and thanked God for it and broke it, and he

said, 'This is my body, which is for you; do this as a memorial of me.' In the same way he took the cup after supper, and said, 'This cup is the new covenant in my blood. Whenever you drink it, do this as a memorial of me.' Until the Lord comes, therefore, every time you eat this bread and drink this cup, you are proclaiming his death.

This is the word of the Lord.

SEQUENCE (*Shorter Form*)
(*The* Sequence *may be said or sung.*)

Behold the bread of angels, sent
For pilgrims in their banishment,
The bread for God's true children meant,
    That may not unto dogs be given:

Oft in the olden types foreshadowed;
In Isaac on the altar bowed,
And in the ancient paschal food,
    And in the manna sent from heaven.

Come then, good shepherd, bread divine,
Still show to us thy mercy sign;
Oh, feed us still, still keep us thine;
So may we see thy glories shine
    In fields of immortality;

O thou, the wisest, mightiest, best,
Our present food, our future rest,
Come, make us each thy chosen guest,
Co-heirs of thine, and comrades blest
    With saints whose dwelling is with thee.

GOSPEL ACCLAMATION   (*Jn 6:51-52*)

Allelluia, alleluia!
I am the living bread which has come down from heaven,
says the Lord.
Anyone who eats this bread will live for ever. Alleluia!

GOSPEL   (*Lk 9:11-17*)

A reading from the Holy Gospel according to Luke.

They all ate as much as they wanted.

Jesus made the crowds welcome and talked to them about the kingdom of God; and he cured those who were in need of healing.

It was late afternoon when the Twelve came to him and said, 'Send the people away, and they can go to the villages and farms round about to find lodging and food; for we are in a lonely

place here.' He replied, 'Give them something to eat yourselves.'
But they said, 'We have no more than five loaves and two fish,
unless we are to go ourselves and buy food for all these people.'
For there were about five thousand men. But he said to his
disciples, 'Get them to sit down in parties of about fifty.' They
did so and made them all sit down. Then he took the five loaves
and the two fish, raised his eyes to heaven, and said the blessing
over them; then he broke them and handed them to his
disciples to distribute among the crowd. They all ate as much as
they wanted, and when the scraps remaining were collected they
filled twelve baskets.

This is the Gospel of the Lord.

PROFESSION OF FAITH — *pages 15-16*

PRAYER OVER THE GIFTS

Lord,
may the bread and cup we offer
bring your Church the unity and peace they signify.

PREFACE OF THE HOLY EUCHARIST I

Father, all-powerful and ever-living God,
we do well always and everywhere to give you thanks
through Jesus Christ our Lord.

He is the true and eternal priest
who established this unending sacrifice.
He offered himself as a victim for our deliverance
and taught us to make this offering in his memory.
As we eat his body which he gave for us,
we grow in strength.
As we drink his blood which he poured out for us,
we are washed clean.

Now, with angels and archangels,
and the whole company of heaven,
we sing the unending hymn of your praise:

Holy, holy, holy...

COMMUNION ANTIPHON   *(Jn 6:57)*

**Whoever eats my flesh and drinks my blood will live in me
and I in him, says the Lord.**

PRAYER AFTER COMMUNION

Lord Jesus Christ,
you give us your body and blood in the eucharist

as a sign that even now we share your life.
May we come to possess it completely in the kingdom
where you live for ever and ever.

REFLECTION

The Church has reserved the consecrated bread and
occasionally wine in a tabernacle from the earliest times.
Today theological concerns tend to link the reserved sacrament
more closely with the celebration of the Eucharist. At the last
supper, Jesus took, blessed, broke and gave the bread to his
disciples to eat. Similarly with the wine. Reserving the
sacrament enables the Church to give the sacred gifts for the
communion of those who are sick and also allows the Church
to worship Jesus in the Blessed Sacrament.

<hr>

═══ 13 JUNE ═══
11th SUNDAY IN ORDINARY TIME

Today we resume the reading of the gospel of Luke which we
had been hearing until the first Sunday of Lent. We shall
continue with it for the next five and a half months until the
end of November. We hear it thus read every three years. It is a
gospel with unique appeal which has delighted artists, poets,
musicians and ordinary folk throughout the ages. Dante called
Luke 'the scribe of Christ's gentleness'. It is through his eyes
that Jesus will be made real for us over the coming months.

ENTRANCE ANTIPHON   *(Ps 26:7.9)*

**Lord, hear my voice when I call to you. You are my help; do
not cast me off, do not desert me, my Saviour God.**

GREETING, PENITENTIAL RITE, GLORIA — *pages 7-14*

OPENING PRAYER

Let us pray

[for the grace to follow Christ more closely]

Almighty God,
our hope and our strength,
without you we falter.
Help us to follow Christ
and to live according to your will.

or

Let us pray
    [to the Father whose love gives us strength to follow his Son]
God our Father,
we rejoice in the faith that draws us together,
aware that selfishness can drive us apart.
Let your encouragement be our constant strength.
Keep us one in the love that has sealed our lives,
help us to live as one family
the gospel we profess.

FIRST READING   (2 S 12:7-10.13)

A reading from the second book of Samuel.

The Lord forgives your sin; you are not to die.

Nathan said to David, 'The Lord the God of Israel says this, "I
anointed you king over Israel; I delivered you from the hands of
Saul; I gave you your master's house to you, his wives into your arms;
I gave you the House of Israel and of Judah; and if this were not
enough, I would add as much again for you. Why have you shown
contempt for the Lord, doing what displeases him? You have
struck down Uriah the Hittite with the sword, taken his wife for
your own, and killed him with the sword of the Ammonites. So
now the sword will never be far from your House, since you
have shown contempt for me and taken the wife of Uriah the
Hittite to be your wife." '

    David said to Nathan, 'I have sinned against the Lord.' Then
Nathan said to David, 'The Lord, for his part, forgives your sin;
you are not to die.'

    This is the word of the Lord.

RESPONSORIAL PSALM   (Ps 31:1-2.5.7.11)

℟   **Forgive, Lord, the guilt of my sin.**

1.   Happy the man whose offence is forgiven
     whose sin is remitted.
     O happy the man to whom the Lord
     imputes no guilt,
     in whose spirit is no guile. ℟

2.   But now I have acknowledged my sins:
     my guilt I did not hide.
     I said: 'I will confess
     my offence to the Lord.'
     And you, Lord, have forgiven
     the guilt of my sin. ℟

3. You are my hiding place, O Lord;
    you save me from distress.
    You surround me with cries of deliverance. ℟

4. Rejoice, rejoice in the Lord,
    exult, you just!
    O come, ring out your joy,
    all you upright of heart. ℟

SECOND READING   *(Gal 2:16.19-21)*

A reading from the letter of St Paul to the Galatians.

I live now, not with my own life but with the life of Christ who lives in me.

We acknowledge that what makes a man righteous is not obedience to the Law, but faith in Jesus Christ. We had to become believers in Christ Jesus no less than you had, and now we hold that faith in Christ rather than fidelity to the Law is what justifies us, and that no one can be justified by keeping the Law. In other words, through the Law I am dead to the Law, so that now I can live for God. I have been crucified with Christ, and I live now not with my own life but with the life of Christ who lives in me. The life I now live in this body I live in faith: faith in the Son of God who loved me and who sacrificed himself for my sake. I cannot bring myself to give up God's gift: if the Law can justify us, there is no point in the death of Christ.

    This is the word of the Lord.

GOSPEL ACCLAMATION   *(Jn 14:6)*

Alleluia, alleluia!
I am the Way, the Truth and the Life, says the Lord;
no one can come to the Father except through me.
Alleluia!

or   *(1 Jn 4:10)*

Alleluia, alleluia!
God so loved us when he sent his Son
to be the sacrifice that takes our sins away.
Alleluia!

GOSPEL   *(Lk 7:36-8:3)*

(For Shorter Form, read between ♦ ◀)

A reading from the holy Gospel according to Luke.

Her many sins have been forgiven, or she would not have shown such great love.

♦One of the Pharisees invited Jesus to a meal. When he arrived at the Pharisee's house and took his place at table, a woman came in, who had a bad name in the town. She had heard he was dining with the Pharisee and had brought with her an alabaster jar of ointment. She waited behind him at his feet, weeping, and her tears fell on his feet, and she wiped them away with her hair; then she covered his feet with kisses and anointed them with the ointment.

When the Pharisee who had invited him saw this, he said to himself, 'If this man were a prophet, he would know who this woman is that is touching him and what a bad name she has.' Then Jesus took him up and said, 'Simon, I have something to say to you.' 'Speak, Master,' was the reply. 'There was once a creditor who had two men in his debt; one owed him five hundred denarii, the other fifty. They were unable to pay, so he pardoned them both. Which of them will love him more?' 'The one who was pardoned more, I suppose,' answered Simon. Jesus said, 'You are right.'

Then he turned to the woman. 'Simon', he said, 'you see this woman? I came into your house, and you poured no water over my feet, but she has poured out her tears over my feet and wiped them away with her hair. You gave me no kiss, but she has been covering my feet with kisses ever since I came in. You did not anoint my head with oil, but she has anointed my feet with ointment. For this reason I tell you that her sins, her many sins, must have been forgiven her, or she would not have shown such great love. It is the man who is forgiven little who shows little love.' Then he said to her, 'Your sins are forgiven.' Those who were with him at table began to say to themselves, 'Who is this man, that he even forgives sins?' But he said to the woman, 'Your faith has saved you; go in peace.'◄

Now after this he made his way through towns and villages, preaching, and proclaiming the Good News of the kingdom of God. With him went the Twelve, as well as certain women who had been cured of evil spirits and ailments: Mary surnamed the Magdalene, from whom seven demons had gone out, Joanna the wife of Herod's steward Chuza, Susanna, and several others who provided for them out of their own resources.

◄This is the Gospel of the Lord.◄

PROFESSION OF FAITH — *pages 15-16*

PRAYER OVER THE GIFTS
Lord God, in this bread and wine
you give us food for body and spirit.
May the eucharist renew our strength
and bring us health of mind and body.

PREFACE OF SUNDAYS IN ORDINARY TIME — *pages 22-25*

COMMUNION ANTIPHON   *(Ps 26:4)*

One thing I seek: to dwell in the house of the Lord all the days of my life.

or   *(Jn 17:11)*

Father, keep in your name those you have given me, that they may be one as we are one, says the Lord.

PRAYER AFTER COMMUNION

Lord, may this eucharist
accomplish in your Church
the unity and peace it signifies.

SOLEMN BLESSING — *pages 57-58*

REFLECTION

> Luke's gospel is the gospel of mercy and compassion. Its aim is to show how the life of Jesus is extended and paralleled in the life of the Church. The author's aim is to show that the life, destiny and teaching of Jesus is the pattern for the Christian community.

======= 20 JUNE =======

12th SUNDAY IN ORDINARY TIME

> Luke's gospel has been described as the gospel of the Holy Spirit. In its pages the Spirit is presented as working in human beings and bringing about salvation. Salvation already exists where people treat one another according to the values of the Kingdom of God: justice, truth, mercy, respect, love and peace, to name but a few.

ENTRANCE ANTIPHON   *(Ps 27:8-9)*

God is the strength of his people. In him, we his chosen live in safety. Save us, Lord, who share in your life, and give us your blessing; be our shepherd for ever.

GREETING, PENITENTIAL RITE, GLORIA — *pages 7-14*

OPENING PRAYER

Let us pray
    [that we may grow in the love of God]

Father, guide and protector of your people,
grant us an unfailing respect for your name,
and keep us always in your love.

or

Let us pray
    [to God whose fatherly love keeps us safe]
God of the universe,
we worship you as Lord.
God, ever close to us,
we rejoice to call you Father.
From this world's uncertainty we look to your covenant.
Keep us one in your peace, secure in your love.

FIRST READING   (Zc 12:10-11; 13:1)

A reading from the prophet Zechariah.

They will look on the one whom they have pierced.

It is the Lord who speaks: 'Over the House of David and the
citizens of Jerusalem I will pour out a spirit of kindness and
prayer. They will look on the one whom they have pierced; they
will mourn for him as for an only son, and weep for him as
people weep for a first-born child. When that day comes, there
will be great mourning in Judah, like the mourning of Hadad-
rimmon in the plain of Megiddo. When that day comes, a
fountain will be opened for the House of David and the citizens
of Jerusalem, for sin and impurity.'

    This is the word of the Lord.

RESPONSORIAL PSALM   (Ps 62:2-6. 8-9)

℞   **For you my soul is thirsting, O God, my God.**

1.   O God, you are my God, for you I long;
     for you my soul is thirsting.
     My body pines for you
     like a dry, weary land without water. ℞

2.   So I gaze on you in the sanctuary
     to see your strength and your glory.
     For your love is better than life,
     my lips will speak your praise. ℞

3.   So I will bless you all my life,
     in your name I will lift up my hands.
     My soul shall be filled as with a banquet,
     my mouth shall praise you with joy. ℞

4.   For you have been my help;
     in the shadow of your wings I rejoice.
     My soul clings to you;
     your right hand holds me fast. ℞

SECOND READING   *(Gal 3:26-29)*

A reading from the letter of St Paul to the Galatians.

All baptised in Christ, you have all clothed yourselves in Christ.

You are, all of you, sons of God through faith in Christ Jesus. All baptised in Christ, you have all clothed yourselves in Christ, and there are no more distinctions between Jew and Greek, slave and free, male and female, but all of you are one in Christ Jesus. Merely by belonging to Christ you are the posterity of Abraham, the heirs he was promised.

This is the word of the Lord.

GOSPEL ACCLAMATION   *(Jn 8:12)*

Alleluia, alleluia!
I am the light of the world, says the Lord,
anyone who follows me
will have the light of life.
Alleluia!
or   *(Jn 10:27)*
Alleluia, alleluia!
The sheep that belong to me listen to my voice,
says the Lord,
I know them and they follow me.
Alleluia!

GOSPEL   *(Lk 9:18-24)*

A reading from the holy Gospel according to Luke.

You are the Christ of God. The Son of Man is destined to suffer grievously.

One day when Jesus was praying alone in the presence of his disciples he put this question to them, 'Who do the crowds say I am?' And they answered, 'John the Baptist; others Elijah; and others say one of the ancient prophets come back to life.' 'But you,' he said 'who do you say I am?' It was Peter who spoke up. 'The Christ of God' he said. But he gave them strict orders not to tell anyone anything about this.

'The Son of Man' he said 'is destined to suffer grievously, to be rejected by the elders and chief priests and scribes and to be put to death, and to be raised up on the third day.'

Then to all he said, 'If anyone wants to be a follower of mine, let him renounce himself and take up his cross every day and follow me. For anyone who wants to save his life will lose it; but anyone who loses his life for my sake, that man will save it.'

This is the Gospel of the Lord.

PROFESSION OF FAITH — *pages 15-16*

PRAYER OVER THE GIFTS
Lord,
receive our offering,
and may this sacrifice of praise
purify us in mind and heart
and make us always eager to serve you.

PREFACE OF SUNDAYS IN ORDINARY TIME — *pages 22-25*

COMMUNION ANTIPHON   (Ps 144:15)
**The eyes of all look to you, O Lord, and you give them food
in due season.**
or   (Jn 10:11.15)
I am the Good Shepherd; I give my life for my sheep, says the Lord.

PRAYER AFTER COMMUNION
Lord,
you give us the body and blood of your Son
to renew your life within us.
In your mercy, assure our redemption
and bring us to the eternal life
we celebrate in this eucharist.

SOLEMN BLESSING — *pages 57-58*

REFLECTION
>   Luke's is the most colourful of all the gospels. His unique genius
>   for characterisation has been well remarked upon. Some of the
>   most memorable people from the time of the Lord come from
>   his pen – Mary (from the stories of Jesus' infancy); the good
>   thief; Zachary, Elizabeth, Zacchaeus, the good Samaritan etc.

27 JUNE
13th SUNDAY IN ORDINARY TIME

Luke is particularly sensitive to people's weakness and he presents them as interacting with a very compassionate Jesus. He portrays Jesus as someone who has a special concern for those who are sick, in trouble and on the margins of respectable society.

ENTRANCE ANTIPHON   *(Ps 46:2)*

All nations, clap your hands. Shout with a voice of joy to God.

GREETING, PENITENTIAL RITE, GLORIA — *pages 7-14*

OPENING PRAYER

Let us pray

[that Christ may be our light]

Father,
you call your children
to walk in the light of Christ.
Free us from darkness
and keep us in the radiance of your truth.

or

Let us pray

[for the strength to reject the darkness of sin]

Father in heaven,
the light of Jesus
has scattered the darkness of hatred and sin.
Called to that light
we ask for your guidance.
Form our lives in your truth, our hearts in your love.

FIRST READING   *(1 K 19:16.19-21)*

A reading from the first book of the Kings.

Elisha rose and followed Elijah.

The Lord said to Elijah: 'Go, you are to anoint Elisha son of Shaphat, of Abel Meholah, as prophet to succeed you.'

Leaving there, Elijah came on Elisha son of Shaphat as he was ploughing behind twelve yoke of oxen, he himself being with the twelfth. Elijah passed near to him and threw his cloak over him. Elisha left his oxen and ran after Elijah. 'Let me kiss my father and mother, then I will follow you' he said. Elijah answered, 'Go, go back; for have I done anything to you?' Elisha turned away, took the pair of oxen and slaughtered them. He used the plough for cooking the oxen, then gave to his men, who ate. He then rose, and followed Elijah and became his servant.

This is the word of the Lord.

RESPONSORIAL PSALM   *(Ps 15:1-2. 5.7-11)*

℞   **O Lord, it is you who are my portion.**

1.   Preserve me, God, I take refuge in you.
     I say to the Lord: 'You are my God.'
     O Lord, it is you who are my portion and cup;
     it is you yourself who are my prize. ℞

2.   I will bless the Lord who gives me counsel,
     who even at night directs my heart.
     I keep the Lord ever in my sight:
     since he is at my right hand, I shall stand firm. ℞

3.   And so my heart rejoices, my soul is glad;
     even my body shall rest in safety.
     For you will not leave my soul among the dead,
     nor let your beloved know decay. ℞

4.   You will show me the path of life,
     the fullness of joy in your presence,
     at your right hand happiness for ever. ℞

SECOND READING   *(Gal 5:1.13-18)*

A reading from the letter of St Paul to the Galatians.
You were called to liberty.

When Christ freed us, he meant us to remain free. Stand firm, therefore, and do not submit again to the yoke of slavery.

My brothers, you were called, as you know, to liberty; but be careful, or this liberty will provide an opening for self-indulgence. Serve one another, rather, in works of love, since the whole of the Law is summarised in a single command: Love your neighbour as yourself. If you go snapping at each other and tearing each other to pieces, you had better watch or you will destroy the whole community.

Let me put it like this: if you are guided by the Spirit you will be in no danger of yielding to self-indulgence, since self-indulgence is the opposite of the Spirit, the Spirit is totally against such a thing, and it is precisely because the two are so opposed that you do not always carry out your good intentions. If you are led by the Spirit, no law can touch you.

This is the word of the Lord.

GOSPEL ACCLAMATION   *(1 S 3:9; Jn 6:68)*
Alleluia, alleluia!
Speak, Lord, your servant is listening:
you have the message of eternal life. Alleluia!

GOSPEL   *(Lk 9:51-62)*
A reading from the holy Gospel according to Luke.

Jesus resolutely took the road for Jerusalem. I will follow you wherever you go.

As the time drew near for him to be taken up to heaven, Jesus resolutely took the road for Jerusalem and sent messengers ahead of him. These set out, and they went into a Samaritan village to make preparations for him, but the people would not receive him because he was making for Jerusalem. Seeing this, the disciples James and John said, 'Lord, do you want us to call down fire from heaven to burn them up?' But he turned and rebuked them, and they went off to another village.

As they travelled along they met a man on the road who said to him, 'I will follow you wherever you go.' Jesus answered, 'Foxes have holes and the birds of the air have nests, but the Son of Man has nowhere to lay his head.'

Another to whom he said, 'Follow me,' replied, 'Let me go and bury my father first.' But he answered, 'Leave the dead to bury their dead; your duty is to go and spread the news of the kingdom of God.'

Another said, 'I will follow you, sir, but first let me go and say good-bye to my people at home.' Jesus said to him, 'Once the hand is laid on the plough, no one who looks back is fit for the kingdom of God.'

This is the Gospel of the Lord.

PROFESSION OF FAITH — *pages 15-16*

PRAYER OVER THE GIFTS
Lord God,
through your sacraments
you give us the power of your grace.
May this eucharist
help us to serve you faithfully.

PREFACE OF SUNDAYS IN ORDINARY TIME — *pages 22-25*

COMMUNION ANTIPHON   *(Ps 102:1)*
O, bless the Lord, my soul, and all that is within me bless his
holy name.

or   *(Jn 17:20-21)*

Father, I pray for them: may they be one in us, so that the world may believe it was you who sent me.

PRAYER AFTER COMMUNION

Lord, may this sacrifice and communion
give us a share in your life
and help us bring your love to the world.

SOLEMN BLESSING — *pages 57-58*

REFLECTION

> The Holy Spirit occupies a prominent place in the gospel of Luke. Jesus is presented as a Spirit filled man. It is the Spirit who is Jesus' guiding light, drawing him into the desert and carrying him through his temptations.
>
> In his gospel the Spirit animates the prayer of Jesus. At Pentecost the fearful disciples are transformed by the Spirit. He implies that the community for which he is writing already has the gift of the Spirit as does this community gathered here today.

---

29 JUNE

STS PETER AND PAUL, APOSTLES

VIGIL MASS

> In the time of Peter and Paul the early Christians celebrated the eucharist in private houses. When numbers became too great they adapted a private house which they called 'the house (of the gathering) of the people.' In the Irish language this sense is maintained in the term *'teach an phobail'*, literally, 'the house of the people'.

ENTRANCE ANTIPHON

Peter the apostle and Paul the teacher of the Gentiles have brought us to know the law of the Lord.

GREETING, PENITENTIAL RITE, GLORIA — *pages 7-14*

OPENING PRAYER

Let us pray
[that the prayers of the apostles will lead us to salvation]
Lord our God,
encourage us through the prayers of Saints Peter and Paul.
May the apostles who strengthened the faith of the infant Church
help us on our way of salvation.

or

Let us pray
> [to be true to the faith
> which has come to us through the apostles Peter and Paul]

Father in heaven,
the light of your revelation brought Peter and Paul
the gift of faith in Jesus your Son.
Through their prayers
may we always give thanks for your life
given us in Christ Jesus,
and for having been enriched by him
in all knowledge and love.

FIRST READING   *(Acts 3:1-10)*

A reading from the Acts of the Apostles.

I will give you what I have: in the name of Jesus stand up and walk!

Once, when Peter and John were going up to the Temple for the prayers at the ninth hour, it happened that there was a man being carried past. He was a cripple from birth; and they used to put him down every day near the Temple entrance called the Beautiful Gate so that he could beg from the people going in. When this man saw Peter and John on their way into the Temple he begged from them. Both Peter and John looked straight at him and said, 'Look at us.' He turned to them expectantly, hoping to get something from them, but Peter said, 'I have neither silver nor gold, but I will give you what I have: in the name of Jesus Christ the Nazarene, walk!' Peter then took him by the hand and helped him to stand up. Instantly his feet and ankles became firm, he jumped up, stood, and began to walk, and he went with them into the Temple, walking and jumping and praising God. Everyone could see him walking and praising God, and they recognised him as the man who used to sit begging at the Beautiful Gate of the Temple. They were all astonished and unable to explain what had happened to him.

This is the word of the Lord.

RESPONSORIAL PSALM   *(Ps 18:2-5)*

℟ **Their word goes forth through all the earth.**

1. The heavens proclaim the glory of God
    and the firmament shows forth the work of his hands.
    Day unto day takes up the story
    and night unto night makes known the message. ℟

(continued)

2.   No speech, no word, no voice is heard
     yet their span extends through all the earth,
     their words to the utmost bounds of the world. ℟

℟   **Their word goes forth through all the earth.**

SECOND READING   *(Gal 1:11-20)*

A reading from the letter of St Paul to the Galatians.

God specially chose me while I was still in my mother's womb.

The Good News I preached is not a human message that I was given
by men, it is something I learnt only through a revelation of Jesus
Christ. You must have heard of my career as a practising Jew,
how merciless I was in persecuting the Church of God, how much
damage I did to it, how I stood out among other Jews of my generation,
and how enthusiastic I was for the traditions of my ancestors.

     Then God, who had specially chosen me while I was still in
my mother's womb, called me through his grace and chose to
reveal his Son to me, so that I might preach the Good News
about him to the pagans. I did not stop to discuss this with any
human being, nor did I go up to Jerusalem to see those who
were already apostles before me, but I went off to Arabia at once
and later went straight back from there to Damascus. Even when
after three years I went up to Jerusalem to visit Cephas and
stayed with him for fifteen days, I did not see any of the other
apostles; I only saw James, the brother of the Lord, and I swear
before God that what I have just written is the literal truth.

     This is the word of the Lord.

GOSPEL ACCLAMATION   *(Jn 21:17)*

Alleluia, alleluia!
Lord, you know everything;
you know I love you.
Alleluia!

GOSPEL   *(Jn 21:15-19)*

A reading from the holy Gospel according to John.

Feed my lambs, feed my sheep.

After Jesus had shown himself to his disciples, and eaten with
them, he said to Simon Peter, 'Simon son of John, do you love
me more than these others do?' He answered, 'Yes, Lord, you
know I love you.' Jesus said to him, 'Feed my lambs,' A second
time he said to him, 'Simon son of John, do you love me?' He
replied, 'Yes, Lord, you know I love you.' Jesus said to him, 'Look
after my sheep.' Then he said to him a third time, 'Simon son of

John, do you love me?' Peter was upset that he asked him the third time, "Do you love me?" and said, 'Lord, you know everything; you know I love you.' Jesus said to him, 'Feed my sheep.

'I tell you most solemnly,
when you were young
you put on your own belt
and walked where you liked;
but when you grow old
you will stretch out your hands,
and somebody else will put a belt round you
and take you where you would rather not go.'

In these words he indicated the kind of death by which Peter would give glory to God. After this he said, 'Follow me.'

This is the Gospel of the Lord.

PROFESSION OF FAITH — *pages 15-16*

PRAYER OVER THE GIFTS

Lord, we present these gifts
on this feast of the apostles Peter and Paul.
Help us to know our own weakness
and to rejoice in your saving power.

PREFACE OF SAINTS PETER AND PAUL — *page 277*

COMMUNION ANTIPHON   *(Jn 21:15.17)*

Simon, son of John, do you love me more than these? Lord, you know all things; you know that I love you.

PRAYER AFTER COMMUNION

Father,
you give us light by the teaching of your apostles.
In this sacrament we have received
fill us with your strength.

SOLEMN BLESSING — *page 277*

REFLECTION

The honouring of saints has its roots in the Jewish background of Christianity. From the Hebrew scriptures it is clear that the Jewish people had a particular respect for the bodies of those who had died. The cult of the saints especially through the veneration of their relics is an important aspect of our Judaeo-Christian heritage.

MASS DURING THE DAY

Peter was a humble fisherman. Paul was an educated theologian as well as a tentmaker and initially a persecutor of 'The Way of Jesus of Nazareth.' Both of them were chosen to carry out complementary roles in the emerging young Church. Both sealed what they taught and believed with their lives as did the one whom they preached.

ENTRANCE ANTIPHON

These men, conquering all human frailty, shed their blood and helped the Church to grow. By sharing the cup of the Lord's suffering, they became the friends of God.

GREETING, PENITENTIAL RITE, GLORIA — *pages 7-14*

OPENING PRAYER

Let us pray
    [that we will remain true to the faith of the apostles]

God our Father,
today you give us the joy
of celebrating the feast of the apostles Peter and Paul.
Through them your Church first received the faith.
Keep us true to their teaching.

or

Let us pray
    [one with Peter and Paul in our faith
    in Christ the Son of the living God]

Praise to you, the God and Father of our Lord Jesus Christ,
who in your great mercy
have given us new birth and hope
through the power of Christ's resurrection.

Through the prayers of the apostles Peter and Paul
may we who receive this faith through their preaching
share their joy in following the Lord
to the unfading inheritance
reserved for us in heaven.

FIRST READING   *(Acts 12:1-11)*
A reading from the Acts of the Apostles.
Now I know the Lord really did save me from Herod.
King Herod started persecuting certain members of the Church.
He beheaded James the brother of John, and when he saw that

this pleased the Jews he decided to arrest Peter as well. This was
during the days of Unleavened Bread, and he put Peter in prison,
assigning four squads of four soldiers each to guard him in turns.
Herod meant to try Peter in public after the end of Passover week.
All the time Peter was under guard the Church prayed to God for
him unremittingly.

On the night before Herod was to try him, Peter was sleeping
between two soldiers, fastened with double chains, while guards
kept watch at the main entrance to the prison. Then suddenly
the angel of the Lord stood there, and the cell was filled with
light. He tapped Peter on the side and woke him. 'Get up!' he
said 'Hurry!' — and the chains fell from his hands. The angel then
said, 'Put on your belt and sandals.' After he had done this, the
angel next said, 'Wrap your cloak round you and follow me.'
Peter followed him, but had no idea that what the angel did was
all happening in reality; he thought he was seeing a vision. They
passed through two guard posts one after the other, and reached
the iron gate leading to the city. This opened of its own accord;
they went through it and had walked the whole length of one
street when suddenly the angel left him. It was only then that
Peter came to himself. 'Now I know it is all true,' he said. 'The Lord
really did send his angel and has saved me from Herod and from
all that the Jewish people were so certain would happen to me.'

This is the word of the Lord.

RESPONSORIAL PSALM   *(Ps 33:2-9)*

℟   **From all my terrors the Lord set me free.**

or **The angel of the Lord rescues those who revere him.**

1.   I will bless the Lord at all times,
         his praise always on my lips;
     in the Lord my soul shall make its boast.
         The humble shall hear and be glad. ℟

2.   Glorify the Lord with me.
         Together let us praise his name.
     I sought the Lord and he answered me;
         from all my terrors he set me free. ℟

3.   Look towards him and be radiant;
         let your faces not be abashed.
     This poor man called; the Lord heard him
         and rescued him from all his distress. ℟   *(continued)*

4. The angel of the Lord is encamped
    around those who revere him, to rescue them.
    Taste and see that the Lord is good.
    He is happy who seeks refuge in him. ℟

℟   **From all my terrors the Lord set me free.**

or **The angel of the Lord rescues those who revere him.**

SECOND READING   *(2 Tm 4:6-8.17-18)*
A reading from the second letter of St Paul to Timothy

All there is to come now is the crown of righteousness reserved for me.

My life is already being poured away as a libation, and the time
has come for me to be gone. I have fought the good fight to the
end; I have run the race to the finish; I have kept the faith; all
there is to come now is the crown of righteousness reserved for
me, which the Lord, the righteous judge, will give to me on that
Day; and not only to me but to all those who have longed for
his Appearing.

    The Lord stood by me and gave me power, so that through
me the whole message might be proclaimed for all the pagans to
hear; and so I was rescued from the lion's mouth. The Lord will
rescue me from all evil attempts on me, and bring me safely to
his heavenly kingdom. To him be glory for ever and ever. Amen.

    This is the word of the Lord.

GOSPEL ACCLAMATION   *(Mt 16:18)*
Alleluia, alleluia!
You are Peter and on this rock I will build my Church.
And the gates of the underworld can never hold out against it.
Alleluia!

GOSPEL   *(Mt 16:13-19)*
A reading from the holy Gospel according to Matthew.

You are Peter, and I will give you the keys of the kingdom of heaven.

When Jesus came to the region of Caesarea Philippi he put this
question to his disciples, 'Who do people say the Son of Man is?'
And they said, 'Some say he is John the Baptist, some Elijah, and
others Jeremiah or one of the prophets.' 'But you,' he said 'who
do you say I am?' Then Simon Peter spoke up, 'You are the Christ,'
he said 'the Son of the living God.' Jesus replied, 'Simon son of
Jonah, you are a happy man! Because it was not flesh and blood
that revealed this to you but my Father in heaven. So I now say
to you: You are Peter and on this rock I will build my Church.
And the gates of the underworld can never hold out against it. I

will give you the keys of the kingdom of heaven: whatever you bind on earth shall be considered bound in heaven; whatever you loose on earth shall be considered loosed in heaven.'

This is the Gospel of the Lord.

PROFESSION OF FAITH — *pages 15-16*

PRAYER OVER THE GIFTS

Lord, may your apostles join their prayers to our offering and help us to celebrate this sacrifice in love and unity.

PREFACE OF SAINTS PETER AND PAUL

Father, all-powerful and ever-living God,
we do well always and everywhere to give you thanks.

You fill our hearts with joy
as we honour your great apostles:
Peter, our leader in the faith,
and Paul, its fearless preacher.

Peter raised up the Church
from the faithful flock of Israel.
Paul brought your call to the nations,
and became the teacher of the world.
Each in his chosen way gathered into unity
the one family of Christ.
Both shared a martyr's death
and are praised throughout the world.

Now, with the apostles and all the angels and saints,
we praise you for ever:
Holy, holy, holy...

COMMUNION ANTIPHON   *(Mt 16:16.18)*

Peter said: You are the Christ, the Son of the living God. Jesus answered: You are Peter the rock on which I will build my Church.

PRAYER AFTER COMMUNION

Lord, renew the life of your Church
with the power of this sacrament.
May the breaking of bread
and the teaching of the apostles
keep us united in your love.

SOLEMN BLESSING

Bow your heads and pray for God's blessing.
The Lord has set you firm within his Church,

which he built upon the rock of Peter's faith.
May he bless you with a faith that never falters. **Amen**.

The Lord has given you knowledge of the faith
through the labours and preaching of Saint Paul.
May his example inspire you to lead others to Christ
by the manner of your life. **Amen**.

May the keys of Peter, and the words of Paul,
their undying witness and their prayers,
lead you to the joy of that eternal home
which Peter gained by his cross, and Paul by the sword. **Amen**.

May almighty God bless you,
the Father, and the Son, ✠ and the Holy Spirit. **Amen**.

REFLECTION
> Simon of Bethsaida and Saul of Tarsus, both seemed unlikely
> candidates to be entrusted with the task which they were
> eventually given. Simon Peter's judgement and loyalty were
> questionable. Saul's intense opposition to the emerging Church
> made him the focus of suspicion. Yet it was these two that the
> Lord called. They answered and their lives were transformed.

━━━━━━━━━━━━ 4 JULY ━━━━━━━━━━━━

14th SUNDAY IN ORDINARY TIME

> The images of harvest and labourers are presented in the scriptures
> today to portray the idea of working in order to bring about the
> Kingdom of God. Everyone is invited to play their part in this task
> whether ordained or lay, married or single, in religious life or outside
> it. All are equally invited to make the Kingdom a reality in their
> own life and in the community in which they find themselves.

ENTRANCE ANTIPHON   *(Ps 47:10-11)*
**Within your temple, we ponder your loving kindness, O God.
As your name, so also your praise reaches to the ends of the
earth; your right hand is filled with justice.**

GREETING, PENITENTIAL RITE, GLORIA — *pages 7-14*

OPENING PRAYER
Let us pray
  [for forgiveness through the grace of Jesus Christ]
Father, through the obedience of Jesus,

your servant and your Son,
you raised a fallen world.
Free us from sin
and bring us the joy that lasts for ever.

or

Let us pray

> [for greater willingness
> to serve God and our fellow man]

Father, in the rising of your Son
death gives birth to new life.
The sufferings he endured restored hope to a fallen world.
Let sin never ensnare us
with empty promises of passing joy.
Make us one with you always,
so that our joy may be holy,
and our love may give life.

FIRST READING   *(Is 66:10-14)*

A reading from the prophet Isaiah.

Towards her I send flowing peace, like a river.

Rejoice, Jerusalem,
be glad for her, all you who love her!
Rejoice, rejoice for her,
all you who mourned her!

That you may be suckled, filled,
from her consoling breast,
that you may savour with delight
her glorious breasts.

For thus says the Lord:
Now towards her I send flowing
peace, like a river,
and like a stream in spate
the glory of the nations.

At her breast will her nurslings be carried
and fondled in her lap.
Like a son comforted by his mother
will I comfort you.
And by Jerusalem you will be comforted.

At the sight your heart will rejoice,
and your bones flourish like the grass.
To his servants the Lord will reveal his hand.

> This is the word of the Lord.

RESPONSORIAL PSALM   *(Ps 65:1-7.16.20)*

℞   **Cry out with joy to God all the earth.**

1. Cry out with joy to God all the earth,
    O sing to the glory of his name.
    O render him glorious praise.
    Say to God: How tremendous your deeds! ℞

2. 'Before you all the earth shall bow;
    shall sing to you, sing to your name!'
    Come and see the works of God,
    tremendous his deeds among men. ℞

3. He turned the sea into dry land,
    they passed through the river dry-shod.
    Let our joy then be in him;
    he rules for ever by his might. ℞

4. Come and hear, all who fear God.
    I will tell what he did for my soul.
    Blessed be God who did not reject my prayer
    nor withhold his love from me. ℞

SECOND READING   *(Gal 6:14-18)*

A reading from the letter of St Paul to the Galatians.

The marks on my body are those of the Lord Jesus.

The only thing I can boast about is the cross of our Lord Jesus
Christ, through whom the world is crucified to me, and I to the
world. It does not matter if a person is circumcised or not; what
matters is for him to become an altogether new creature. Peace
and mercy to all who follow this rule, who form the Israel of God.

I want no more trouble from anybody after this; the marks
on my body are those of Jesus. The grace of our Lord Jesus Christ
be with your spirit, my brothers. Amen.

This is the word of the Lord.

GOSPEL ACCLAMATION   *(Jn 15:15)*

Alleluia, alleluia!
I call you friends, says the Lord,
because I have made known to you
everything I have learnt from my Father.
Alleluia!

or   *(Col 3:15-16)*

Alleluia, alleluia!
May the peace of Christ reign in your hearts,
because it is for this that you were called together

**as parts of one body.
Alleluia!**

GOSPEL *(Lk 10:1-12.17-20)*

(For Shorter Form, *read between* ▶ ◀)

A reading from the holy Gospel according to Luke.

Your peace will rest on that man.

▶The Lord appointed seventy-two others and sent them out ahead of him, in pairs, to all the towns and places he himself was to visit. He said to them, 'The harvest is rich but the labourers are few, so ask the Lord of the harvest to send labourers to his harvest. Start off now, but remember, I am sending you out like lambs among wolves. Carry no purse, no haversack, no sandals. Salute no one on the road. Whatever house you go into, let your first words be, "Peace to this house!" And if a man of peace lives there, your peace will go and rest on him; if not, it will come back to you. Stay in the same house, taking what food and drink they have to offer, for the labourer deserves his wages; do not move from house to house. Whenever you go into a town where they make you welcome, eat what is set before you. Cure those in it who are sick, and say, "The kingdom of God is very near to you."◀ But whenever you enter a town and they do not make you welcome, go out into its streets and say, "We wipe off the very dust of your town that clings to our feet, and leave it with you. Yet be sure of this: the kingdom of God is very near." I tell you, that on that day it will not go as hard with Sodom as with that town.'

The seventy-two came back rejoicing. 'Lord', they said, 'even the devils submit to us when we use your name.' He said to them, 'I watched Satan fall like lightning from heaven. Yes, I have given you power to tread underfoot serpents and scorpions and the whole strength of the enemy; nothing shall ever hurt you. Yet do not rejoice that the spirits submit to you; rejoice rather that your names are written in heaven.'

This is the Gospel of the Lord.

PROFESSION OF FAITH — *pages 15-16*

PRAYER OVER THE GIFTS

Lord,
let this offering to the glory of your name
purify us and bring us closer to eternal life.

PREFACE OF SUNDAYS IN ORDINARY TIME — *pages 22-25*

COMMUNION ANTIPHON   *(Ps 33:9)*
**Taste and see the goodness of the Lord; blessed is he who
hopes in God.**
or   *(Mt 11:28)*
**Come to me, all you that labour and are burdened, and I will
give you rest, says the Lord.**

PRAYER AFTER COMMUNION
Lord, may we never fail to praise you
for the fullness of life and salvation
you give us in this eucharist.

SOLEMN BLESSING — *pages 57-58*

REFLECTION
> Marriage is a sacrament. This means that through the love and
> respect which each one has for the other, God's love and
> respect is communicated to both. Each one is the principal
> means through which God's love is revealed to the other. This
> may appear an enormous task for any human being but it is
> the Spirit of God who empowers those who take on the task.

═══════════════ 11 JULY ═══════════════

15th SUNDAY IN ORDINARY TIME

'Vocation', meaning a call by God, is for everyone in the
Church. It has frequently been used in the narrow sense of a
call to the religious life and/or to the priesthood. It is not that
certain words are heard but rather that a voice is discerned.
And it is the persons themselves who are in the best position
to discern what God's call for them may be. Once the call has
been discerned, the next step is the generosity to respond.

ENTRANCE ANTIPHON   *(Ps 16:15)*
**In my justice I shall see your face, O Lord; when your glory
appears, my joy will be full.**

GREETING, PENITENTIAL RITE, GLORIA — *pages 7-14*

OPENING PRAYER
Let us pray
     [that the gospel may be our rule of life]
God our Father,

your light of truth
guides us to the way of Christ.
May all who follow him
reject what is contrary to the gospel.

or

Let us pray
     [to be faithful to the light we have received,
        to the name we bear]

Father, let the light of your truth
guide us to your kingdom
through a world filled with lights contrary to your own.
Christian is the name and the gospel we glory in.
May your love make us what you have called us to be.

FIRST READING   *(Dt 30:10-14)*

A reading from the book of Deuteronomy.

The Word is very near to you for your observance.

Moses said to the people: 'Obey the voice of the Lord your God,
keeping those commandments and laws of his that are written
in the Book of this Law, and you shall return to the Lord your
God with all your heart and soul.

'For this Law that I enjoin on you today is not beyond your
strength or beyond your reach. It is not in heaven, so that you
need to wonder, "Who will go up to heaven for us and bring it
down to us, so that we may hear it and keep it?" Nor is it
beyond the seas, so that you need to wonder, "Who will cross
the seas for us and bring it back to us, so that we may hear it and
keep it?" No, the Word is very near to you, it is in your mouth
and in your heart for your observance.'

This is the word of the Lord.

RESPONSORIAL PSALM   *(Ps 68:14.17.30-31.33-34.36-37)*

℟   **Seek the Lord, you who are poor,**
    and your hearts will revive.

1.   This is my prayer to you,
     my prayer for your favour.
     In your great love, answer me, O God,
     with your help that never fails:
     Lord, answer, for your love is kind;
     in your compassion, turn towards me. ℟

2.   As for me in my poverty and pain
     let your help, O God, lift me up.   *(continued)*

I will praise God's name with a song;
I will glorify him with thanksgiving. ℟

℟   **Seek the Lord, you who are poor,**
    and your hearts will revive.

3. The poor when they see it will be glad
    and God-seeking hearts will revive;
    for the Lord listens to the needy
    and does not spurn his servants in their chains. ℟

4. For God will bring help to Zion
    and rebuild the cities of Judah.
    The sons of his servants shall inherit it;
    those who love his name shall dwell there. ℟

SECOND READING   *(Col 1:15-20)*

A reading from the letter of St Paul to the Colossians.

All things were created through Christ and for him.

Christ Jesus is the image of the unseen God
and the first-born of all creation,
for in him were created
all things in heaven and on earth:
everything visible and everything invisible,
Thrones, Dominations, Sovereignties, Powers —
all things were created through him and for him.
Before anything was created, he existed,
and he holds all things in unity.
Now the Church is his body,
he is its head.

As he is the Beginning,
he was first to be born from the dead,
so that he should be first in every way;
because God wanted all perfection
to be found in him
and all things to be reconciled through him and for him,
everything in heaven and everything on earth,
when he made peace
by his death on the cross.

    This is the word of the Lord.

GOSPEL ACCLAMATION   *(Jn 10:27)*

Alleluia, alleluia!
The sheep that belong to me listen to my voice,
says the Lord,
I know them and they follow me. Alleluia!

or   *(cf. Jn 6:63-68)*
Alleluia, alleluia!
Your words are spirit, Lord,
and they are life:
you have the message of eternal life. Alleluia!

GOSPEL   *(Lk 10:25-37)*
A reading from the holy Gospel according to Luke.
Who is my neighbour?

There was a lawyer who, to disconcert Jesus, stood up and said to him, 'Master, what must I do to inherit eternal life?' He said to him, 'What is written in the law? What do you read there?' He replied, 'You must love the Lord your God with all your heart, with all your soul, with all your strength, and with all your mind, and your neighbour as yourself.' 'You have answered right,' said Jesus, 'do this and life is yours.'

But the man was anxious to justify himself and said to Jesus, 'And who is my neighbour?' Jesus replied, 'A man was once on his way down from Jerusalem to Jericho and fell into the hands of brigands; they took all he had, beat him and then made off, leaving him half dead. Now a priest happened to be travelling down the same road, but when he saw the man, he passed by on the other side. In the same way a Levite who came to the place saw him, and passed by on the other side. But a Samaritan traveller who came upon him was moved with compassion when he saw him. He went up and bandaged his wounds, pouring oil and wine on them. He then lifted him on to his own mount, carried him to the inn and looked after him. Next day, he took out two denarii and handed them to the innkeeper. "Look after him," he said "and on my way back I will make good any extra expense you have." Which of these three, do you think, proved himself a neighbour to the man who fell into the brigands' hands?' 'The one, who took pity on him' he replied. Jesus said to him, 'Go, and do the same yourself.'

This is the Gospel of the Lord.

PROFESSION OF FAITH — *pages 15-16*

PRAYER OVER THE GIFTS
Lord, accept the gifts of your Church.
May this eucharist
help us grow in holiness and faith.

PREFACE OF SUNDAYS IN ORDINARY TIME — *pages 22-25*

COMMUNION ANTIPHON   *(Ps 83:4-5)*
**The sparrow even finds a home, the swallow finds a nest
wherein to place her young, near to your altars, Lord of hosts,
my King, my God! How happy they who dwell in your house!
For ever they are praising you.**

or   *(Jn 6:57)*
**Whoever eats my flesh and drinks my blood will live in me
and I in him, says the Lord.**

PRAYER AFTER COMMUNION
Lord, by our sharing in the mystery of this eucharist,
let your saving love grow within us.

SOLEMN BLESSING — *pages 57-58*

REFLECTION
> The single life is one way through which a significant number
> of people respond to God's call. While the majority of people
> opt for marriage their path through life is equally esteemed in
> the Christian community. Many who have not had the care of
> a spouse and family have given generously of their time and
> talents to the wider family of the Church. Both paths are part
> of the rich tapestry of Christian vocation.

———————————— 18 JULY ————————————

16th SUNDAY IN ORDINARY TIME

> Religious communities make up a small percentage of the Christian
> population but nevertheless play a dynamic and central role in
> the spreading of the Kingdom of God. To belong to a religious society
> is a call to witness with one's life to what one believes in. The
> most effective form of witness is the testimony of a person's life.

ENTRANCE ANTIPHON   *(Ps 53:6.8)*
**God himself is my help. The Lord upholds my life. I will offer
you a willing sacrifice; I will praise your name, O Lord, for its
goodness.**

GREETING, PENITENTIAL RITE, GLORIA — *pages 7-14*

OPENING PRAYER
Let us pray
    [to be kept faithful in the service of God]
Lord, be merciful to your people.

Fill us with your gifts
and make us always eager to serve you
in faith, hope, and love.

or

Let us pray
    [that God will continue to bless us
    with his compassion and love]

Father,
let the gift of your life
continue to grow in us,
drawing us from death to faith, hope, and love.
Keep us alive in Christ Jesus.
Keep us watchful in prayer
and true to his teaching
till your glory is revealed in us.

FIRST READING   *(Gen 18:1-10)*

A reading from the book of Genesis.

Lord, do not pass your servant by.

The Lord appeared to Abraham at the Oak of Mamre while he
was sitting by the entrance of the tent during the hottest part of
the day. He looked up, and there he saw three men standing near
him. As soon as he saw them he ran from the entrance of the tent
to meet them, and bowed to the ground. 'My Lord,' he said 'I
beg you, if I find favour with you, kindly do not pass your servant
by. A little water shall be brought; you shall wash your feet and
lie down under the tree. Let me fetch a little bread and you shall
refresh yourselves before going further. That is why you have
come in your servant's direction.' They replied, 'Do as you say.'

    Abraham hastened to the tent to find Sarah. 'Hurry,' he said
'knead three bushels of flour and make loaves.' Then running to
the cattle Abraham took a fine and tender calf and gave it to the
servant, who hurried to prepare it. Then taking cream, milk and
the calf he had prepared, he laid all before them, and they ate
while he remained standing near them under the tree.

    'Where is your wife Sarah? they asked him. 'She is in the tent'
he replied. Then his guest said, 'I shall visit you again next year
without fail and your wife will then have a son.'

    This is the word of the Lord.

RESPONSORIAL PSALM   *(Ps 14:2-5)*

℟   **The just will live in the presence of the Lord.**

1. Lord, who shall dwell on your holy mountain?
    He who walks without fault;
    he who acts with justice
    and speaks the truth from his heart;
    he who does not slander with his tongue. ℟

2. He who does no wrong to his brother,
    who casts no slur on his neighbour,
    who holds the godless in disdain,
    but honours those who fear the Lord. ℟

3. He who keeps his pledge, come what may;
    who takes no interest on a loan
    and accepts no bribes against the innocent.
    Such a man will stand firm for ever. ℟

SECOND READING   *(Col 1:24-28)*

A reading from the letter of St Paul to the Colossians.

A mystery hidden for centuries has now been revealed to God's saints.

It makes me happy to suffer for you, as I am suffering now, and in my body to do what I can to make up all that has still to be undergone by Christ for the sake of his body, the Church. I became the servant of the Church when God made me responsible for delivering God's message to you, the message which was a mystery hidden for generations and centuries and has now been revealed to his saints. It was God's purpose to reveal it to them and to show all the rich glory of this mystery to pagans. The mystery is Christ among you, your hope of glory: this is the Christ we proclaim, this is the wisdom in which we thoroughly train everyone and instruct everyone, to make them all perfect in Christ.

     This is the word of the Lord.

GOSPEL ACCLAMATION   *(cf. Acts 16:14)*

Alleluia, alleluia!
Open our heart, O Lord,
to accept the words of your Son. Alleluia!

or   *(cf. Lk 8:15)*

Alleluia, alleluia!
Blessed are those who,
with a noble and generous heart,
take the word of God to themselves
and yield a harvest through their perseverance. Alleluia!

GOSPEL   (Lk 10:38-42)

A reading from the holy Gospel according to Luke.

Martha welcomed Jesus into her house. Mary has chosen the better part.

Jesus came to a village, and a woman named Martha welcomed
him into her house. She had a sister called Mary, who sat down
at the Lord's feet and listened to him speaking. Now Martha
who was distracted with all the serving said, 'Lord, do you not
care that my sister is leaving me to do the serving all by myself?
Please tell her to help me.' But the Lord answered: 'Martha,
Martha,' he said 'you worry and fret about so many things, and
yet few are needed, indeed only one. It is Mary who has chosen
the better part; it is not to be taken from her.'

This is the Gospel of the Lord.

PROFESSION OF FAITH — *pages 15-16*

PRAYER OVER THE GIFTS

Lord, bring us closer to salvation
through these gifts which we bring in your honour.
Accept the perfect sacrifice you have given us,
bless it as you blessed the gifts of Abel.

PREFACE OF SUNDAYS IN ORDINARY TIME — *pages 22-25*

COMMUNION ANTIPHON   (Ps 110:4-5)

**The Lord keeps in our minds the wonderful things he has
done. He is compassion and love; he always provides for his
faithful.**

or   (Apo 3:20)

**I stand at the door and knock, says the Lord. If anyone hears
my voice and opens the door, I will come in and sit down to
supper with him, and he with me.**

PRAYER AFTER COMMUNION

Merciful Father,
may these mysteries
give us new purpose
and bring us to a new life in you.

SOLEMN BLESSING — *pages 57-58*

REFLECTION

> Religious life has been called a radical response to the Jesus
> who appears on the pages of the gospels. Radical means 'to the
> very roots'. Religious congregations are made up of people

who have been attracted by the gospel message and who freely
opt to bring that message to the women and men of their own
day. This is the task of the Church and this is why religious
communities are at the heart of the Church. It is a call that
whoever can would do well to answer.

25 JULY

17th SUNDAY IN ORDINARY TIME

The call to the Christian priesthood is a call to service. The gift
of the priesthood is not given primarily to the individual but
to the whole Church. Like the call to the religious life the one
who is called to the priesthood is invited to affirm by their
lifestyle that faith that one believes in. Let those who can
accept this task, accept it.

ENTRANCE ANTIPHON   *(Ps 67:6-7.36)*
**God is in his holy dwelling; he will give a home to the lonely,
he gives power and strength to his people.**

GREETING, PENITENTIAL RITE, GLORIA — *pages 7-14*

OPENING PRAYER
Let us pray
    [that we will make good use of the gifts
    that God has given us]

God our Father and protector,
without you nothing is holy,
nothing has value.
Guide us to everlasting life
by helping us to use wisely
the blessings you have given to the world.

or
Let us pray
    [for the faith to recognise God's presence in our world]

God our Father,
open our eyes to see your hand at work
in the splendour of creation,
in the beauty of human life.
Touched by your hand our world is holy.
Help us to cherish the gifts that surround us,
to share your blessings with our brothers and sisters,
and to experience the joy of life in your presence.

FIRST READING   *(Gen 18:20-32)*

A reading from the book of Genesis.

I trust my Lord will not be angry, but give me leave to speak.

The Lord said, 'How great an outcry there is against Sodom and Gomorrah! How grievous is their sin! I propose to go down and see whether or not they have done all that is alleged in the outcry against them that has come up to me. I am determined to know.'

The men left there and went to Sodom while Abraham remained standing before the Lord. Approaching him he said, 'Are you really going to destroy the just man with the sinner? Perhaps there are fifty just men in the town. Will you really overwhelm them, will you not spare the place for the fifty just men in it? Do not think of doing such a thing: to kill the just man with the sinner, treating just and sinner alike! Do not think of it! Will the judge of the whole earth not administer justice?' The Lord replied, 'If at Sodom I find fifty just men in the town, I will spare the whole place because of them.'

Abraham replied, 'I am bold indeed to speak like this to my Lord, I who am dust and ashes. But perhaps the fifty just men lack five: will you destroy the whole city for five?' 'No', he replied, 'I will not destroy it if I find forty-five just men there.' Again Abraham said to him, 'Perhaps there will only be forty there.' 'I will not do it' he replied 'for the sake of the forty.'

Abraham said, 'I trust my Lord will not be angry, but give me leave to speak: perhaps there will only be thirty there.' 'I will not do it' he replied 'if I find thirty there.' He said, 'I am bold indeed to speak like this, but perhaps there will only be twenty there.' 'I will not destroy it' he replied 'for the sake of the twenty.' He said, 'I trust my Lord will not be angry if I speak once more: perhaps there will only be ten.' 'I will not destroy it' he replied 'for the sake of the ten.'

This is the word of the Lord.

RESPONSORIAL PSALM   *(Ps 137:1-3.6-8)*

℞   **On the day I called,**
     you answered me, O Lord.

1.   I thank you, Lord, with all my heart,
     you have heard the words of my mouth.
     Before the angels I will bless you.
     I will adore before your holy temple.   ℞

2.   I thank you for your faithfulness and love
     which excel all we ever knew of you.   *(continued)*

On the day I called, you answered;
you increased the strength of my soul. ℟

℟ **On the day I called,
you answered me, O Lord.**

3. The Lord is high yet he looks on the lowly
and the haughty he knows from afar.
Though I walk in the midst of affliction
you give me life and frustrate my foes. ℟

4. You stretch out your hand and save me,
your hand will do all things for me.
Your love, O Lord, is eternal,
discard not the work of your hands. ℟

SECOND READING   *(Col 2:12-14)*
A reading from the letter of St Paul to the Colossians.
He has brought you to life with him, he has forgiven us all our sins.
You have been buried with Christ, when you were baptised; and
by baptism, too, you have been raised up with him through your
belief in the power of God who raised him from the dead. You
were dead, because you were sinners and had not been circumcised:
he has brought you to life with him, he has forgiven us all our sins.

He has overridden the Law, and cancelled every record of
the debt that we had to pay; he has done away with it by nailing
it to the cross.

This is the word of the Lord.

GOSPEL ACCLAMATION   *(Jn 1:14.12)*
**Alleluia, alleluia!
The Word was made flesh and lived among us;
to all who did accept him
he gave power to become children of God. Alleluia!**
or   *(Rm 8:15)*
**Alleluia, alleluia!
The spirit you received is the spirit of sons,
and it makes us cry out, 'Abba, Father!' Alleluia!**

GOSPEL   *(Lk 11:1-13)*
A reading from the holy Gospel according to Luke.
Ask, and it will be given to you.
Once Jesus was in a certain place praying, and when he had
finished, one of his disciples said, 'Lord, teach us to pray, just as
John taught his disciples.' He said to them, 'Say this when you pray:

"Father, may your name be held holy,
your kingdom come;
give us each day our daily bread,
and forgive us our sins,
for we ourselves forgive each one who is in debt to us.
And do not put us to the test." '

He also said to them, 'Suppose one of you has a friend and goes to him in the middle of the night to say, "My friend, lend me three loaves because a friend of mine on his travels has just arrived at my house and I have nothing to offer him"; and the man answers from inside the house, "Do not bother me. The door is bolted now, and my children and I are in bed; I cannot get up to give it to you," I tell you, if the man does not get up and give it him for friendship's sake, persistence will be enough to make him get up and give his friend all he wants.

'So I say to you: Ask, and it will be given to you; search, and you will find; knock, and the door will be opened to you. For the one who asks always receives; the one who searches always finds; the one who knocks will always have the door opened to him. What father among you would hand his son a stone when he asked for bread? Or hand him a snake instead of a fish? Or hand him a scorpion if he asked for an egg? If you then, who are evil, know how to give your children what is good, how much more will the heavenly Father give the Holy Spirit to those who ask him!'

This is the Gospel of the Lord.

PROFESSION OF FAITH — *pages 15-16*

PRAYER OVER THE GIFTS
Lord,
receive these offerings
chosen from your many gifts.
May these mysteries make us holy
and lead us to eternal joy.

PREFACE OF SUNDAYS IN ORDINARY TIME — *pages 22-25*

COMMUNION ANTIPHON   *(Ps 102:2)*
O, bless the Lord, my soul, and remember all his kindness.
or   *(Mt 5:7-8)*
Happy are those who show mercy; mercy shall be theirs. Happy are the pure of heart, for they shall see God.

PRAYER AFTER COMMUNION

Lord, we receive the sacrament
which celebrates the memory
of the death and resurrection of Christ your Son.
May this gift bring us closer to our eternal salvation.

SOLEMN BLESSING — *pages 57-58*

REFLECTION

> In the Church there is a diversity of ministry: lay, religious and
> priestly but a unity of mission, the proclamation and realisation
> of the Kingdom of God. It is by Baptism and Confirmation
> that this mission is entrusted to all. The Holy Spirit is the one
> who empowers each to carry out their individual mission and
> that of the community of the Church.

═══════════════ 1 AUGUST ═══════════════

18th SUNDAY IN ORDINARY TIME

> Prayer in the Christian tradition is first of all addressed to God
> the Father. God is the Father of the Lord Jesus, the Christ as
> well as our Father. This is true of most of the Church's liturgical
> prayer. Christian prayer may also be directed towards Jesus,
> especially by calling on his holy name. One of the most ancient
> examples of prayer is: 'Lord Jesus Christ, Son of God, have mercy
> on us sinners.'

ENTRANCE ANTIPHON   *(Ps 69:2.6)*

**God, come to my help. Lord, quickly give me assistance. You
are the one who helps me and sets me free: Lord, do not be
long in coming.**

GREETING, PENITENTIAL RITE, GLORIA — *pages 7-14*

OPENING PRAYER

Let us pray

[for the gift of God's forgiveness and love]

Father of everlasting goodness,
our origin and guide,
be close to us
and hear the prayers of all who praise you.
Forgive our sins and restore us to life.
Keep us safe in your love.
or

Let us pray
[to the Father whose kindness never fails]

God our Father,
gifts without measure flow from your goodness
to bring us your peace.
Our life is your gift.
Guide our life's journey,
for only your love makes us whole.
Keep us strong in your love.

FIRST READING (Qo 1:2; 2:21-23)

A reading from the book of Ecclesiastes.

What does a man gain for all his toil?

Vanity of vanities, the Preacher says. Vanity of vanities. All is vanity!

For so it is that a man who has laboured wisely, skilfully and successfully must leave what is his own to someone who has not toiled for it at all. This, too, is vanity and great injustice; for what does he gain for all the toil and strain that he has undergone under the sun? What of all his laborious days, his cares of office, his restless nights? This, too, is vanity.

This is the word of the Lord.

RESPONSORIAL PSALM (Ps 89:3-6.12-14.17)

℟ **O Lord, you have been our refuge**
   from one generation to the next.

1. You turn men back into dust
   and say: 'Go back, sons of men.'
   To your eyes a thousand years
   are like yesterday, come and gone,
   no more than a watch in the night. ℟

2. You sweep men away like a dream,
   like grass which springs up in the morning.
   In the morning it springs up and flowers:
   by evening it withers and fades. ℟

3. Make us know the shortness of our life
   that we may gain wisdom of heart.
   Lord, relent! Is your anger for ever?
   Show pity to your servants. ℟

4. In the morning, fill us with your love;
   we shall exult and rejoice all our days.
   Let the favour of the Lord be upon us:
   give success to the work of our hands. ℟

SECOND READING   *(Col 3:1-5.9-11)*

A reading from the letter of St Paul to the Colossians.

You must look for the things that are in heaven, where Christ is.

Since you have been brought back to true life with Christ, you must look for the things that are in heaven, where Christ is, sitting at God's right hand. Let your thoughts be on heavenly things, not on the things on the earth, because you have died, and now the life you have is hidden with Christ in God. But when Christ is revealed – and he is your life – you too will be revealed in all your glory with him.

That is why you must kill everything in you that belongs only to earthly life: fornication, impurity, guilty passion, evil desires and especially greed, which is the same thing as worshipping a false god; and never tell each other lies. You have stripped off your old behaviour with your old self, and you have put on a new self which will progress towards true knowledge the more it is renewed in the image of its creator; and in that image there is no room for distinction between Greek and Jew, between the circumcised or the uncircumcised, or between barbarian and Scythian, slave and free man. There is only Christ: he is everything and he is in everything.

This is the word of the Lord.

GOSPEL ACCLAMATION   *(Jn 17:17)*

Alleluia, alleluia!
Your word is truth, O Lord,
consecrate us in the truth.
Alleluia!

or   *(Mt 5:3)*

Alleluia, alleluia!
How happy are the poor in spirit;
theirs is the kingdom of heaven.
Alleluia!

GOSPEL   *(Lk 12:13-21)*

A reading from the holy Gospel according to Luke.

This hoard of yours, whose will it be?

A man in the crowd said to Jesus, 'Master, tell my brother to give me a share of our inheritance.' 'My friend,' he replied 'who appointed me your judge, or the arbitrator of your claims?' Then he said to them, 'Watch, and be on your guard against avarice of any kind, for a man's life is not made secure by what he owns, even when he has more than he needs.'

Then he told them a parable: 'There was once a rich man who, having had a good harvest from his land, thought to himself, "What am I to do? I have not enough room to store my crops." Then he said, "This is what I will do: I will pull down my barns and build bigger ones, and store all my grain and my goods in them, and I will say to my soul: My soul, you have plenty of good things laid by for many years to come; take things easy, eat, drink, have a good time." But God said to him, "Fool! This very night the demand will be made for your soul; and this hoard of yours, whose will it be then?" So it is when a man stores up treasure for himself in place of making himself rich in the sight of God.'

This is the Gospel of the Lord.

PROFESSION OF FAITH — *pages 15-16*

PRAYER OVER THE GIFTS

Merciful Lord,
make holy these gifts,
and let our spiritual sacrifice
make us an everlasting gift to you.

PREFACE OF SUNDAYS IN ORDINARY TIME - *pages 22-25*

COMMUNION ANTIPHON   *(Wis 16:20)*

You gave us bread from heaven, Lord: a sweet-tasting bread that was very good to eat.

or   *(Jn 6:35)*

The Lord says: I am the bread of life. A man who comes to me will not go away hungry, and no one who believes in me will thirst.

PRAYER AFTER COMMUNION

Lord, you give us the strength of new life
by the gift of the eucharist.
Protect us with your love
and prepare us for eternal redemption.

REFLECTION

The richness of the Church's tradition of prayer can be seen from some of the many biblical titles given to Jesus which may be used in prayer: Son of God, Word of God, Lord, Saviour, Lamb of God, King, Beloved Son, Son of the virgin, Good Shepherd, our life, our light, our hope, our resurrection, friend of humankind.

8 AUGUST
19th SUNDAY IN ORDINARY TIME

In the Hebrew Scriptures which we sometimes call the Old Testament, the personal name for God is Yahweh. It was considered too holy to be pronounced. It could be written but never spoken. When speaking or reading from the scriptures the speaker would replace it with 'the LORD'. We can take it that this is the practice which Jesus himself would have grown up with too.

ENTRANCE ANTIPHON   *(Ps 73:20.19.22.23)*

Lord, be true to your covenant, forget not the life of your poor ones for ever. Rise up, O God, and defend your cause; do not ignore the shouts of your enemies.

GREETING, PENITENTIAL RITE, GLORIA — *pages 7-14*

OPENING PRAYER

Let us pray
    [in the Spirit
    that we may grow in the love of God]

Almighty and ever-living God,
your Spirit made us your children,
confident to call you Father.
Increase your Spirit within us
and bring us to our promised inheritance.

or

Let us pray
    [that through us
    others may find the way to life in Christ]

Father, we come, reborn in the Spirit,
to celebrate our sonship in the Lord Jesus Christ.
Touch our hearts,
help them grow toward the life you have promised.
Touch our lives,
make them signs of your love for all.

FIRST READING   *(Wis 18:6-9)*

A reading from the book of Wisdom.

By the same act with which you took vengeance on our foes you made us glorious by calling us to you.

That night had been foretold to our ancestors, so that, once they saw what kind of oaths they had put their trust in

they would joyfully take courage.
This was the expectation of your people,
the saving of the virtuous and the ruin of their enemies;
for by the same act with which you took vengeance on our foes
you made us glorious by calling us to you.
The devout children of worthy men offered sacrifice in secret
and this divine pact they struck with one accord:
that the saints would share the same blessings and dangers alike;
and forthwith they had begun to chant the hymns of the fathers.

    This is the word of the Lord.

RESPONSORIAL PSALM   *(Ps 32:1.12.18-20.22)*

℟ **Happy are the people the Lord has chosen as his own.**

1. Ring out your joy to the Lord, O you just;
    for praise is fitting for loyal hearts.
    They are happy, whose God is the Lord,
    the people he has chosen as his own. ℟

2. The Lord looks on those who revere him,
    on those who hope in his love,
    to rescue their souls from death,
    to keep them alive in famine. ℟

3. Our soul is waiting for the Lord.
    The Lord is our help and our shield.
    May your love be upon us, O Lord,
    as we place all our hope in you. ℟

SECOND READING   *(Heb 11:1-2.8-19)*

(For Shorter Form, *read between* ♦ ♦*)*

A reading from the letter to the Hebrews.

Abraham looked forward to a city founded, designed and built by God.

♦Only faith can guarantee the blessings that we hope for, or
prove the existence of the realities that at present remain unseen.
It was for faith that our ancestors were commended.

    It was by faith that Abraham obeyed the call to set out for a
country that was the inheritance given to him and his descendants,
and that he set out without knowing where he was going. By faith
he arrived, as a foreigner, in the Promised Land, and lived there
as if in a strange country, with Isaac and Jacob, who were heirs
with him of the same promise. They lived there in tents while he
looked forward to a city founded, designed and built by God.

    It was equally by faith that Sarah, in spite of being past the
age, was made able to conceive, because she believed that he

who had made the promise would be faithful to it. Because of this, there came from one man, and one who was already as good as dead himself, more descendants than could be counted, as many as the stars of heaven or the grains of sand on the seashore. ◖

All these died in faith, before receiving any of the things that had been promised, but they saw them in the far distance and welcomed them, recognising that they were only strangers and nomads on earth. People who use such terms about themselves make it quite plain that they are in search of their real homeland. They can hardly have meant the country they came from, since they had the opportunity to go back to it; but in fact they were longing for a better homeland, their heavenly homeland. That is why God is not ashamed to be called their God, since he has founded the city for them.

It was by faith that Abraham, when put to the test, offered up Isaac. He offered to sacrifice his only son even though the promises had been made to him and he had been told: it is through Isaac that your name will be carried on. He was confident that God had the power even to raise the dead; and so, figuratively speaking, he was given back Isaac from the dead.

◖This is the word of the Lord. ◖

GOSPEL ACCLAMATION   *(cf. Mt 11:25)*
Alleluia, alleluia!
Blessed are you, Father,
Lord of heaven and earth,
for revealing the mysteries of the kingdom
to mere children. Alleluia!
or   *(Mt 24:42.44)*
Alleluia, alleluia!
Stay awake and stand ready,
because you do not know the hour
when the Son of Man is coming. Alleluia!

GOSPEL   *(Lk 12:32-48)*
(For Shorter Form, *read between* ◖ ◖*)*
A reading from the holy Gospel according to Luke.

You too must stand ready.

◖Jesus said to his disciples:◖ 'There is no need to be afraid, little flock, for it has pleased your Father to give you the kingdom.

'Sell your possessions and give alms. Get yourselves purses that do not wear out, treasure that will not fail you, in heaven where no thief can reach it and no moth destroy it. For where your treasure is, there will your heart be also.

❧'See that you are dressed for action and have your lamps lit. Be like men waiting for their master to return from the wedding feast, ready to open the door as soon as he comes and knocks. Happy those servants whom the master finds awake when he comes. I tell you solemnly, he will put on an apron, sit them down at table and wait on them. It may be in the second watch he comes, or in the third, but happy those servants if he finds them ready. You may be quite sure of this, that if the householder had known at what hour the burglar would come, he would not have let anyone break through the wall of his house. You too must stand ready, because the Son of Man is coming at an hour you do not expect.'❧

Peter said, 'Lord, do you mean this parable for us, or for everyone?' The Lord replied, 'What sort of steward, then, is faithful and wise enough for the master to place him over his household to give them their allowance of food at the proper time? Happy that servant if his master's arrival finds him at this employment. I tell you truly, he will place him over everything he owns. But as for the servant who says to himself, "My master is taking his time coming", and sets about beating the menservants and the maids, and eating and drinking and getting drunk, his master will come on a day he does not expect and at an hour he does not know. The master will cut him off and send him to the same fate as the unfaithful.

'The servant who knows what his master wants, but has not even started to carry out those wishes, will receive very many strokes of the lash. The one who did not know, but deserves to be beaten for what he has done, will receive fewer strokes. When a man has had a great deal given him, a great deal will be demanded of him; when a man has had a great deal given him on trust, even more will be expected of him.'

❧This is the Gospel of the Lord.❧

PROFESSION OF FAITH — *pages 15-16*

PRAYER OVER THE GIFTS

God of power,
giver of the gifts we bring,
accept the offering of your Church
and make it the sacrament of our salvation.

PREFACE OF SUNDAYS IN ORDINARY TIME — *pages 22-25*

COMMUNION ANTIPHON   (Ps 147:12.14)

Praise the Lord, Jerusalem; he feeds you with the finest wheat.

or   (Jn 6:52)

The bread I shall give is my flesh for the life of the world, says the Lord.

PRAYER AFTER COMMUNION

Lord, may the eucharist you give us
bring us to salvation
and keep us faithful to the light of your truth.

SOLEMN BLESSING — *pages 57-58*

REFLECTION

> Of all the names and titles given to him in the scriptures and
> the tradition of the Church, the name which contains
> everything is that of Jesus. The name itself means 'Yahweh
> saves'. The tradition of the Church tells us that this name is the
> only one that contains the presence of the one it signifies. To
> call on the name of Jesus is to call him within us.

═══════════ 15 AUGUST ═══════════

THE ASSUMPTION
OF THE BLESSED VIRGIN MARY

VIGIL MASS

> The Liturgy of the Word has its origins in both the preaching
> of the apostles and the service of the synagogue. From the Acts
> of the Apostles we know that the disciples gathered together to
> remember what had happened. Among them was Mary the mother
> of Jesus. On these occasions one of them would preach. Some of
> the parts of our present gospels were formed in this type of preaching.

ENTRANCE ANTIPHON

**All honour to you, Mary! Today you were raised above the
choirs of angels to lasting glory with Christ.**

GREETING, PENITENTIAL RITE, GLORIA — *pages 7-14*

OPENING PRAYER

Let us pray
  [that the Virgin Mary will help us
  with her prayers]

Almighty God,
you gave a humble virgin
the privilege of being the mother of your Son,
and crowned her with the glory of heaven.
May the prayers of the Virgin Mary
bring us to the salvation of Christ
and raise us up to eternal life.

or

Let us pray
   [with Mary to the Father,
   in whose presence she now dwells]

Almighty Father of our Lord Jesus Christ,
you have revealed the beauty of your power
by exalting the lowly virgin of Nazareth
and making her the mother of our Saviour.
May the prayers of this woman clothed with the sun
bring Jesus to the waiting world
and fill the void of incompletion
with the presence of her child,
who lives and reigns with you and the Holy Spirit,
one God, for ever and ever.

FIRST READING   *(Ch 15:3-4.15-16;16:1-2)*
A reading from the first book of Chronicles.
They brought in the ark of God and set it inside the tent which David
had pitched for it.
David gathered all Israel together in Jerusalem to bring the ark of
God up to the place he had prepared for it. David called together
the sons of Aaron and the sons of Levi. And the Levites carried
the ark of God with the shafts on their shoulders, as Moses had
ordered in accordance with the word of the Lord.

   David then told the heads of the Levites to assign duties for
their kinsmen as cantors, with their various instruments of
music, harps and lyres and cymbals, to play joyful tunes. They
brought the ark of God in and put it inside the tent that David
had pitched for it; and they offered holocausts before God, and
communion sacrifices. And when David had finished offering
holocausts and communion sacrifices, he blessed the people in
the name of the Lord.

   This is the word of the Lord.

RESPONSORIAL PSALM   *(Ps 131:6-7.9-10.13-14)*

℟ **Go up, Lord, to the place of your rest,
   you and the ark of your strength.**

1. At Ephrata we heard of the ark;
    we found it in the plains of Yearim.
    'Let us go to the place of his dwelling;
    let us go to kneel at his footstool.' ℟

2. Your priests shall be clothed with holiness:
    your faithful shall ring out their joy.
    For the sake of David your servant
    do not reject your anointed. ℟

3. For the Lord has chosen Zion;
    he has desired it for his dwelling:
    'This is my resting-place for ever,
    here have I chosen to live.' ℟

SECOND READING   *(1 Cor 15:54-57)*

A reading from the first letter of St Paul to the Corinthians.

He gave us victory through our Lord Jesus Christ.

When this perishable nature has put on imperishability, and
when this mortal nature has put on immortality, then the words
of scripture will come true: Death is swallowed up in victory. Death,
where is your victory? Death, where is your sting? Now the sting
of death is sin, and sin gets its power from the Law. So let us
thank God for giving us the victory through our Lord Jesus Christ.

This is the word of the Lord.

GOSPEL ACCLAMATION   *(Lk 11:28)*

**Alleluia, alleluia!
Happy are those who hear the word of God, and keep it.
Alleluia!**

GOSPEL   *(Lk 11:27-28)*

A reading from the holy Gospel according to Luke.

Happy the womb that bore you!

As Jesus was speaking, a woman in the crowd raised her voice
and said, 'Happy the womb that bore you and the breasts you
sucked!' But he replied, 'Still happier those who hear the word
of God and keep it!'

This is the Gospel of the Lord.

PROFESSION OF FAITH — *pages 15-16*

PRAYER OVER THE GIFTS

Lord,
receive this sacrifice of praise and peace
in honour of the assumption of the Mother of God.
May our offering bring us pardon
and make our lives a thanksgiving to you.

PREFACE OF THE ASSUMPTION — *page 309*

COMMUNION ANTIPHON   *(cf. Lk 11:27)*

**Blessed is the womb of the Virgin Mary; she carried the Son of
the eternal Father.**

PRAYER AFTER COMMUNION

God of mercy,
we rejoice because Mary, the mother of our Lord,
was taken into the glory of heaven.
May the holy food we receive at this table
free us from evil.

SOLEMN BLESSING — *page 310*

REFLECTION

Mary was an eyewitness to many of the events of Jesus' life.
She was, therefore, a link between Jesus and those gatherings
of disciples who assembled to remember the events of his public
ministry. She handed on the faith to the new generation. The
writers of the gospels who were not themselves eyewitnesses
could not otherwise have succeeded in drawing up a faithful
picture of what had happened.

MASS DURING THE DAY

On this day the Church celebrates the tradition that at the end
of her earthly life the Blessed Virgin Mary was assumed into
heavenly glory. Some strands record that Mary died while
others attest that this took place while she was still alive. The
earliest references to this belief date from the Fourth Century
yet it wasn't until 1950 that Pope Pius XII defined it as an
article of faith. This date has been observed as a feastday of
Mary since the beginning of the Seventh Century.

ENTRANCE ANTIPHON   *(Rv 12:1)*
**A great sign appeared in heaven: a woman clothed with the
sun, the moon beneath her feet, and a crown of twelve stars
on her head.**

or

**Let us rejoice in the Lord and celebrate this feast in honour of
the Virgin Mary, at whose assumption the angels rejoice,
giving praise to the Son of God.**

GREETING, PENITENTIAL RITE, GLORIA — *pages 7-14*

OPENING PRAYER
Let us pray
    [that we will join Mary, the mother of the Lord,
    in the glory of heaven]
All-powerful and ever-living God,
you raised the sinless Virgin Mary, mother of your Son,
body and soul to the glory of heaven.
May we see heaven as our final goal
and come to share her glory.

or

Let us pray
    [that with the help of Mary's prayers
    we too may reach our heavenly home]
Father in heaven,
all creation rightly gives you praise,
for all life and all holiness come from you.

In the plan of your wisdom
she who bore the Christ in her womb
was raised body and soul in glory to be with him in heaven.

May we follow her example in reflecting your holiness
and join in her hymn of endless life and praise.

FIRST READING   *(Rv 11:19;12:1-6.10)*

A reading from the book of the Apocalypse.

A woman adorned with the sun, standing on the moon.

The sanctuary of God in heaven opened, and the ark of the covenant
could be seen inside it. Now a great sign appeared in heaven: a
woman, adorned with the sun, standing on the moon, and with
the twelve stars on her head for a crown. She was pregnant, and
in labour, crying aloud in the pangs of childbirth. Then a second
sign appeared in the sky, a huge red dragon which had seven
heads and ten horns, and each of the seven heads crowned with
a coronet. Its tail dragged a third of the stars from the sky and
dropped them to the earth, and the dragon stopped in front of
the woman as she was having the child, so that he could eat it as
soon as it was born from its mother. The woman brought a
male child into the world, the son who was to rule all the nations
with an iron sceptre, and the child was taken straight up to God
and to his throne, while the woman escaped into the desert, where
God had made a place of safety ready. Then I heard a voice shout
from heaven, "Victory and power and empire for ever have been
won by our God, and all authority for his Christ."

    This is the word of the Lord.

RESPONSORIAL PSALM   *(Ps 44:10-12.16)*

℟ **On your right stands the queen,**
    in garments of gold.

1. The daughters of kings are among your loved ones.
    On your right stands the queen in gold of Ophir.
    Listen, O daughter, give ear to my words:
    forget your own people and your father's house. ℟

2. So will the king desire your beauty:
    he is your lord, pay homage to him.
    They are escorted amid gladness and joy;
    they pass within the palace of the king. ℟

SECOND READING   *(1 Cor 15:20-27)*

A reading from the first letter of St Paul to the Corinthians.

Christ as the first-fruits and then those who belong to him.

Christ has been raised from the dead, the first-fruits of all who
have fallen asleep. Death came through one man and in the

same way the resurrection of the dead has come through one man. Just as all die in Adam, so all will be brought to life in Christ; but all of them in their proper order: Christ as the first-fruits and then, after the coming of Christ, those who belong to him. After that will come the end, when he hands over the kingdom to God the Father, having done away with every sovereignty, authority and power. For he must be king until he has put all his enemies under his feet and the last of the enemies to be destroyed is death, for everything is to be put under his feet — though when it is said that everything is subjected, this clearly cannot include the One who subjected everything to him.

This is the word of the Lord.

GOSPEL ACCLAMATION

Alleluia, alleluia!
Mary has been taken up into heaven;
all the choirs of angels are rejoicing. Alleluia!

GOSPEL   *(Lk 1:39-56)*
A reading from the holy Gospel according to Luke.

The Almighty has done great things for me, he has exalted the lowly.

Mary set out and went as quickly as she could to a town in the hill country of Judah. She went into Zechariah's house and greeted Elizabeth. Now as soon as Elizabeth heard Mary's greeting, the child leapt in her womb and Elizabeth was filled with the Holy Spirit. She gave a loud cry and said, "Of all women you are the most blessed, and blessed is the fruit of your womb. Why should I be honoured with a visit from the mother of my Lord? For the moment your greeting reached my ears, the child in my womb leapt for joy. Yes, blessed is she who believed that the promise made to her by the Lord would be fulfilled."

And Mary said:

"My soul proclaims the greatness of the Lord
and my spirit exults in God my saviour;
because he has looked upon his lowly handmaid.
Yes, from this day forward all generations will call me blessed,
for the Almighty has done great things for me.
Holy is his name,
and his mercy reaches from age to age for those who fear him.
He has shown the power of his arm,
he has routed the proud of heart.
He has pulled down princes from their thrones and exalted

the lowly.
The hungry he has filled with good things, the rich sent
    empty away.
He has come to the help of Israel his servant, mindful of his
    mercy
— according to the promise he made to our ancestors —
of his mercy to Abraham and to his descendants for ever."
Mary stayed with Elizabeth about three months and then went
back home.

This is the Gospel of the Lord.

PROFESSION OF FAITH — *pages 15-16*

PRAYER OVER THE GIFTS

Lord, receive this offering of our service.
You raised the Virgin Mary to the glory of heaven.
By her prayers, help us to seek you
and to live in your love.

PREFACE OF THE ASSUMPTION

Father, all-powerful and ever-living God,
we do well always and everywhere to give you thanks,
through Jesus Christ our Lord.

Today the virgin Mother of God was taken up into heaven
to be the beginning and the pattern of the Church in its perfection,
and a sign of hope and comfort for your people
    on their pilgrim way.
You would not allow decay to touch her body,
for she had given birth to your Son, the Lord of all life,
in the glory of the incarnation.

In our joy we sing to your glory
with all the choirs of angels:
Holy, holy, holy...

COMMUNION ANTIPHON   *(Lk 1:48-49)*
**All generations will call me blessed, for the Almighty has
done great things for me.**

PRAYER AFTER COMMUNION

Lord,
may we who receive this sacrament of salvation
be led to the glory of heaven
by the prayers of the Virgin Mary.

SOLEMN BLESSING

Born of the Blessed Virgin Mary,
the Son of God redeemed humankind.
May he enrich you with his blessings. **Amen**.

You received the author of life through Mary.
May you always rejoice in her loving care. **Amen**.

You have come to rejoice at Mary's feast.
May you be filled with the joys of the Spirit
and the gifts of your eternal home. **Amen**.

May almighty God bless you,
the Father, and the Son, ✠ and the Holy Spirit. **Amen**.

REFLECTION

> The *Magnificat* is the prayer which Luke puts on the lips of
> Mary. It is a revolutionary prayer at a number of levels: moral
> – scattering the proud; social – putting down the mighty and
> exalting the lowly and economic – filling the hungry and
> sending the rich away empty. The image which it paints of
> God is one who vindicates the weak against the powerful.

━━━━━ 22 AUGUST ━━━━━

21st SUNDAY IN ORDINARY TIME

> 'Who is Jesus?' is a question which Luke seeks to answer in his gospel
> and in the Acts of the Apostles. To answer this question he sometimes
> finds it necessary to correct an inadequate view of Jesus. As in
> the case of the two disciples on the road to Emmaus who are
> demoralised about the events surrounding Jesus' crucifixion. It
> is by returning to Jerusalem, which is also a journey back to the
> risen Lord, that they begin to have the question answered.

ENTRANCE ANTIPHON   *(Ps 85:1-3)*

**Listen, Lord, and answer me. Save your servant who trusts in
you. I call to you all day long, have mercy on me, O Lord.**

GREETING, PENITENTIAL RITE, GLORIA — *pages 7-14*

OPENING PRAYER

Let us pray
    [that God will make us one in mind and heart]

Father,
help us to seek the values

that will bring us lasting joy in this changing world.
In our desire for what you promise
make us one in mind and heart.

or

Let us pray
[with minds fixed on eternal truth]

Lord our God,
all truth is from you,
and you alone bring oneness of heart.

Give your people the joy
of hearing your word in every sound
and of longing for your presence more than for life itself.
May all the attractions of a changing world
serve only to bring us
the peace of your kingdom which this world does not give.

FIRST READING   *(Is 66:18-21)*

A reading from the prophet Isaiah.

They will bring all your brothers from all the nations.

The Lord says this: I am coming to gather the nations of every
language. They shall come to witness my glory. I will give them a
sign and send some of their survivors to the nations: to Tarshish,
Put, Lud, Moshech, Rosh, Tubal, and Javan, to the distant
islands that have never heard of me or seen my glory. They will
proclaim my glory to the nations. As an offering to the Lord they
will bring all your brothers, on horses, in chariots, in litters, on
mules, on dromedaries, from all the nations to my holy
mountain in Jerusalem, says the Lord, like Israelites bringing
oblations in clean vessels to the Temple of the Lord. And of
some of them I will make priests and Levites, says the Lord.

    This is the word of the Lord.

RESPONSORIAL PSALM   *(Ps 116)*

℞   **Go out to the whole world;
    proclaim the Good News.**

or   **Alleluia!**

1.   O praise the Lord, all you nations,
     acclaim him all you peoples!   ℞

2.   Strong is his love for us;
     he is faithful for ever.   ℞

SECOND READING   (Heb 12:5-7.11-13)

A reading from the letter to the Hebrews.

The Lord trains the one that he loves.

Have you forgotten that encouraging text in which you are addressed as sons? My son, when the Lord corrects you, do not treat it lightly; but do not get discouraged when he reprimands you. For the Lord trains the ones that he loves and he punishes all those that he acknowledges as his sons. Suffering is part of your training; God is treating you as his sons. Has there ever been any son whose father did not train him? Of course, any punishment is most painful at the time, and far from pleasant; but later, in those on whom it has been used, it bears fruit in peace and goodness. So hold up your limp arms and steady your trembling knees and smooth out the path you tread; then the injured limb will not be wrenched, it will grow strong again.

　　This is the word of the Lord.

GOSPEL ACCLAMATION   (Jn 14:23)

Alleluia, alleluia!
If anyone loves me he will keep my word,
and my Father will love him,
and we shall come to him.
Alleluia!

or   (Jn 14:6)

Alleluia, alleluia!
I am the Way, the Truth and the Life, says the Lord;
no one can come to the Father except through me.
Alleluia!

GOSPEL   (Lk 13:22-30)

A reading from the holy Gospel according to Luke.

Men from east and west will come to take their places at the feast in the kingdom of God.

Through towns and villages Jesus went teaching, making his way to Jerusalem. Someone said to him, 'Sir, will there be only a few saved?' He said to them, 'Try your best to enter by the narrow door, because I tell you, many will try to enter and will not succeed.

　　'Once the master of the house has got up and locked the door, you may find yourself knocking on the door, saying, "Lord, open to us" but he will answer, "I do not know where you come from." Then you will find yourself saying, "We once ate and drank in your company; you taught in our streets" but he will reply, "I do not know where you come from. Away from me, all you wicked men!"

'Then there will be weeping and grinding of teeth, when you see Abraham and Isaac and Jacob and all the prophets in the kingdom of God, and yourselves turned outside. And men from east and west, from north and south, will come to take their places at the feast in the kingdom of God.

'Yes, there are those now last who will be first, and those now first who will be last.'

This is the Gospel of the Lord.

PROFESSION OF FAITH — *pages 15-16*

PRAYER OVER THE GIFTS

Merciful God,
the perfect sacrifice of Jesus Christ
made us your people.
In your love,
grant peace and unity to your Church.

PREFACE OF SUNDAYS IN ORDINARY TIME — *pages 22-25*

COMMUNION ANTIPHON   *(Ps 103:13-15)*

Lord, the earth is filled with your gift from heaven; man grows bread from earth, and wine to cheer his heart.

or   *(Jn 6:55)*

The Lord says: The man who eats my flesh and drinks my blood will live for ever; I shall raise him to life on the last day.

PRAYER AFTER COMMUNION

Lord,
may this eucharist increase within us
the healing power of your love.
May it guide and direct our efforts
to please you in all things.

SOLEMN BLESSING — *pages 57-58*

REFLECTION

The stranger who meets the two disciples on the road to Emmaus journeys with them, talks with them and eventually shares a meal with them. By his closeness to them he transforms failure into fidelity. The assurance of the presence of Jesus with his community today is the inspiration that can equally transform our failures.

29 AUGUST
22nd SUNDAY IN ORDINARY TIME

The parables of Luke's gospel appear towards the end of Jesus'
ministry when some of the crowds are abandoning him, perhaps
from fear of the establishment or for reasons of respectability.
The 'harsh ones' are a last warning that such a path is the direct
opposite to true discipleship which by contrast is portrayed as
remaining with Jesus who remains with his followers.

ENTRANCE ANTIPHON   *(Ps 85:3.5)*
**I call to you all day long, have mercy on me, O Lord. You are
good and forgiving, full of love for all who call to you.**

GREETING, PENITENTIAL RITE, GLORIA — *pages 7-14*

OPENING PRAYER
Let us pray
    [that God will increase our faith
    and bring to perfection the gifts he has given us]
Almighty God,
every good thing comes from you.
Fill our hearts with love for you,
increase our faith,
and by your constant care
protect the good you have given us.
or
Let us pray
    [to God who forgives all who call upon him]
Lord God of power and might,
nothing is good which is against your will,
and all is of value which comes from your hand.
Place in our hearts a desire to please you
and fill our minds with insight into love,
so that every thought may grow in wisdom
and all our efforts may be filled with your peace.

FIRST READING   *(Si 3:17-20.28-29)*
A reading from the book of Ecclesiasticus.
Behave humbly, and then you will find favour with the Lord.
My son, be gentle in carrying out your business,
and you will be better loved than a lavish giver.
The greater you are, the more you should behave humbly,

and then you will find favour with the Lord;
for great though the power of the Lord is,
he accepts the homage of the humble.
There is no cure for the proud man's malady,
since an evil growth has taken root in him.
The heart of a sensible man will reflect on parables,
an attentive ear is the sage's dream.

   This is the word of the Lord.

RESPONSORIAL PSALM   *(Ps 67:4-7.10-11)*

℞   **In your goodness, O God,
     you prepared a home for the poor.**

1.   The just shall rejoice at the presence of God,
     they shall exult and dance for joy.
     O sing to the Lord, make music to his name;
     rejoice in the Lord, exult at his presence. ℞

2.   Father of the orphan, defender of the widow,
     such is God in his holy place.
     God gives the lonely a home to live in;
     he leads the prisoners forth into freedom. ℞

3.   You poured down, O God, a generous rain:
     when your people were starved you gave them new life.
     It was there that your people found a home,
     prepared in your goodness, O God, for the poor. ℞

SECOND READING   *(Heb 12:18-19.22-24)*

A reading from the letter to the Hebrews.

You have come to Mount Zion and the city of the living God.

What you have come to is nothing known to the senses: not a
blazing fire, or a gloom turning to total darkness, or a storm; or
trumpeting thunder or the great voice speaking which made
everyone that heard it beg that no more should be said to them.
But what you have come to is Mount Zion and the city of the
living God, the heavenly Jerusalem where the millions of angels
have gathered for the festival, with the whole Chuch in which
everyone is a 'first-born son' and a citizen of heaven. You have
come to God himself, the supreme Judge, and been placed with
spirits of the saints who have been made perfect; and to Jesus,
the mediator who brings a new covenant.

   This is the word of the Lord.

GOSPEL ACCLAMATION   (Jn 14:23)
Alleluia, alleluia!
If anyone loves me he will keep my word,
and my Father will love him,
and we shall come to him. Alleluia!

or   (Mt 11:29)

Alleluia, alleluia!
Shoulder my yoke and learn from me,
for I am gentle and humble in heart. Alleluia!

GOSPEL   (Lk 14:1.7-14)
A reading from the holy Gospel according to Luke.

Everyone who exalts himself will be humbled, and the man who humbles himself will be exalted.

On a sabbath day Jesus had gone for a meal to the house of one of the leading Pharisees; and they watched him closely. He then told the guests a parable, because he had noticed how they picked the places of honour. He said this, 'When someone invites you to a wedding feast, do not take your seat in the place of honour. A more distinguished person than you may have been invited, and the person who invited you both may come and say, "Give up your place to this man." And then, to your embarrassment, you would have to go and take the lowest place. No; when you are a guest, make your way to the lowest place and sit there, so that, when your host comes, he may say, "My friend, move up higher." In that way, everyone with you at the table will see you honoured. For everyone who exalts himself will be humbled, and the man who humbles himself will be exalted.'

Then he said to his host, 'When you give a lunch or a dinner, do not ask your friends, brothers, relations or rich neighbours, for fear they repay your courtesy by inviting you in return. No; when you have a party, invite the poor, the crippled, the lame, the blind; that they cannot pay you back means that you are fortunate, because repayment will be made to you when the virtuous rise again.'

This is the Gospel of the Lord.

PROFESSION OF FAITH — *pages 15-16*

PRAYER OVER THE GIFTS
Lord, may this holy offering
bring us your blessing
and accomplish within us
its promise of salvation.

PREFACE OF SUNDAYS IN ORDINARY TIME — *pages 22-25*

COMMUNION ANTIPHON   *(Ps 30:20)*

O Lord, how great is the depth of the kindness which you have shown to those who love you.

or   *(Mt 5:9-10)*

Happy are the peacemakers; they shall be called sons of God. Happy are they who suffer persecution for justice's sake; the kingdom of heaven is theirs.

PRAYER AFTER COMMUNION

Lord, you renew us at your table with the bread of life.
May this food strengthen us in love
and help us to serve you in each other.

SOLEMN BLESSING — *pages 57-58*

REFLECTION

> Jesus met opposition from the religious teachers of his day especially in his presentation of God's mercy. In the parable of the lost sheep Luke directs Jesus' words against those who opposed him on this point. He uses it to explain why Jesus, in the name of God, seeks out sinners and rejoices in their conversion. This message is for us today as much as it was for Jesus' first hearers and later for Luke's community

—————— 5 SEPTEMBER ——————

23rd SUNDAY IN ORDINARY TIME

'The Kingdom of God' is a term which we frequently meet in Luke's gospel. It is a metaphor used by Jesus to refer to God's reign in the world being accepted by humankind. The kingdom is not identical with the Church. Wherever the values which Jesus lived and preached are operating, even though the Church may not be established in that place, the Kingdom is already there.

ENTRANCE ANTIPHON   *(Ps 118:137.124)*

Lord, you are just, and the judgements you make are right. Show mercy when you judge me, your servant.

GREETING, PENITENTIAL RITE, GLORIA — *pages 7-14*

OPENING PRAYER

Let us pray
  [that we may realise the freedom God has given us
  in making us his sons and daughters]

God our Father,
you redeem us
and make us your children in Christ.
Look upon us,
give us true freedom
and bring us to the inheritance you promised.

or

Let us pray
  [to our just and merciful God]

Lord our God,
in you justice and mercy meet.
With unparalleled love you have saved us from death
and drawn us into the circle of your life.

Open our eyes to the wonders this life sets before us,
that we may serve you free from fear
and address you as God our Father.

FIRST READING   (Ws 9:13-18)

A reading from the book of Wisdom.

Who can divine the will of the Lord?

'What man can know the intentions of God?
Who can divine the will of the Lord?
The reasonings of mortals are unsure
and our intentions unstable;
for a perishable body presses down the soul,
and this tent of clay weighs down the teeming mind.
It is hard enough for us to work out what is on earth,
laborious to know what lies within our reach;
who, then, can discover what is in the heavens
As for your intention, who could have learnt it, had you not
    granted Wisdom
and sent your holy spirit from above?
Thus have the paths of those on earth been straightened
and men been taught what pleases you,
and saved, by Wisdom.'

    This is the word of the Lord.

RESPONSORIAL PSALM   *(Ps 89:3-6.12-14.17)*

℟ **O Lord, you have been our refuge**
    from one generation to the next.

1. You turn men back into dust
    and say: 'Go back, sons of men.'
    To your eyes a thousand years
    are like yesterday, come and gone,
    no more than a watch in the night. ℟

2. You sweep men away like a dream,
    like grass which springs up in the morning.
    In the morning it springs up and flowers:
    by evening it withers and fades. ℟

3. Make us know the shortness of our life
    that we may gain wisdom of heart.
    Lord, relent! Is your anger for ever.
    Show pity to your servants. ℟

4. In the morning, fill us with your love;
    we shall exult and rejoice all our days.
    Let the favour of the Lord be upon us:
    give success to the work of our hands. ℟

SECOND READING   *(Phm 9-10.12-17)*

A reading from the letter of St Paul to Philemon.

Have him back, not as a slave any more, but as a dear brother.

This is Paul writing, an old man now and, what is more, still a
prisoner of Christ Jesus. I am appealing to you for a child of
mine, whose father I became while wearing these chains: I mean
Onesimus. I am sending him back to you, and with him — I
could say — a part of my own self. I should have liked to keep
him with me; he could have been a substitute for you, to help
me while I am in the chains that the Good News has brought
me. However, I did not want to do anything without your
consent; it would have been forcing your act of kindness, which
should be spontaneous. I know you have been deprived of
Onesimus for a time, but it was only so that you could have him
back for ever, not as a slave any more, but something much
better than a slave, a dear brother; especially dear to me, but
how much more to you, as a blood-brother as well as a brother
in the Lord. So if all that we have in common means anything to
you, welcome him as you would me.

This is the word of the Lord.

GOSPEL ACCLAMATION   *(Jn 15:15)*
Alleluia, alleluia!
I call you friends, says the Lord,
because I have made known to you
everything I have learnt from my Father. Alleluia!
or   *(Ps 118:135)*
Alleluia, alleluia!
Let your face shine on your servant,
and teach me your decrees. Alleluia!

GOSPEL   *(Lk 14:25-33)*
A reading from the holy Gospel according to Luke.
None of you can be my disciple unless he gives up all his possessions.
Great crowds accompanied Jesus on his way and he turned and
spoke to them. 'If any man comes to me without hating his
father, mother, wife, children, brothers, sisters, yes and his own
life too, he cannot be my disciple. Anyone who does not carry
his cross and come after me cannot be my disciple.

　　'And indeed, which of you here, intending to build a tower,
would not first sit down and work out the cost to see if he had
enough to complete it? Otherwise, if he laid the foundation and
then found himself unable to finish the work, the onlookers
would all start making fun of him and saying, 'Here is a man
who started to build and was unable to finish.' Or again, what
king marching to war against another king would not first sit
down and consider whether with ten thousand men he could
stand up to the other who advanced against him with twenty
thousand? If not, then while the other king was still a long way
off, he would send envoys to sue for peace. So in the same way,
none of you can be my disciple unless he gives up all his
possessions.'

　　This is the Gospel of the Lord.

PROFESSION OF FAITH — *pages 15-16*

PRAYER OVER THE GIFTS
God of peace and love,
may our offering bring you true worship
and make us one with you.

PREFACE OF SUNDAYS IN ORDINARY TIME — *pages 22-25*

COMMUNION ANTIPHON   *(Ps 41:2-3)*
Like a deer that longs for running streams, my soul longs for
you, my God. My soul is thirsting for the living God.

or   (Jn 8:12)

**I am the light of the world, says the Lord; the man who
follows me will have the light of life.**

PRAYER AFTER COMMUNION

Lord, your word and your sacrament
give us food and life.
May this gift of your Son
lead us to share his life for ever.

SOLEMN BLESSING — *pages 57-58*

REFLECTION

> One of the mysterious aspects of the Kingdom of God is that
> on the one hand it is already here and, on the other, it has not
> yet arrived. The message of a number of kingdom parables is
> that the kingdom spreads silently and unobtrusively. In spite
> of apparently weak beginnings and feeble efforts the kingdom
> is taking root wherever people treat one another with respect
> and love.

━━━━━━━━━━━ 12 SEPTEMBER ━━━━━━━━━━━

24th SUNDAY IN ORDINARY TIME

The Christian assembly is an assembly of disciples of Jesus. A
disciple is literally one who is learning. Learning requires
openness of mind and heart. The scripture readings and the
prayers of today's liturgy are a powerful force for teaching and
learning about the way of Jesus.

ENTRANCE ANTIPHON   (Si 36:18)

**Give peace, Lord, to those who wait for you and your
prophets will proclaim you as you deserve. Hear the prayers
of your servant and of your people Israel.**

GREETING, PENITENTIAL RITE, GLORIA — *pages 7-14*

OPENING PRAYER

Let us pray
    [that God will keep us faithful in his service]

Almighty God,
our creator and guide,
may we serve you with all our heart
and know your forgiveness in our lives.

or

Let us pray
    [for the peace which is born of faith and hope]

Father in heaven, Creator of all,
look down upon your people in their moments of need,
for you alone are the source of our peace.
Bring us to the dignity which distinguishes the poor in spirit
and show us how great is the call to serve,
that we may share in the peace of Christ
who offered his life in the service of all.

FIRST READING   *(Ex 32:7-11.13-14)*

A reading from the book of Exodus.

The Lord relented and did not bring on his people the disaster he had
threatened.

The Lord spoke to Moses, 'Go down now, because your people
whom you brought out of Egypt have apostatised. They have
been quick to leave the way I marked out for them; they have
made themselves a calf of molten metal and have worshipped it
and offered it sacrifice. "Here is your God, Israel," they have
cried "who brought you up from the land of Egypt!" I can see
how headstrong these people are! Leave me, now, my wrath
shall blaze out against them and devour them; of you, however,
I will make a great nation.'

    But Moses pleaded with the Lord his God. 'Lord,' he said,
'why should your wrath blaze out against this people of yours
whom you brought out of the land of Egypt with arm
outstretched and mighty hand? Remember Abraham, Isaac and
Jacob, your servants to whom by your own self you swore and
made this promise: I will make your offspring as many as the
stars of heaven, and all this land which I promised I will give to
your descendants, and it shall be their heritage for ever.' So the
Lord relented and did not bring on the people the disaster he
had threatened.

    This is the word of the Lord.

RESPONSORIAL PSALM   *(Ps 50:3-4.12-13.17.19)*

℟   I will leave this place and go to my father.

1.   Have mercy on me, God, in your kindness.
     In your compassion blot out my offence.
     O wash me more and more from my guilt
     and cleanse me from my sin. ℟

2. A pure heart create for me, O God,
    put a steadfast spirit within me.
    Do not cast me away from your presence,
    nor deprive me of your holy spirit. ℟

3. O Lord, open my lips
    and my mouth shall declare your praise.
    My sacrifice is a contrite spirit;
    a humbled, contrite heart you will not spurn. ℟

SECOND READING   *(1 Tm 1:12-17)*

A reading from the first letter of St Paul to Timothy.

Christ Jesus came into the world to save sinners.

I thank Christ Jesus our Lord, who has given me strength, and
who judged me faithful enough to call into his service even
though I used to be a blasphemer and did all I could to injure
and discredit the faith. Mercy, however, was shown me, because
until I became a believer I had been acting in ignorance; and the
grace of our Lord filled me with faith and with the love that is in
Christ Jesus. Here is a saying that you can rely on and nobody
should doubt: that Christ Jesus came into the world to save
sinners. I myself am the greatest of them; and if mercy has been
shown to me, it is because Jesus Christ meant to make me the
greatest evidence of his inexhaustible patience for all the other
people who would later have to trust in him to come to eternal
life. To the eternal King, the undying, invisible and only God, be
honour and glory for ever and ever. Amen.

This is the word of the Lord.

GOSPEL ACCLAMATION   *(cf. Eph 1:17.18)*

Alleluia, alleluia!
May the Father of our Lord Jesus Christ
enlighten the eyes of our mind,
so that we can see what hope his call holds for us. Alleluia!
or   *(2 Cor 5:19)*
Alleluia, alleluia!
God in Christ was reconciling the world to himself,
and he has entrusted to us the news that they are reconciled.
Alleluia!

GOSPEL   *(Lk 15:1-32)*

(For Shorter Form, *read between* ◆ ◀*)*

A reading from the holy Gospel according to Luke.

There will be rejoicing in heaven over one repentant sinner.

▶The tax collectors and the sinners were all seeking the company of Jesus to hear what he had to say, and the Pharisees and the scribes complained. 'This man' they said 'welcomes sinners and eats with them.' So he spoke this parable to them:

'What man among you with a hundred sheep, losing one, would not leave the ninety-nine in the wilderness and go after the missing one till he found it? And when he found it, would he not joyfully take it on his shoulders and then, when he got home, call together his friends, and neighbours? "Rejoice with me," he would say "I have found my sheep that was lost." In the same way, I tell you, there will be more rejoicing in heaven over one repentant sinner than over ninety-nine virtuous men who have no need of repentance.

'Or again, what woman with ten drachmas would not, if she lost one, light a lamp and sweep out the house and search thoroughly till she found it? And then, when she had found it, call together her friends and neighbours? "Rejoice with me," she would say "I have found the drachma I lost." In the same way, I tell you, there is rejoicing among the angels of God over one repentant sinner.'◀

He also said, 'A man had two sons. The younger said to his father, 'Father, let me have the share of the estate that would come to me." So the father divided the property between them. A few days later the younger son got together everything he had and left for a distant country where he squandered his money on a life of debauchery.

'When he had spent it all, that country experienced a severe famine, and now he began to feel the pinch, so he hired himself out to one of the local inhabitants who put him on his farm to feed the pigs. And he would willingly have filled his belly with the husks the pigs were eating but no one offered him anything. Then he came to his senses and said, "How many of my father's paid servants have more food than they want, and here am I dying of hunger! I will leave this place and go to my father and say: Father, I have sinned against heaven and against you; I no longer deserve to be called your son; treat me as one of your paid servants." So he left the place and went back to his father.

'While he was still a long way off, his father saw him and was moved with pity. He ran to the boy, clasped him in his arms and kissed him tenderly. Then his son said, "Father, I have sinned against heaven and against you. I no longer deserve to be called your son." But the father said to his servants, "Quick! Bring out the best robe and put it on him; put a ring on his finger and sandals on his feet. Bring the calf we have been fattening, and kill it; we are going to have a feast, a celebration, because this son of mine was dead and has come back to life; he was lost and is found." And they began to celebrate.

'Now the elder son was out in the fields, and on his way back, as he drew near the house, he could hear music and dancing. Calling one of the servants he asked what it was all about. "Your brother has come" replied the servant "and your father has killed the calf we had fattened because he has got him back safe and sound." He was angry then and refused to go in, and his father came out to plead with him; but he answered his father, "Look, all these years I have slaved for you and never once disobeyed your orders, yet you never offered me so much as a kid for me to celebrate with my friends. But, for this son of yours, when he comes back after swallowing up your property — he and his women — you kill the calf we had been fattening."

'The father said, "My son, you are with me always and all I have is yours. But it was only right we should celebrate and rejoice, because your brother here was dead and has come to life; he was lost and is found." '

◆This is the Gospel of the Lord.◀

PROFESSION OF FAITH — *pages 15-16*

PRAYER OVER THE GIFTS
Lord, hear the prayers of your people
and receive our gifts.
May the worship of each one here
bring salvation to all.

PREFACE OF SUNDAYS IN ORDINARY TIME — *pages 22-25*

COMMUNION ANTIPHON   (Ps 35:8)
O God, how much we value your mercy! All humankind can gather under your protection.
or   (cf 1 Cor 10:16)
The cup that we bless is a communion with the blood of Christ; and the bread that we break is a communion with the body of the Lord.

PRAYER AFTER COMMUNION
Lord, may the eucharist you have given us
influence our thoughts and actions.
May your Spirit guide and direct us in your way.

SOLEMN BLESSING — *pages 57-58*

REFLECTION

The demands which Jesus makes in Luke's gospel are first a call to repentance, which means an invitation to change one's attitude. Secondly, a call to faith. Faith has been described as the human response to God's revelation in Jesus Christ. And thirdly, a call to discipleship, which may be summed up as a call to be 'with' Jesus.

===== 19 SEPTEMBER =====

25th SUNDAY IN ORDINARY TIME

At every Mass we recite the Lord's prayer. The liturgy of the Church uses this prayer also each day at morning prayer and evening prayer. It is Jesus' response to the request of his disciples to teach them how to pray. In Matthew's account it contains seven petitions and in Luke's five. The Church has used Matthew's version in its liturgical celebration.

ENTRANCE ANTIPHON

I am the Saviour of all people, says the Lord. Whatever their troubles, I will answer their cry, and I will always be their Lord.

GREETING, PENITENTIAL RITE, GLORIA — *pages 7-14*

OPENING PRAYER

Let us pray
    [that we will grow in the love of God
    and of one another]
Father, guide us, as you guide creation
according to your law of love.
May we love one another
and come to perfection
in the eternal life prepared for us.

or

Let us pray
    [to the Lord who is a God of love to all peoples]

Father in heaven,
the perfection of justice is found in your love
and all humankind is in need of your law.
Help us to find this love in each other
that justice may be attained
through obedience to your law.

FIRST READING   (Am 8:4-7)

A reading from the prophet Amos.

Against those who 'buy up the poor for money.'

Listen to this, you who trample on the needy
and try to suppress the poor people of the country,
you who say, 'When will New Moon be over
so that we can sell our corn,
and sabbath, so that we can market our wheat?
Then by lowering the bushel, raising the shekel,
by swindling and tampering with the scales,
we can buy up the poor for money,
and the needy for a pair of sandals,
and get a price even for the sweeping of the wheat.'
The Lord swears it by the pride of Jacob,
'Never will I forget a single thing you have done.'

       This is the word of the Lord.

RESPONSORIAL PSALM   (Ps 112:1-2.4-8)

℟   **Praise the Lord, who raises the poor.**

or   **Alleluia!**

1.   Praise, O servants of the Lord,
     praise the name of the Lord!
     May the name of the Lord be blessed
     both now and for evermore! ℟

2.   High above all nations is the Lord,
     above the heavens his glory.
     Who is like the Lord, our God,
     who has risen on high to his throne
     yet stoops from the heights to look down,
     to look down upon heaven and earth? ℟

3.   From the dust he lifts up the lowly,
     from the dungheap he raises the poor
     to set him in the company of princes,
     yes, with the princes of his people. ℟

SECOND READING   (1 Tm 2:1-8)

A reading from the first letter of St Paul to Timothy.

There should be prayers offered for everyone to God, who wants
everyone to be saved.

My advice is that, first of all, there should be prayers offered for
everyone — petitions, intercessions and thanksgiving — and
especially for kings and others in authority, so that we may be

able to live religious and reverent lives in peace and quiet. To do this is right, and will please God our saviour: he wants everyone to be saved and reach full knowledge of the truth. For there is only one God, and there is only one mediator between God and humankind, himself a man, Christ Jesus, who sacrificed himself as a ransom for them all. He is the evidence of this, sent at the appointed time, and I have been named a herald and apostle of it and — I am telling the truth and no lie — a teacher of the faith and the truth to the pagans.

In every place, then, I want the men to lift their hands up reverently in prayer, with no anger or argument.

This is the word of the Lord.

GOSPEL ACCLAMATION   *(cf. Acts 16:14)*
Alleluia, alleluia!
Open our heart, O Lord,
to accept the words of your Son,
Alleluia!
or   *(2 Cor 8:9)*
Alleluia, alleluia!
Jesus Christ was rich,
but he became poor for your sake,
to make you rich out of his poverty.
Alleluia!

GOSPEL   *(Lk 16:1-13)*
(For Shorter Form, *read between* ▶ ◀*)*
A reading from the holy Gospel according to Luke.
You cannot be the slave both of God and of money.
▶Jesus said to his disciples,◀ 'There was a rich man and he had a steward who was denounced to him for being wasteful with his property. He called for the man and said, "What is this I hear about you? Draw me up an account of your stewardship because you are not to be my steward any longer." Then the steward said to himself, "Now that my master is taking the stewardship from me, what am I to do? Dig? I am not strong enough. Go begging? I should be too ashamed. Ah, I know what I will do to make sure that when I am dismissed from office there will be some to welcome me into their homes."

'Then he called his master's debtors one by one. To the first he said, "How much do you owe my master?" "One hundred measures of oil" was the reply. The steward said, "Here, take your bond; sit down straight away and write fifty." To another he said, "And you, sir, how much do you owe?" "One hundred measures of wheat" was the reply. The steward said, "Here, take your bond and write eighty."

'The master praised the dishonest steward for his astuteness. For the children of this world are more astute in dealing with their own kind than are the children of light.

'And so I tell you this: use money, tainted as it is, to win you friends, and thus make sure that when it fails you, they will welcome you into the tents of eternity. ▸The man who can be trusted in little things can be trusted in great; the man who is dishonest in little things can be dishonest in great. If then you cannot be trusted with money, that tainted thing, who will trust you with genuine riches? And if you cannot be trusted with what is not yours, who will give you what is your very own?

'No servant can be the slave of two masters: he will either hate the first and love the second, or treat the first with respect and the second with scorn. You cannot be the slave both of God and of money.'

This is the Gospel of the Lord.◂

PROFESSION OF FAITH — *pages 15-16*

PRAYER OVER THE GIFTS

Lord, may these gifts which we now offer
to show our belief and our love
be pleasing to you.
May they become for us
the eucharist of Jesus Christ your Son,
who is Lord for ever and ever.

PREFACE OF SUNDAYS IN ORDINARY TIME — *pages 22-25*

COMMUNION ANTIPHON   (Ps 118:4-5)

You have laid down your precepts to be faithfully kept. May my footsteps be firm in keeping your commands.

or   (Jn 10:14)

I am the Good Shepherd, says the Lord; I know my sheep, and mine know me.

PRAYER AFTER COMMUNION

Lord, help us with your kindness.
Make us strong through the eucharist.
May we put into action
the saving mystery we celebrate.

SOLEMN BLESSING — *pages 57-58*

REFLECTION

From a very early stage the Church completed the Lord's prayer with a special formula giving glory to God. One of the most ancient of Christian documents the *Didache* which may go back to the First Century contains the ending: 'For yours are the power and the glory for ever.' 'The kingdom' was added by another ancient document *The Apostolic Constitutions* from the Fourth Century and this is the formula which is retained today in inter-Church prayer.

---

26 SEPTEMBER

26th SUNDAY IN ORDINARY TIME

The Lord's prayer has been described as a summary of the whole gospel. Saint Augustine maintained that there is nothing in all the prayers found in the scriptures which is not included in the Lord's prayer. Each person has their own particular needs which they may bring before the Father. The Lord's prayer may be said as an expression of the foundation of all further desires.

ENTRANCE ANTIPHON   *(Dan 3:31.29.30.43.42)*

O Lord, you had just cause to judge men as you did: because we sinned against you and disobeyed your will. But now show us your greatness of heart, and treat us with your unbounded kindness.

GREETING, PENITENTIAL RITE, GLORIA — *pages 7-14*

OPENING PRAYER

Let us pray
    [for God's forgiveness
    and for the happiness it brings]
Father, you show your almighty power
in your mercy and forgiveness.
Continue to fill us with your gifts of love.
Help us to hurry toward the eternal life you promise
and come to share in the joys of your kingdom.
or
Let us pray
    [for the peace of the kingdom
    which we have been promised]
Father of our Lord Jesus Christ,

in your unbounded mercy
you have revealed the beauty of your power
through your constant forgiveness of our sins.
May the power of this love be in our hearts
to bring your pardon and your kingdom to all we meet.

FIRST READING   *(Am 6:1.4-7)*

A reading from the prophet Amos.

Those who sprawl and those who bawl will be exiled.

The almighty Lord says this:

> Woe to those ensconced so snugly in Zion
> and those who feel so safe on the mountain of Samaria.
> Lying on ivory beds
> and sprawling on their divans,
> they dine on lambs from the flock,
> and stall-fattened veal;
> they bawl to the sound of the harp,
> they invent new instruments of music like David,
> they drink wine by the bowlful,
> and use the finest oil for anointing themselves,
> but about the ruin of Joseph they do not care at all.
> That is why they will be the first to be exiled;
> the sprawlers' revelry is over.

This is the word of the Lord.

RESPONSORIAL PSALM   *(Ps 145:6-10)*

℟ **My soul, give praise to the Lord.**

or **Alleluia!**

1. It is the Lord who keeps faith for ever,
   who is just to those who are oppressed.
   It is he who gives bread to the hungry,
   the Lord, who sets prisoners free. ℟

2. It is the Lord who gives sight to the blind,
   who raises up those who are bowed down.
   It is the Lord who loves the just,
   the Lord, who protects the stranger. ℟

3. He upholds the widow and orphan
   but thwarts the path of the wicked.
   The Lord will reign for ever,
   Zion's God, from age to age. ℟

SECOND READING   (1 Tm 6:11-16)

A reading from the first letter of St Paul to Timothy.

Do all that you have been told until the Appearing of the Lord.

As a man dedicated to God, you must aim to be saintly and religious, filled with faith and love, patient and gentle. Fight the good fight of the faith and win for yourself the eternal life to which you were called when you made your profession and spoke up for the truth in front of many witnesses. Now, before God the source of all life and before Jesus Christ, who spoke up as a witness for the truth in front of Pontius Pilate, I put to you the duty of doing all that you have been told, with no faults or failures, until the Appearing of our Lord Jesus Christ,

> who at the due time will be revealed
> by God, the blessed and only Ruler of all,
> the King of kings and the Lord of lords,
> who alone is immortal,
> whose home is in inaccessible light,
> whom no man has seen and no man is able to see:
> to him be honour and everlasting power. Amen.

This is the word of the Lord.

GOSPEL ACCLAMATION   (Jn 10:27)

Alleluia, alleluia!
The sheep that belong to me listen to my voice,
says the Lord,
I know them and they follow me. Alleluia!

or   (2 Cor 8:9)

Alleluia, alleluia!
Jesus Christ was rich,
but he became poor for your sake,
to make you rich out of his poverty. Alleluia!

GOSPEL   (Lk 16:19-31)

A reading from the holy Gospel according to Luke.

Good things came your way, just as bad things came the way of Lazarus. Now he is being comforted here while you are in agony.

Jesus said to the Pharisees: 'There was a rich man who used to dress in purple and fine linen and feast magnificently every day. And at his gate there lay a poor man called Lazarus, covered with sores, who longed to fill himself with the scraps that fell from the rich man's table. Dogs even came and licked his sores. Now the poor man died and was carried away by the angels to the bosom of Abraham. The rich man also died and was buried.

'In his torment in Hades he looked up and saw Abraham a long way off with Lazarus in his bosom. So he cried out, "Father Abraham, pity me and send Lazarus to dip the tip of his finger in water and cool my tongue, for I am in agony in these flames." "My son," Abraham replied "remember that during your life good things came your way, just as bad things came the way of Lazarus. Now he is being comforted here while you are in agony. But that is not all: between us and you a great gulf has been fixed, to stop any crossing from your side to ours."

'The rich man replied, "Father, I beg you then to send Lazarus to my father's house, since I have five brothers, to give them warning so that they do not come to this place of torment too." "They have Moses and the prophets," said Abraham "let them listen to them." "Ah no, father Abraham," said the rich man "but if someone comes to them from the dead, they will repent." Then Abraham said to him, "If they will not listen either to Moses or to the prophets, they will not be convinced even if someone should rise from the dead." '

This is the Gospel of the Lord.

PROFESSION OF FAITH — *pages 15-16*

PRAYER OVER THE GIFTS

God of mercy,
accept our offering
and make it a source of blessing for us.

PREFACE OF SUNDAYS IN ORDINARY TIME — *pages 22-25*

COMMUNION ANTIPHON   (Ps 118: 49-50)

O Lord, remember the words you spoke to me, your servant, which made me live in hope and consoled me when I was downcast.

or   (1 Jn 3:16)

This is how we know what love is: Christ gave up his life for us; and we too must give up our lives for our brothers.

PRAYER AFTER COMMUNION

Lord, may this eucharist
in which we proclaim the death of Christ
bring us salvation
and make us one with him in glory,
for he is Lord for ever and ever.

SOLEMN BLESSING — *pages 57-58*

REFLECTION

> Saint Thomas Aquinas said of the Our Father: 'The Lord's
> prayer is the most perfect of prayers. In it we ask not only for
> all the things we can rightly desire, but also in the order that
> they should be desired.' This prayer encourages us to ask the
> Father for what we need. To do so is in itself a declaration of faith.

---

3 OCTOBER

27th SUNDAY IN ORDINARY TIME

> Today's liturgy invites us to focus on forgiveness. The gospel
> passage follows immediately on Jesus' urging his apostles to
> exercise unlimited forgiveness. He answers their objection by
> focusing on faith. Real faith will empower them to forgive to
> this degree.

ENTRANCE ANTIPHON   (Est 13:9.10-11)

**O Lord, you have given everything its place in the world, and
no one can make it otherwise. For it is your creation, the
heavens and the earth and the stars: your are the Lord of all.**

GREETING, PENITENTIAL RITE, GLORIA — *pages 7-14*

OPENING PRAYER

Let us pray

> [that God will forgive our failings
> and bring us peace]

Father,
your love for us
surpasses all our hopes and desires.
Forgive our failings,
keep us in your peace
and lead us in the way of salvation.

or

Let us pray

> [before the face of God, in trusting faith]

Almighty and eternal God,
Father of the world to come,
your goodness is beyond what our spirit can touch
and your strength is more than the mind can bear.
Lead us to seek beyond our reach
and give us the courage to stand before your truth.

FIRST READING   *(Hab 1:2-3; 2:2-4)*

A reading from the prophet Habakkuk.

The upright man will live by his faithfulness.

How long, Lord, am I to cry for help
while you will not listen;
to cry 'Oppression!' in your ear
and you will not save?
Why do you set injustice before me,
why do you look on where there is tyranny?
Outrage and violence, this is all I see,
all is contention, and discord flourishes.
Then the Lord answered and said,

> 'Write the vision down,
> inscribe it on tablets
> to be easily read,
> since this vision is for its own time only:
> eager for its own fulfilment, it does not deceive;
> if it comes slowly, wait,
> for come it will, without fail.
> See how he flags, he whose soul is not at rights,
> but the upright man will live by his faithfulness.'

This is the word of the Lord.

RESPONSORIAL PSALM   *(Ps 94:1-2.6-9)*

℟   **O that today you would listen to his voice!
    Harden not your hearts.**

1. Come, ring out our joy to the Lord;
    hail the rock who saves us.
    Let us come before him, giving thanks,
    with songs let us hail the Lord. ℟

2. Come in; let us bow and bend low;
    let us kneel before the God who made us
    for he is our God and we
    the people who belong to his pasture,
    the flock that is led by his hand. ℟

3. O that today you would listen to his voice!
    'Harden not your hearts as at Meribah,
    as on that day at Massah in the desert
    when your fathers put me to the test;
    when they tried me, though they saw my work.' ℟

SECOND READING   *(2 Tm 1:6-8.13-14)*
A reading from the second letter of St Paul to Timothy.
Never be ashamed of witnessing to our Lord.

I am reminding you to fan into a flame the gift that God gave you when I laid my hands on you. God's gift was not a spirit of timidity, but the Spirit of power, and love, and self-control. So you are never to be ashamed of witnessing to the Lord, or ashamed of me for being his prisoner; but with me, bear the hardships for the sake of the Good News, relying on the power of God.

Keep as your pattern the sound teaching you have heard from me, in the faith and love that are in Christ Jesus. You have been trusted to look after something precious; guard it with the help of the Holy Spirit who lives in us.

This is the word of the Lord.

GOSPEL ACCLAMATION   *(1 Sam 3:9; Jn 6:68)*
Alleluia, alleluia!
Speak, Lord, your servant is listening:
you have the message of eternal life.
Alleluia!

or   *(1 Pt 1:25)*

Alleluia, alleluia!
The word of the Lord remains for ever:
What is this word?
It is the Good News that has been brought to you.
Alleluia!

GOSPEL   *(Lk 17:5-10)*
A reading from the holy Gospel according to Luke.
If only you had faith!

The Apostles said to the Lord, 'Increase our faith.' The Lord replied, 'Were your faith the size of a mustard seed you could say to this mulberry tree, "Be uprooted and planted in the sea," and it would obey you.

'Which of you, with a servant ploughing or minding sheep, would say to him when he returned from the fields, "Come and have your meal immediately?" Would he not be more likely to say, "Get my supper laid; make yourself tidy and wait on me while I eat and drink. You can eat and drink yourself afterwards?" Must he be grateful to the servant for doing what he was told? So with you: when you have done all you have been told to do, say, "We are merely servants: we have done no more than our duty." '

This is the Gospel of the Lord.

PROFESSION OF FAITH — *pages 15-16*

PRAYER OVER THE GIFTS

Father, receive these gifts
which our Lord Jesus Christ
has asked us to offer in his memory.
May our obedient service
bring us to the fullness of your redemption.

PREFACE OF SUNDAYS IN ORDINARY TIME — *pages 22-25*

COMMUNION ANTIPHON   (*Lm 3:25*)

The Lord is good to those who hope in him, to those who are searching for his love.

or   (*cf. 1 Cor 10:17*)

Because there is one bread, we, though many, are one body, for we all share in the one loaf and in the one cup.

PRAYER AFTER COMMUNION

Almighty God,
let the eucharist we share
fill us with your life.
May the love of Christ
which we celebrate here
touch our lives and lead us to you.

SOLEMN BLESSING — *pages 57-58*

REFLECTION

Forgiveness is an important part of love. It is not the same as turning a blind eye to wrongdoing or putting up with an unjust situation. When someone asks for forgiveness as brothers and sisters of the Lord we must forgive them. This is the example of Jesus and of Stephen the first Christian martyr, both of whom died forgiving their enemies. It is also the consequence of saying the Lord's prayer and meaning it.

10 OCTOBER
28th SUNDAY IN ORDINARY TIME

Every eucharistic celebration begins with the assembled people acknowledging their sins and asking for God's forgiveness. This is followed by a prayer in which the president of the assembly asks the Lord to absolve the sins of all. Having thus been reconciled with God and with one another we can proceed to the table of God's word and then to the table of his body and blood.

ENTRANCE ANTIPHON   *(Ps 129:3-4)*

If you, O Lord, laid bare our guilt, who could endure it? But you are forgiving, God of Israel.

GREETING, PENITENTIAL RITE, GLORIA — *pages 7-14*

OPENING PRAYER

Let us pray
[that God will help us to love one another]

Lord,
our help and guide
make your love the foundation of our lives.
May our love for you express itself
in our eagerness to do good for others.

or

Let us pray
[in quiet for the grace of sincerity]

Father in heaven,
the hand of your loving kindness
powerfully yet gently guides all the moments of our day.
Go before us in our pilgrimage of life,
anticipate our needs and prevent our falling.
Send your Spirit to unite us in faith,
that sharing in your service,
we may rejoice in your presence.

FIRST READING   *(2 Kg 5:14-17)*

A reading from the second book of the Kings.

Naaman returned to Elisha and acknowledged the Lord.

Naaman the leper went down and immersed himself seven times in the Jordan, as Elisha had told him to do. And his flesh became clean once more like the flesh of a little child.

Returning to Elisha with his whole escort, he went in and stood before him. 'Now I know' he said 'that there is no God in all the earth except in Israel. Now, please, accept a present from your servant.' But Elisha replied, 'As the Lord lives, whom I serve, I will accept nothing.' Naaman pressed him to accept, but he refused. Then Naaman said, 'Since your answer is "No," allow your servant to be given as much earth as two mules may carry, because your servant will no longer offer holocaust or sacrifice to any god except the Lord.'

This is the word of the Lord.

RESPONSORIAL PSALM   *(Ps 97:1-4)*

℞ **The Lord has shown his salvation to the nations.**

1. Sing a new song to the Lord
   for he has worked wonders.
   His right hand and his holy arm
   have brought salvation. ℞

2. The Lord has made known his salvation;
   has shown his justice to the nations.
   He has remembered his truth and love
   for the house of Israel. ℞

3. All the ends of the earth have seen
   the salvation of our God.
   Shout to the Lord all the earth,
   ring out your joy. ℞

SECOND READING   *(2 Tm 2:8-13)*

A reading from the second letter of St Paul to Timothy.

If we hold firm, then we shall reign with Christ.

Remember the Good News that I carry, 'Jesus Christ risen from the dead, sprung from the race of David'; it is on account of this that I have my own hardships to bear, even to being chained like a criminal—but they cannot chain up God's news. So I bear it all for the sake of those who are chosen, so that in the end they may have the salvation that is in Christ Jesus and the eternal glory that comes with it.

Here is a saying that you can rely on:
If we have died with him, then we shall live with him.
If we hold firm, then we shall reign with him.
If we disown him, then he will disown us.
We may be unfaithful, but he is always faithful,
for he cannot disown his own self.
This is the word of the Lord.

GOSPEL ACCLAMATION   *(cf. Jn 6:63.68)*
Alleluia, alleluia!
Your words are spirit, Lord,
and they are life:
you have the message of eternal life. Alleluia!
or   *(1 Th 5:18)*
Alleluia, alleluia!
For all things give thanks,
because this is what God expects you to do in Christ Jesus.
Alleluia!

GOSPEL   *(Lk 17:11-19)*
A reading from the holy Gospel according to Luke.
No one has come back to give praise to God, except this foreigner.

On the way to Jerusalem Jesus travelled along the border between Samaria and Galilee. As he entered one of the villages, ten lepers came to meet him. They stood some way off and called to him, 'Jesus! Master! Take pity on us.' When he saw them he said, 'Go and show yourselves to the priests.' Now as they were going away they were cleansed. Finding himself cured, one of them turned back praising God at the top of his voice and threw himself at the feet of Jesus and thanked him. The man was a Samaritan. This made Jesus say, 'Were not all ten made clean? The other nine, where are they? It seems that no one has come back to give praise to God, except this foreigner.' And he said to the man, 'Stand up and go on your way. Your faith has saved you.'

    This is the Gospel of the Lord.

PROFESSION OF FAITH — *pages 15-16*

PRAYER OVER THE GIFTS
Lord,
accept the prayers and gifts
we offer in faith and love.
May this eucharist bring us to your glory.

PREFACE OF SUNDAYS IN ORDINARY TIME — *pages 22-25*

COMMUNION ANTIPHON   *(Ps 33:11)*
The rich suffer want and go hungry, but nothing shall be lacking to those who fear the Lord.
or   *(1Jn 3:2)*
When the Lord is revealed we shall be like him, for we shall see him as he is.

PRAYER AFTER COMMUNION
Almighty Father,
may the body and blood of your Son
give us a share in his life,
for he is Lord for ever and ever.

SOLEMN BLESSING — *pages 57-58*

REFLECTION

> The Church celebrates two sacraments of healing, namely, the
> Sacrament of Penance and the Sacrament of Anointing of
> those who are sick. Jesus who forgave the sins of the paralytic
> man and restored him to bodily health is the pattern for these
> two. Through the power of the Holy Spirit his work of healing
> and salvation is continued in the Church in every age.

===== 17 OCTOBER =====

29th SUNDAY IN ORDINARY TIME

> The Sundays of the year allow the Christian Church to ponder
> the mysteries of the Lord. One of these mysteries is the
> forgiveness of God. Those who approach the Sacrament of
> Penance obtain pardon from God's mercy for the offences
> which they have committed against him. At the same time they
> are reconciled with the Church.

ENTRANCE ANTIPHON   *(Ps 16:6.8)*
**I call upon you, God, for you will answer me; bend your ear
and hear my prayer. Guard me as the pupil of your eye; hide
me in the shade of your wings.**

GREETING, PENITENTIAL RITE, GLORIA — *pages 7-14*

OPENING PRAYER
Let us pray
  [for the gift of simplicity and joy
  in our service of God and man]
Almighty and ever-living God,
our source of power and inspiration,
give us strength and joy
in serving you as followers of Christ,
who lives and reigns with you and the Holy Spirit,
one God, for ever and ever.

or

Let us pray
    [to the Lord who bends close to hear our prayer]
Lord our God, Father of all,
you guard us under the shadow of your wings
and search into the depths of our hearts.

Remove the blindness that cannot know you
and relieve the fear that would hide us from your sight.

FIRST READING   *(Ex 17:8-13)*

A reading from the book of Exodus.

As long as Moses kept his arms raised, Israel had the advantage.

The Amalekites came and attacked Israel at Rephidim. Moses
said to Joshua, 'Pick out men for yourself, and tomorrow
morning march out to engage Amalek. I, meanwhile, will stand
on the hilltop, the staff of God in my hand.' Joshua did as Moses
told him and marched out to engage Amalek, while Moses and
Aaron and Hur went up to the top of the hill. As long as Moses
kept his arms raised, Israel had the advantage; when he let his
arms fall, the advantage went to Amalek. But Moses' arms grew
heavy, so they took a stone and put it one on one side, one on
the other; and his arms remained firm till sunset. With the edge
of the sword Joshua cut down Amalek and his people.

    This is the word of the Lord.

RESPONSORIAL PSALM   *(Ps 120)*

℞   Our help is in the name of the Lord
      who made heaven and earth.

1.   I lift up my eyes to the mountains:
      from where shall come my help?
      My help shall come from the Lord
      who made heaven and earth. ℞

2.   May he never allow you to stumble!
      Let him sleep not, your guard.
      No, he sleeps not nor slumbers,
      Israel's guard. ℞

3.   The Lord is your guard and your shade;
      at your right side he stands.
      By day the sun shall not smite you
      nor the moon in the night. ℞

4.   The Lord will guard you from evil,
he will guard your soul.
The Lord will guard your going and coming
both now and for ever. ℟

SECOND READING   *(2 Tm 3:14-4:2)*

A reading from the second letter of St Paul to Timothy.

The man who is dedicated to God becomes fully equipped and ready for
any good work.

You must keep to what you have been taught and know to be
true; remember who your teachers were, and how, ever since you
were a child, you have known the holy scriptures — from these
you can learn the wisdom that leads to salvation through faith
in Christ Jesus. All scripture is inspired by God and can
profitably be used for teaching, for refuting error, for guiding
people's lives and teaching them to be holy. This is how the man
who is dedicated to God becomes fully equipped and ready for
any good work.

Before God and before Christ Jesus who is to be judge of the
living and the dead, I put this duty to you, in the name of his
Appearing and of his kingdom: proclaim the message and,
welcome or unwelcome, insist on it. Refute falsehood, correct
error, call to obedience — but do all with patience and with the
intention of teaching.

This is the word of the Lord.

GOSPEL ACCLAMATION   *(cf. Eph. 1:17-18)*

Alleluia, alleluia!
May the Father of our Lord Jesus Christ
enlighten the eyes of our mind,
so that we can see what hope his call holds for us. Alleluia!
or   *(Heb 4:12)*
Alleluia, alleluia!
The word of God is something alive and active;
it can judge secret emotions and thoughts. Alleluia!

GOSPEL   *(Lk 18:1-8)*

A reading from the holy Gospel according to Luke.

God will see justice done to his chosen who cry to him.

Jesus told his disciples a parable about the need to pray
continually and never lose heart. 'There was a judge in a certain
town' he said 'who had neither fear of God nor respect for man.
In the same town there was a widow who kept on coming to

him and saying, "I want justice from you against my enemy!" For a long time he refused, but at last he said to himself, "Maybe I have neither fear of God nor respect for man, but since she keeps pestering me I must give this widow her just rights, or she will persist in coming and worry me to death." '

And the Lord said, 'You notice what the unjust judge has to say? Now will not God see justice done to his chosen who cry to him day and night even when he delays to help them? I promise you, he will see justice done to them, and done speedily. But when the Son of Man comes, will he find any faith on earth?'

This is the Gospel of the Lord.

PROFESSION OF FAITH — *pages 15-16*

PRAYER OVER THE GIFTS
Lord God,
may the gifts we offer
bring us your love and forgiveness
and give us freedom to serve you with our lives.

PREFACE OF SUNDAYS IN ORDINARY TIME — *pages 22-25*

COMMUNION ANTIPHON   (Ps 32:18-19)
See how the eyes of the Lord are on those who fear him, on those who hope in his love, that he may rescue them from death and feed them in time of famine.
or   (Mk 10:45)
The Son of Man came to give his life as a ransom for many.

PRAYER AFTER COMMUNION
Lord,
may this eucharist help us to remain faithful.
May it teach us the way of eternal life.

SOLEMN BLESSING — *pages 57-58*

REFLECTION
> The Sacrament of Confession is so called because it reflects both meanings of the word 'confess'. In the first place, the disclosure of sins to a priest is an essential element of this sacrament. Secondly, it is also a confession — an acknowledgement and praise of the holiness of God and of his mercy towards sinful humankind.

24 OCTOBER
30th SUNDAY IN ORDINARY TIME

The community of the Church strongly recommends that the faithful celebrate the Sacrament of Reconciliation at least once every year. It is called the Sacrament of Reconciliation because it makes present to the recipient the love of God who reconciles. To live by this merciful love is to be prepared to be reconciled with one's sister and brother.

ENTRANCE ANTIPHON   *(Ps 104:3-4)*

Let hearts rejoice who search for the Lord. Seek the Lord and his strength, seek always the face of the Lord.

GREETING, PENITENTIAL RITE, GLORIA — *pages 7-14*

OPENING PRAYER

Let us pray
     [for the strength to do God's will]

Almighty and ever living God,
strengthen our faith, hope, and love.
May we do with loving hearts
what you ask of us
and come to share the life you promise.

or

Let us pray
     [in humble hope for salvation]

Praised be you, God and Father of our Lord Jesus Christ.
There is no power for good
which does not come from your covenant,
and no promise to hope in
that your love has not offered.
Strengthen our faith to accept your covenant
and give us the love to carry out your command.

FIRST READING   *(Si 35:12-14.16-19)*

A reading from the book of Ecclesiasticus.

The humble man's prayer pierces the clouds.

The Lord is a judge
who is no respecter of personages.
He shows no respect of personages to the detriment of a poor man,
he listens to the plea of the injured party.

He does not ignore the orphan's supplication,
nor the widow's as she pours out her story.
The man who with his whole heart serves God will be accepted,
his petitions will carry to the clouds.
The humble man's prayer pierces the clouds,
until it arrives he is inconsolable,
nor will he desist until the Most High takes notice of him,
acquits the virtuous and delivers judgement.
And the Lord will not be slow,
nor will he be dilatory on their behalf.

This is the word of the Lord.

RESPONSORIAL PSALM   *(Ps 32:2-3.17-19.23)*

℟   **This poor man called; the Lord heard him.**

1.   I will bless the Lord at all times,
      his praise always on my lips;
      in the Lord my soul shall make its boast.
      The humble shall hear and be glad.   ℟

2.   The Lord turns his face against the wicked
      to destroy their remembrance from the earth.
      The just call and the Lord hears
      and rescues them in all their distress.   ℟

3.   The Lord is close to the broken-hearted;
      those whose spirit is crushed he will save.
      The Lord ransoms the souls of his servants.
      Those who hide in him shall not be condemned.   ℟

SECOND READING   *(2 Tm 4:6-8.16-18)*
A reading from the second letter of St Paul to Timothy.
All there is to come now is the crown of righteousness reserved for me.
My life is already being poured away as a libation, and the time has
come for me to be gone. I have fought the good fight to the end;
I have run the race to the finish; I have kept the faith; all there is
to come now is the crown of righteousness reserved for me, which
the Lord, the righteous judge, will give to me on that Day; and not
only to me but to all those who have longed for his Appearing.

The first time I had to present my defence, there was not a
single witness to support me. Every one of them deserted me —
may they not be held accountable for it. But the Lord stood by
me and gave me power, so that through me the whole message
might be proclaimed for all the pagans to hear; and so I was
rescued from the lion's mouth. The Lord will rescue me from all

evil attempts on me, and bring me safely to his heavenly kingdom. To him be glory for ever and ever. Amen.

This is the word of the Lord.

GOSPEL ACCLAMATION   (cf. Mt 11:25)
Alleluia, alleluia!
Blessed are you, Father,
Lord of heaven and earth,
for revealing the mysteries of the kingdom
to mere children. Alleluia!
or   (2 Cor 5:19)
Alleluia, alleluia!
God in Christ was reconciling the world to himself,
and he has entrusted to us the news that they are reconciled.
Alleluia!

GOSPEL   (Lk 18:9-14)
A reading from the holy Gospel according to Luke.
The publican went home at rights with God; the Pharisee did not.
Jesus spoke the following parable to some people who prided themselves on being virtuous and despised everyone else. 'Two men went up to the Temple to pray, one a Pharisee, the other a tax collector. The Pharisee stood there and said this prayer to himself, "I thank you, God, that I am not grasping, unjust, adulterous like the rest of mankind, and particularly that I am not like this tax collector here. I fast twice a week; I pay tithes on all I get." The tax collector stood some distance away, not daring even to raise his eyes to heaven; but he beat his breast and said, "God, be merciful to me, a sinner." This man, I tell you, went home again at rights with God; the other did not. For everyone who exalts himself will be humbled, but the man who humbles himself will be exalted.'

This is the Gospel of the Lord.

PROFESSION OF FAITH — *pages 15-16*

PRAYER OVER THE GIFTS
Lord God of power and might,
receive the gifts we offer
and let our service give you glory.

PREFACE OF SUNDAYS IN ORDINARY TIME — *pages 22-25*

COMMUNION ANTIPHON   (Ps 19:6)
We will rejoice at the victory of God and make our boast in
his great name.

or   *(Eph 5:2)*

**Christ loved us and gave himself up for us as a fragrant offering
to God.**

PRAYER AFTER COMMUNION

Lord, bring to perfection within us
the communion we share in this sacrament.
May our celebration have an effect in our lives.

SOLEMN BLESSING — *pages 57-58*

REFLECTION

> Every sincere act of worship or devotion revives the spirit of
> conversion and repentance within us and in this way contributes
> to the forgiveness of our sins. Conversion is a daily challenge
> and a life-long project. Reading sacred scripture, joining in the
> prayer of the Church, especially the Our Father, all are indications
> of a humble desire to receive God's forgiveness.

─────────────── **31 OCTOBER** ───────────────

31st SUNDAY IN ORDINARY TIME

> One of the intentions behind the reforms of the liturgy which
> the Second Vatican Council (1962-1965) undertook was to present
> the mysteries of the Lord Jesus throughout the yearly cycle. Of
> these the most fundamental is that victory which God the Father
> gave to Jesus by raising him to a new life and which is variously
> termed resurrection, exaltation, vindication glorification etc. Every
> Sunday is primarily the day on which this mystery is celebrated.

ENTRANCE ANTIPHON

**Do not abandon me, Lord. My God, do not go away from me!
Hurry to help me, Lord, my Saviour.**

GREETING, PENITENTIAL RITE, GLORIA — *pages 7-14*

OPENING PRAYER

Let us pray
    [that our lives will reflect our faith]
God of power and mercy,
only with your help
can we offer you fitting service and praise.
May we live the faith we profess
and trust your promise of eternal life.

or

Let us pray
[in the presence of God, the source of every good]

Father in heaven, God of power and Lord of mercy,
from whose fullness we have received,
direct our steps in our everyday efforts.
May the changing moods of the human heart
and the limits which our failings impose on hope
never blind us to you, source of every good.

Faith gives us the promise of peace
and makes known the demands of love.
Remove the selfishness that blurs the vision of faith.

FIRST READING   *(Wis 11:22-12:2)*

A reading from the book of Wisdom.

You are merciful to all because you love all that exists.

In your sight, Lord, the whole world is like a grain of dust that
    tips the scales,
like a drop of morning dew falling on the ground.
Yet you are merciful to all, because you can do all things
and overlook men's sins so that they can repent.
Yes, you love all that exists, you hold nothing of what you have
    made in abhorrence,
for had you hated anything, you would not have formed it.
And how, had you not willed it, could a thing persist,
how be conserved if not called forth by you?
You spare all things because all things are yours, Lord,
    lover of life,
you whose imperishable spirit is in all.
Little by little, therefore, you correct those who offend,
you admonish and remind them of how they have sinned,
so that they may abstain from evil and trust in you, Lord.

    This is the word of the Lord.

RESPONSORIAL PSALM   *(Ps 144:1-2.8-11.13-14)*

℟ **I will bless your name for ever,
    O God my King.**

1. I will give you glory, O God my King,
    I will bless your name for ever.
    I will bless you day after day
    and praise your name for ever. ℟

2. The Lord is kind and full of compassion,
    slow to anger, abounding in love.   *(continued)*

How good is the Lord to all,
compassionate to all his creatures. ℟

℟ **I will bless your name for ever,
O God my King.**

3. All your creatures shall thank you, O Lord,
and your friends shall repeat their blessing.
They shall speak of the glory of your reign
and declare your might, O God. ℟

4. The Lord is faithful in all his words
and loving in all his deeds.
The Lord supports all who fall
and raises all who are bowed down. ℟

SECOND READING   (2 Th 1:11-2:2)

A reading from the second letter of St Paul
to the Thessalonians.
The name of Christ will be glorified in you and you in him.

We pray continually that our God will make you worthy of his call,
and by his power fulfil all your desires for goodness and complete
all that you have been doing through faith; because in this way
the name of our Lord Jesus Christ will be glorified in you and
you in him, by the grace of our God and the Lord Jesus Christ.

    To turn now, brothers, to the coming of our Lord Jesus Christ
and how we shall all be gathered round him: please do not get
excited too soon or alarmed by any prediction or rumour or any
letter claiming to come from us, implying that the Day of the
Lord has already arrived.

    This is the word of the Lord.

GOSPEL ACCLAMATION   (Lk 19:38;2:14)
**Alleluia, alleluia!
Blessings on the King who comes,
in the name of the Lord!
Peace in heaven
and glory in the highest heavens!
Alleluia!**
or   (Jn 3:16)
**Alleluia, alleluia!
God loved the world so much
that he gave his only Son,
so that everyone who believes in him
may have eternal life.
Alleluia!**

GOSPEL (Lk 19:1-10)

A reading from the holy Gospel according to Luke.

The Son of Man has come to seek out and save what was lost.

Jesus entered Jericho and was going through the town when a man whose name was Zacchaeus made his appearance; he was one of the senior tax collectors and a wealthy man. He was anxious to see what kind of man Jesus was, but he was too short and could not see him for the crowd; so he ran ahead and climbed a sycamore tree to catch a glimpse of Jesus who was to pass that way. When Jesus reached the spot he looked up and spoke to him: 'Zacchaeus, come down. Hurry, because I must stay at your house today.' And he hurried down and welcomed him joyfully. They all complained when they saw what was happening. 'He has gone to stay at a sinner's house' they said. But Zacchaeus stood his ground and said to the Lord, 'Look, sir, I am going to give half my property to the poor, and if I have cheated anybody I will pay him back four times the amount.' And Jesus said to him, 'Today salvation has come to this house, because this man too is a son of Abraham; for the Son of Man has come to seek out and save what was lost.'

This is the Gospel of the Lord.

PROFESSION OF FAITH — *pages 15-16*

PRAYER OVER THE GIFTS

God of mercy,
may we offer a pure sacrifice
for the forgiveness of our sins.

PREFACE OF SUNDAYS IN ORDINARY TIME — *pages 22-25*

COMMUNION ANTIPHON (Ps 15:11)

Lord, you will show me the path of life and fill me with joy in your presence.

or (Jn 6:58)

As the living Father sent me, and I live because of the Father, so he who eats my flesh and drinks my blood will live because of me.

PRAYER AFTER COMMUNION

Lord, you give us new hope in this eucharist.
May the power of your love
continue its saving work among us
and bring us to the joy you promise.

SOLEMN BLESSING — *pages 57-58*

REFLECTION

> The Lord's Prayer, the Our Father, links two essential aspects of
> life, namely, asking for forgiveness and granting forgiveness. It
> is an example of the type of world which he prayed for in the
> phrase 'Your kingdom come.' At its heart it suggests that to
> have some appreciation of what it costs another to forgive us
> and what it means when they do, it is necessary to have forgiven
> someone else beforehand. 'Forgive us our failings as we forgive
> those who fail us.' Do we really want this prayer to be answered?

---

1 NOVEMBER

ALL SAINTS

> Since the Eighth Century the celebration of the feast of all the
> saints of the Church, both known and unknown, has been kept
> on this day. Originally it was celebrated on the first Sunday
> after Pentecost. In the Churches of the Eastern part of Christianity
> it is still kept on that day. In the scriptures the term 'saints' is frequently
> used to refer to the living members of the Christian community.

ENTRANCE ANTIPHON

**Let us all rejoice in the Lord and keep a festival in honour of
all the saints. Let us join with the angels in joyful praise to
the Son of God.**

GREETING, PENITENTIAL RITE, GLORIA — *pages 7-14*

OPENING PRAYER

Let us pray

> [that the prayers of all the saints
> will bring us forgiveness for our sins]

Father, all-powerful and ever-living God,
today we rejoice in the holy men and women
of every time and place.
May their prayers bring us your forgiveness and love.

or

Let us pray

> [as we rejoice and keep festival
> in honour of all the saints]

God our Father,
source of all holiness,

the work of your hands is manifest in your saints,
the beauty of your truth is reflected in their faith.

May we who aspire to have part in their joy
be filled with the Spirit that blessed their lives,
so that having shared their faith on earth
we may also know their peace in your kingdom.

FIRST READING   *(Apo 7:2-4.9-14)*

A reading from the book of the Apocalypse.

*I saw a huge number, impossible to count, of people from every nation,
race, tribe and language.*

I, John, saw another angel rising where the sun rises, carrying the
seal of the living God; he called in a powerful voice to the four
angels whose duty was to devastate land and sea, 'Wait before
you do any damage on land or at sea or to the trees, until we
have put the seal on the foreheads of the servants of our God.'
Then I heard how many were sealed: a hundred and forty-four
thousand, out of all the tribes of Israel.

    After that I saw a huge number, impossible to count, of people
from every nation, race, tribe and language; they were standing
in front of the throne and in front of the Lamb, dressed in white
robes and holding palms in their hands. They shouted aloud,
'Victory to our God, who sits on the throne, and to the Lamb!'
And all the angels who were standing in a circle round the
throne, surrounding the elders and the four animals, prostrated
themselves before the throne, and touched the grounds with
their foreheads, worshipping God with these words: 'Amen.
Praise and glory and wisdom and thanksgiving and honour and
power and strength to our God for ever and ever. Amen.'

    One of the elders then spoke, and asked me, 'Do you know
who these people are, dressed in white robes, and where they
have come from?' I answered him, 'You can tell me, my Lord.'
Then he said, 'These are the people who have been through the
great persecution, and they have washed their robes white again
in the blood of the Lamb.'

    This is the word of the Lord.

RESPONSORIAL PSALM   *(Ps 23:1-6)*

℞ **Such are the men who seek your face, O Lord.**

1. The Lord's is the earth and its fullness,
   the world and all its peoples.
   It is he who set it on the seas;
   on the waters he made it firm. ℞

(continued)

2. Who shall climb the mountain of the Lord?
    Who shall stand in his holy place?
    The man with clean hands and pure heart,
    who desires not worthless things. ℟

℟ **Such are the men who seek your face, O Lord.**

3. He shall receive blessings from the Lord
    and reward from the God who saves him.
    Such are the men who seek him,
    seek the face of the God of Jacob. ℟

SECOND READING   (1 Jn 3:1-3)
A reading from the first letter of St John.
We shall see God as he really is.
Think of the love that the Father has lavished on us,
by letting us be called God's children;
and that is what we are.
Because the world refused to acknowledge him,
therefore it does not acknowledge us.
My dear people, we are already the children of God
but what we are to be in the future has not yet been revealed;
all we know is, that when it is revealed
we shall be like him
because we shall see him as he really is.
Surely everyone who entertains this hope
must purify himself, must try to be as pure as Christ.
        This is the word of the Lord.

GOSPEL ACCLAMATION   (Mt 11:28)
Alleluia, alleluia!
Come to me, all you who labour and are overburdened,
and I will give you rest, says the Lord.
Alleluia!

GOSPEL   (Mt 5:1-12)
A reading from the holy Gospel according to Matthew.
Rejoice and be glad, for your reward will be great in heaven.
Seeing the crowds, Jesus went up the hill. There he sat down and
was joined by his disciples. Then he began to speak. This is what
he taught them:

    'How happy are the poor in spirit;
    theirs is the kingdom of heaven.
    Happy the gentle:

they shall have the earth for their heritage.
Happy those who mourn:
they shall be comforted.
Happy those who hunger and thirst for what is right:
they shall be satisfied.
Happy the merciful:
they shall have mercy shown them.
Happy the pure in heart:
they shall see God.
Happy the peacemakers:
they shall be called sons of God.
Happy those who are persecuted in the cause of right:
theirs is the kingdom of heaven.

'Happy are you when people abuse you and persecute you and
speak all kinds of calumny against you on my account. Rejoice
and be glad, for your reward will be great in heaven.'

This is the Gospel of the Lord.

PROFESSION OF FAITH — *pages 15-16*

PRAYER OVER THE GIFTS

Lord, receive our gifts in honour of the holy men and women
who live with you in glory.
May we always be aware
of their concern to help and save us.

PREFACE OF ALL SAINTS

Father, all-powerful and ever-living God,
we do well always and everywhere to give you thanks.

Today we keep the festival of your holy city,
the heavenly Jerusalem, our mother.
Around your throne
the saints, our brothers and sisters,
sing your praise for ever.
Their glory fills us with joy,
and their communion with us in your Church
gives us inspiration and strength
as we hasten on our pilgrimage of faith,
eager to meet them.

With their great company and all the angels
we praise your glory
as we cry out with one voice:

Holy, holy, holy...

COMMUNION ANTIPHON   *(Mt 5:8-10)*

Happy are the pure of heart for they shall see God. Happy the peacemakers; they shall be called sons of God. Happy are they who suffer persecution for justice' sake; the kingdom of heaven is theirs.

PRAYER AFTER COMMUNION

Father, holy one,
we praise your glory reflected in the saints.
May we who share at this table
be filled with your love
and prepared for the joy of your kingdom,
where Jesus is Lord for ever and ever.

SOLEMN BLESSING

Bow your heads and pray for God's blessing.

God is the glory and joy of all his saints,
whose memory we celebrate today.
May his blessing be with you always.
Amen.

May the prayers of the saints deliver you from present evil;
may their example of holy living
turn your thoughts to the service of God and neighbour.
Amen.

God's holy Church rejoices that her children
are one with the saints in lasting peace.
May you come to share with them
in all the joys of our Father's house.
Amen.

May almighty God bless you,
the Father, and the Son, ✠ and the Holy Spirit.
Amen.

REFLECTION

The beatitudes are one summary of the gospel. In them the Good News is proclaimed. It is that God is giver and that humankind can only receive. They are a means towards living with the same motivation that inspired Jesus. In the final beatitude the reward is none other than God himself. This is the inheritance of the saints.

7 NOVEMBER
32nd SUNDAY IN ORDINARY TIME

As we approach the end of the Liturgical Year our celebrations contain many references to the end of time. Our attention is directed towards what has yet to be. The Letter to the Hebrews boldly states that Jesus the Christ is the same yesterday, today and for ever. Whatever the future brings we can be confident that God who did not desert us in the past will remain faithful.

ENTRANCE ANTIPHON   *(Ps 87:3)*
Let my prayer come before you, Lord; listen and answer me.

GREETING, PENITENTIAL RITE, GLORIA — *pages 7-14*

OPENING PRAYER

Let us pray
    [for health of mind and body]

God of power and mercy,
protect us from all harm.
Give us freedom of spirit
and health in mind and body
to do your work on earth.

or

Let us pray
    [that our prayer rise like incense
    in the presence of the Lord]

Almighty Father,
strong is your justice and great is your mercy.
Protect us in the burdens and challenges of life.
Shield our minds from the distortion of pride
and enfold our desire with the beauty of truth.

Help us to become more aware of your loving design
so that we may more willingly give our lives in service to all.

FIRST READING   *(2 Mac 7:1-2.9-14)*
A reading from the second book of Maccabees.
The King of the world will raise us up to live again for ever.

There were seven brothers who were arrested with their mother. The king tried to force them to taste pig's flesh, which the Law forbids, by torturing them with whips and scourges. One of them, acting as spokesman for the others, said, 'What are you trying to find out from us? We are prepared to die rather than break the Law of our ancestors.'

With his last breath the second brother exclaimed, 'Inhuman fiend, you may discharge us from this present life, but the King of the world will raise us up, since it is for his laws that we die, to live again for ever.'

After him, they amused themselves with the third, who on being asked for his tongue promptly thrust it out and boldly held out his hands, with these honourable words, 'It was heaven that gave me these limbs; for the sake of his laws I disdain them; from him I hope to receive them again.' The king and his attendants were astounded at the young man's courage and his utter indifference to suffering.

When this one was dead they subjected the fourth to the same savage torture. When he neared his end he cried, 'Ours is the better choice, to meet death at men's hands, yet relying on God's promise that we shall be raised up by him; whereas for you there can be no resurrection, no new life.'

This is the word of the Lord.

RESPONSORIAL PSALM   (Ps 16:1.5-6.8.15)

℞   I shall be filled, when I awake,
    with the sight of your glory, O Lord.

1. Lord, hear a cause that is just,
    pay heed to my cry.
    Turn your ear to my prayer:
    no deceit is on my lips. ℞

2. I kept my feet firmly in your paths;
    there was no faltering in my steps.
    I am here and I call, you will hear me, O God.
    Turn your ear to me; hear my words. ℞

3. Guard me as the apple of your eye.
    Hide me in the shadow of your wings.
    As for me, in my justice I shall see your face
    and be filled, when I awake, with the sight of your glory. ℞

SECOND READING   (2 Th 2:16-3:5)

A reading from the second letter of St Paul
to the Thessalonians.

May the Lord strengthen you in everything good that you do or say.

May our Lord Jesus Christ himself, and God our Father who has given us his love and, through his grace, such inexhaustible comfort and such sure hope, comfort you and strengthen you in everything good that you do or say.

Finally, brothers, pray for us; pray that the Lord's message may spread quickly, and be received with honour as it was among you; and pray that we may be preserved from the interference of bigoted and evil people, for faith is not given to everyone. But the Lord is faithful, and he will give you strength and guard you from the evil one, and we, in the Lord, have every confidence that you are doing and will go on doing all that we tell you. May the Lord turn your hearts towards the love of God and the fortitude of Christ.

This is the word of the Lord.

GOSPEL ACCLAMATION   *(Lk 21:36)*

Alleluia, alleluia!
Stay awake, praying at all times
for the strength to stand with confidence
before the Son of Man.
Alleluia!
or   *(Apo 1:5-6)*

Alleluia, alleluia!
Jesus Christ is the First-born from the dead;
to him be glory and power for ever and ever.
Alleluia!

GOSPEL   *(Lk 20:27-38)*

(For Shorter Form, *read between* ♦ ◀*)*

A reading from the holy Gospel according to Luke.

He is God, not of the dead, but of the living.

♦Some Sadducees—those who say that there is no resurrection—approached Jesus and they put this question to him,◀ 'Master, we have it from Moses in writing, that if a man's married brother dies childless, the man must marry the widow to raise up children for his brother. Well, then, there were seven brothers. The first, having married a wife, died childless. The second and then the third married the widow. And the same with all the seven, they died leaving no children. Finally the woman herself died. Now, at the resurrection, to which of them will she be wife since she had been married to all seven?'

♦Jesus replied, 'The children of this world take wives and husbands, but those who are judged worthy of a place in the other world and in the resurrection from the dead do not marry because they can no longer die, for they are the same as the angels, and being children of the resurrection they are sons of God. And Moses himself implies that the dead rise again, in the passage about the bush where he calls the Lord the God of Abraham, the God of Isaac and the God of Jacob. Now he is God, not of the dead, but of the living; for to him all are in fact alive.'

This is the Gospel of the Lord.◆

PROFESSION OF FAITH — *pages 15-16*

PRAYER OVER THE GIFTS

God of mercy,
in this eucharist we proclaim the death of the Lord.
Accept the gifts we present
and help us follow him with love,
for he is Lord for ever and ever.

PREFACE OF SUNDAYS IN ORDINARY TIME — *pages 22-25*

COMMUNION ANTIPHON   (Ps 22:1-2)
The Lord is my shepherd; there is nothing I shall want. In green pastures he gives me rest, he leads me beside the waters of peace.

or   (Lk 24:35)

The disciples recognised the Lord Jesus in the breaking of bread.

PRAYER AFTER COMMUNION

Lord,
we thank you for the nourishment you give us
through your holy gift.
Pour out your Spirit upon us
and in the strength of this food from heaven
keep us single-minded in your service.

SOLEMN BLESSING — *pages 57-58*

REFLECTION

Hope is a frame of mind which makes all the difference in the person who has it. Where there is no hope life becomes intolerable. Hope is therefore one of the best gifts that a person can receive. The hope of the Church is based on God's actions in the past. We have no reason to doubt that God will not continue as he began.

14 NOVEMBER
33rd SUNDAY IN ORDINARY TIME

Belief in an afterlife is something which developed only gradually
in the Hebrew Bible. Our Jewish people who are our fathers
and mothers in faith came to realise late in their history that
God is the God of those who have died as well as of those who
are alive. God's plan for each human being is not thwarted by
death, but as in the case of Jesus, overcomes it.

ENTRANCE ANTIPHON   *(Jer 29:11.12.14)*

**The Lord says: my plans for you are peace and not disaster;
when you call to me, I will listen to you, and I will bring you
back to the place from which I exiled you.**

GREETING, PENITENTIAL RITE, GLORIA — *pages 7-14*

OPENING PRAYER

Let us pray
　　[that God will help us to be faithful]

Father of all that is good,
keep us faithful in serving you,
for to serve you is our lasting joy.

or

Let us pray
　　[with hearts that long for peace]

Father in heaven,
ever-living source of all that is good,
from the beginning of time you promised man salvation
through the future coming of your Son, our Lord Jesus Christ.

Help us to drink of his truth
and expand our hearts with the joy of his promises,
so that we may serve you in faith and in love
and know for ever the joy of your presence.

FIRST READING   *(Mal 3:19-20)*

A reading from the prophet Malachi.

For you the sun of righteousness will shine out.

The day is coming now, burning like a furnace; and all the
arrogant and the evil-doers will be like stubble. The day that is
coming is going to burn them up, says the Lord of hosts, leaving
them neither root nor stalk. But for you who fear my name, the
sun of righteousness will shine out with healing in its rays.

　　This is the word of the Lord.

RESPONSORIAL PSALM   *(Ps 97:5-9)*

℟   **The Lord comes to rule the peoples with fairness.**

1.   Sing psalms to the Lord with the harp
      with the sound of music.
      With trumpets and the sound of the horn
      acclaim the King, the Lord. ℟

2.   Let the sea and all within it, thunder;
      the world, and all its peoples.
      Let the rivers clap their hands
      and the hills ring out their joy
      at the presence of the Lord. ℟

3.   For the Lord comes,
      he comes to rule the earth.
      He will rule the world with justice
      and the peoples with fairness. ℟

SECOND READING   *(2 Th 3:7-12)*

A reading from the second letter of St Paul
to the Thessalonians.

Do not let anyone have food if he refuses to work.

You know how you are supposed to imitate us: now we were not
idle when we were with you, nor did we ever have our meals at
anyone's table without paying for them; no, we worked night
and day, slaving and straining, so as not to be a burden on any
of you. This was not because we had no right to be, but in order
to make ourselves an example for you to follow.

We gave you a rule when we were with you: not to let
anyone have any food if he refused to do any work. Now we
hear that there are some of you who are living in idleness, doing
no work themselves but interfering with everyone else's. In the
Lord Jesus Christ, we order and call on people of this kind to go
on quietly working and earning the food that they eat.

This is the word of the Lord.

GOSPEL ACCLAMATION   *(Lk 21:36)*
Alleluia, alleluia!
Stay awake, praying at all times
for the strength to stand with confidence
before the Son of Man. Alleluia!
or   *(Lk 21:28)*
Alleluia, alleluia!
Stand erect, hold your heads high,

because your liberation is near at hand. Alleluia!

GOSPEL *(Lk 21:5-19)*

A reading from the holy Gospel according to Luke.

Your endurance will win you your lives.

When some were talking about the Temple, remarking how it was adorned with fine stonework and votive offerings, Jesus said, 'All these things you are staring at now — the time will come when not a single stone will be left on another: everything will be destroyed.' And they put to him this question: 'Master', they said 'when will this happen, then, and what sign will there be that this is about to take place?'

'Take care not to be deceived', he said 'because many will come using my name and saying, "I am he", and, "The time is near at hand." Refuse to join them. And when you hear of wars and revolutions, do not be frightened, for this is something that must happen but the end is not so soon'. Then he said to them, 'Nation will fight against nation, and kingdom against kingdom. There will be great earthquakes and plagues and famines here and there; there will be fearful sights and great signs from heaven.

'But before all this happens, men will seize you and persecute you; they will hand you over to the synagogues and to imprisonment, and bring you before kings and governors because of my name — and that will be your opportunity to bear witness. Keep this carefully in mind: you are not to prepare your defence, because I myself shall give you an eloquence and a wisdom that none of your opponents will be able to resist or contradict. You will be betrayed even by parents and brothers, relations and friends; and some of you will be put to death. You will be hated by all on account of my name, but not a hair of your head will be lost. Your endurance will win you your lives.'

This is the Gospel of the Lord.

PROFESSION OF FAITH — *pages 15-16*

PRAYER OVER THE GIFTS

Lord God,
may the gifts we offer
increase our love for you
and bring us to eternal life.

PREFACE OF SUNDAYS IN ORDINARY TIME — *pages 22-25*

COMMUNION ANTIPHON *(Ps 72:28)*

It is good for me to be with the Lord and to put my hope in him.

or   (Mk 11:23.24)
**I tell you solemnly, whatever you ask for in prayer, believe
that you have received it, and it will be yours, says the Lord.**

PRAYER AFTER COMMUNION
Father, may we grow in love
by the eucharist we have celebrated
in memory of the Lord Jesus,
who is Lord for ever and ever.

SOLEMN BLESSING — *pages 57-58*

REFLECTION
> Authentic Christianity discovers the unity between this life and
> the next. To concentrate on one and neglect the other is to
> create an imbalance. In the past perhaps too much attention
> was directed to the afterlife to the detriment of improving the
> quality of life here on earth. Today the opposite may be the
> case. It is the same God who is Lord of both.

═══════════════ 21 NOVEMBER ═══════════════

OUR LORD JESUS CHRIST,
UNIVERSAL KING

> On the last Sunday of the Liturgical Year, today, we celebrate
> the feast of Our Lord Jesus Christ, Universal King. It was instituted
> by Pope Pius XI in 1925 at the close of the Jubilee Year. Jesus was
> questioned at his trial: are you a king? His answer serves to highlight
> how different his kingship is from that of human rulers.

ENTRANCE ANTIPHON   (Apoc 5:12; 1:6)
**The Lamb who was slain is worthy to receive strength and
divinity, wisdom and power and honour: to him be glory and
power for ever.**

GREETING, PENITENTIAL RITE, GLORIA — *pages 7-14*

OPENING PRAYER
Let us pray
        [that all will acclaim Jesus as Lord]
Almighty and merciful God,
you break the power of evil
and make all things new

in your Son Jesus Christ, the King of the universe.
May all in heaven and earth acclaim your glory
and never cease to praise you.

or

Let us pray
> [that the kingdom of Christ
> may live in our hearts and come to our world]

Father all-powerful, God of love,
you have raised our Lord Jesus Christ from death to life,
resplendent in glory as King of creation.

Open our hearts,
free all the world to rejoice in his peace,
to glory in his justice, to live in his love.
Bring all mankind together in Jesus Christ your Son,
whose kingdom is with you and the Holy Spirit,
one God, for ever and ever.

FIRST READING   *(2 S 5:1-3)*

A reading from the second book of Samuel.

They anointed David king of Israel.

All the tribes of Israel came to David at Hebron. 'Look' they said 'we are your own flesh and blood. In days past when Saul was our king, it was you who led Israel in all their exploits; and the Lord said to you, "You are the man who shall be shepherd of my people Israel, you shall be the leader of Israel." ' So all the elders of Israel came to the king at Hebron, and King David made a pact with them at Hebron in the presence of the Lord, and they anointed David king of Israel.

This is the word of the Lord.

RESPONSORIAL PSALM   *(Ps 121:1-5)*

℟ **I rejoiced when I heard them say:**
   'Let us go to God's house.'

1. I rejoiced when I heard them say:
   'Let us go to God's house.'
   And now our feet are standing
   within your gates, O Jerusalem. ℟

2. Jerusalem is built as a city
   strongly compact.
   It is there that the tribes go up,
   the tribes of the Lord. ℟

(continued)

3. For Israel's law it is,
    there to praise the Lord's name.
    There were set the thrones of judgement
    of the house of David. ℞

℞ I rejoiced when I heard them say:
   'Let us go to God's house.'

SECOND READING   *(Col 1:12-20)*

A reading from the letter of St Paul to the Colossians.

He has created a place for us in the kingdom of the Son that he loves.

We give thanks to the Father who has made it possible for you to
join the saints and with them to inherit the light.

Because that is what he has done: he has taken us out of the
power of darkness and created a place for us in the kingdom of
the Son that he loves, and in him, we gain our freedom, the
forgiveness of our sins.

He is the image of the unseen God
and the first-born of all creation,
for in him were created
all things in heaven and on earth:
everything visible and everything invisible,
Thrones, Dominations, Sovereignties, Powers —
all things were created through him and for him.
Before anything was created, he existed,
and he holds all things in unity.
Now the Church is his body,
he is its head.
As he is the Beginning,
he was first to be born from the dead,
so that he should be first in every way;
because God wanted all perfection
to be found in him
and all things to be reconciled through him and for him,
everything in heaven and everything on earth,
when he made peace
by his death on the cross.

This is the word of the Lord.

GOSPEL ACCLAMATION   *(Mk 11:9-10)*

Alleluia, alleluia!
Blessings on him who comes in the name of the Lord!
Blessings on the coming kingdom of our father David!
Alleluia!

GOSPEL   (Lk 23:35-43)

A reading from the holy Gospel according to Luke.

Lord, remember me when you come into your kingdom.

The people stayed there before the cross watching Jesus. As for the leaders, they jeered at him. 'He saved others', they said 'let him save himself if he is the Christ of God, the Chosen One'. The soldiers mocked him too, and when they approached to offer him vinegar they said, 'If you are the king of the Jews, save yourself'. Above him there was an inscription: 'This is the King of the Jews.'

One of the criminals hanging there abused him. 'Are you not the Christ?' he said. 'Save yourself and us as well.' But the other spoke up and rebuked him. 'Have you no fear of God at all?' he said, 'You got the same sentence as he did, but in our case we deserved it: we are paying for what we did. But this man has done nothing wrong. Jesus,' he said 'remember me when you come into your kingdom.' 'Indeed, I promise you,' he replied 'today you will be with me in paradise.'

This is the Gospel of the Lord.

PROFESSION OF FAITH — *pages 15-16*

PRAYER OVER THE GIFTS

Lord, we offer you the sacrifice
by which your Son reconciles mankind.
May it bring unity and peace to the world.

PREFACE OF CHRIST THE KING

Father, all-powerful and every-living God,
we do well always and everywhere to give you thanks.

You anointed Jesus Christ, your only Son, with the oil of
        gladness,
as the eternal priest and universal King.

As priest he offered his life on the altar of the cross
and redeemed the human race
by this one perfect sacrifice of peace.

As King he claims dominion over all creation,
that he may present to you, his almighty Father,
an eternal and universal kingdom:
a kingdom of truth and life,
a kingdom of holiness and grace,
a kingdom of justice, love, and peace.

And so, with all the choirs of angels in heaven
we proclaim your glory

and join in their unending hymn of praise:
Holy, holy, holy...

COMMUNION ANTIPHON   *(Ps 28:8-11)*
The Lord will reign for ever and will give his people the gift of peace.

PRAYER AFTER COMMUNION
Lord, you give us Christ, the King of all creation,
as food for everlasting life.
Help us to live by the gospel
and bring us to the joy of his kingdom,
where he lives and reigns for ever and ever.

REFLECTION
> For Luke what was written over the cross of Jesus was a
> statement of fact. This is the King of the Jews. An indication of
> the values which underlie his kingdom is got from the events
> surrounding the scene. Jesus bears with mockery and abuse,
> accepts the questioning of the Jewish leaders, the soldiers and
> a criminal beside him and dies forgiving his enemies.

━━━━━━━━━ **28 NOVEMBER** ━━━━━━━━━

FIRST SUNDAY OF ADVENT

> The new year of the Church begins with the image of 'coming'
> or 'arrival' which is what Advent means. The Lord has come
> already at Bethlehem. He comes each day into the lives of
> those who open their heart to receive him. He will come again
> in glory on the last day.

ENTRANCE ANTIPHON   *(Ps 24:1-3)*
**To you, my God, I lift my soul, I trust in you; let me never
come to shame. Do not let my enemies laugh at me. No one
who waits for you is ever put to shame.**

GREETING, PENITENTIAL RITE — *pages 7-13*

The Gloria is omitted.

OPENING PRAYER
Let us pray
     [that we may take Christ's coming seriously]
All-powerful God,

increase our strength of will for doing good
that Christ may find an eager welcome at his coming
and call us to his side in the kingdom of heaven
where he lives and reigns with you and the Holy Spirit,
one God for ever and ever.

or

Let us pray

> [in Advent time
> with longing and waiting
> for the coming of the Lord]

Father in heaven,
our hearts desire the warmth of your love
and our minds are searching for the light of your Word.

Increase our longing for Christ our Saviour
and give us the strength to grow in love,
that the dawn of his coming
may find us rejoicing in his presence
and welcoming the light of his truth.

FIRST READING   *(Is 2:1-5)*

A reading from the prophet Isaiah.

The Lord gathers all nations together into the eternal peace of God's
kingdom.

The vision of Isaiah son of Amoz, concerning Judah and
    Jerusalem.
In the days to come
the mountain of the Temple of the Lord
shall tower above the mountains
and be lifted higher than the hills.
All the nations will stream to it,
peoples without number will come to it; and they will say:

> 'Come, let us go up to the mountain of the Lord,
>   to the Temple of the God of Jacob
>   that he may teach us his ways
>   so that we may walk in his paths;
>   since the Law will go out from Zion,
>   and the oracle of the Lord from Jerusalem.'

He will wield authority over the nations
and adjudicate between many peoples;
these will hammer their swords into ploughshares,
their spears into sickles.

Nation will not lift sword against nation,
there will be no more training for war.
O House of Jacob, come,
let us walk in the light of the Lord.

   This is the word of the Lord.

RESPONSORIAL PSALM   *(Ps 121:1-2.4-5.6-9)*

℟ **I rejoiced when I heard them say:**
   'Let us go to God's house.'

1. I rejoiced when I heard them say:
    'Let us go to God's house.'
    And now our feet are standing
    within your gates, O Jerusalem. ℟

2. It is there that the tribes go up,
    the tribes of the Lord.
    For Israel's law it is,
    there to praise the Lord's name.
    There were set the thrones of judgement
    of the house of David. ℟

3. For the peace of Jerusalem pray:
    'Peace be to your homes!
    May peace reign in your walls,
    in your palaces, peace!' ℟

4. For love of my brethren and friends
    I say: 'Peace upon you!'
    For love of the house of the Lord
    I will ask for your good. ℟

SECOND READING   *(Rm 13:11-14)*
A reading from the letter of St Paul to the Romans.
Our salvation is near.

You know 'the time' has come: you must wake up now: our
salvation is even nearer than it was when we were converted.
The night is almost over, it will be daylight soon — let us give
up all the things we prefer to do under cover of the dark; let us
arm ourselves and appear in the light. Let us live decently as
people do in the daytime: no drunken orgies, no promiscuity or
licentiousness, and no wrangling or jealousy. Let your armour be
the Lord Jesus Christ.

   This is the word of the Lord.

GOSPEL ACCLAMATION   *(Ps 84:8)*

Alleluia, alleluia!
Let us see, O Lord, your mercy
and give us your saving help.
Alleluia!

GOSPEL   *(Mt 24:27-44)*

A reading from the holy Gospel according to Matthew.

Stay awake so that you may be ready.

Jesus said to his disciples: 'As it was in Noah's day, so will it be when the Son of Man comes. For in those days before the Flood people were eating, drinking, taking wives, taking husbands, right up to the day Noah went into the ark, and they suspected nothing till the Flood came and swept all away. It will be like this when the Son of Man comes. Then of two men in the fields one is taken, one left; of two women at the millstone grinding, one is taken, one left.

'So stay awake, because you do not know the day when your master is coming. You may be quite sure of this that if the householder had known at what time of night the burglar would come, he would have stayed awake and would not have allowed anyone to break through the wall of his house. Therefore, you too must stand ready because the Son of Man is coming at an hour you do not expect.'

This is the Gospel of the Lord.

PROFESSION OF FAITH — *pages 15-16*

PRAYER OVER THE GIFTS

Father, from all you give us
we present this bread and wine.
As we serve you now,
accept our offering
and sustain us with your promise of eternal life.

PREFACE OF ADVENT I — *page 18*

COMMUNION ANTIPHON   *(Ps 84:13)*

The Lord will shower his gifts, and our land will yield its fruit.

PRAYER AFTER COMMUNION

Father, may our communion
teach us to love heaven.
May its promise and hope
guide our way on earth.

SOLEMN BLESSING — *page 56*

REFLECTION

Throughout this year we will hear the gospel of Matthew read
on most Sundays outside the special liturgical seasons of
Advent, Christmas, Lent and Easter. This gospel which at
present is dated to the 80s or 90s of the First Century adapted
earlier sources such as the gospel of Mark to meet the needs of
a developing and changing situation. This reminds us that the
gospel needs to be constantly reinterpreted to address the
people of every generation in their new situations.

---

30 NOVEMBER

SAINT ANDREW, APOSTLE
(Patron of Scotland)

Andrew from Bethsaida in Galilee was a fisherman like his
brother Simon Peter. He appears in several incidents in the
gospel. Various traditions have emerged about him, especially
the one that his martyrdom was upon a cross shaped like the
letter X which in Greek is the first letter of the name of Christ.
He is the patron of Scotland, Greece and Russia.

ENTRANCE ANTIPHON   *(cf. Mt 4:18-19)*

**By the Sea of Galilee the Lord saw two brothers, Peter and
Andrew. He called them: come and follow me, and I will
make you fishers of men.**

GREETING, PENITENTIAL RITE, GLORIA — *pages 7-14*

OPENING PRAYER

Lord, in your kindness hear our petitions.
You called Andrew the apostle
to preach the gospel and guide your Church in faith.
May he always be our friend in your presence
to help us with his prayers.

FIRST READING   *(Ws 3:1-9)*

A reading from the book of Wisdom.

He accepted them as a holocaust.

The souls of the virtuous are in the hands of God,
no torment shall ever touch them.
In the eyes of the unwise, they did appear to die,

their going looked like a disaster,
their leaving us, like annihilation;
but they are in peace.
If they experienced punishment as men see it,
their hope was rich with immortality;
slight was their affliction, great will their blessings be.
God has put them to the test
and proved them worthy to be with him;
he has tested them like gold in a furnace,
and accepted them as a holocaust.
When the time comes for his visitation they will shine out;
as sparks run through the stubble, so will they.
They shall judge nations, rule over peoples,
and the Lord will be their king for ever.
They who trust in him will understand the truth,
those who are faithful will live with him in love;
for grace and mercy await those he has chosen.

This is the word of the Lord.

RESPONSORIAL PSALM *(Ps 30:3-4.6.8.17.21)*

℟ **Into your hands, O Lord,
I commend my spirit.**

1. Be a rock of refuge for me,
   a mighty stronghold to save me,
   for you are my rock, my stronghold.
   For your name's sake, lead me and guide me. ℟

2. Into your hands I commend my spirit.
   It is you who will redeem me, Lord.
   As for me, I trust in the Lord;
   let me be glad and rejoice in your love. ℟

3. Let your face shine on your servant.
   Save me in your love.
   You hide them in the shelter of your presence
   from the plotting of men. ℟

SECOND READING *(Rm 10:9-18)*

A reading from the letter of St Paul to the Romans.

Faith comes from what is preached, and what is preached comes from
the word of Christ.

If your lips confess that Jesus is Lord and if you believe in your
heart that God raised him from the dead, then you will be saved.
By believing from the heart you are made righteous; by confessing

with your lips you are saved. When scripture says: those who
believe in him will have no cause for shame, it makes no
distinction between Jew and Greek: all belong to the same Lord
who is rich enough, however many ask his help, for everyone
who calls on the name of the Lord will be saved.

But they will not ask his help unless they believe in him,
and they will not believe in him unless they have heard of him
and they will not hear of him unless they get a preacher, and
they will never have a preacher unless one is sent, but as
scripture says: The footsteps of those who bring good news are a
welcome sound. Not everyone, of course, listens to the Good
News. As Isaiah says: Lord, how many believed what we
proclaimed? So faith comes from what is preached, and what is
preached comes from the word of Christ.

Let me put the question: is it possible that they did not hear?
Indeed they did; in the words of the psalm, their voice has gone
out through all the earth, and their message to the ends of the world.

This is the word of the Lord.

GOSPEL ACCLAMATION   (Mt 4:19)
Alleluia, alleluia!
Follow me, says the Lord,
and I will make you into fishers of men.
Alleluia!

GOSPEL   (Mt 4:18-22)
A reading from the holy Gospel according to Matthew.
And they left their nets at once and followed him.
As Jesus was walking by the Sea of Galilee he saw two brothers,
Simon, who was called Peter, and his brother Andrew; they were
making a cast in the lake with their net, for they were fishermen.
And he said to them, 'Follow me and I will make you fishers of
men.' And they left their nets at once and followed him.

Going on from there he saw another pair of brothers, James
son of Zebedee and his brother John; they were in their boat
with their father Zebedee, mending their nets, and he called them.
At once, leaving the boat and their father, they followed him.

This is the Gospel of the Lord.

PROFESSION OF FAITH — *pages 15-16*

PRAYER OVER THE GIFTS
All-powerful God,
may these gifts we bring on the feast of Saint Andrew

be pleasing to you
and give life to all who receive them.

PREFACE OF THE APOSTLES I
Father, all-powerful and ever-living God,
we do well always and everywhere to give you thanks.

You are the eternal Shepherd
who never leaves his flock untended.
Through the apostles
you watch over us and protect us always.
You made them shepherds of the flock
to share in the work of your Son,
and from their place in heaven they guide us still.

And so, with all the choirs of angels in heaven
we proclaim your glory
and join in their unending hymn of praise:
Holy, holy, holy Lord…

COMMUNION ANTIPHON   *(Jn 1:41-42)*
**Andrew told his brother Simon: we have found the Messiah,
the Christ; and he brought him to Jesus.**

PRAYER AFTER COMMUNION
Lord,
may the sacrament we have received give us courage
to follow the example of Andrew the apostle.
By sharing in Christ's suffering
may we live with him for ever in glory,
for he is Lord for ever and ever.

SOLEMN BLESSING
May God who founded his Church upon the apostles
bless you through the prayers of Saint Andrew. **Amen.**

May God inspire you to follow the example of the apostles,
and give witness to the truth before all people. **Amen.**

The teaching of the apostles has strengthened your faith.
May their prayers lead you
to your true and eternal home. **Amen.**

May almighty God bless you,
the Father, and the Son, ✠ and the Holy Spirit. **Amen.**

REFLECTION
    An apostle is literally one who has been sent. Every Christian is
    sent to hand on the faith which they have received. And so

every Christian is in this sense an apostle. The missionary outreach
of the Christian Church is also an expression of the Church's
apostolic character. To be a Christian is to be a missionary.

---

5 DECEMBER

SECOND SUNDAY OF ADVENT

The season of Advent falls into two parts. The first which continues
to December 16 evokes the themes and persons of the Hebrew
Scriptures who prepared the people of Israel for the coming of
the Messiah. During the second stage the mood of preparation
intensifies and becomes anticipation for the birth of the Wonder-
Counsellor, Mighty-God, Everlasting Father and Prince of Peace.

ENTRANCE ANTIPHON   *(cf. Is 30.19-30)*

**People of Zion, the Lord will come to save all nations, and
your hearts will exult to hear his majestic voice.**

GREETING, PENITENTIAL RITE — *pages 7-13*

The Gloria *is omitted.*

OPENING PRAYER

Let us pray
    [that nothing may hinder us
    from receiving Christ with joy]

God of power and mercy
open our hearts in welcome.
Remove the things that hinder us from receiving Christ with joy,
so that we may share his wisdom
and become one with him
when he comes in glory,
for he lives and reigns with you and the Holy Spirit,
one God, for ever and ever.

or

Let us pray
    [in Advent time
    for the coming Saviour to teach us wisdom]

Father in heaven,
the day draws near when the glory of your Son
will make radiant the night of the waiting world.
May the lure of greed not impede us from the joy

which moves the hearts of those who seek him.
May the darkness not blind us
to the vision of wisdom
which fills the minds of those who find him.

FIRST READING   *(Is 11:1-10)*

A reading from the prophet Isaiah.

He judges the wretched with integrity.

A shoot springs from the stock of Jesse,
a scion thrusts from his roots:
on him the spirit of the Lord rests,
a spirit of wisdom and insight,
a spirit of counsel and power,
a spirit of knowledge and of the fear of the Lord.
(The fear of the Lord is his breath.)
He does not judge by appearances,
he gives no verdict of hearsay,
but judges the wretched with integrity,
and with equity gives a verdict for the poor of the land.
His word is a rod that strikes the ruthless;
his sentences bring death to the wicked.

Integrity is the loincloth round his waist,
faithfulness the belt about his hips.

The wolf lives with the lamb,
the panther lies down with the kid,
calf and lion cub feed together
with a little boy to lead them.
The cow and the bear make friends,
their young lie down together.
The lion eats straw like the ox.
The infant plays over the cobra's hole;
into the viper's lair
the young child puts his hand.
They do no hurt, no harm,
on all my holy mountain,
for the country is filled with the knowledge of the Lord
as the waters swell the sea.
That day, the root of Jesse
shall stand as signal to the peoples.
It will be sought out by the nations
and its home will be glorious.

This is the word of the Lord.

RESPONSORIAL PSALM   *(Ps 71:1-2.7-8.12-13.17)*

℞ **In his days justice shall flourish
and peace till the moon fails.**

1. O God, give your judgement to the king,
    to a king's son your justice,
    that he may judge your people in justice
    and your poor in right judgement. ℞

2. In his days justice shall flourish
    and peace till the moon fails.
    He shall rule from sea to sea,
    from the Great River to earth's bounds. ℞

3. For he shall save the poor when they cry
    and the needy who are helpless.
    He will have pity on the weak
    and save the lives of the poor. ℞

4. May his name be blessed for ever
    and endure like the sun.
    Every tribe shall be blessed in him,
    all nations bless his name. ℞

SECOND READING   *(Rm 15:4-9)*

A reading from the letter of St Paul to the Romans.

Christ is the saviour of all.

Everything that was written long ago in the scriptures was meant
to teach us something about hope from the examples scripture
gives of how people who did not give up were helped by God.
And may he who helps us when we refuse to give up, help you
all to be tolerant with each other, following the example of
Christ Jesus, so that united in mind and voice you may give
glory to the God and Father of our Lord Jesus Christ.

It can only be to God's glory, then, for you to treat each
other in the same friendly way as Christ treated you. The reason
Christ became the servant of circumcised Jews was not only so
that God could faithfully carry out the promises made to the
patriarchs, it was also to get the pagans to give glory to God for
his mercy, as scripture says in one place: For this I shall praise
you among the pagans and sing your name.

This is the word of the Lord.

GOSPEL ACCLAMATION   *(Lk 3:4.6)*

**Alleluia, alleluia!
Prepare a way for the Lord,**

make his paths straight,
and all mankind shall see the salvation of God.
Alleluia!

GOSPEL *(Mt 3:1-12)*

A reading from the holy Gospel according to Matthew.

Repent, for the kingdom of heaven is close at hand.

In due course John the Baptist appeared; he preached in the wilderness of Judaea and this was his message: 'Repent, for the kingdom of heaven is close at hand.' This was the man the prophet Isaiah spoke of when he said:

A voice cries in the wilderness:
Prepare a way for the Lord,
make his paths straight.

This man John wore a garment made of camel-hair with a leather belt round his waist, and his food was locusts and wild honey. Then Jerusalem and all Judaea and the whole Jordan district made their way to him, and as they were baptised by him in the river Jordan they confessed their sins. But when he saw a number of Pharisees and Sadducees coming for baptism he said to them, 'Brood of vipers, who warned you to fly from the retribution that is coming? But if you are repentant, produce the appropriate fruit, and do not presume to tell yourselves, "We have Abraham for our father," because, I tell you, God can raise children for Abraham from these stones. Even now the axe is laid to the roots of the trees, so that any tree which fails to produce good fruit will be cut down and thrown on the fire. I baptise you in water for repentance, but the one who follows me is more powerful than I am, and I am not fit to carry his sandals; he will baptise you with the Holy Spirit and fire. His winnowing-fan is in his hand; he will clear his threshing-floor and gather his wheat into the barn; but the chaff he will burn in a fire that will never go out.'

This is the Gospel of the Lord.

PROFESSION OF FAITH — *pages 15-16*

PRAYER OVER THE GIFTS

Lord,
we are nothing without you.
As you sustain us with your mercy,
receive our prayers and offerings.

PREFACE OF ADVENT I — *page 18*

COMMUNION ANTIPHON   (Jn 1:12)

Rise up, Jerusalem, stand on the heights, and see the joy that is coming to you from God.

PRAYER AFTER COMMUNION

Father, you give us food from heaven.
By our sharing in this mystery,
teach us to judge wisely the things of earth
and to love the things of heaven.

SOLEMN BLESSING — *pages 56*

REFLECTION

> The advent wreath is a rich symbol which expresses some of
> the truths of the Jewish Christian tradition. The circle without
> beginning or end suggests God who was, who is and who will
> be. The green branches symbolise life. The candles light and
> the gradual unfolding of God's plan for humankind.

─────────── 8 DECEMBER ───────────

THE IMMACULATE CONCEPTION OF THE BLESSED VIRGIN MARY

The formal document of Pope Pius IX of 1854 in which he
defined the dogma of the Immaculate Conception declares:
'From the first moment of her conception, the Blessed Virgin
Mary was, by the singular grace and privilege of Almighty God,
and in view of the merits of Jesus Christ, Saviour of
humankind, kept free from all stain of original sin.' From the
Seventh Century the feast of Mary's conception was celebrated.

ENTRANCE ANTIPHON   (Is 61:10)

**I exult for joy in the Lord, my soul rejoices in my God; for he
has clothed me in the garment of salvation and robed me in
the cloak of justice, like a bride adorned with her jewels.**

GREETING, PENITENTIAL RITE, GLORIA — *pages 7-14*

OPENING PRAYER

Let us pray
    [that through the prayers of the sinless Virgin Mary,
    God will free us from our sins]

Father, you prepared the Virgin Mary
to be the worthy mother of your Son.

You let her share beforehand
in the salvation Christ would bring by his death,
and kept her sinless from the first moment of her conception.
Help us by her prayers
to live in your presence without sin.

or

Let us pray
    [on this feast of Mary
    who experienced the perfection of God's saving power]

Father,
the image of the Virgin is found in the Church.
Mary had a faith that your Spirit prepared
and a love that never knew sin,
for you kept her sinless from the first moment of her conception.

Trace in our actions the lines of her love,
in our hearts her readiness of faith.
Prepare once again a world for your Son
who lives and reigns with you and the Holy Spirit,
one God, for ever and ever.

FIRST READING   *(Gen 3:9-15.20)*

A reading from the book of Genesis.

I will make you enemies of each other; your offspring and her offspring.

After Adam had eaten of the tree, the Lord God called to him.
'Where are you?' he asked. 'I heard the sound of you in the
garden', he replied. 'I was afraid because I was naked, so I hid.'
'Who told you that you were naked?' he asked. 'Have you been
eating of the tree I forbade you to eat?' The man replied, 'It was
the woman you put with me; she gave me the fruit, and I ate it.'
Then the Lord God asked the woman, 'What is this you have
done?' The woman replied, 'The serpent tempted me and I ate.'

    Then the Lord God said to the serpent, 'Because you have
done this,

    'Be accursed beyond all cattle,
    all wild beasts.
    You shall crawl on your belly and eat dust
    every day of your life.
    I will make you enemies of each other:
    you and the woman,
    your offspring and her offspring.
    It will crush your head
    and you will strike its heel.'

The man named his wife 'Eve' because she was the mother of all those who live.

This is the word of the Lord.

RESPONSORIAL PSALM   (Ps 97:1-4)

℟ **Sing a new song to the Lord
for he has worked wonders.**

1. Sing a new song to the Lord
    for he has worked wonders.
    His right hand and his holy arm
    have brought salvation. ℟

2. The Lord has made known his salvation;
    has shown his justice to the nations.
    He has remembered his truth and love
    for the house of Israel. ℟

3. All the ends of the earth have seen
    the salvation of our God.
    Shout to the Lord all the earth,
    ring out your joy. ℟

SECOND READING   (Eph 1:3-6.11-12)

A reading from the letter of St Paul to the Ephesians.
Before the world was made, God chose us in Christ.

Blessed be God the Father of our Lord Jesus Christ,
who has blessed us with all the spiritual blessings of heaven in
    Christ.
Before the world was made, he chose us, chose us in Christ,
to be holy and spotless, and to live through love in his presence,
determining that we should become his adopted sons, through
    Jesus Christ
for his own kind purposes,
to make us praise the glory of his grace,
his free gift to us in the Beloved.
And it is in him that we were claimed as God's own,
chosen from the beginning,
under the predetermined plan of the one who guides all things
as he decides by his own will;
chosen to be,
for his greater glory,
the people who would put their hopes in Christ before he came.

This is the word of the Lord.

GOSPEL ACCLAMATION   *(Lk 1:28)*

Alleluia, alleluia!
Hail, Mary, full of grace; the Lord is with thee!
Blessed art thou among women. Alleluia!

GOSPEL   *(cf. Lk 1:26-38)*

A reading from the holy Gospel according to Luke.

You are to conceive and bear a Son.

The angel Gabriel was sent by God to a town in Galilee called
Nazareth, to a virgin betrothed to a man named Joseph, of the
House of David; and the virgin's name was Mary. He went in
and said to her, 'Rejoice, so highly favoured! The Lord is with
you.' She was deeply disturbed by these words and asked herself
what this greeting could mean, but the angel said to her, 'Mary,
do not be afraid; you have won God's favour. Listen! You are to
conceive and bear a son, and you must name him Jesus. He will
be great and will be called Son of the Most High. The Lord God
will give him the throne of his ancestor David; he will rule over
the House of Jacob for ever and his reign will have no end.' Mary
said to the angel, 'But how can this come about, since I am a
virgin?' 'The Holy Spirit will come upon you' the angel
answered, 'and the power of the Most High will cover you with
its shadow. And so the child will be holy and will be called Son
of God. Know this too: your kinswoman Elizabeth has, in her
old age, herself conceived a son, and she whom people called
barren is now in her sixth month; for nothing is impossible to
God.' 'I am the handmaid of the Lord' said Mary, 'let what you
have said be done to me.' And the angel left her.

This is the Gospel of the Lord.

PROFESSION OF FAITH — *pages 15-16*

PRAYER OVER THE GIFTS

Lord, accept this sacrifice
on the feast of the sinless Virgin Mary.
You kept her free from sin
from the first moment of her life.
Help us by her prayers,
and free us from our sins.

PREFACE OF THE IMMACULATE CONCEPTION

Father, all-powerful and ever-living God,
we do well always and everywhere to give you thanks.
You allowed no stain of Adam's sin

to touch the Virgin Mary.
Full of grace, she was to be a worthy mother of your Son,
your sign of favour to the Church at its beginning,
and the promise of its perfection as the bride of Christ, radiant
in beauty.

Purest of virgins, she was to bring forth your Son,
the innocent lamb who takes away our sins.
You chose her from all women to be our advocate with you
and our pattern of holiness.

In our joy we sing to your glory
with all the choirs of angels:
Holy, holy, holy...

COMMUNION ANTIPHON
**All honour to you, Mary! From you arose the sun of justice,
Christ our God.**

PRAYER AFTER COMMUNION
Lord our God,
in your love, you chose the Virgin Mary
and kept her free from sin.
May this sacrament of your love
free us from our sins.

SOLEMN BLESSING
Born of the Blessed Virgin Mary,
the Son of God redeemed humankind.
May he enrich you with his blessings. **Amen**.

You received the author of life through Mary.
May you always rejoice in her loving care. **Amen**.

You have come to rejoice at Mary's feast.
May you be filled with the joys of the Spirit
and the gifts of your eternal home. **Amen**.

May almighty God bless you,
the Father, and the Son, ✠ and the Holy Spirit. **Amen**.

REFLECTION
Today's feast celebrates Mary's acceptance of God's plan for
her. It also celebrates the salvation of the entire human race,
including hers also, which her Son brought about. By declaring
that she was redeemed in advance of the rest of humanity the
Church is simply calling our attention to God's saving plan for
the future mother of the Saviour.

12 DECEMBER
THIRD SUNDAY OF ADVENT

The first word of today's liturgy calls on us to rejoice at the imminent birth of the Messiah. That his name is Emmanuel serves to underline the cause of our joy, God's presence with his people for ever. Matthew's gospel begins and closes with this consoling truth.

ENTRANCE ANTIPHON   *(Ph 4:4-5)*

Rejoice in the Lord always; again I say, rejoice! The Lord is near.

GREETING, PENITENTIAL RITE — *pages 7-13*

The Gloria is omitted.

OPENING PRAYER

Let us pray
    [that God will fill us with joy
    at the coming of Christ]

Lord God,
may we, your people,
who look forward to the birthday of Christ
experience the joy of salvation
and celebrate that feast with love and thanksgiving.

or

Let us pray
    [this Advent
    for joy and hope in the coming Lord]

Father of our Lord Jesus Christ,
ever faithful to your promises
and ever close to your Church:
the earth rejoices in hope of the Saviour's coming
and looks forward with longing
to his return at the end of time.

Prepare our hearts and remove the sadness
that hinders us from feeling the joy and hope
which his presence will bestow,
for he is Lord for ever and ever.

FIRST READING   (Is 35:1-6.10)

A reading from the prophet Isaiah.
God himself is coming to save you.

Let the wilderness and the dry-lands exult,
let the wasteland rejoice and bloom,
let it bring forth flowers like the jonquil,
let it rejoice and sing for joy.

The glory of Lebanon is bestowed on it,
the splendour of Carmel and Sharon;
they shall see the glory of the Lord,
the splendour of our God.

Strengthen all weary hands,
steady all trembling knees
and say to all faint hearts,
'Courage! Do not be afraid.

'Look your God is coming,
vengeance is coming,
the retribution of God;
he is coming to save you.'

Then the eyes of the blind shall be opened,
the ears of the deaf unsealed,
then the lame shall leap like a deer
and the tongues of the dumb sing for joy,
for those the Lord has ransomed shall return.

They will come to Zion shouting for joy,
everlasting joy in their faces;
joy and gladness will go with them
and sorrow and lament be ended.

This is the word of the Lord.

RESPONSORIAL PSALM   (Ps 145:6-10)

℟   Come, Lord, and save us.

1.   It is the Lord who keeps faith for ever,
     who is just to those who are oppressed.
     It is he who gives bread to the hungry,
     the Lord, who sets prisoners free. ℟

2.   It is the Lord who gives sight to the blind,
     who raises up those who are bowed down,
     the Lord, who protects the stranger
     and upholds the widow and orphan. ℟

3.   It is the Lord who loves the just
      but thwarts the path of the wicked.
      The Lord will reign for ever,
      Zion's God, from age to age. ℞

SECOND READING   *(Jm 5:7-10)*

A reading from the letter of St James.

Do not lose heart, for the Lord's coming will be soon.

Be patient, brothers, until the Lord's coming. Think of a farmer:
how patiently he waits for the precious fruit of the ground until
it has had the autumn rains and the spring rains! You too have
to be patient; do not lose heart, because the Lord's coming will
be soon. Do not make complaints against one another, brothers,
so as not to be brought to judgement yourselves; the Judge is
already to be seen waiting at the gates. For your example,
brothers, in submitting with patience, take the prophets who
spoke in the name of the Lord.

      This is the word of the Lord.

GOSPEL ACCLAMATION   *(Is 61:1)*

Alleluia, alleluia!
The spirit of the Lord has been given to me.
He has sent me to bring good news to the poor.
Alleluia!

GOSPEL   *(Mt 11:2-11)*

A reading from the holy Gospel according to Matthew.

Are you the one who is to come, or have we got to wait for someone else?

John in his prison had heard what Christ was doing and he sent
his disciples to ask him, 'Are you the one who is to come, or
have we got to wait for someone else?' Jesus answered, 'Go back
and tell John what you hear and see; the blind see again, and the
lame walk, lepers are cleansed, and the deaf hear, and the dead
are raised to life and the Good News is proclaimed to the poor;
and happy is the man who does not lose faith in me.'

      As the messengers were leaving, Jesus began to talk to the
people about John: 'What did you go out into the wilderness to
see? A reed swaying in the breeze? No? Then what did you go
out to see? A man wearing fine clothes? Oh no, those who wear
fine clothes are to be found in palaces. Then what did you go
out for? To see a prophet? Yes, I tell you, and much more than a
prophet: he is the one of whom scripture says: Look, I am going
to send my messenger before you; he will prepare your way

before you. I tell you solemnly, of all the children born of
women, a greater than John the Baptist has never been seen; yet
the least in the kingdom of heaven is greater than he is.'

This is the Gospel of the Lord.

PROFESSION OF FAITH — *pages 15-16*

PRAYER OVER THE GIFTS
Lord,
may the gift we offer in faith and love
be a continual sacrifice in your honour
and truly become our eucharist and our salvation.

PREFACE OF ADVENT I — *page 18*

COMMUNION ANTIPHON   *(cf. Is 35:4)*
**Say to the anxious: be strong and fear not, our God will come
to save us.**

PRAYER AFTER COMMUNION
God of mercy,
may this eucharist bring us your divine help,
free us from our sins,
and prepare us for the birthday of our Saviour,
who is Lord for ever and ever.

SOLEMN BLESSING — *page 56*

REFLECTION
Today's gospel presents John the Baptist rethinking his views
of what the Messiah would be. From prison he discovers that
the one he has called Christ is not assuming a politically
powerful role. Hence his sending messengers to Jesus with the
question: are you the Messiah, really?

19 DECEMBER
FOURTH SUNDAY OF ADVENT

Joseph does not figure prominently in the scriptures or in the liturgy. Yet popular devotion has appreciated his role in the events surrounding the birth of the child, the son of Mary. He is asked to recognise the child as his own and so guarantee its legal status. His acceptance of his role and Mary's similar acceptance of hers is a model for Christian discipleship.

ENTRANCE ANTIPHON   (Is 45:8)

Let the clouds rain down the Just One, and the earth bring forth a Saviour.

GREETING, PENITENTIAL RITE — *pages 7-13*

The Gloria is omitted.

OPENING PRAYER

Let us pray
[as Advent draws to a close,
that Christ will truly come into our hearts]

Lord,
fill our hearts with your love,
and as you revealed to us by an angel
the coming of your Son as man,
so lead us through his suffering and death
to the glory of his resurrection,
for he lives and reigns with you and the Holy Spirit,
one God, for ever and ever.

or

Let us pray
[as Advent draws to a close
for the faith that opens our lives
to the Spirit of God]

Father, all-powerful God,
your eternal Word took flesh on our earth
when the Virgin Mary placed her life
at the service of your plan.

Lift our minds in watchful hope
to hear the voice which announces his glory
and open our minds to receive the Spirit
who prepares us for his coming.

FIRST READING   (Is 7:10-14)

A reading from the prophet Isaiah.
The maiden is with child.

The Lord spoke to Ahaz and said, 'Ask the Lord your God for a
sign for yourself coming either from the depths of Sheol or from
the heights above.' 'No,' Ahaz answered 'I will not put the Lord
to the test.'

Then Isaiah said:

'Listen now, House of David:
are you not satisfied with trying the patience of men
without trying the patience of God, too?
The Lord himself, therefore,
will give you a sign.
It is this: the maiden is with child
and will soon give birth to a son
whom she will call Emmanuel,
a name which means "God-is-with-us".'

This is the word of the Lord.

RESPONSORIAL PSALM   (Ps 23:1-6)

℞ Let the Lord enter!
    He is the king of glory.

1. The Lord's is the earth and its fullness,
    the world and all its peoples.
    It is he who set it on the seas;
    on the waters he made it firm. ℞

2. Who shall climb the mountain of the Lord?
    Who shall stand in his holy place?
    The man with clean hands and pure heart,
    who desires not worthless things. ℞

3. He shall receive blessings from the Lord
    and reward from the God who saves him.
    Such are the men who seek him,
    seek the face of the God of Jacob. ℞

SECOND READING   (Rm 1:1-7)

A reading from the letter of St Paul to the Romans.
Jesus Christ, descendant of David, Son of God.

From Paul, a servant of Christ Jesus who has been called to be
an apostle, and specially chosen to preach the Good News that
God promised long ago through his prophets in the scriptures.

This news is about the Son of God, who, according to the human nature he took, was a descendant of David: it is about Jesus Christ our Lord who, in the order of the spirit, the spirit of holiness that was in him, was proclaimed Son of God in all his power through his resurrection from the dead. Through him we received grace and our apostolic mission to preach the obedience of faith to all pagan nations in honour of his name. You are one of these nations, and by his call belong to Jesus Christ. To you all, then, who are God's beloved in Rome, called to be saints, may God our Father and the Lord Jesus Christ send grace and peace.

This is the word of the Lord.

GOSPEL ACCLAMATION   (Mt 1:23)

Alleluia, alleluia!
The virgin will conceive and give birth to a son
and they will call him Emmanuel,
a name which means 'God-is-with-us'.
Alleluia!

GOSPEL   (Mt 1:18-24)

A reading from the holy Gospel according to Matthew.

Jesus is born of Mary who was betrothed to Joseph, son of David.

This is how Jesus Christ came to be born. His mother Mary was betrothed to Joseph; but before they came to live together she was found to be with child through the Holy Spirit. Her husband Joseph, being a man of honour and wanting to spare her publicity, decided to divorce her informally. He had made up his mind to do this when the angel of the Lord appeared to him in a dream, and said 'Joseph son of David, do not be afraid to take Mary home as your wife, because she has conceived what is in her by the Holy Spirit. She will give birth to a son and you must name him Jesus, because he is the one who is to save his people from their sins.' Now all this took place to fulfil the words spoken by the Lord through the prophet:

The virgin will conceive and give birth to a son
and they will call him Emmanuel,

a name which means 'God-is-with-us'. When Joseph woke up he did what the angel of the Lord had told him to do: he took his wife to his home.

This is the Gospel of the Lord.

PROFESSION OF FAITH — *pages 15-16*

PRAYER OVER THE GIFTS

Lord, may the power of the Spirit,
which sanctified Mary the mother of your Son,
make holy the gifts we place upon this altar.

PREFACE OF ADVENT II

Father, all-powerful and ever-living God,
we do well always and everywhere to give you thanks
through Jesus Christ our Lord.

His future coming was proclaimed by all the prophets.
The virgin mother bore him in her womb with love
      beyond all telling.
John the Baptist was his herald
and made him known when at last he came.

In his love Christ has filled us with joy
as we prepare to celebrate his birth,
so that when he comes he may find us watching in prayer,
our hearts filled with wonder and praise.

And so, with all the choirs of angels in heaven
we proclaim your glory
and join in their unending hymn of praise:
Holy, holy, holy...

COMMUNION ANTIPHON   (Is 7:14)

**The Virgin is with child, and shall bear a son, and she will
call him Emmanuel.**

PRAYER AFTER COMMUNION

Lord, in this sacrament
we receive the promise of salvation;
as Christmas draws near
make us grow in faith and love
to celebrate the coming of Christ our Saviour,
who is Lord for ever and ever.

SOLEMN BLESSING — *page 56*

REFLECTION

During the second part of Advent, that is from December 17
onwards, the ancient *O Antiphons* are used daily as the gospel
acclamation at the Eucharist and as the antiphon for the
Magnificat at evening prayer. These were already in use by the
Eighth Century and together form a tapestry of titles for Jesus
in the mystery of his incarnation: Wisdom, Lord, Root of Jesse,
Key of David, Rising Sun, King and Emmanuel.

25 DECEMBER

THE NATIVITY OF OUR LORD

VIGIL MASS

The feast of Christmas replaced an earlier pre-Christian feast of the winter solstice. The connection with the birth of Jesus is made by the prophet Malachi who declares: 'But for you who fear my name the sun of righteousness shall rise with healing in its wings.'

ENTRANCE ANTIPHON   (cf. Ex 16:6-7)

Today you will know that the Lord is coming to save us, and in the morning you will see his glory.

GREETING, PENITENTIAL RITE, GLORIA — *pages 7-14*

OPENING PRAYER

Let us pray
   [that Christmas morning will find us at peace]

God our Father,
every year we rejoice
as we look forward to this feast of our salvation.
May we welcome Christ as our Redeemer,
and meet him with confidence when he comes to be our judge,
who lives and reigns with you and the Holy Spirit,
one God, for ever and ever.

or

Let us pray
   [and be ready to welcome the Lord]

God of endless ages, Father of all goodness,
we keep vigil for the dawn of salvation
and the birth of your Son.

With gratitude we recall his humanity,
the life he shared with the sons of men.
May the power of his divinity
help us answer his call to forgiveness and life.

FIRST READING   (Is 62:1-5)

A reading from the prophet Isaiah.

The Lord takes delight in you.

About Zion I will not be silent,
about Jerusalem I will not grow weary,
until her integrity shines out like the dawn

and her salvation flames like a torch.

The nations then will see your integrity,
all the kings your glory,
and you will be called by a new name,
one which the mouth of the Lord will confer.
You are to be a crown of splendour in the hand of the Lord,
a princely diadem in the hand of your God;
no longer are you to be named 'Forsaken',
nor your land 'Abandoned',
but you shall be called 'My Delight'
and your land 'The Wedded';
for the Lord takes delight in you
and your land will have its wedding.

Like a young man marrying a virgin,
so will the one who built you wed you,
and as the bridegroom rejoices in his bride,
so will your God rejoice in you.

   This is the word of the Lord.

RESPONSORIAL PSALM   (Ps 88:4-5.16-17.27.29)

℟ **I will sing for ever of your love, O Lord.**

1. 'I have made a covenant with my chosen one;
    I have sworn to David my servant:
    I will establish your dynasty for ever
    and set up your throne through all ages.' ℟

2. Happy the people who acclaim such a king,
    who walk, O Lord, in the light of your face,
    who find their joy every day in your name,
    who make your justice the source of their bliss. ℟

3   'He will say to me: "You are my father,
    my God, the rock who saves me."
    I will keep my love for him always;
    for him my covenant shall endure.' ℟

SECOND READING   (Acts 13:16-17.22-25)
A reading from the Acts of the Apostles.

Paul's witness to Christ, the son of David.

When Paul reached Antioch in Pisidia, he stood up in the
synagogue, held up a hand for silence and began to speak:
   'Men of Israel, and fearers of God, listen! The God of our
nation Israel chose our ancestors, and made our people great

when they were living as foreigners in Egypt; then by divine power he led them out.

'Then he made David their king, of whom he approved in these words, "I have selected David son of Jesse, a man after my own heart, who will carry out my whole purpose." To keep his promise, God has raised up for Israel one of David's descendants, Jesus, as Saviour, whose coming was heralded by John when he proclaimed a baptism of repentance for the whole people of Israel. Before John ended his career he said, "I am not the one you imagine me to be; that one is coming after me and I am not fit to undo his sandal".'

This is the word of the Lord.

GOSPEL ACCLAMATION

Alleluia, alleluia!
Tomorrow there will be an end to the sin of the world
and the saviour of the world will be our king. Alleluia!

GOSPEL *(Shorter Form)*   *(Mt 1:18-25)*

A reading from the holy Gospel according to Matthew.

Mary will give birth to a son and will name him Jesus.

This is how Jesus Christ came to be born. His mother Mary was betrothed to Joseph; but before they came to live together she was found to be with child through the Holy Spirit. Her husband Joseph, being a man of honour and wanting to spare her publicity, decided to divorce her informally. He had made up his mind to do this when the angel of the Lord appeared to him in a dream and said, 'Joseph son of David, do not be afraid to take Mary home as your wife, because she has conceived what is in her by the Holy Spirit. She will give birth to a son and you must name him Jesus, because he is the one who is to save his people from their sins.' Now all this took place to fulfil the words spoken by the Lord through the prophet:

The Virgin will conceive and give birth to a son
and they will call him Emmanuel,

a name which means 'God-is-with-us'. When Joseph woke up he did what the angel of the Lord told him to do: he took his wife to his home and, though he had not had intercourse with her, she gave birth to a son; and he named him Jesus.

This is the Gospel of the Lord.

PROFESSION OF FAITH — *pages 15-16*

(All genuflect at the words, 'and was made man'.)

PRAYER OVER THE GIFTS

Lord, as we keep tonight the vigil of Christmas,
may we celebrate this eucharist
with greater joy than ever
since it marks the beginning of our redemption.

PREFACE OF CHRISTMAS I-III — *page 19*

COMMUNION ANTIPHON   *(cf. Is 40:5)*

**The glory of the Lord will be revealed, and all humankind will
see the saving power of God.**

PRAYER AFTER COMMUNION

Father, we ask you to give us a new birth
as we celebrate the beginning
of your Son's life on earth.
Strengthen us in spirit
as we take your food and drink.

SOLEMN BLESSING — *page 400*

REFLECTION

> The Gospels of Matthew and Luke provide us with an Infancy
> Narrative, an account of events surrounding the birth of the
> Messiah. These appear to have been written later than the
> gospels to which they were appended. They have the same
> function as the rest of the gospel: to evoke faith in the risen
> Lord on the part of their hearers and readers.

MIDNIGHT MASS

The Roman missal provides texts for three separate Masses on
Christmas Day. The original Mass of Christmas was celebrated
at Saint Peter's basilica. Then in the middle of the Fifth Century
a Mass was celebrated first 'at cockcrow' then at midnight at
the basilica of Santa Maria Maggiore where there was erected a
replica of the crib at Bethlehem. In the early Thirteenth Century,
Francis of Assisi began the devotion of the Christmas crib.

ENTRANCE ANTIPHON   *(Ps 2:7)*

**The Lord said to me: You are my Son; this day have I begotten
you.**
or

Let us all rejoice in the Lord, for our Saviour is born to the world. True peace has descended from heaven.

GREETING, PENITENTIAL RITE, GLORIA — *pages 7-14*

OPENING PRAYER

Let us pray
[in the peace of Christmas midnight
that our joy in the birth of Christ
will last for ever]

Father,
you make this holy night radiant
with the splendour of Jesus Christ our light.
We welcome him as Lord, the true light of the world.
Bring us to eternal joy in the kingdom of heaven,
where he lives and reigns with you and the Holy Spirit,
one God, for ever and ever.

or

Let us pray
[with joy and hope
as we await the dawning of the Father's Word]

Lord our God,
with the birth of your Son,
your glory breaks on the world.

Through the night hours of the darkened earth
we your people watch for the coming of your promised Son.
As we wait, give us a foretaste of the joy that you will grant us
when the fullness of his glory has filled the earth,
who lives and reigns with you for ever and ever.

FIRST READING *(Is 9:1-7)*

A reading from the prophet Isaiah.

A Son is given to us.

The people that walked in darkness
has seen a great light;
on those who live in a land of deep shadow
a light has shone.
You have made their gladness greater,
you have made their joy increase;
they rejoice in your presence
as men rejoice at harvest time,
as men are happy when they are dividing the spoils.
For the yoke that was weighing on him,

the bar across his shoulders,
the rod of his oppressor,
these you break as on the day of Midian.
For all the footgear of battle,
every cloak rolled in blood,
is burnt, and consumed by fire.
For there is a child born for us,
a son given to us
and dominion is laid on his shoulders;
and this is the name they give him:
Wonder-Counsellor, Mighty-God,
Eternal-Father, Prince-of-Peace.
Wide is his dominion
in a peace that has no end,
for the throne of David
and for his royal power,
which he establishes and makes secure
in justice and integrity.
From this time onwards and for ever,
the jealous love of the Lord of hosts will do this.

This is the word of the Lord.

RESPONSORIAL PSALM   (Ps 95:1-3.11-13)

℟   Today a saviour has been born to us;
      he is Christ the Lord.

1.   O sing a new song to the Lord,
      sing to the Lord all the earth.
      O sing to the Lord, bless his name. ℟

2.   Proclaim his help day by day,
      tell among the nations his glory
      and his wonders among all the peoples. ℟

3.   Let the heavens rejoice and earth be glad,
      let the sea and all within it thunder praise,
      let the land and all it bears rejoice,
      all the trees of the wood shout for joy
      at the presence of the Lord for he comes,
      he comes to rule the earth. ℟

4.   With justice he will rule the world,
      he will judge the peoples with his truth. ℟

SECOND READING   (Tt 2:11-14)
A reading from the letter of St Paul to Titus.
God's grace has been revealed to the whole human race.

God's grace has been revealed, and it has made salvation
possible for the whole human race and taught us that what we
have to do is to give up everything that does not lead to God,
and all our worldly ambitions; we must be self-restrained and
live good and religious lives here in this present world, while we
are waiting in hope for the blessing which will come with the
Appearing of the glory of our great God and saviour Christ Jesus.
He sacrificed himself for us in order to set us free from all
wickedness and to purify a people so that it could be his very
own and would have no ambition except to do good.

    This is the word of the Lord.

GOSPEL ACCLAMATION   (Lk 2:10-11)
Alleluia, alleluia!
I bring you news of great joy:
today a saviour has been born to us, Christ the Lord.
Alleluia!

GOSPEL   (Lk 2:1-14)
A reading from the holy Gospel according to Luke.
Today a saviour has been born to you.

Caesar Augustus issued a decree for a census of the whole world
to be taken. This census — the first — took place while
Quirinius was governor of Syria, and everyone went to his own
town to be registered. So Joseph set out from the town of
Nazareth in Galilee and travelled up to Judaea, to the town of
David called Bethlehem, since he was of David's House and line,
in order to be registered together with Mary, his betrothed, who
was with child. While they were there the time came for her to
have her child, and she gave birth to a son, her first-born. She
wrapped him in swaddling clothes, and laid him in a manger
because there was no room for them at the inn. In the
countryside close by there were shepherds who lived in the fields
and took it in turns to watch their flocks during the night. The
angel of the Lord appeared to them and the glory of the Lord
shone round them. They were terrified, but the angel said, 'Do
not be afraid. Listen, I bring you news of great joy, a joy to be
shared by the whole people. Today in the town of David a
saviour has been born to you; he is Christ the Lord. And here is
a sign for you: you will find a baby wrapped in swaddling

clothes and lying in a manger.' And suddenly with the angel there was a great throng of the heavenly host, praising God and singing:

'Glory to God in the highest heaven,
and peace to men who enjoy his favour.'

This is the Gospel of the Lord.

PROFESSION OF FAITH — *pages 15-16*
(All genuflect at the words, 'and was made man).'

PRAYER OVER THE GIFTS

Lord,
accept our gifts on this joyful feast of our salvation.
By our communion with God made man,
may we become more like him
who joins our lives to yours,
for he is Lord for ever and ever.

PREFACE OF CHRISTMAS I-III — *page 19*

COMMUNION ANTIPHON   *(Jn 1:14)*
The Word of God became man; we have seen his glory.

PRAYER AFTER COMMUNION

God our Father,
we rejoice in the birth of our Saviour.
May we share his life completely
by living as he has taught.

SOLEMN BLESSING

When he came to us as man,
the Son of God scattered the darkness of this world,
and filled this holy night (day) with his glory.
May the God of infinite goodness
scatter the darkness of sin
and brighten your hearts with holiness. **Amen.**

God sent his angels to shepherds
to herald the great joy of our Saviour's birth.
May he fill you with joy
and make you heralds of his gospel. **Amen.**

When the Word became man,
earth was joined to heaven.
May he give you his peace and good will,
and fellowship with all the heavenly host. **Amen**

May almighty God bless you,
the Father, and the Son, ✠ and the Holy Spirit. **Amen.**

REFLECTION

> Although Luke's Gospel has the appearance of being a 'Life of
> Christ' this is not what the author intended. His work is a
> proclamation designed to arouse faith on the part of
> Theophilus to whom it is addressed. He may be an individual
> or a symbol for every 'friend of God' as his name implies. This
> is true also of the stories surrounding Jesus' birth.

DAWN MASS

> The third Mass to be added to the Roman liturgy of Christmas
> Day was the Dawn Mass. It was originally celebrated at the
> church of Anastasia, a martyr whose feast day was kept on
> December 25. In imitation of Easter and the Epiphany,
> Christmas was provided with an octave, a week of celebration
> to underline its special significance for the Church.

ENTRANCE ANTIPHON   *(cf. Is 9:2,6; Lk 1:33)*

**A light will shine on us this day, the Lord is born for us: he
shall be called Wonderful God, Prince of peace, Father of the
world to come; and his kingship will never end.**

GREETING, PENITENTIAL RITE, GLORIA — *pages 7-14*

OPENING PRAYER

Let us pray

> [that the love of Christ
> will be a light to the world]

Father,
we are filled with the new light
by the coming of your Word among us.
May the light of faith
shine in our words and actions.

or

Let us pray

> [for the peace that comes from the Prince of Peace]

Almighty God and Father of light,
a child is born for us and a son is given to us.
Your eternal Word leaped down from heaven

in the silent watches of the night,
and now your Church is filled with wonder
at the nearness of her God.

Open our hearts to receive his life
and increase our vision with the rising of dawn,
that our lives may be filled with his glory and his peace,
who lives and reigns for ever and ever.

FIRST READING   (Is 62:11-12)
A reading from the prophet Isaiah.
Look, your saviour comes.

This the Lord proclaims
to the ends of the earth:

> Say to the daughter of Zion, 'Look,
> your saviour comes,
> the prize of his victory with him,
> his trophies before him.'
> They shall be called 'The Holy People',
> 'The Lord's Redeemed'.
> And you shall be called 'The-sought-after',
> 'City-not-forsaken'.

This is the word of the Lord.

RESPONSORIAL PSALM   (Ps 96:1.6.11-12)

℟ This day new light will shine upon the earth:
   the Lord is born for us.

1. The Lord is king, let earth rejoice,
   the many coastlands be glad.
   The skies proclaim his justice;
   all peoples see his glory. ℟

2. Light shines forth for the just
   and joy for the upright of heart.
   Rejoice, you just, in the Lord;
   give glory to his holy name.

SECOND READING   (Tt 3:4-7)
A reading from the letter of St Paul to Titus.
It was for no reason except his own compassion that he saved us.

When the kindness and love of God our saviour for mankind
were revealed, it was not because he was concerned with any
righteous actions we might have done ourselves; it was for no
reason except his own compassion that he saved us, by means of

the cleansing water of rebirth and by renewing us with the Holy Spirit which he has so generously poured over us through Jesus Christ our saviour. He did this so that we should be justified by his grace, to become heirs looking forward to inheriting eternal life.

This is the word of the Lord.

GOSPEL ACCLAMATION   *(Lk 2:14)*
Alleluia, alleluia!
Glory to God in the highest heaven,
and peace to men who enjoy his favour.
Alleluia!

GOSPEL   *(Lk 2:15-20)*
A reading from the holy Gospel according to Luke.
The shepherds found Mary and Joseph and the baby.

Now when the angels had gone from them into heaven, the shepherds said to one another, 'Let us go to Bethlehem and see this thing that has happened which the Lord has made known to us.' So they hurried away and found Mary and Joseph, and the baby lying in the manger. When they saw the child they repeated what they had been told about him, and everyone who heard it was astonished at what the shepherds had to say. As for Mary, she treasured all these things and pondered them in her heart. And the shepherds went back glorifying and praising God for all they had heard and seen; it was exactly as they had been told.

This is the Gospel of the Lord.

PROFESSION OF FAITH — *pages 15-16*
(All genuflect at the words, 'and was made man.'*)*

PRAYER OVER THE GIFTS
Father, may we follow the example of your Son
who became man and lived among us.
May we receive the gift of divine life
through these offerings here on earth.

PREFACE OF CHRISTMAS I-III — *page 19*

COMMUNION ANTIPHON   *(cf. Zc 9:9)*
Daughter of Zion, exult; shout aloud, daughter of Jerusalem!
Your King is coming, the Holy One, the Saviour of the world.

PRAYER AFTER COMMUNION
Lord, with faith and joy
we celebrate the birthday of your Son.
Increase our understanding and our love

of the riches you have revealed in him,
who is Lord for ever and ever.

SOLEMN BLESSING — *page 400*

REFLECTION

> Luke's portrait of Jesus, including his accounts of the
> childhood of Jesus, is kerygmatic. He wants to impress on his
> hearers that the person he is writing about is worthy to be
> preached. That he has significance for every human being in
> every age. He clearly depicts Jesus as proclaiming himself and
> the Kingdom of God in this way, when he has Jesus declare:
> 'This is what I was sent for' (Lk 4:43).

MASS DURING THE DAY

> The Church has kept the feast of the birth of the Lord from at
> least the Fourth Century. Jesus was born in a particular place,
> at a particular time and to a particular mother. This is the
> kernel of the event when all the myths have been stripped
> away. These are the hard facts. Mary, whom St Jerome calls
> 'mother and midwife', is a witness to this event.

ENTRANCE ANTIPHON   *(Is 9:6)*

**A child is born for us, a son given to us; dominion is laid on
his shoulder, and he shall be called Wonderful-Counsellor.**

GREETING, PENITENTIAL RITE, GLORIA — *pages 7-14*

OPENING PRAYER

Let us pray

> [for the glory promised by the birth of Christ]

Lord God,
we praise you for creating man,
and still more for restoring him in Christ.
Your Son shared our weakness:
may we share his glory,
for he lives and reigns with you and the Holy Spirit,
one God, for ever and ever.

or

Let us pray

> [in the joy of Christmas
> because the Son of God lives among us]

God of love, Father of all,
the darkness that covered the earth
has given way to the bright dawn of your Word made flesh.

Make us a people of this light.
Make us faithful to your Word,
that we may bring your life to the waiting world.

FIRST READING   (Is 52:7-10)

A reading from the prophet Isaiah.

All the ends of the earth shall see the salvation of our God.

How beautiful on the mountains,
are the feet of one who brings good news,
who heralds peace, brings happiness,
proclaims salvation,
and tells Zion,
'Your God is king!'
Listen! Your watchmen raise their voices,
they shout for joy together,
for they see the Lord face to face,
as he returns to Zion.
Break into shouts of joy together,
you ruins of Jerusalem;
for the Lord is consoling his people,
redeeming Jerusalem.
The Lord bares his holy arm
in the sight of all the nations,
and all the ends of the earth shall see
the salvation of our God.

    This is the word of the Lord.

RESPONSORIAL PSALM   (Ps 97:1-6)

℟   **All the ends of the earth have seen
     the salvation of our God.**

1.   Sing a new song to the Lord
     for he has worked wonders.
     His right hand and his holy arm
     have brought salvation. ℟

2.   The Lord has made known his salvation;
     has shown his justice to the nations.
     He has remembered his truth and love
     for the house of Israel. ℟   *(continued)*

3.   All the ends of the earth have seen
     the salvation of our God.
     Shout to the Lord all the earth,
     ring out your joy. ℟

℟   **All the ends of the earth have seen
     the salvation of our God.**

4.   Sing psalms to the Lord with the harp,
     with the sound of music.
     With trumpets and the sound of the horn
     acclaim the King, the Lord. ℟

SECOND READING   *(Heb 1:1-6)*

A reading from the letter to the Hebrews.

God has spoken to us through his Son.

At various times in the past and in various different ways, God
spoke to our ancestors through the prophets; but in our own
time, the last days, he has spoken to us through his Son, the Son
that he has appointed to inherit everything and through whom
he made everything there is. He is the radiant light of God's glory
and the perfect copy of his nature, sustaining the universe by his
powerful command; and now that he has destroyed the defilement
of sin, he has gone to take his place in heaven at the right hand
of divine Majesty. So he is now as far above the angels as the
title which he has inherited is higher than their own name.

     God has never said to any angel: You are my Son, today I
have become your father, or: I will be a father to him and he a
son to me. Again, when he brings the First-born into the world,
he says: Let all the angels of God worship him.

     This is the word of the Lord.

GOSPEL ACCLAMATION

**Alleluia, alleluia!
A hallowed day has dawned upon us.
Come, you nations, worship the Lord,
for today a great light has shone down upon the earth.
Alleluia!**

GOSPEL   *(Jn 1:1-18)*

(*For* Shorter Form, *read between* ◆ ◆)

A reading from the holy Gospel according to John.

The Word was made flesh, and lived among us.

◆In the beginning was the Word:
the Word was with God

and the Word was God.
He was with God in the beginning.
Through him all things came to be,
not one thing had its being but through him.
All that came to be had life in him
and that life was the light of men,
a light that shines in the dark,
a light that darkness could not overpower.◀

A man came, sent by God.
His name was John.
He came as a witness,
as a witness to speak for the light,
so that everyone might believe through him.
He was not the light,
only a witness to speak for the light.
▶The Word was the true light
that enlightens all men;
and he was coming into the world.
He was in the world
that had its being through him,
and the world did not know him.
He came to his own domain
and his own people did not accept him.
But to all who did accept him
he gave power to become children of God,
to all who believe in the name of him
who was born not out of human stock
or urge of the flesh
or will of man
but of God himself.
The Word was made flesh,
he lived among us,
and we saw his glory,
the glory that is his as the only Son of the Father,
full of grace and truth.◀

John appears as his witness. He proclaims:
'This is the one of whom I said:
He who comes after me
ranks before me
because he existed before me.'
Indeed, from his fullness we have, all of us, received —
yes, grace in return for grace,

since, though the Law was given through Moses,
grace and truth have come through Jesus Christ.
No one has ever seen God;
it is the only Son, who is nearest to the Father's heart,
who has made him known.

◗This is the Gospel of the Lord.◖

PROFESSION OF FAITH — *pages 15-16*
(*All genuflect at the words,* 'and was made man).

PRAYER OVER THE GIFTS
Almighty God,
the saving work of Christ
made our peace with you.
May our offering today
renew that peace within us
and give you perfect praise.

PREFACE OF CHRISTMAS I-III — *page 19*

COMMUNION ANTIPHON   (Ps 97:3)
All the ends of the earth have seen the saving power of God.

PRAYER AFTER COMMUNION
Father,
the child born today is the Saviour of the world.
He made us your children.
May he welcome us into your kingdom
where he lives and reigns with you for ever and ever.

SOLEMN BLESSING — *page 400*

REFLECTION
The stories relating to Jesus' birth and childhood are later than
the other parts of the gospels to which they are now attached.
This does not take away from their importance, written as they
are in the light of the Resurrection. They are evidence of a post-
Easter faith which seeks to read the significance of the paschal
mystery of the suffering, death and resurrection of the Lord
into the earlier events of his life.

26 DECEMBER
THE HOLY FAMILY

Since 1969 the first Sunday after Christmas has been kept as
the feast of the Holy Family of Jesus, Mary and Joseph, a devotion
which greatly increased in the popular imagination in the
Seventeenth Century. The scriptures and the liturgy give very
little emphasis to the private life of Jesus, dominated as they both
are with his public ministry. Today's feast is an exception. The
details of their family life are lost. The significance enduring.

ENTRANCE ANTIPHON   *(Lk 2:16)*

**The shepherds hastened to Bethlehem, where they found
Mary and Joseph, and the baby lying in a manger.**

GREETING, PENITENTIAL RITE, GLORIA — *pages 7-14*

OPENING PRAYER

Let us pray
    [for peace in our families]
Father, help us to live as the holy family,
united in respect and love.
Bring us to the joy and peace of your eternal home.
or
Let us pray
    [as the family of God,
    who share in his life]

Father in heaven, creator of all,
you ordered the earth to bring forth life
and crowned its goodness by creating the family of man.
In history's moment when all was ready,
you sent your Son to dwell in time,
obedient to the laws of life in our world.

Teach us the sanctity of human love,
show us the value of family life,
and help us to live in peace with all
that we may share in your life for ever.

FIRST READING   *(Si 3:2-6.12-14)*

A reading from the Book of Ecclesiasticus.

He who fears the Lord respects his parents.

The Lord honours the father in his children,
and upholds the rights of a mother over her sons.

Whoever respects his father is atoning for his sins,
he who honours his mother is like someone amassing a fortune.
Whoever respects his father will be happy with children
        of his own,
he shall be heard on the day when he prays.
Long life comes to him who honours his father,
he who sets his mother at ease is showing obedience to the Lord.
My son, support your father in his old age,
do not grieve him during his life.
Even if his mind should fail, show him sympathy,
do not despise him in your health and strength;
for kindness to a father shall not be forgotten
but will serve as reparation for your sins.

>   This is the word of the Lord.

RESPONSORIAL PSALM   *(Ps 127:1-5)*

℞   **O blessed are those who fear the Lord**
     and walk in his ways!

1.   O blessed are those who fear the Lord
     and walk in his ways!
     By the labour of your hands you shall eat.
     You will be happy and prosper. ℞

2.   Your wife like a fruitful vine
     in the heart of your house;
     your children like shoots of the olive,
     around your table. ℞

3.   Indeed thus shall be blessed
     the man who fears the Lord.
     May the Lord bless you from Zion
     all the days of your life! ℞

SECOND READING   *(Col 3:12-17)*

A reading from the letter of St Paul to the Colossians.

Family life in the Lord.

You are God's chosen race, his saints; he loves you and you should
be clothed in sincere compassion, in kindness and humility,
gentleness and patience. Bear with one another; forgive each other
as soon as a quarrel begins. The Lord has forgiven you; now you
must do the same. Over all these clothes, to keep them together
and complete them, put on love. And may the peace of Christ
reign in your hearts, because it is for this that you were called
together as parts of one body. Always be thankful.

Let the massage of Christ, in all its richness, find a home with you. Teach each other, and advise each other, in all wisdom. With gratitude in your hearts sing psalms and hymns and inspired songs to God; and never say or do anything except in the name of the Lord Jesus, giving thanks to God the Father through him.

This is the word of the Lord.

GOSPEL ACCLAMATION *(Col 3:15. 16)*

Alleluia, alleluia!
May the peace of Christ reign in your hearts;
let the message of Christ find a home with you.
Alleluia!

GOSPEL *(Mt 2:13-15.19-23)*

A reading from the holy Gospel according to Matthew.

Take the child and his mother and escape into Egypt.

After the wise men had left, the angel of the Lord appeared to Joseph in a dream and said, 'Get up, take the child and his mother with you, and escape into Egypt, and stay there until I tell you, because Herod intends to search for the child and do away with him.' So Joseph got up and, taking the child and his mother with him, left that night for Egypt, where he stayed until Herod was dead. This was to fulfil what the Lord had spoken through the prophet:

I called my son out of Egypt.

After Herod's death, the angel of the Lord appeared in a dream to Joseph in Egypt and said, 'Get up, take the child and his mother with you and go back to the land of Israel, for those who wanted to kill the child are dead'. So Joseph got up and, taking the child and his mother with him, went back to the land of Israel. But when he learnt that Archelaus had succeeded his father Herod as ruler of Judaea he was afraid to go there, and being warned in a dream he left to the region of Galilee. There he settled in a town called Nazareth. In this way the words spoken through the prophets were to be fulfilled:

He will be called a Nazarene.

This is the Gospel of the Lord.

PROFESSION OF FAITH — *pages 15-16*

PRAYER OVER THE GIFTS

Lord,
accept this sacrifice
and through the prayers of Mary, the virgin Mother of God,

and of her husband, Joseph,
unite our families in peace and love.

PREFACE OF CHRISTMAS I-III — *page 19*

COMMUNION ANTIPHON   *(Ba 3:38)*

Our God has appeared on earth, and lived among men.

PRAYER AFTER COMMUNION

Eternal Father,
we want to live as Jesus, Mary, and Joseph,
in peace with you and one another.
May this communion strengthen us
to face the troubles of life.

SOLEMN BLESSING — *page 400*

REFLECTION

Matthew presents Jesus going into exile like his people did some
six centuries earlier. He is a displaced person. The narrative
about Herod serves to remind the hearers of Matthew's
community that the shadow of the cross stretches right back to
Jesus' first moments on earth. But that is good news because it
implies that God's saving plan, symbolised by the cross, is
close at hand.

DEVOTIONAL PRAYERS

THANKSGIVING AFTER COMMUNION

Adoration. I adore you present in me, Incarnate Word, only-begotten Son and splendour of the Father, born of Mary. I thank you, sole Master and Truth, for your supreme condescension in coming to me, ignorant and sinful as I am. With Mary I offer you to the Father: through you, with you, in you, may there be eternal praise, thanksgiving and supplication for peace to humankind. Enlighten my mind; make me a docile disciple of the Church; grant that I may live of faith; give me an understanding of the Scriptures. Make me your ardent apostle. Let the light of your Gospel, O Divine Master, shine to the farthest bounds of the world.

Resolution. O Jesus, you are the Way which I must follow; the perfect model which I must imitate. In presenting myself at the judgment I want to be found similar to you.

O divine model of humility and obedience, make me similar to you.

O perfect example of mortification and purity, make me similar to you.

O Jesus, poor and patient, make me similar to you.

O exemplar of charity and ardent zeal, make me similar to you.

Petition. O Jesus, my Life, my joy and source of all good, I love you. Above all, I ask of you that I may love you more and more and the souls redeemed by your Blood.

You are the vine and I am the branch: I want to stay united to you always so as to bring forth many fruits.

You are the source: pour out an ever greater abundance of grace to sanctify my soul.

You are my head; I, your member: communicate to me your Holy Spirit with all his gifts.

May your kingdom come through Mary.

Console and save those dear to me. Free the souls in purgatory.

SPIRITUAL COMMUNION

My Jesus, I believe that you are truly present in the Blessed
Sacrament. I love you above all things and I desire you in my
soul. As I cannot now receive you sacramentally, come at least
spiritually into my heart. I embrace you and unite myself
entirely to you. Do not let me leave you ever.

TO JESUS, THE DIVINE MASTER

Jesus, Divine Master, I adore you as the Word Incarnate sent by
the Father to instruct humankind in life-giving truths. You are
uncreated *Truth*, the only Master. You alone have words of
eternal life. I thank you for having ignited in me the light of
reason and the light of faith, and for having called me to the
light of glory. I believe, submitting my whole mind to you and
to the Church, and I condemn all that the Church condemns.
Master, show me the treasures of your wisdom, let me know the
Father, make me your true disciple. Increase my faith so that I
may attain to the eternal vision in heaven.

PRAYER OF ST FRANCIS

Lord, make me an instrument of your peace:
where there is hatred let me sow love,
where there is injury let me sow pardon,
where there is doubt let me sow faith,
where there is despair let me give hope,
where there is darkness let me give light,
where there is sadness let me give joy.

O Divine Master, grant that I may
not try to be comforted but to comfort,
not try to be understood but to understand,
not try to be loved but to love.

Because it is in giving that we receive,
it is in forgiving that we are forgiven,
and it is in dying that we are born to eternal life.

THE DIVINE PRAISES

Blessed be God.
Blessed be His holy Name.

Blessed be the Name of Jesus.
Blessed be His most Sacred Heart.
Blessed be His most precious Blood.
Blessed be Jesus in the most holy Sacrament of the Altar.
Blessed be the Holy Spirit, the Paraclete.
Blessed be the great Mother of God, Mary most holy.
Blessed be her holy and immaculate conception.
Blessed be her glorious assumption.
Blessed be the name of Mary, Virgin and Mother.
Blessed be St Joseph, her most chaste spouse.
Blessed be God in His angels and in His saints.

SOUL OF CHRIST

Soul of Christ, sanctify me,
Body of Christ, save me.
Blood of Christ, inebriate me.
Water from the side of Christ, wash me.
Passion of Christ, strengthen me.
O good Jesus, hear me.
Within your wounds hide me.
Permit me not to be separated from you.
From the malignant enemy defend me.
In the hour of my death call me
And bid me come to you,
That with your saints I may praise you
For ever and ever. Amen.

CONSECRATION TO THE MOST HOLY TRINITY

O divine Trinity, Father, Son and Holy Spirit, present and active in the Church and the depths of my soul, I adore you, I thank you, I love you! And through the hands of Mary most holy, my Mother, I offer, give, and consecrate myself entirely to You for life and for eternity.

To You, heavenly Father, I offer, give and consecrate myself as Your child.

To You, Jesus Master, I offer, give and consecrate myself as Your brother (sister) and disciple.

To You, Holy Spirit, I offer, give and consecrate myself as "a living temple" to be consecrated and sanctified.

O Mary, Mother of the Church and my Mother, teach me to live, through the liturgy and the sacraments, in ever more intimate union with the three Divine Persons, so that my whole life may be a "glory be to the Father, to the Son and to the Holy Spirit." Amen.

PRAYER TO THE HOLY SPIRIT

O divine Holy Spirit, eternal Love of the Father and of the Son, I adore you, I thank you, I love you, and I ask you pardon for all the times I have grieved you in myself and in my neighbour.

Descend with many graces during the holy ordination of bishops and priests, during the consecration of men and women religious, during the reception of Confirmation by all the faithful; be light, sanctity and zeal.

To you, O Spirit of Truth, I consecrate my mind, imagination and memory; enlighten me. May I know Jesus Christ our Master and understand his Gospel and the teaching of holy Church. Increase in me the gifts of wisdom, knowledge, understanding and right judgment.

To you, O sanctifying Spirit, I consecrate my will. Guide me in your will, sustain me in the observance of the commandments, in the fulfilment of my duties. Grant me the gifts of courage and reverence.

To you, O life-giving Spirit, I consecrate my heart. Guard and increase the divine life in me. Grant me the gift of filial love. Amen.

ACT OF SUBMISSION TO THE WILL OF GOD

My God, I do not know what will happen to me today. I only know that nothing will happen to me that was not foreseen by you and directed to my greater good from all eternity. This is enough for me.

I adore your holy, eternal and unfathomable designs. I submit to them with all my heart for love of you. I make a sacrifice of my whole being to you and join my sacrifice to that of Jesus, my divine Saviour.

In his name and by his infinite merits, I ask you to give me patience in my sufferings and perfect submission, so that everything you want or permit to happen will result in your greater glory and my sanctification. Amen.

INVOCATIONS TO THE DIVINE MASTER

Jesus Master, sanctify my mind and increase my faith.

Jesus, teaching in the Church, draw everyone to your school.

Jesus Master, deliver me from error, from vain thoughts, and from eternal darkness.

O Jesus, Way between the Father and us, I offer you everything and look to you for everything.

O Jesus, Way of sanctity, make me your faithful imitator.

O Jesus Way, render me perfect as the Father who is in heaven.

O Jesus Life, live in me, so that I may live in you.

O Jesus Life, do not permit me to separate myself from you.

O Jesus Life, grant that I may live eternally in the joy of your love.

O Jesus Truth, may I be light for the world.

O Jesus Way, may I be an example and model for others.

O Jesus Life, may my presence bring grace and consolation everywhere.

TO RECALL GOD'S PRESENCE

I believe, my God, that I am in your presence, that you are looking at me and listening to my prayers.

You are so great and so holy: I adore you.

You have given me all: I thank you.

You have been so offended by me: I ask your pardon with all my heart.

You are so merciful: and I ask of you all the graces which you know are beneficial to me.

ACT OF FAITH

O my God, I firmly believe that you are one God in three Divine Persons; Father, Son, and Holy Spirit; I believe that your divine Son became man and died for our sins, and that he will come to judge the living and the dead. I believe these and all truths which the holy catholic Church teaches, because you have revealed them who can neither deceive nor be deceived.

ACT OF HOPE

O my God, relying on your infinite goodness and promises, I hope to obtain pardon of my sins, the help of your grace, and life everlasting, through the merits of Jesus Christ, my Lord and Redeemer.

ACT OF LOVE

O my God, I love you above all things, with my whole heart and soul, because you are all good and worthy of all love. I love my neighbour as myself for the love of you. I forgive all who have injured me and I ask pardon of all whom I have injured.

ACT OF CONTRITION

My God, I am heartily sorry for having offended you, and I detest all my sins, because of your just punishment, but most of all because they offend you, my God, who are all good and deserving of all my love. I firmly resolve, with the help of your grace, to sin no more and to avoid the near occasions of sin.

PRAYERS TO OUR LADY

The Angelus

Angel of the Lord declared unto Mary.
And she conceived of the holy Spirit.
Hail Mary....

Behold the handmaid of the Lord.
Be it done unto me according to thy word.
Hail Mary...

And the Word was made flesh,
And dwelt among us.
Hail Mary...

Pray for us, O Holy Mother of God.
That we may be made worthy of the promises of Christ.

Let us pray. Pour forth, we beseech thee, O Lord, thy grace into our hearts, that we, to whom the incarnation of Christ thy Son was made known by the message of an angel, may be brought, by his passion and cross, to the glory of his resurrection. Through the same Christ our Lord. Amen.

REGINA COELI

(This prayer is said instead of the Angelus *from the Easter Vigil until the evening of Pentecost Sunday.)*

O Queen of heaven, rejoice, alleluia!
For he whom thou didst merit to bear, alleluia!
Has risen, as he said, alleluia!
Pray for us to God, alleluia!
Rejoice and be glad, O Virgin Mary, alleluia!
For the Lord has risen indeed, alleluia!

Let us pray. O God, who gavest joy to the world through the resurrection of thy Son our Lord Jesus Christ; grant that we may obtain, through his Virgin Mother, Mary, the joys of everlasting Life. Through the same Christ our Lord. Amen.

THE ROSARY

Joyful Mysteries

The Annunciation
The Visitation
The Nativity
The Presentation in the Temple
The Finding of the Child Jesus
    in the Temple

Luminous Mysteries

Jesus' Baptism in the Jordan
Jesus' Self-manifestation at the
    Wedding Feast of Cana
Jesus' Proclamation of the
    Kingdom of God, with His
    Call to Conversion
The Transfiguration
The Institution of the Holy
    Eucharist

Sorrowful Mysteries

The Agony in the Garden
The Scourging at the Pillar
The Crowning with Thorns
Jesus Carries His Cross
Jesus Dies on the Cross

Glorious Mysteries

The Resurrection
The Ascension
The Coming of the Holy Spirit
The Assumption of Our Lady
    into Heaven
The Coronation of Our Lady
    and the Glory of All the
    Saints

SALVE REGINA

Hail, holy Queen, mother of mercy, hail, our life, our sweetness, and our hope. To you do we cry, banished children of Eve. To you do we send up our sighs, mourning and weeping in this vale of tears. Turn then, most gracious advocate, your eyes of mercy towards us, and after this our exile show to us the blessed fruit of your womb, Jesus. O Clement, O loving, O sweet Virgin Mary.

ST BERNARD'S PRAYER

Remember, O most gracious Virgin Mary, that never was it known that anyone who fled to your protection, implored your help or sought your intercession, was left unaided. Inspired with this confidence, I fly to you, O Virgin of virgins, my Mother. To you I come, before you I stand, sinful and sorrowful. O Mother of the Word Incarnate! Despise not my petitions, but in your mercy hear and answer me. Amen.

SONG OF MARY (The Magnificat)

My soul proclaims the greatness of the Lord,
my spirit rejoices in God, my Saviour;
for he has looked with favour on his lowly servant,
and from this day all generations will call me blessed.
The Almighty has done great things for me:
holy is his Name.
He has mercy on those who fear him in every generation.
He has shown the strength of his arm,
he has scattered the proud in their conceit.
He has cast down the mighty from their thrones,
and has lifted up the lowly.
He has filled the hungry with good things,
and has sent the rich away empty.
He has come to the help of his servant Israel
for he has remembered his promise of mercy,
the promise he made to our fathers,
to Abraham and his children for ever.

(ICET translation)

The WAY of the CROSS

Holy and merciful Father,
grant that we may follow the way of the cross
in faith and love, so that we may share
in Christ's passion and together with him
reach the glory of your kingdom.
We ask you this through your son Jesus Christ.

FIRST STATION

JESUS IS CONDEMNED TO DEATH

℣   We adore you, O Christ, and we bless you.
℟   Because by your holy cross you have redeemed the world.

So Pilate, wishing to satisfy the crowd, released for them Barabbas; and having scourged Jesus, he delivered him to be crucified (Mk 15:15).

"He came to his own home, and his own people received him not." The whole world — a world made up of Christians, Jews and non-believers — judges its own Creator and Redeemer. It was a judgement passed on Jesus by a small group among those who had followed him: by Judas who, not finding this Messiah up to his expectations, betrayed him to those who were seeking political power and liberation. Peter denied Jesus, while the other disciples fled.

Lord our God, have mercy on us all who have condemned you to death. Your mercy is already manifest in the sublime freedom with which you have borne our ingratitude and rejection.

All:
Our Father...

At the cross her station keeping
Stood the mournful Mother weeping,
Close to Jesus to the last.

SECOND STATION

JESUS TAKES UP HIS CROSS

℣   We adore you, O Christ, and we bless you.
℟   Because by your holy cross you have redeemed the world.

... Jesus went out, bearing his cross, to the place called 'Place of the Skull', which is called in Hebrew Golgotha (Jn 19:17).

Lord, you accept from humankind the same cross of which from all eternity you told your heavenly Father you were ready to bear in freedom and in love. It was not the human race who placed their sins on your shoulders, making of you a scapegoat, but it was you who had freely taken upon yourself our sins: everything you suffered would have otherwise been in vain.

To impose the burden of one's guilt on another is to disclaim any sort of personal culpability. It was not your Father who placed the burden on your shoulders, but the whole Trinity decreed that you should redeem the world lost in sin. You offered yourself to the Father in the Holy Spirit, in order to bring to completion on the cross the work of creation, and the Father — moved by the same Spirit — accepted your sacrifice.

Welcome, beloved Cross! You are the means by which we can finally and effectively show the world the immensity of God's love.

All:
Our Father...

Through her heart, his sorrow sharing,
All his bitter anguish bearing,
Now at length the sword had passed.

THIRD STATION

JESUS FALLS FOR THE FIRST TIME

℣ We adore you, O Christ, and we bless you.
℞ Because by your holy cross you have redeemed the world.

Unless a grain of wheat falls into the earth and dies, it remains alone; but if it dies it bears much fruit (Jn 12:24).

The Bible mentions neither this fall nor the others. But we must remember that Jesus had undergone the appalling Roman scourging, the pain and exhaustion enough to kill anyone.

With repeated blows of the cudgel, the crown of thorns was driven into his sacred head. It is astonishing how our Lord did not lose consciousness when the heavy weight of the cross was placed on his shoulders. His resources were not totally drained.

People of goodwill can surely help the Redeemer as he carries his cross. There are those who wish to do so, and we shall encounter them as we go along.

Let us now ask our Lord to forgive us, for we too have placed unnecessary burdens on his shoulders.

All:
Our Father...

Oh, how sad and sore distressed
Was that Mother highly blest
Of the sole-begotten one!

FOURTH STATION

JESUS MEETS HIS MOTHER

℣   We adore you, O Christ, and we bless you.
℟   Because by your holy cross you have redeemed the world.

Simeon said to Mary, "This child is set for the fall and rising of many in Israel, and for a sign that is spoken against and a sword will pierce through your own soul also" (Lk 2:34-35).

As Mary, the mother, played an essential role in Jesus' conception and birth, likewise she played an essential part in his passion by sharing in his suffering and death. No one is without a companion or a friend, yet on the cross the two criminals crucified with Jesus were of no comfort to him; he needed the presence of the sinless woman, Mary, the ever-Virgin Mother, whom he would make the mother of his mystical body, the Church.

Jesus entrusts to his sorrowful Mother his beloved disciple, John, who would be spiritually united with Peter, the representative of ecclesial unity. Thus, Mary the Immaculate becomes the Mother of the Petrine Church where — on behalf of all believers — she pleads the Holy Spirit by whom she was overshadowed at Nazareth.

All:
Our Father...

Christ above in torment hangs,
She beneath beholds the pangs
of her dying glorious Son.

FIFTH STATION

SIMON OF CYRENE HELPS JESUS CARRY HIS CROSS

℣ We adore you, O Christ, and we bless you.
℟ Because by your holy cross you have redeemed the world.

And they compelled a passer-by, Simon of Cyrene, who was coming in from the country, the father of Alexander and Rufus, to carry his cross (Mk 15:21).

Mary, in the most profound sorrow, accompanies her son on his way to Calvary. Simon, an ordinary man, is not prepared for anything unusual. He is on his way home from work. The evangelists underline the fact that he had to be forced to carry the cross that is too heavy for Jesus.

Even our most feeble "yes" to suffering — despite our resistance and our being unaware of it — becomes a transforming grace, provided that we accept it from the hands of God. Job, a patient man, uttered bitter words for his undeserved fate and great suffering, nevertheless was able to accept everything as coming from God: "The Lord has given and the Lord has taken away. The Lord's name be praised," — this earned him God's justification.

All:
Our Father...

Is there anyone who would not weep,
Whelmed in miseries so deep,
Christ's dear Mother to behold?

SIXTH STATION

VERONICA WIPES THE FACE OF JESUS

℣ We adore you, O Christ, and we bless you.
℟ Because by your holy cross you have redeemed the world.

He had no form or comeliness that we should look at him, and no beauty to attract us. He was despised and rejected by men as one from whom men hide their faces (Is 53:2-3).

Veronica is not mentioned in the Bible, but several women were present along the way to Calvary: women who wished by their presence, not only to profess their faith in the Lord but also to help him unreservedly.

Women in the Gospel are marked by Christ's preferential love of which John, the beloved disciple, was privileged. The Church, the bride of Christ, is therefore graced by the presence of women. In so far as the Church professes her faith and fidelity in loving humility to the Lord, as Veronica did in a gesture of love, Jesus leaves the imprint of his features on all those who are ready to accept it as a peace-token of his love.

Veronica's linen cloth, bearing the features of Jesus, is a sign and a promise to all believers that he will help them who call upon him.

Lord God, imprint in my spirit the sufferings of your Son Jesus.

All:
Our Father...

Can the human heart refrain
From partaking in her pain,
In that Mother's pain untold?

SEVENTH STATION

JESUS FALLS FOR THE SECOND TIME

℣ We adore you, O Christ, and we bless you.
℟ Because by your holy cross you have redeemed the world.

Jesus said to them, 'My soul is very sorrowful, even to death....' And going a little farther, he fell on the ground and prayed that, if it were possible, this hour might pass from him (Mk 14:34-35).

To know that the Son of God's strength should fail him is indeed terrifying, yet it reminds us of what John (3:16) says of him: "God so loved the world that he gave his only Son..." to take upon himself the weight of man's sins and, as man, succumb under it. Humanly speaking, what would the Father have felt upon seeing his Son's sufferings, who in fulfilment of his Father's will gave himself up to death?

We always want to know why God allows so much suffering in the world. There is no easy answer to this. God can only offer a gesture of fatherly love: he loves the world so much that "he gave his only Son" to fall and be crushed under its massive weight.

We should not dwell so much on our own suffering which is nothing compared to what the Son of God suffered for us. Whenever we are able to share in a small way in Christ's suffering, it is indeed a grace.

All:
Our Father...

Bruised, derided, cursed, defiled
She beheld her tender Child
All with bloody scourges rent.

EIGHTH STATION

JESUS COMFORTS THE WOMEN OF JERUSALEM

℣ We adore you, O Christ, and we bless you.
℟ Because by your holy cross you have redeemed the world.

And there followed him a great multitude of the people, and of women who bewailed and lamented him. But Jesus turning to them said, 'Daughters of Jerusalem, do not weep for me, but weep for yourselves and for your children' (Lk 23:27-28).

In this station we are faced with a gnawing question about the role played by the people of Israel in the Passion of Jesus.

We cannot ignore the fact that Israel not only disowned its long-awaited Messiah, but also condemned him to death; we should nonetheless bear in mind that both pagans and Christians are also guilty of his death. Jesus however would not let himself be comforted by the women of Jerusalem: "...weep not for me but for yourselves and for your children."

He foresees the imminent catastrophe which is to befall Jerusalem, and indeed the whole of Israel. The people of Israel could not give solace to the Son of God while he is being condemned.

All:
Our Father...

Let me share with you his pain
who for all my sins was slain
who for me in torment died.

NINTH STATION

JESUS FALLS FOR THE THIRD TIME

℣ We adore you, O Christ, and we bless you.
℞ Because by your holy cross you have redeemed the world.

*Come to me, all who labour and are heavy-laden, and I will give you
rest. Take my yoke upon you, and learn from me; for I am gentle and
lowly in heart, and you will find rest for your souls. For my yoke is
easy, and my burden is light (Mt 11:28-30).*

It would not be inappropriate to think that this third fall of Jesus
came about to the advantage of the people of Israel. Jesus'
greatest pain was possibly the rejection by his own people who
condemned him to the most atrocious death. We should not
forget that his first mission was to gather together the scattered
sheep of Israel. Not having been recognized as the Messiah was
the most poignant defeat and the greatest humiliation he had to
undergo.

This last burden, surely, must redound to Israel's advantage:
how could it be otherwise? The tears of the daughters of
Jerusalem could undoubtedly mingle with the tears of Jesus over
that city whose destruction was imminent (cf. Lk 19:41).

All:
Our Father...

O my Mother, fount of love,
Touch my spirit from above;
Make my heart with yours accord.

TENTH STATION

JESUS IS STRIPPED OF HIS GARMENTS

℣ We adore you, O Christ, and we bless you.
℞ Because by your holy cross you have redeemed the world.

They divided his garments among them, casting lots for them, to decide what each should take (Mk 15:24).

What do clothes matter to a human body which is about to be crucified? Jesus is stripped of his garments to enable the soldiers to work without being hampered.

Since that time in the Garden of Eden, fallen man has been covering himself with all sorts of clothing: from fig leaves and animal skins to the latest fashion of today. On Calvary everything is cast away: the new Adam stands before the Father as he is, having freely taken upon himself the sins and shame of the old Adam.

On the cross man fully manifests himself, and God restores to him his lost dignity — his most precious gift to mankind. In every eucharistic celebration down the centuries he gives to humanity this unadorned body. "The body of Christ" — says the priest as he gives communion — "who takes away the sins of the world": the body which bears your sins and the wounds inflicted on it.

All:
Our Father...

Make me feel as you have felt,
Make my soul to glow and melt
with the love of Christ my Lord.

ELEVENTH STATION

JESUS IS NAILED TO THE CROSS

℣ We adore you, O Christ, and we bless you.
℞ Because by your holy cross you have redeemed the world.

It was the third hour, when they crucified him. And the inscription of the charge against him read, 'The King of the Jews'. And with him they crucified two robbers, one on his right and one on his left (Mk 15:25-27).

"They know not what they do" (Lk 23:34). They nailed him to the cross in order to get rid of him, but in so doing, bonded him the more firmly to the earth. They nailed him down so that he could no longer go away but remain with us forever: neither the Resurrection nor the Ascension could alter this.

No one binds Jesus to sinful humanity; he remains with us, of his own accord, to the very end. And when he returns on judgement day the cross, "the sign of the Son of Man, will appear in heaven" (Mt 24:30).

"All things were created through him and for him" (Col 1:16-17), that is, for the Son whom the Father allows to be nailed to the cross of the world.

Overwhelmed by this unfathomable mystery we can only kneel in grateful adoration.

All:
Our Father...

Holy Mother, pierce me through;
In my heart each wound renew
Of my Saviour crucified.

TWELFTH STATION

JESUS DIES ON THE CROSS

℣ We adore you, O Christ, and we bless you.
℞ Because by your holy cross you have redeemed the world.

And when the sixth hour had come, there was darkness over the whole land until the ninth hour. And at the ninth hour Jesus cried with a loud voice, 'Eloi, Eloi, lama sabachtani?' which means, 'My God, my God, why hast thou forsaken me?' ... And one ran and, filling a sponge full of vinegar, put it on a reed and gave it to him to drink... And Jesus uttered a loud cry, and breathed his last.... And when the centurion, who stood facing him, saw that he thus breathed his last, he said, 'Truly this man was the Son of God' (Mk 15:33-39).

Jesus is suspended between heaven and earth, repudiated by men and forsaken by his Father, thus restoring the unity between them. Extending his arms he reaches out to both the sinner who goes back to him and to the one who turns away from him and yet could not hinder Christ to reach out to him. The vertical beam of the cross bridges the gap between God and man, while the horizontal one embraces the ends of the earth.

Bending his head, Jesus gives up the spirit, the same spirit whom he will breathe on the Church on the day of his Resurrection, and in this way all is truly accomplished.

All:
Our Father...

For the sins of his own nation
She saw him hang in desolation
Till his spirit forth he sent.

THIRTEENTH STATION

JESUS IS TAKEN DOWN FROM THE CROSS

℣ We adore you, O Christ, and we bless you.
℟ Because by your holy cross you have redeemed the world.

Standing by the cross of Jesus were his mother and his mother's sister, Mary the wife of Clopas, and Mary Magdalene... The soldiers came to Jesus and when they saw that he was already dead, they did not break his legs. But one of the soldiers pierced his side with a spear, and at once there came out blood and water. After this Joseph of Arimathea... asked Pilate that he might take away the body of Jesus
(Jn 19:25.32-24.38).

Jesus is taken down from the cross and his mother accepting the pain that his Son bore for the sake of the world — is there to receive him in her bosom. Each of the seven swords which transfixed the heart of the mother was Mary's renewed assent to her Son's sufferings. It is beyond human comprehension that a person should say "yes" to everything, even to the most harrowing pain.

In her unconditional "yes" Mary becomes the "redeemed earth", capable of receiving on her lap the dead body of the Redeemer. This scene wrapped in silence reveals that Christ's Passion was not suffered in vain: Mary in this moment of weariness and infinite sorrow, represents humanity who accepts with gratitude heaven's blessings.

All:
Our Father...

Let me mingle tears with you
Mourning him who mourned for me,
All the days that I may live.

FOURTEENTH STATION

JESUS IS LAID IN THE TOMB

℣ We adore you, O Christ, and we bless you.
℟ Because by your holy cross you have redeemed the world.

When Pilate learned from the centurion that Jesus was dead, he granted the body to Joseph. And he bought a linen shroud, and taking him down, wrapped him in the linen shroud, and laid him in a tomb which had been hewn out of the rock; and he rolled a stone against the entrance of the tomb. Mary Magdalene and Mary the mother of Joses saw where he was laid (Mk 15:45-47).

The fact that Jesus' body — wrapped in a linen shroud lay in the tomb for three days, rules out any possibility of apparent death. He died as all people die. A large stone indicates definitiveness: everything that had been lived until then is now decisively in the past.

Nevertheless Jesus' death — a death which is absolutely real — was different from any other. For this unique death was the ultimate expression of God's infinite love, and love is the only living reality that cannot die.

Love is nothing else but perfect self-oblation and abnegation, in order to give oneself completely to the loved one. Is this not a form of death? And when one loves in a Christian way, placing his life completely at the service of his neighbour, is this not a "dying to self"?

All:
Our Father...

While my body here decays,
May my soul your goodness praise,
Safe in paradise with you. Amen.

"He descended to the dead.
On the third day he rose again.
He ascended into heaven,
and is seated at the right hand of the Father..."
— *Apostles' Creed*

HYMNS

ABIDE WITH ME

1. Abide with me, fast falls the eventide;
   the darkness deepens, Lord, with me abide!
   When other helpers fail, and comforts flee,
   help of the helpless, O abide with me.

2. Swift to its close ebbs our life's little day;
   earth's joys grow dim, its glories pass away;
   change and decay in all around I see;
   O thou who changest not, abide with me.

3. I need thy presence every passing hour;
   what but thy grace can foil the tempter's power?
   Who like thyself my guide and stay can be?
   Through cloud and sunshine, O abide with me.

4. I fear no foe with thee at hand to bless;
   ills have no weight, and tears no bitterness.
   Where is death's sting? Where, grave, thy victory?
   I triumph still if thou abide with me.

5. Hold thou thy Cross before my closing eyes;
   shine through the gloom, and point me to the skies;
   heaven's morning breaks, and earth's vain shadows flee;
   in life, in death, O Lord, abide with me!

— *H.F. Lyte*

AMAZING GRACE

1. Amazing grace! How sweet the sound
   that saved a wretch like me.
   I once was lost, but now I'm found,
   was blind, but now I see.

2. 'Twas grace that taught my heart to fear,
   and grace my fears relieved.
   How precious did that grace appear
   the hour I first believed.

3. Through many dangers, toils and snares
   I have already come.
   'Tis grace hath brought me safe thus far,
   and grace will lead me home.

4. The Lord has promised good to me;
    his word my hope secures.
    He will my shield and portion be
    as long as life endures.

    — *John Newton*

CHRIST BE BESIDE ME

1. Christ be beside me, Christ be before me,
    Christ be behind me, King of my heart.
    Christ be within me, Christ be below me,
    Christ be above me, Never to part.

2. Christ on my right hand, Christ on my left hand.
    Christ all around me, Shield in the strife.
    Christ in my sleeping, Christ in my sitting,
    Christ in my rising, Light of my life.

3. Christ be in all hearts Thinking about me,
    Christ be on all tongues Telling of me.
    Christ be the vision In eyes that see me,
    In ears that hear me, Christ ever be.

    — *St Patrick's Breastplate* — *J. Quinn*

NEARER, MY GOD, TO THEE

1. Nearer, my God, to thee, Nearer to thee!
    E'en though it be a cross that raiseth me,
    Still all my song shall be, Nearer my God to thee,
    Nearer my God to thee, nearer to thee.

2. Though, like the wanderer, the sun gone down,
    Darkness be over me, my rest a stone;
    Yet in my dreams I'd be nearer my God to thee,
    Nearer my God to thee, nearer to thee.

3. There let the way appear steps unto heav'n;
    All that thou sendest me in mercy giv'n,
    Angels to beckon me nearer my God to thee,
    Nearer my God to thee, nearer to thee.

4. Deep in thy sacred heart let me abide
    Thou who hast come for me, suffered and died.
    Sweet shall my weeping be, grief surely leading me,
    Nearer my God to thee, nearer to thee.

    — *S. Adams*

PRAISE TO THE HOLIEST IN THE HEIGHT

1. Praise to the Holiest in the height, And in the depth be praise,
   In all his words most wonderful, most sure in all his ways.

2. O loving wisdom of our God! When all was sin and shame,
   a second Adam to the fight, and to the rescue came.

3. O wisest love! That flesh and blood which did in Adam fail,
   should strive afresh against the foe, should strive and should
   prevail.

4. And that a higher gift than grace should flesh and blood refine,
   God's presence and his very self, and essence all divine.

5. O generous love! that he who smote in man for man the foe,
   the double agony in man for man should undergo.

6. And in the garden secretly, and on the cross on high,
   should teach his brethren, and inspire, to suffer and to die.

7. Praise to the Holiest in the height, and in the depth be praise,
   in all his words most wonderful, most sure in all his ways.

— *John Henry Newman*

PRAISE TO THE LORD, THE ALMIGHTY

1. Praise to the Lord, the Almighty, the King of creation!
   O my soul, praise him, for he is your health and salvation.
   All you who hear, now to his altar draw near,
   join in profound adoration.

2. Praise to the Lord, let us offer our gifts at his altar;
   let not our sins and transgressions, now cause us to falter.
   Christ, the High Priest, bids us all join in his feast;
   victims with him on the altar.

3. Praise to the Lord, oh let all that is in us adore him!
   All that has life and breath, come now in praises before him.
   Let the Amen sound from his people again,
   now as we worship before him.

— *J. Neander – C. Winkworth*

THE LORD'S MY SHEPHERD

1. The Lord's my shepherd, I'll not want.
   He makes me down to lie
   in pastures green. He leadeth me
   the quiet waters by.

2. My soul he doth restore again,
   and me to walk doth make

within the paths of righteousness,
e'en for his own name's sake.

3. Yea, though I walk in death's dark vale,
   yet will I fear no ill.
   For thou art with me, and thy rod
   and staff me comfort still.

4. My table thou hast furnishèd
   in presence of my foes,
   my head thou dost with oil anoint,
   and my cup overflows.

5. Goodness and mercy all my life
   shall surely follow me.
   And in God's house for evermore
   my dwelling place shall be.

— *Ps 22, Scottish Psalter*

TO JESUS CHRIST OUR SOVEREIGN KING

1. To Jesus Christ, our sov'reign King,
   Who is the world's Salvation,
   All praise and homage do we bring,
   And thanks and adoration.

   > *Christ Jesus, victor. Christ Jesus, ruler.*
   > *Christ Jesus, Lord and Redeemer.*

2. Your reign extend, O King benign,
   To ev'ry land and nation;
   For in your kingdom, Lord divine,
   Alone we find salvation.

3. To you and to your Church, great King,
   We pledge our hearts' oblation,
   Until before your throne we sing
   In endless jubilation.

— *M.B. Hellriegel*

WHEN I BEHOLD THE WONDROUS CROSS

1. When I behold the wondrous cross,
   On which the prince of glory died,
   My richest gain I count but loss,
   And pour contempt on all my pride.

2. Forbid it, Lord, that I should boast,
   Save in the death of Christ, my God;
   The vain things that attract me most,
   I sacrifice them to his blood.

3. See, from his dead, his hands, his feet,
    What grief and love flow mingled down;
    Did e'er such love and sorrow meet,
    Or thorns compose so rich a crown?

4. Were all the realm of nature mine,
    It would be offering far too small;
    Love so amazing, so divine,
    Demands my soul, my life, my all.

    — I. Watts

PRAISE, MY SOUL, THE KING OF HEAVEN

1. Praise, my soul, the king of heaven!
    To his feet your tribute bring.
    Ransomed, healed, restored, forgiven,
    who am I his praise to sing?

        Praise him! Praise him! (2x)
        Praise the everlasting king!

2. Praise him for his grace and favour
    to our fathers in distress;
    praise him still the same for ever,
    slow to chide and swift to bless.

3. Fatherlike, he tends and spares us;
    well our feeble frame he knows:
    in his hands he gently bears us,
    rescues us from all our foes.

4. Angels, help us to adore him;
    you behold him face to face;
    sun and moon bow down before him,
    ev'rything in time and space.

    — H.F. Lyte

SOUL OF MY SAVIOUR

1. Soul of my Saviour, sanctify my breast;
    Body of Christ, be thou my saving guest;
    Blood of my Saviour, bathe me in thy tide,
    wash me ye waters, streaming from thy side.

2. Strength and protection may thy passion be;
    O Blessed Jesus, hear and answer me;
    deep in thy wounds, Lord, hide and shelter me;
    so shall I never, never part from thee.

3.   Guard and defend me from the foe malign;
     in death's dread moments make me only thine;
     call me, and bid me come to thee on high,
     where I may praise thee with thy saints for aye.
                                             — *Pope John XXII*

SWEET HEART OF JESUS

1.   Sweet Heart of Jesus, fount of love and mercy,
     today we come, thy blessing to implore;
     O touch our hearts, so cold and so ungrateful,
     and make them, Lord, thine own for evermore.

         Sweet Heart of Jesus, we implore,
         O make us love thee more and more.

2.   Sweet Heart of Jesus, make us know and love thee,
     unfold to us the treasures of thy grace;
     that so our hearts, from things of earth uplifted,
     may long alone to gaze upon thy face.

3.   Sweet Heart of Jesus, make us pure and gentle,
     and teach us how to do thy blessed will;
     to follow close the print of thy dear footsteps,
     and when we fall – Sweet Heart, oh, love us still.

4.   Sweet Heart of Jesus, bless all hearts that love thee,
     and may thine own Heart ever blessèd be;
     bless us, dear Lord, and bless the friends we cherish,
     and keep us true to Mary and to thee.
                                             — *Author Unknown*

SWEET SACRAMENT DIVINE

1.   Sweet sacrament divine, our shepherd and our king,
     Around your earthly shrine, with grateful hearts we sing.
     Jesus to you our voice we raise, in songs of love and joyful
         praise,
     Sweet sacrament divine, sweet sacrament divine.

2.   Sweet sacrament of peace, in you mankind is blessed,
     All pain and sorrows cease, and human hearts find rest.
     Upon your promise we rely: "Who eats this Bread will never
         die",
     Sweet sacrament of peace, sweet sacrament of peace.
                                             — *F. Stanfield*

LORD, ACCEPT THE GIFTS WE OFFER

1. Lord, accept the gifts we offer
   At this Eucharistic feast.
   Bread and wine to be transformed now,
   Through the action of thy priest.
   Take us too Lord, and transform us,
   Be thy grace in us increased.

2. May our souls be pure and spotless
   As this host of wheat so fine,
   May all stain of sin be crushed out,
   Like the grape that forms the wine,
   As we, too, become partakers
   In this sacrifice divine.

3. Take our gifts, almighty Father,
   Living God, eternal, true,
   Which we give, through Christ our Saviour,
   Pleading here for us anew.
   Grant salvation to all present
   And our faith and love renew.

— Sr M. Teresine

HAIL! REDEEMER, KING DIVINE!

1. Hail! Redeemer, King divine!
   Priest and lamb, the throne is thine,
   King whose reign shall never cease,
   Prince of everlasting peace.

   Angels, saints and nations sing:
   Praised be Jesus Christ, our King:
   Lord of life, earth, sky and sea,
   King of love on Calvary.

2. Eucharistic King, what love
   Draws thee daily from above,
   Clad in signs of bread and wine,
   Feed us, lead us, keep us thine.

3. King whose name creation thrills,
   Rule our minds, our hearts, our wills,
   Till in peace each nation rings,
   With thy praises, King of kings.

— P. Brennan

JESUS CHRIST IS RISEN TODAY

1. Jesus Christ is ris'n today, alleluia.
   Our triumphant holy day, alleluia.
   Who did once upon the cross, alleluia.
   Suffer to redeem our loss, alleluia.

2. Hymns of praise then let us sing, alleluia.
   Unto Christ, our heavenly king, alleluia.
   Who endured the cross and grave, alleluia.
   Sinners to redeem and save, alleluia.

3. But the pain which he endured, alleluia.
   Our salvation has procured; alleluia.
   Now above he reigns as king, alleluia.
   Where the angels ever sing, alleluia.

— *J. Arnold*

COME, HOLY GHOST, CREATOR, COME

1. Come, Holy Ghost, Creator, come
   from thy bright heavenly throne.
   Come, take possession of our souls,
   and make them all thine own.

2. Thou who art called the Paraclete,
   best gift of God above,
   the living spring, the living fire,
   sweet unction and true love.

3. Thou who are seven-fold in thy grace,
   finger of God's right hand;
   his promise, teaching little ones
   to speak and understand.

4. O guide our minds with thy blest light,
   with love our hearts inflame;
   and with thy strength, which ne'er decays,
   confirm our mortal frame.

5. Far from us drive our deadly foe;
   true peace unto us bring;
   and through all perils lead us safe
   beneath thy sacred wing.

6. Through thee may we the Father know,
   through thee th' eternal Son,
   and thee the Spirit of them both,
   thrice-blessed Three in One.

7.   All glory to the Father be,
     with his co-equal Son:
     the same to thee great Paraclete,
     while endless ages run.

— *Ascribed to Robanus Maurus*

O COME, EMMANUEL

1.   O come, O come, Emmanuel, To free your captive Israel,
     That mourns in lonely exile here, Until the Son of God
          appear.
               Rejoice, rejoice, O Israel,
               To you shall come Emmanuel.

2.   O royal branch of Jesse's tree, Redeem us all from tyranny;
     From pain of hell your people free, And over death win
          victory.

3.   O come, great daystar, radiance bright, And heal us with your
          glorious light.
     Disperse the gloomy clouds of night, And death's dark
          shadows put to flight.

4.   O key of David's city, come And open wide our heav'nly
          home:
     Make safe the way that leads above, Protect us ever by your
          love.

5.   O come, O come, great Lord of might, Who once appeared on
          Sinai's height,
     And gave your faithful people law, In all the splendour we
          adore.

— *J.M.Neale*

HARK, THE HERALD ANGELS SING

1.   Hark, the herald angels sing, glory to the new-born king;
     peace on earth and mercy mild, God and sinners reconciled:
     joyful all ye nations rise, join the triumph of the skies,
     with the angelic host proclaim, Christ is born in Bethlehem.
               Hark, the herald angels sing,
               Glory to the new-born King.

2.   Christ, by highest heaven adored, Christ, the everlasting Lord,
     late in time behold him come, offspring of a Virgin's womb!
     Veiled in flesh the Godhead see, hail the Incarnate Deity!
     Pleased as man with man to dwell, Jesus, our Emmanuel.

3. Hail the heaven-born Prince of peace! Hail the Son of
     righteousness!
   Light and life to all he brings, risen with healing in his wings;
   mild he lays his glory by, born that man no more may die,
   born to raise the sons of earth, born to give them second
     birth.

— *C. Wesley*

O COME, ALL YE FAITHFUL

1. O come, all ye faithful, joyful and triumphant,
   O come ye, O come ye to Bethlehem;
   Come and behold him, born the king of angels:
      O come, let us adore him (3x)
      Christ the Lord.

2. Born of the Father, light from light eternal,
   Son of the gentle maid our flesh and blood;
   Honour and praise him with the hosts of angels.

3. Sing, choirs of angels, sing in exultation,
   Sing, all ye citizens of heaven above,
   Glory to God in the highest:

4. Now, Lord, we greet you, born this happy morning,
   Jesus to you be glory given, Word of the Father,
   Now in flesh appearing.

— *John Wade, tr F. Oakley*

SILENT NIGHT

1. Silent night, holy night, all is calm, all is bright,
   round yon virgin mother and child; holy infant so tender and
     mild:
   sleep in heavenly peace, sleep in heavenly peace.

2. Silent night, holy night. Shepherds quake at the sight,
   glories stream from heaven afar, heavenly hosts sing alleluia:
   Christ the Saviour is born, Christ the Saviour is born.

3. Silent night, holy night. Son of God, love's pure light,
   radiant beams from thy holy face, with the dawn of redeeming
     grace:
   Jesus, Lord, at thy birth, Jesus, Lord, at thy birth.

— *Joseph Mohr, tr J. Young*

HAIL, QUEEN OF HEAV'N

1. Hail, Queen of heav'n, the ocean star,
    guide of the wand'rer here below;
    thrown on life's surge, we claim thy care;
    save us from peril and from woe.
    Mother of Christ, star of the sea,
    pray for the wanderer, pray for me.

2. O gentle, chaste and spotless maid,
    we sinners make our prayers through thee;
    remind thy Son that he has paid
    the price of our iniquity.
    Virgin most pure, star of the sea,
    pray for the sinner, pray for me.

3. Sojourners in this vale of tears,
    to thee, blest advocate, we cry;
    pity our sorrows, calm our fears,
    and soothe with hope our misery.
    Refuge in grief, star of the sea,
    pray for the mourner, pray for me.

4. And while to him who reigns above,
    in Godhead One, in Persons Three,
    the source of life, of grace, of love,
    homage we pay on bended knee,
    do thou, bright Queen, star of the sea,
    pray for thy children, pray for me.

                                        — *John Lingard*

I'LL SING A HYMN TO MARY

1. I'll sing a hymn to Mary, the Mother of my God,
    the Virgin of all virgins, of David's royal blood.
    O teach me, holy Mary, a loving song to frame,
    when wicked men blaspheme thee, to love and bless thy
        name.

2. O noble Tower of David, of gold and ivory,
    the Ark of God's own promise, the gate of heav'n to me,
    to live and not to love thee would fill my soul with shame;
    when wicked men blaspheme thee, I'll love and bless thy
        name.

3. The saints are high in glory, with golden crowns so bright;
   but brighter far is Mary, upon her throne of light.
   O that which God did give thee, let mortal ne'er disclaim;
   when wicked men blaspheme thee I'll love and bless thy
   name.

4. But in the crown of Mary, there lies a wondrous gem,
   as Queen of all the angels, which Mary shares with them:
   no sin hath e'er defiled thee, so doth our faith proclaim;
   when wicked men blaspheme thee I'll love and bless thy
   name.

— John Wyse

THE BELLS OF THE ANGELUS

1. The bells of the angelus, Call us to pray
   In sweet tones announcing, The sacred Ave.

   > *Ave, Ave, Ave, Maria;*
   > *Ave, Ave, Ave, Maria;*

2. An angel of mercy, Led Bernadette's feet
   Where flows the deep torrent, Our Lady to greet.

3. She prayed to our mother, That God's will be done,
   She prayed for his glory, That his kingdom come.

4. Immaculate Mary Your praises we sing
   Who reign now with Christ, Our redeemer and king.

5. In heaven the blessed Your glory proclaim,
   On earth now your children Invoke your fair name.

HAIL GLORIOUS SAINT PATRICK

1. Hail glorious Saint Patrick, dear saint of our isle,
   On us thy poor children bestow a sweet smile,
   And now thou art high in the mansions above,
   On Erin's green valleys look down in thy love.

2. Ever bless and defend the dear land of our birth,
   Where shamrock still blooms as when thou wert on earth,
   Our hearts shall still burn wheresoever we roam,
   For God and Saint Patrick, and our native home.

— Sr Agnes